Charles Evans Hughes and the Supreme Court

CHARLES EVANS HUGHES

and the

SUPREME COURT

by

Samuel Hendel

Member of the New York Bar; Assistant Professor of Government
at the College of the City of New York

1951

KING'S CROWN PRESS, COLUMBIA UNIVERSITY

NEW YORK

PUBLISHED IN GREAT BRITAIN, CANADA, AND INDIA

BY GEOFFREY CUMBERLEGE, OXFORD UNIVERSTY PRESS

LONDON, TORONTO, AND BOMBAY

MANUFACTURED IN THE UNITED STATES OF AMERICA

To CLARA

PREFACE

The public career of Charles Evans Hughes began very early in the twentieth century and ended just before Pearl Harbor. In that career is written a vital segment of the history of our century. It was a career which in point of personal eminence, diversity of experience and significance to American society few men have ever rivalled. In its course, Charles Evans Hughes was governor of the State of New York, an Associate Justice of the United States Supreme Court, Republican candidate for the presidency of the United States, acknowledged leader of the American bar, Secretary of State, a Judge of the Permanent Court of International Justice, and Chief Justice of the United States.

Paradoxically, in the process of writing this record across the pages of American history, Mr. Hughes was both extolled as a great liberal and a fearless champion of public rights against special privileges, and denounced as a deadly conservative and the greatest champion of property rights of our time. To some he was preeminently a man of balance and sanity who displayed impartiality and judicial quality of mind. To others he was characterized by extreme views and narrowness of understanding, unteachable stubbornness, and arid self-righteousness. Calumny and hyperbole are no doubt the penalty and dubious reward of public service. But the extreme opposing forms these took in the case of Mr. Hughes suggest what study reveals, that is, that few men have more successfully eluded simple and unequivocal characterization.

It is not part of the purpose of this volume to draw a full life portrait of Mr. Hughes. Its purpose is at once more limited and more inclusive. Some attention will be devoted to the career of Mr. Hughes other than to his work as a member of the Court because no man ever brought greater wealth and diversity of experience to the Chief Justiceship than he did; and this experience, sometimes in obvious and palpable ways, and sometimes in subtle and imponderable ways, had a profound effect upon his decisions. Primarily, however, this book will be concerned with an analysis of the contribution of Associate Justice and later Chief Justice Hughes to the solution of important *constitutional* issues that came before the Supreme Court. So delimited, the area to be canvassed is still large because the two periods of Mr. Hughes' service on the Court were periods of great ferment in American history. The first, from October, 1910, to June, 1916, coincided with a considerable part of the New Free- dom of Woodrow Wilson and preceded America's entry into war. The second, from February, 1930, to June, 1941, coincided with the New Deal of Franklin D. Roosevelt and preceded America's entry into a second world war. Both these periods were marked by legislative innovations involving great extensions of governmental power over the economy and challenging traditional conceptions of the rights of the states and of individuals. The latter was par- ticularly a period of great crisis for the nation and produced a funda- mental challenge to the Court itself.

Intelligent analysis of the contribution of Mr. Hughes in the de- velopment of constitutional doctrine involves a great deal more than some insight into the mainsprings of his action and an analysis of his decisions. This contribution cannot be appraised in isolation from the historic development of which it formed a part. To be sure, stare decisis has never been a rigid rule of the Court but tradition and con- tinuity are fundamental in the judicial process and to a significant degree are the bases for its existence and prestige. Particularly did concern for the tradition, continuity and prestige of the Court loom large in the thinking of Mr. Hughes. It is in historic context, there- fore, that the judicial endeavors of Mr. Hughes will be appraised.

Nor is that enough. Justices cannot divorce themselves, if they would, from the social milieu into which they are born and in which they are nurtured. The very concepts of justice and reasonableness, which are frequently the tests of constitutionality, are derived from and dependent upon society. The Olympian impartiality of Plato's guardians, schooled in abstract justice and wisdom, poses an impos- sible ideal for this mundane world. To trace, therefore, the impact, whenever discernible, of political, economic and social conflict upon the decisions of the Court is a legitimate part of the task of this book.

Finally, an analysis of the judicial record of even so distinguished a jurist as Charles Evans Hughes would be of little more than his- toric interest and importance unless it served as the basis for reassessing the value, to our functioning democracy, of that extraordinary American institution of judicial review.

I am indebted to Professor Walter R. Sharp and Dean Morton Gottschall of the College of the City of New York for their confidence and encouragement; and to Professors Noel T. Dowling, Henry Steele Commager and Arthur W. Macmahon of Columbia University for their counsel and criticism. In light of the controversial nature of aspects of this study, I must emphasize, however, that responsibility for interpretations and conclusions is mine.

I am thankful to my brother, Stanley Hendel, for his generous help with many laborious tasks. And to my wife, Clara, I owe immeasurable gratitude for sympathy, encouragement, assistance, and advice.

S. H.

New York City
October, 1950

CONTENTS

I. The Making of a Justice

1 "LEARNING, WISDOM AND CHARACTER"   I

II. Associate Justice of the United States Supreme Court

2 THE RECONCILIATION OF LIBERTY AND AUTHORITY   16
3 DUE PROCESS, EQUAL PROTECTION AND THE POLICE
   POWER   23
4 PUBLIC CONTRACTS, THE CONTRACT CLAUSE AND THE
   POLICE POWER   36
5 THE CONTROL OF COMMERCE: NATIONAL AND STATE
   POWER   46
6 A SUMMARY EVALUATION   64

III. The Years Between

7 PRIVATE CITIZEN AND PUBLIC SERVANT   68
8 A HISTORIC DEBATE   78

IV. Chief Justice of the United States

9   THE SETTING   91
10 PROCEDURAL DUE PROCESS AND GOVERNMENTAL POWER   95
11 DUE PROCESS AFFECTING ECONOMIC INTERESTS   116
12 INTELLECTUAL LIBERTY UNDER THE CONSTITUTION   137
13 EQUALITY BEFORE THE LAW AND THE POLICE POWER   159
14 PRIVATE CONTRACTS, THE CONTRACT CLAUSE AND THE
    POLICE POWER   168

15   THE FEDERAL SYSTEM: TAX IMMUNITY OF GOVERN-
     MENTAL INSTRUMENTALITIES   185

V.   Chief Justice of the United States: the Constitution, "Road or Gate?"

16   SOME IMPORTANT FEDERAL LEGISLATION   197
17   THE DELEGATION OF LEGISLATIVE POWER   211
18   THE CONTROL OF COMMERCE   227
19   THE COURT UNDER ATTACK   246
20   THE END OF AN ERA: REEXAMINATION AND RETREAT   255

VI.   Charles Evans Hughes and Judicial Review

21   AN EVALUATION   276

Notes   297

Table of Cases   329

Index   333

I. The Making of a Justice

CHAPTER I

"LEARNING, WISDOM AND CHARACTER"

INTRODUCTORY

Judicial review is the virtually unique power enjoyed by judges of American courts, and ultimately and conclusively, by Justices of the Supreme Court of the United States to declare invalid and unenforceable the laws of sovereign legislative bodies, national and state.

The compatibility of this power with the theory and practice of democracy has been the subject of sharp and persistent controversy. It is argued that this power is indispensable to the working of our federal system, gives assurance of greater justice and reasonableness in the enactment and administration of our laws, and, far from impeding democracy, safeguards it by protecting civil liberties and the tradition and continuity of our institutions against the force of temporary but overbearing majorities. On the other hand, there are many who assail this power as undemocratic in theory, challenging the capacity of the people for self-government, and anti-democratic in practice, frustrating the will of the majority and impeding the peaceful conciliation of our economic and social conflicts.

The judicial career of Charles Evans Hughes which, with some hiatus, spanned seventeen years of ferment and crisis in our history furnishes a laboratory test from which may be derived some fundamental insight into the nature of the judicial process and the value of judicial review.

This is true, however, only if it is recognized that the judge, in passing upon the constitutionality of legislation, is not simply and invariably an instrument of the law denuded of a will of his own. In the light of the history of judicial review, the dictum of Chief

Justice Marshall, in 1824, cannot seriously be regarded as describing the judicial practice in constitutional cases. He then wrote:

Judicial power, as contradistinguished from the power of the laws, has no existence. Courts are the mere instruments of the law, and can will nothing. . . . Judicial power is never exercised for the purpose of giving effect to the will of the judge; always for the purpose of giving effect to the will of the legislature; or, in other words, to the will of the law.[1]

It cannot now be denied that "the Courts are free in marking the limits of the individual's immunities to shape their judgment in accordance with reason and justice."[2] That duty, Justice Holmes has said, is inevitable.[3] Especially is this true in regard to legislation challenged as deprivations of life, liberty or property without due process of law, when reasonableness and justice are the avowed tests of constitutionality.

Yet it must be obvious that reason and justice do not speak with one loud, clear voice. The influences which place judges on one or another side of constitutionality are, to be sure, often unconscious reaching far beyond and beneath verbal and technical manifestations of difference. And because the influences may be manifold and varied, and frequently subtle and tenuous, understanding may call for the skill of the psychoanalyst as well as that of the lawyer. Here it is possible only to draw some of the sharper, clearer lines of influence in the making of a justice.

EARLY YEARS

Charles Evans Hughes was born in Glens Falls, New York, on April 11, 1862.[4] His father, a Welshman who had migrated to America, was a Baptist preacher. His mother, before her marriage, had been a school teacher. Charles Evans Hughes was a scholarly and serious-minded youngster, who at an early age evolved what he called "The Charles Evans Hughes Plan of Study" to guide his reading and research. At the age of thirteen, while attending a public grammar school in New York City, he wrote themes on "The Limitations of the Human Mind" and "The Evils of Light Literature," and his commencement oration was titled "Self-help," which suggest both his unusual precocity and extreme seriousness.

At fourteen he was admitted to Madison College (now Colgate University). It was then his intention to prepare for the ministry. Two years later he transferred to Brown University in Providence, Rhode Island, where he decided upon a career at the bar, and displayed, apparently for the first time, an interest in some of the lighter diversions of youth. At the age of nineteen he was graduated with fourth highest honors in a class of forty-three and was elected to Phi Beta Kappa. Lacking the financial means immediately to enter law school, he took a position teaching Greek, French and mathematics at a small academy. Upon his arrival at the academy, it is said, his youthful appearance proved such a shock to the authorities that he soon thereafter cultivated a beard which was to remain so striking an aspect of his physiognomy.

After serving a year at the academy he succeeded in obtaining a scholarship to Columbia Law School. He was graduated with highest honors from that institution in 1884. His outstanding record won him an annual fellowship for three years at the law school and a connection with the prominent law firm of Chamberlin, Carter and Hornblower. Within a few years he became a partner in the firm. A short time later he married Antoinette Carter, the daughter of one of the partners.

In 1891, principally because of failing health, he decided to accept a post as professor of law at Cornell University. Two years later he returned to the practice of law but continued for some years as a special lecturer both at Cornell and New York Law School.

PUBLIC CAREER

The public career of Charles Evans Hughes began in 1905 with his designation, at the suggestion of Henry W. Taft, the younger brother of William Howard Taft, as counsel to the Stevens Committee set up by the New York legislature to investigate gas rates. He plunged into the investigation with tremendous energy and displayed a phenomenal ability to master complex and technical data to the point of expertise. It is said that he had a photographic mind which enabled him to recall material he had fleetingly scanned. He revealed, among other things, that the Consolidated Gas Company was charging rates based upon a valuation which included heavily watered stock. His work led to a rate reduction for private consumers from $1.00 to 80 cents per thousand cubic feet and saved the city over $800,000 for lighting the city's streets alone.

When, later that year, the legislature set up the Armstrong Committee to investigate the insurance companies, Hughes was its logical choice for counsel. Revealing a remarkable ability to grasp the intricacies of insurance and high finance, Mr. Hughes over a period of three and one-half months and in fifty-seven public hearings subjected the leaders of the insurance and financial world to withering examination.[5] Under his merciless probing, it was exposed that part of the profits of underwriting syndicates, used by the insurance companies, found their way into the pockets of insurance executives; that huge salaries, improper personal expenditures and nepotism, on the part of executives and at the expense of stockholders, were commonplace; that clandestine lobbying activities were being carried on; and that concentration of the business of insurance had grown very great. Some months after the completion of the investigation the New York legislature enacted a series of laws to reform the conduct of the insurance business in the light of the Hughes disclosures.[6]

While the investigation was still under way, the Republican party sought the consent of Mr. Hughes to name him as its candidate for mayor of New York City but he refused. The following year, however, partly through the influence of President Theodore Roosevelt he was nominated by acclamation as the Republican party candidate for governor of New York State.[7] In this connection President Theodore Roosevelt commented in a letter to Henry Cabot Lodge:

Hughes' nomination is an excellent thing for the morale of the Republican party, and he is identified in the public mind as a reformer, but a sane and sincere reformer, who really has fought against the very evils which Hearst denounces, while yet free from any taint of demagogy.[8]

In his speech formally accepting the nomination, Mr. Hughes stressed "decent government" as "the supreme issue of this campaign." He promised an honest and unbossed administration and, in a special appeal to labor, pledged support of "every practical measure for the real benefit of labor." [9] Mr. Hughes was the only candidate on the state ticket of the Republican party to escape defeat. He won by a margin of 57,897 votes over the candidate of the Democratic party and the Independence League, William Randolph Hearst. His earlier exposures of corrupt business practices did not apparently militate against his receiving generous Wall Street support. In 1908, Mr. Hughes was reelected governor and served until October 10, 1910 when he was sworn in as an Associate Justice of the United States Supreme Court.

PHILOSOPHY OF GOVERNMENT

The philosophy of government that formed an integral part of the thinking of Mr. Hughes which he carried with him to the bench was forged out of the imponderable blending of his personality with his experience as a lawyer, public investigator and governor. As the chief executive of the most populous state in the Union, confronted with a host of unprecedented problems engendered by the development of an industrial society, that philosophy was necessarily influenced and tested in the crucible of the practical application of theory to the art of effective government. It is to be found expressed in his speeches, public documents and in the legislation to which he gave leadership or support.

It was a philosophy that held, as a basic tenet, that the security of our democracy was primarily safeguarded by the intelligence and public spirit of a free people, particularly as evinced in the selection of honest and competent public officers. In his inaugural address delivered on January 1, 1907,[10] Governor Hughes said that our form of government was not primarily safeguarded by constitutional guarantees but by "the intelligence and public spirit of its citizens and its ability to call to the work of administration men of single-minded devotion to the public interests, who make unselfish service to the State a point of knightly honor." [11] The emphasis he placed upon "the highest administrative standards" was reflected in his insistence that while political discussion centered largely on changing existing law, "the matter of chief consequence at all times is the conduct of government under the laws that we have," and this he regarded as "the severest test of democracy." [12] It was at least in part for this reason that he urged that the provision of the state constitution outlawing gambling be implemented by applying that prohibition to race-track gambling.

Apart from the "intelligence and public spirit" of the people, which were primary, how could greater honesty and efficiency in public office be assured? To achieve these ends he proposed that largesse in dispensing public favors and in supporting partisan workers at public expense be curtailed. "Partisan encumbrances," he said, "to a great extent account for administrative palsy." [13] In addition, he supported legislation to curb the use of corporate funds for political purposes and favored extension of the civil service. To weaken the hold of the machine, he urged the direct primary and greater secrecy of ballot. He maintained, however, that the chief safeguard against administrative inefficiency lay in greater accountability to the people and this he thought required greater concentration of responsibility and the short ballot.

These, however, were essentially negative measures. To attract competent men to public office more was necessary. One important means by which this could be accomplished, he maintained, was by conferring upon legislators and administrators adequate authority to govern and not curbing them by too minute definition of their powers in constitutions and laws. "Now it is true," he added,

that in the unchecked discretion of legislatures and administrative officers lie the opportunities of tyranny. But on the other hand there is no greater mistake than to withhold the power to do well in the fear of ill. There is no adequate power that cannot be abused.[14]

The emphasis he placed upon the primary importance of honest and efficient government did not lead Mr. Hughes to ignore the necessity for an extension of governmental activities to cope with the problems of modern life. A second fundamental tenet of his philosophy was expressed in his belief in progressive social legislation, effected, however, only upon a "just" balance of personal freedom and public interest and only after careful investigation and full knowledge of the pertinent facts.

This was a constantly recurring note he struck in support of or opposition to public measures. He recognized that social progress had brought in its wake glaring inequalities which had created discontent and "strained the democratic relation." He recognized, too, that there were many areas in which public control in the public interest had become a matter of necessity. But, he insisted, respect must be accorded to individual freedom as well as community interest, for common interest cannot be preserved if individual incentive is paralyzed. The line may be difficult to draw, he said, but the principle is clear: "Restrictions, to be justified, must be such as are essential to the maintenance of wholesome life and to prevent the liberty of some from accomplishing the enthraldom of all." [15] And such restrictions must not be adopted on the basis of sentiment or prejudice but only when warranted by the facts. Consistent with these principles, he sponsored the creation of the Wainwright Commission whose investigation into the social aspects of occupational injury and disease led to the enactment of the New York workmen's compensation law which served as the model for similar enactments in other states. So, too, he urged the passage of an anti-child labor law, the setting up of public service commissions to regulate utility rates, and supported legislation to conserve waterways and forest preserves free from private exploitation.

Consistent, too, with these principles, he vetoed the bills to reduce railroad rates to two cents per mile and to reduce the fare to Coney Island to five cents. Neither of these measures, he said, was opposed by him in principle. What he censured was the manner in which the reductions were effected, that is, by legislative "fiat" without prior investigation, which, in his opinion, made any conclusion regarding the justice of the proposals impossible. In his message vetoing the two cents per mile railroad bill, he stated:

The passage of the bill was not preceded by legislative investigation or suitable inquiry under the authority of the State. Nor is the fixing of this rate predicated on reports or statistics officially collated which would permit a fair conclusion as to the justice of its operation with reference to the railroads within its purview. . . . Where the matter requires investigation in order that a just result may be reached, the obvious course is to create a body which can investigate, with expert assistance, as summarily as possible, and which shall have adequate power to make appropriate orders. Such a body has been created in this State through the Public Service Commissions Law recently enacted.[16]

Similarly, in rejecting the Coney Island fare reduction bill, he said:

Whether a five-cent fare is a fair one depends upon facts and not upon sentiment, desire, or prejudice. . . . The proper way to deal with these matters is to provide for investigation in which the whole subject can be considered, specious claims sifted out, and a result just both to the corporations and to the public arrived at.[17]

The conviction of Governor Hughes, reflected in his vetoes, that a full knowledge of the facts is inseparable from the process of rendering justice was repeatedly voiced in his public statements. In an address at Chautauqua, in 1907, he said that progressive democracy depended upon the reign of reason, and "reason demands the facts." [18] In a lecture he delivered at Yale University in 1910, shortly before he became an Associate Justice of the high Court, he stressed the importance of opposition not only to the tyranny of a despot but also to that of a majority. The individual, he said, is to be highly prized, "who demands the facts, who is willing to stand or fall by the facts, who forms his convictions deliberately and adheres to them tenaciously, who courts patient inquiry and 'plays fair.' " [19]

In the area of intergovernmental, as distinguished from intra-societal, relations a third vital tenet of Mr. Hughes' philosophy of government lay in his concern for an appropriate division of national and state power. Such a division, he believed, while rendering federal power adequate to the solution of problems national in scope, particularly in relation to interstate commerce, should not destroy the essential duality of our federal system. It was his deep conviction that it was necessary to the permanence of free institutions that each community should attend to its particular affairs. Through the powers and responsibilities of local administration, he believed, independence, public spirit and capacity for self-government were developed, which not only appertained to local government but made possible the support of the central government.[20] There were two dangers, he thought:

The one is that serious evils of national scope may go unchecked because Federal power is not exercised. The other lies in an unnecessary exercise of Federal power, burdening the central authority with an attempted control which would result in the impairment of proper local autonomy, and extending it so widely as to defeat its purpose. It must be remembered that an evil is not the proper subject of Federal cognizance merely because it may exist in many States. All sorts of evils exist in many States which should be corrected by the exercise of local power, and they are not evils of Federal concern although they may be widespread.

On the other hand, it cannot be regarded as a policy of unwise centralization that, wherever there is a serious evil demanding governmental correction which afflicts interstate commerce and hence is beyond the control of the State, the power of Congress should unhesitatingly be exercised.[21]

This deep interest of Governor Hughes in maintaining the essential bases and prerogatives of state power was reflected in his opposition to ratification of the proposed income tax amendment. In his message of January 5, 1910, submitting the joint resolution of Congress to the state legislature, he placed his opposition squarely on this ground.[22] He believed that the national government should be given the power to tax ordinary incomes "to equip it with the means of meeting national exigencies." He pointed out, however, that the comprehensive sweep of the proposed power extended not only to incomes from ordinary real and personal property but to incomes "from whatever source derived." The effect would be "to place the borrowing capacity of the State and of its governmental agencies at the mercy of the Federal taxing power" and "an impairment of the essential rights of the State." The immunity which state securities had theretofore enjoyed had enabled the state to market them at low interest cost. "To permit such securities to be the subject of Federal taxation is to place such limitations upon the borrowing power of the State as to make the performance of the functions of local government a matter of Federal grace."

To the argument that the scope of the amendment might be limited by construction in the Supreme Court, Governor Hughes answered that this could not be assured and that, in any event, no amendment should be approved which was so worded as to afford the opportunity for violation of the fundamental conditions of state authority. He concluded, "While we may desire that the Federal government may be equipped with all necessary powers in order that it may perform its national function, we must be equally solicitous to secure the essential bases of State government."

The reconciliation of a grant of adequate power to the national government to meet national exigencies with the preservation of the "essential bases of State government" was to be one of the cardinal problems with which Mr. Hughes was compelled to deal, again and again, as an Associate Justice and as Chief Justice of the United States.

Of commanding importance, in the light of the nature of this study, was a fourth basic tenet of Mr. Hughes' philosophy of government—unqualified acceptance of the authority of the Supreme Court as the final arbiter of all constitutional questions. This, he maintained, was implicit in the theory of our Constitution, operated to safeguard our separation of powers and federal systems and to subordinate the will of an existing majority to the will of the people as expressed in our Constitution. In January, 1908, he stated,

In this country progress cannot be made save in harmony with our constitutional system. The Constitution in its entirety must be observed. . . . The functions of each department of government—executive, legislative, and judicial—are defined, and the responsibilities of each department are fixed. The people have not only marked out the spheres and limited the powers of their representatives, but the provisions of our Constitution are also checks upon the hasty and inconsiderate action of the people themselves. According to our system, the controlling will of the people is found in constitutional provisions, as interpreted and applied by the courts, and these must remain effective until the people change them by amending the Constitution in the prescribed manner.[23]

He recognized, he said the following month, that differences of opinion, influenced by differences in economic and political theory, were bound to exist with regard to the appropriate spheres of federal and state authority. These differences had to be resolved, "and for that purpose we have a final arbiter in the Supreme Court." Let the people debate such matters, but, he added, "We secure our peace and confidence by loyal acceptance of the decisions of our umpires." [24]

Finally, basic to the philosophy of Charles Evans Hughes was the conviction, developed out of experience, that the final authority of the Supreme Court in interpreting and enforcing the Constitution, must be reconciled with the establishment of administrative agencies vested with adequate powers to cope with complex problems of day-to-day regulation. The most complete exposition of his views with regard to the appropriate roles of courts and administrative agencies occurred under unusual circumstances. His proposal that public service commissions be established to regulate utility rates, with finality attaching to determinations of fact supported by evidence, met the fierce opposition of a section of the New York bar. On May 3, 1907, in Hughes' presence, Mr. John V. Stanchfield, a distinguished lawyer, before the Elmira Chamber of Commerce, made a scathing attack upon the bill. Discarding the speech he had prepared for the occasion, Governor Hughes delivered an extemporaneous reply.[25]

So that there could be no misunderstanding concerning his regard for the courts, he said, "I reckon him one of the worst enemies of the community who will talk lightly of the dignity of the bench." He, too, was opposed to any direct or indirect assault upon the courts. But, he added,

no more insidious assault could be made upon the independence and esteem of the judiciary than to burden it with these questions of administration,—questions which lie close to the public impatience, and in regard to which the people are going to insist on having administration by officers directly accountable to them.

The Court should consider questions of basic constitutional right, such as the right to hold property without being deprived of it without due process of law or not to be subjected to assumptions of arbitrary power. But it would make a "mere mockery" of regulation to say that

all these matters of detail which will be brought before the commission, —matters requiring men to give their entire attention to the subject, to get their information in a variety of ways, to have hearings of those interested, and to deal with questions from a practical standpoint,— should, at the option of the corporations, be taken into court.

Furthermore, if that policy should succeed it would swamp the courts with administrative burdens and expose them to hostile, and, perhaps, violent criticism.

It was in the course of this extemporaneous speech that Governor Hughes made probably the most frequently, if partially, quoted statement concerning the essential nature of the power of judicial review, namely, "*We are under a Constitution, but the Constitution is what the judges say it is* [my italics], and the judiciary is the safeguard of our liberty and of our property under the Constitution."

It has sometimes been suggested that this statement, under the circumstances, did not reflect Mr. Hughes' real judgment. It is interesting to observe, therefore, that in a formal address delivered by him on September 5, 1908, more than one year later, he expressed an almost identical view:

Congress may pass laws, but the Supreme Court interprets and construes them, and determines their validity. *The Constitution, with its guarantees of liberty and its grants of Federal power, is finally what the Supreme Court determines it to mean* [my italics].[26]

Whatever may be said of the earlier statement, the later one was delivered under circumstances that make it impossible to deny that in implying that constitutional interpretation depended, in the final analysis, not upon some inexorable mandate of the Constitution as law, but upon the qualities of the judges as men, he was then expressing his considered opinion. This remark came in the course of an address delivered in support of the election of William Howard Taft to the presidency, which Hughes said was "most important" in its relation to the judiciary. His appeal for votes was based squarely on the ground that "it is not improbable that the next president will appoint at least four judges of the United States Supreme Court" to which he added:

Upon the *learning, wisdom, and character* [my italics] of the judges of the Supreme Court rests not merely the just determination of the important matters of private right which come before that august tribunal, but to a very large degree the course of our political history and the development and security of our institutions.[27]

Such, then, was the measure of the man who, on April 25, 1910, was nominated as an Associate Justice of the United States Supreme Court. In known detail, it was compounded out of a preacher background with its emphasis on rectitude and serious-mindedness; high intellectual capacity; training in the law; experience at the bar in association with a prominent law firm in the representation of important corporate clients; and public service both as an investigator of the corrupt and shabby uses of great wealth, and as the governor of a state facing the acute problems engendered by a heterogeneous population and the need to adapt government to the demands of twentieth-century industrial civilization. The philosophy evolved placed emphasis upon honesty, efficiency and responsibility in public office; sought social progress on the basis of a "fair" balance of public and private interest; saw strength in the maintenance of the essential duality of our federal system; defended the final authority of the Supreme Court on all issues of constitutionality; and evinced an appreciation for the need of the administrative process in the practical art of government. And, it was this accumulated store of "learning, wisdom and character," rather than any specific mandates of the Constitution, as Charles Evans Hughes discerned, that were primary in the making of the justice and of his decisions.

Nomination to the Supreme Court

In announcing the nomination of Charles Evans Hughes to the Supreme Court, President William Howard Taft stated,

I am very much delighted to secure Governor Hughes for the Supreme Court Bench. He is a man of wide experience, and it is a mighty valuable thing to have on that bench a man of affairs. Governor Hughes is forty-eight years old . . . and if he retires from service on the bench at seventy he will have had twenty-two years of solid usefulness.[28]

The nomination of Charles Evans Hughes as an Associate Justice of the Supreme Court in 1910 was received, with but few important exceptions, with acclaim and approved by members of Congress of both parties with rivalling cordiality. (This was in marked contrast, as will be seen, to the bitter dispute evoked in Congress and in the press with his nomination in 1930 as Chief Justice of the United States.) Several members of the Court commented favorably, if tersely. Chief Justice Fuller stated simply, "I am delighted," and Justice Harlan called it "a fine appointment." [29] Henry Cabot Lodge wrote to Theodore Roosevelt, "It is an excellent appointment. He is under sixty-five years old, and he takes the Marshall and not the Taney view of the Constitution." [30] Theodore Roosevelt replied from Christiania,

Hughes' nomination is excellent, and I think he will make a fine judge. I only hope that he has awakened to the fact that unless we are content ical change in the attitude of our judges to public questions. I verily to face disaster to the judiciary in the future, there must be a very rad-believe that the conduct of the bench, in failing to move with the times, and in continually sticking on minor points of the law rather than turning to broad principles of justice and equity, is one of the chief elements in producing the present popular discontent. I do hope Hughes will realize this.[31]

The conservative and liberal press alike joined in the praise. The New York *Times* believed the appointment of a man of his "balance and sanity of judgment" would strengthen the Court.[32] The New York *Daily Tribune* editorially affirmed that "the appointment of Charles E. Hughes as an associate justice of the Supreme Court will be universally approved as a fitting recognition of high attainments and notable public service." [33]

The *World*, a liberal organ, agreed that "Mr. Taft could not have made a better or a more popular selection," and added, "In every part of the country Mr. Hughes is looked upon by Republicans and Democrats alike as a progressive statesman and a fearless champion of public rights against special privilege." [34] The *Wall Street Journal* commented that "his addresses and his vetoes while governor reveal the perfect impartiality and the absolutely judicial quality of his mind." [35]

Among the few dissenting voices raised was that of Hughes' erstwhile opponent for the governorship, William Randolph Hearst. His New York *American*, espousing a now unfamiliar editorial position, recalled Governor Hughes' vetoes of the five-cent fare and his formal argument against the income tax and the two-cent railroad rate bills, and added, "[It] is no more nor less than truth to say that the record of Governor Hughes' executive indorsements and vetoes amply justifies the apprehension that the natural bias and trend of his mind is all in favor of the corporate view." [36]

In even more vigorous dissent from the general acclaim that greeted the nomination was William Jennings Bryan. Condemning Hughes' action in regard to the fare and income tax measures, and adding the charge that Hughes in 1908 was the chief defender of the Republican party's inaction on trust regulation, he insisted that "no one who will examine his record can doubt that he is in close sympathy with the exploiting corporations." Hughes was, Bryan charged,

a shining illustration of that peculiar type of citizen developed in this country during the present generation—the citizen who personally opposes vice and is a punisher of small crimes, but who shows no indignation at the larger forms of legalized robbery.[37]

Senator Borah, on the other hand, although he had led the movement for an income tax law, said, "I strongly approve the selection of Governor Hughes for the Supreme bench. . . . I have the utmost confidence in his legal attainments and honesty." [38] And to the *Nation*, assailing Bryan's attack on the appointment, it appeared that,

Both in the matter of insurance legislation and in the creation of the Public Service Commissions, Mr. Hughes has shown himself to be as far removed as possible from the type of the corporation standpatter against which alone any such criticism as that of Mr. Bryan has force.[39]

On October 13, a few days after Hughes had taken his oath of office as an Associate Justice, the *Nation* again commented,

One can distinctly see the coming of a New Statism to offset or withstand the New Nationalism; and of that movement Gov. Hughes has been a leading prophet and exponent. . . . [We] gratefully acknowledge that he has ennobled our public life and quickened our hope in democracy.[40]

On May 2, 1910, the nomination was unanimously confirmed by the Senate, but since the October term of 1909 was nearing its close and Mr. Hughes was concerned with important tasks as governor, with the approval of the President, he did not resign his state office until some months later when he was sworn in as an Associate Justice of the United States Supreme Court.

II. Associate Justice of the United States Supreme Court

CHAPTER 2

THE RECONCILIATION OF LIBERTY AND AUTHORITY

THE AMERICAN PROBLEM

From earliest times men have sought to set limits upon collective interference with individual independence and to give those limits the force of law. These have been found in "immemorial custom," or the will of God, or natural law, or "higher law," or "right reason," or the social compact. All such attempts have proved inadequate because the reason of men has detected behind the mask of "law" the will and purposes of men. While, under our system, as under any democratic system, the freedom of individuals and minorities is basically protected against majorities by the spirit and tradition of our people and the self-restraint of the majority, the unique contribution of American jurisprudence was to predicate the immediate protection of the individual against society upon a written constitution, having the force of primary law. Unique, too, is the system of dual sovereignty involving a division of powers between the nation and the states which also finds protection in a written constitution. Although this Constitution avowedly possesses no supernatural sanction, yet, strangely perhaps, as Woodrow Wilson discerned, "The divine right of kings never ran a more prosperous course than did this unquestioned prerogative of the Constitution to receive universal homage." [1]

The provisions of the Constitution, however, are not self-effectu-

ating, and early in our history it was established that the ultimate
arbiter of all questions of constitutionality whether in relation to
individual right or national and state power was the Supreme Court
of the United States.[2] And once this authority was recognized, generally speaking, the sanctity attached to the Constitution has with a
similar awe attached to the high civil priests of constitutional interpretation, the Justices of the Supreme Court.

Under this scheme of government the authority of the federal
government generally derives from granted powers and that of the
states from the reservation of sovereign power commonly referred
to as the police power. The central task of the Court, throughout its
history, has been to reconcile these powers with prohibitions either
expressed in the Constitution, or in the case of the states, implied from
the nature of certain delegations to Congress.

Among the more important of the constitutional limitations, with
which Justice Hughes found himself concerned during his initial
tenure on the bench, are those imposed upon the states by the involuntary servitude, due process, equal protection and contract clauses
of the Constitution. These are dealt with in the immediately ensuing
chapters. The most important of these grants of power to Congress
with which Mr. Hughes dealt during this period is that empowering
Congress to regulate interstate commerce. The nature and scope of
this affirmative grant of power, and the extent to which this affects
the power of states over commerce, interstate and intrastate, although
both are subject to due process and other limitations, are for the
sake of convenience separately treated under a single heading in a
later chapter.

It would be fatuous to believe that in applying the Constitution
to the resolution of great social and economic conflicts the task of
the Court is the simple one of invoking the clear and precise language
of the Constitution. For the fact is that many of the delegations and
limitations of power are found in broad and general clauses admitting
of a variety of interpretations. That fact permits inarticulate and un-
avowed considerations, conscious or unconscious, to play an important part in determinations of constitutionality. One of the primary
purposes of this book is to shed light upon these considerations particularly as they affected Mr. Hughes.

In demarcating the area of authority, national and state, from that of liberty, the task of the Court is further complicated by the fact that these are not antithetical conceptions. To regard them as such would be to accept the Hobbesian view that liberty is simply the absence of law. While it is true that virtually every law curtails the liberty of some, it may in that very process, as Locke saw, enhance the freedom of others. Thus, for example, the National Labor Relations Act, in restricting the freedom that employers theretofore enjoyed in dismissing employees, enlarged the freedom of those employees to organize and bargain collectively with their employers. Liberty, therefore, as fully as authority, must be considered by the Court in a social context, and how this was done by Justice Hughes and the Court of which he was a part is an appropriate concern of this study.

Justice Hughes, who took his oath of office on October 10, 1910, as an Associate Justice of the Supreme Court of the United States, brought to the tasks of his position high intelligence, broad legal capacity and administrative experience. For almost six years, and specifically until June 10, 1916, he served on the bench in such manner that, despite occasional criticism of his decisions, his resignation evoked the nearly universal acclaim that had greeted his designation.[3]

In this period he wrote 151 opinions for the Court and dissented in only 32 cases.[4] In only nine instances was there any dissent from his decisions and in only three of these did more than one Justice dissent. Within the Court, in this period, the fairly clear and steadfast alignments, which were to characterize the early New Deal and the present Court, did not emerge, so that to a very significant degree the work of Justice Hughes has been appropriately described as "almost equally a record of the opinions and utterances of the Court as a whole."[5]

Yet there were significant differences among the Justices in point of emphasis and contribution and some fundamental disagreements, and these are explored in the pages that follow.

An Illustration: Involuntary Servitude

The problem of demarcation between national and state power, the uses to which law may be put in relation to freedom, and the process of balancing antithetical social interests involved in most discussions of freedom are well illustrated by one of the earliest of Mr. Hughes' decisions as a member of the Court. Here the authority of the state to promote the interests of its inhabitants confronted not only a specific prohibition of the Constitution but of an Act of Congress as well. The case, *Bailey* v. *Alabama*,[6] involved the validity of an Alabama statute which provided that any person who, with intent to injure or defraud, entered into a written contract for the performance of service, and thereby obtained money from his employer, and with like intent failed to perform such service, was guilty of a crime and punishable as in the case of theft. An amendment to the statute made the refusal or failure to perform the service without just cause and without refunding the money prima facie evidence of the intent to injure or defraud. While the presumption might be negated by evidence, the law did not permit the employee-defendant to testify that he had not intended to defraud.

In this instance, a Negro, Bailey, made a contract with an employer to work at $12 a month for a year. He received $15 in advance. He worked a little more than a month and left without refunding the money. Upon this evidence Bailey was sentenced to pay a fine of $30 and costs and, in default of such payment, to imprisonment at hard labor for 136 days. The statute upon which the conviction was based was challenged as a violation of the provision against involuntary servitude contained in the Thirteenth Amendment of the United States Constitution and of the Act of Congress passed for its enforcement. That Amendment reads as follows:

Section 1. Neither slavery nor involuntary servitude, except as a punishment for crime whereof the party shall have been duly convicted, shall exist within the United States, or any place subject to their jurisdiction.

Section 2. Congress shall have power to enforce this article by appropriate legislation.

Justice Hughes, speaking for a majority of the Court, regarded the statute as simply a means of compelling an employee-debtor to work off his debt. He said,

We cannot escape the conclusion that although the statute, by its terms, is to punish fraud, still its natural and inevitable effect is to expose to conviction for crime those who simply fail or refuse to perform contracts for personal service in liquidation of a debt, and judging its purpose by its effect that it seeks in this way to provide the means of compulsion through which performance of such service may be secured.

The claim that it was within the province of the state to punish for fraud and to set up presumptions of fraud was, in relation to the statute in issue, dismissed as an indirect attempt to transgress the constitutional prohibition against involuntary servitude.

He declared, furthermore, that the law was in conflict with an Act of Congress, passed pursuant to authority granted in the Amendment, which declared null and void all laws of any state by which any attempt should be made to establish or maintain, "directly or indirectly, the voluntary or involuntary service or labor of any persons as peons in liquidation of any debt or obligation." Peonage, he said, was descriptive of a condition known to history, the essence of which "is compulsory service in payment of a debt." The prohibition, therefore, "necessarily embraces all legislation which seeks to compel the service or labor by making it a crime to refuse or fail to perform it." With a regard for practical realities, he added, "Such laws would furnish the readiest means of compulsion," and these would be "peculiarly effective as against the poor and ignorant, its most likely victims."

Justice Holmes, joined by Justice Lurton, dissented. Justice Holmes argued that even on the assumption that the statute made a mere refusal to work according to contract a crime, it did not violate the Thirteenth Amendment. The Amendment, he said, did not outlaw contracts for labor nor deprive the state of the right to declare the breach of such contracts, without excuse, criminal. Furthermore, he maintained, involuntary servitude as a punishment for crime was expressly excepted from the prohibition of the Amendment, and added, "If the contract is one that ought not to be made, prohibit it. But if it is a perfectly fair and proper contract, I can see no reason why the State should not throw its weight on the side of performance."

But the fact is, he insisted, that the statute did not make a mere breach of a contract to labor a crime but punished fraud. So, also, he argued, the amendment to the statute, which made failure to perform or return the money prima facie evidence of fraudulent intent, did not raise a conclusive presumption but merely warranted sending the case to the jury. Such a rule was not unreasonable since "an unjustified departure from the promised service without re-payment may be declared a sufficient case to go to the jury for their judgment."

Justice Hughes, in his opinion, agreed that the prima facie rule did not make it the *duty* of the jury to convict, when there was no other evidence but the breach of the contract and the failure to pay the debt. But, he demurred, "The point is that, in such a case, the statute *authorizes* the jury to convict." He agreed, too, with Justice Holmes that the time and circumstances of the departure may be such as to raise a strong inference of fraudulent intent but this did not require a special statutory presumption since, even before its enactment, timing and circumstances could have been presented as evidence to the jury. It was clear, therefore, that "plainly the ob-ject of the statute was to hit cases which were destitute of such in-ferences, and to provide that the mere breach of the contract and the mere failure to pay the debt might do duty in their absence."

It was likewise true, Justice Hughes conceded, that the Court had frequently recognized the power of legislatures to provide that proof of one fact should be prima facie evidence of another in issue but, he contended, this was so only when the inference was not purely arbitrary and there was a rational relation between the two facts. Moreover, where the fact, the existence of which is made the basis of the statutory presumption, fell within the scope of a constitutional provision it could not be used, he insisted, as a means of indirect escape from constitutional restrictions.

On some of the technical issues in dispute Justice Hughes would appear to be on firmer ground than the distinguished libertarian. In asserting that he could see no reason why the state should not throw its "weight on the side of performance," Justice Holmes failed adequately to recognize the distinction between ordinary civil penalty and criminal punishment for breach of contract. The for-mer, while it seeks to induce compliance, accepts the possibility of breach as a normal incident of the contractual relation, while the latter, for all practical purposes, bars a breach and compels com-pliance. When applied to a contract for labor, this is the essence of peonage.[7] Viewed in terms of practical consequences, "To entrust to the master the powerful weapon of the criminal law would render the laborer's service in a real sense involuntary servitude." [8]

Justice Hughes would appear to be on stronger ground, too, when he suggests the absence of a rational inferential relation between the mere fact of quitting service, without repayment of a debt, and an intent to defraud. If the known facts of experience are considered, obviously many impoverished individuals borrow sums of money with the intention of repayment, through labor, only to quit for a variety of reasons among which the intention to defraud offers only one possible explanation. And it must be borne in mind that the law of the state, in this instance, did not permit the laborer to testify that he did not intend to defraud. Under these circumstances, the inference finds its only real support in legislative fiat and "works a disguised change in the substantive law and authorizes punishment" for the mere act of quitting without repayment of the debt.[9]

But it must be apparent that the differences between the Justices cannot be explained on technical grounds alone. The language of the Thirteenth Amendment, and of the Act of Congress passed under its authority, were sufficiently clouded in ambiguity, as applied to the facts in this case, to yield, on analyses, to either interpretation. Basically, the differing conceptions of constitutionality derived from differing philosophies and conceptions of the public interest. To Justice Holmes, whatever the evil consequences in particular cases, public interest was generally served by extending broad latitude to local legislation against claims of unconstitutionality and by insistence upon the scrupulous execution of contracts freely entered into. "Breach of a legal contract without excuse," he wrote in this case, "is wrong conduct, even if the contract is for labor." [10] To Justice Hughes, on the other hand, there was "no more important concern than to safeguard the freedom of labor upon which alone can enduring prosperity be based," and it was this conviction, I suggest, that probably supplies the fundamental rationale for his decision preventing the circumvention of the restrictions of the Thirteenth Amendment and the Act of Congress through nicely calculated schemes.

CHAPTER 3

DUE PROCESS, EQUAL PROTECTION AND THE POLICE POWER

Due Process of Law

The "due process" clauses of the United States Constitution have been the most fecund source through which national and state legislation has been invalidated by courts of the land. The Fifth Amendment, which limits the exercise of federal power, provides, in part: "No person shall . . . be deprived of life, liberty, or property, without due process of law." And the Fourteenth Amendment, in virtually identical language, denies to the states authority to "deprive any person of life, liberty, or property, without due process of law."

The fundamental historic significance of the due process requirement, dating back to its first explicit formulation in the Statute of Westminster in 1354, is that it imposed *procedural* requirements deemed essential to the process of administering impartial justice in any governmental action affecting life, liberty or property.

The historic transformation through which the purely procedural limitations imposed by the due process clauses have been extended to the imposition of *substantive* restrictions on the powers of government will be traced in connection with the decisions of Mr. Hughes as Chief Justice of the United States.[1] For present purposes it is sufficient to note that substantive content as well as procedure fall under the constitutional scrutiny of the Court.

It is obvious that not every deprivation of life, liberty or property through the action of government violates the constitutional bar. There may be a valid deprivation of liberty, and even of life, for the commission of crime, and property is taken, without offending the Constitution, by taxation and in other ways. Virtually every piece of legislation restricts the liberty of some. The due process limitation must be applied compatibly with the delegated powers vested in the federal government and the police power of the states. How, then, does the Court determine whether particular deprivations are without due process of law? In essence, it has been established that the basic substantive due process inquiry for the Court is whether the legislation is fair and reasonable or arbitrary and unreasonable. How was this judgment applied to the solution of specific conflicts before the Court?

Railroad Regulation. A vast industrial machine inevitably renders some of the human material concerned in its construction and operation expendable. Particularly is this true in the case of our great network of railroads in connection with which accidental injury to employees is commonplace. To reduce the burden of such injury to themselves, railroad corporations frequently contracted with employees, who ordinarily had no real choice but to agree, that in the event of injury such employees would accept a company provided relief or benefit plan in lieu of any right of recovery, ordinarily more substantial, under the common law liability of the company in negligence.

One month after his decision in the BAILEY case, Justice Hughes, in *Chicago, B.&Q.R.R.* v. *McGuire*,[2] had the occasion to pass upon the constitutional validity of a state statute designed to prevent the enforcement of such contracts. An Iowa law barred a railroad corporation from setting up, as a defense to an action in negligence brought against it by an employee, any contract of insurance, benefit or indemnity entered into by the employee prior to injury or its acceptance by such employee after injury.

Justice Hughes, speaking for a unanimous Court, rejected the contention that the statute violated the due process clause by reason of the restraint it laid upon liberty of contract and denied that the liberty protected by this Amendment was absolute. It must be judged, he said, in a social context in terms of reasonableness.

There is no absolute freedom to do as one wills or to contract as one chooses. The guaranty of liberty does not withdraw from legislative supervision the wide department of activity which consists of the making of contracts, or deny to government the power to provide restrictive safeguards. Liberty implies the absence of arbitrary restraint, not immunity from reasonable regulations and prohibitions imposed in the interests of the community.

The particular regulation, he continued, was clearly within the province of the police power of the state. It may be upset, therefore, as a denial of "liberty" only if it is "arbitrary and has no reasonable relation to a purpose which it is competent for government to effect." He added that "where there is reasonable relation to an object within the governmental authority, the exercise of the legislative discretion is not subject to judicial review." He cautioned that

the scope of judicial inquiry in deciding the question of *power* is not to be confused with the scope of legislative considerations in dealing with the matter of policy. Whether the enactment is wise or unwise, whether it is based on sound economic theory, whether it is the best means to achieve the desired result, whether, in short, the legislative discretion within its prescribed limits should be exercised in a particular manner, are matters for the judgment of the legislature, and the earnest conflict of serious opinion does not suffice to bring them within the range of judicial cognizance.

Specifically, in dealing with the employer-employee relationship, said Justice Hughes, the legislature necessarily has wide discretion in seeking to protect health and safety, and promote peace and good order through regulations designed to insure wholesome conditions of work and freedom from oppression. Legislatures, too, may give recognition to the lack of equality between employers and employees and to the fact that their interests may be to a certain extent conflicting, and that in the absence of such equality, or when the public health required, one party to the contract might be protected against himself.

It is obvious that the reasoning of Justice Hughes in this case evinced a grasp of the practical realities of industrial relations. The distinction drawn, however, between *power* and *policy* presents great difficulties which will be the subject of extended discussion at a later point.[3] For the present, it may be noted that although the distinction may be real it is no easy task to distinguish between legislation within the province of the state which is "unwise" or "based on unsound economic theory" but constitutional from legislation which is "arbitrary and has no reasonable relation to a purpose which it is competent for government to effect" and unconstitutional.

Social Legislation. The difficulty in distinguishing between power and policy is well illustrated in the problem of determining the extent to which a state might go in proscribing or penalizing harmless conduct as an aid in the effectuation of legitimate social ends. In three decisions delivered by Justice Hughes a unanimous Court agreed in deciding that if the ends were legitimate, means reasonably adapted to achieve those ends must be upheld, whatever their adverse effect upon innocent behavior.

In the first, *Purity Extract & Tonic Co.* v. *Lynch,*[4] the central question was whether a state might prohibit the sale of malt liquors generally, including such as are non-intoxicating, in aid of the enforcement of its prohibition law. Upholding its right to do so, Justice Hughes reasoned that since the state, in the exercise of its police power, could prohibit the selling of intoxicating liquors it might adopt such measures having reasonable relation to that end as it thought necessary to make its action effective. "It does not follow," he said, "that because a transaction separately considered is innocuous it may not be included in a prohibition the scope of which is regarded as essential in the legislative judgment to accomplish a purpose within the admitted power of the Government." A contrary conclusion logically pressed "would save the nominal power while preventing its effective exercise."

In his second opinion, *Sturges & Burn Manufacturing Co.* v. *Beauchamp,*[5] Justice Hughes sustained the validity of a state statute which prohibited the employment of children under sixteen years of age in various hazardous occupations and made the employer liable for injuries upon a mere finding of violation of the statute without permitting the defense that the employer acted in good faith relying upon the representation of the minor as to his age. Since the state could prohibit the employment of persons of tender years in dangerous occupations, he said, "it could select means appropriate to make its prohibition effective and could compel employers, at their peril, to ascertain whether those they employed were in fact under the age specified."

In the third case, *Price* v. *Illinois,*[6] Justice Hughes held for the Court that a state might validly prohibit the sale of food preservatives containing boric acid although the harmful effects of such acid were "debatable." This power derived, he said, from the rights of the state to protect health and unless, therefore, the prohibition was "palpably unreasonable and arbitrary" it must be sustained. "If it be debatable, the legislature is entitled to its own judgment."

The growth of huge industrial enterprises, possessed of great and integrated economic power, led to an increasing recognition that whatever the legal fiction of freedom of contract in the relations between employers and employees, in reality, the bulk of employees did not enjoy an equality of bargaining power with their employers. The demand for the state-protected right of self-organization for labor, free from the hazard of dismissal, was persistently raised. It culminated, during the New Deal years, in the passage of the National Labor Relations Act and many state labor relations acts guaranteeing this right. These acts were sustained as constitutional.

Earlier, however, in *Adair* v. *United States*,[7] decided before Mr. Hughes became a member, a divided Court had invalidated a Congressional statute making it a crime for an interstate carrier to discharge an employee because of his membership in a labor organization as a deprivation of liberty (into which freedom of contract had been incorporated) without due process of law.

In 1915 the issue was again before the Court in relation to a Kansas statute which made it a criminal offense for an employer to require, as a condition of employment, that an employee enter into an agreement not to become a member of any labor organization while so employed. The case, *Coppage* v. *Kansas*,[8] produced three opinions. A majority of the Court, largely on the authority of the ADAIR case, which was held indistinguishable in principle, invalidated the Kansas statute as violative of the due process clause of the Fourteenth Amendment. The Court reaffirmed the doctrine, however, on the score of "reason" as well and argued that included in the concepts of liberty and property was the right to make contracts of personal employment by which labor is exchanged for money.

The majority further maintained, per Justice Pitney, that it was not a legitimate object for the exercise of the police power to seek to strengthen labor organizations which "are not public institutions . . . such as would render the maintenance of their membership a matter of direct concern to the general welfare." Inequalities in bargaining power were dismissed by the Court as necessary concomitants of the right of private property.

Justice Holmes dissented in a brief opinion. A workman, he said, may naturally believe that only by belonging to a union can he secure a fair contract. In typically Holmesian language, he affirmed, "If that belief, whether right or wrong, may be held by a reasonable man, it seems to me that it may be enforced by law in order to establish the equality of position between the parties in which liberty of contract begins." He made no attempt to distinguish the ADAIR case from the one before the Court and urged that the former be flatly overruled.

Justice Day wrote a separate, lengthy dissenting opinion with which Justice Hughes alone concurred. He denied that the ADAIR case controlled, and argued that "the cases are entirely different, and the decision of the questions controlled by different principles." He emphasized the fact that in the ADAIR case the Court had confined itself to ruling that the Act, in so far as it sought to penalize the discharge of an employee for union membership, was illegal. There was nothing in the statute before the Court, he insisted, that prevented an employer from discharging one in his service at will. What it did seek to proscribe was the exaction of an *agreement*. Because one may dismiss an employee for union membership, it did not follow that he had a constitutional right, against the authority of the state, to insert in a contract of employment any stipulation he chose. Labor organizations, he pointed out, are legal, and the right to join them, as against coercive action of the employer, may be a legitimate subject of protection by the state.

Nor was it improper for the state, in the exercise of its police power, to consider the relative positions of employers and employees.

Certainly it can be no substantial objection to the exercise of the police power that the legislature has taken into consideration the necessities, the comparative abilities, and the relative situation of the contracting parties. While all stand equal before the law, and are alike entitled to its protection, it ought not to be a reasonable objection that one motive which impelled an enactment was to protect those who might otherwise be unable to protect themselves.

The position taken by Mr. Hughes in this case is of especial interest for several reasons. It was to Mr. Hughes, as Chief Justice, that the task later fell of writing the prevailing opinion in the case sustaining the right of self-organization of labor under the National Labor Relations Act.[9] It is interesting to observe, too, that as was to be so frequently the case, Justice Hughes showed, in joining the Day dissent, a great reluctance to overrule a precedent of the Court even at the expense of straining logic and reason. "Stability in judicial opinions," he was later to write, "is of no little importance in maintaining respect for the Court's work." [10]

The strain upon reason and logic involved in the attempt to distinguish the ADAIR case is, I believe, fairly obvious. If, as Justices Day and Hughes reasoned, the relative situation of the parties to a labor contract, and the right of employees to join labor organizations, as against the coercive action of employers, are legitimate subjects of consideration and protection by the state, it is difficult to discern how the two cases cited are "controlled by different principles." The exaction of an agreement not to join a union is an even lesser hindrance, *per se*, to union membership than the discharge for union membership. And if the state may not prevent the latter, which Justices Day and Hughes appear to accept, there would seem to be no substantial ground upon which it may impede the former. Particularly, it may be asked, how is the attempted distinction to be reconciled with the principle enunciated by Justice Hughes in the PURITY EXTRACT and STURGES cases that if the end sought to be served by the state is legitimate within the exercise of its police power, it could select means appropriate to effectuate the end even at the expense of proscribing relatively harmless activity?

Another type of social legislation, upon the constitutionality of which the Court repeatedly passed, was that designed to preserve the human agents in the industrial process from the wastage and impairment induced by excessive hours of labor. As early as 1898, in *Holden* v. *Hardy*,[11] a divided Court had sustained the constitutional validity of a Utah statute limiting hours of labor in underground mines and in smelting to eight in any one day. In *Lochner* v. *New York*,[12] however, the Court, by a vote of five to four, declared invalid a New York statute restricting the hours of labor of bakers to no more than ten hours in any day or sixty in any week. Applied exclusively to women, on the other hand, a unanimous Court, only three years later, in *Muller* v. *Oregon*,[13] upheld an Oregon law prohibiting their employment in factories or laundries for more than ten hours in any day.

One month after its decision in the COPPAGE case the Court, in an opinion by Justice Hughes, in *Miller* v. *Wilson*,[14] unanimously ruled constitutional a California law which forbade the employment of women in selected establishments for more than eight hours a day, or forty-eight hours a week, against the claims that, as applied to a chambermaid in a hotel, it was a deprivation of liberty, that is, freedom of contract, without due process of law and a denial of equal protection of the laws.

Reiterating an often expressed principle, Justice Hughes said, "As the liberty of contract guaranteed by the Constitution is freedom from arbitrary restraint—not immunity to safeguard the public interest—the question is whether the restrictions of the statute have reasonable relation to a proper purpose."

In regard to the particular legislation, the recent decisions of the Court upholding other statutes limiting the hours of labor of women were considered "decisive." Especially pertinent, he found, was the MULLER case from which he quoted extensively in stressing the legitimacy of a special concern by the state in the welfare of women.

It was argued, however, that the legislation in this case, as distinguished from that in the MULLER case, carried a shorter work day and work week to an arbitrary and unconstitutional extreme. This argument he rejected on the ground that the limitations of the statute did not take the case "out of the domain of legislative discretion." He cautioned, however, that "this is not to imply that a limitation of the hours of labor of women might not be pushed to a wholly indefensible extreme."

Nor was the law arbitrary because of its classifications, exclusions or omissions since the legislature, he said, was not bound, in order to support the constitutional validity of its regulation, to extend it to all cases which it might possibly reach, but was free to recognize degrees of harm and confine its restrictions to those classes of cases where the need was deemed to be clearest.

The general principles reaffirmed in this case, apart from those deemed peculiarly applicable to the case of women, were that liberty of contract did not carry immunity from legislation reasonably adapted to safeguarding a public interest, that considerable discretion in serving such interest must be accorded the legislative judgment, and that classification and exclusion would not be deemed arbitrary simply because they were motivated by a desire to deal with those cases where, in the discretion of the legislature, the need was most acute. Few Justices of the Court have ever dissented from this general formulation. It is significant, therefore, that in the particular cases involving limitations upon the hours of labor to come before the Court it was able to arrive at varying conclusions in regard to constitutionality, culminating in its unanimous decision, in 1941, sustaining the restrictions of the Fair Labor Standards Act of 1938 upon the employment of *both men and women* to forty-four and finally to forty hours per week.[15] In terms of the thinking of the Court in 1915, and for many years thereafter, there is little reason to doubt that this statute pushed limitation "to a wholly indefensible extreme." It must be apparent, therefore, that the gyrations of the Court were possible because whether legislation of this character is "arbitrary" or bears a "reasonable relation to a proper purpose" generally involves a fundamental value judgment not susceptible of determination by reference to ordinary legal principles in regard to which judges may possess special competence.

Equal Protection of the Laws

The Fourteenth Amendment to the United States Constitution debars the state, not only from depriving any person of life, liberty and property without due process of law, but also from denying "to any person within its jurisdiction the equal protection of the laws." A law may, of course, violate both the due process and equal protection clauses of the Constitution. Even in the absence of an equal protection limitation, which is the case in regard to an exercise of federal power, the Court has said that if the discrimination of federal law is "gross" enough, it "is equivalent to confiscation and subject under [the due process clause of] the Fifth Amendment to challenge and annulment." [16] It may well be, therefore, that, lacking an equal protection clause applicable to the states, the Court might have arrived at many of the same conclusions through the medium of the due process clause. On the other hand, it is probably correct to suggest that equality receives at least somewhat greater protection against state legislation, in the presence of an equal protection clause, than in the case of federal legislation, in its absence.

"Equality" and "non-discrimination" are the essence of equal protection of the laws. But these do not enjoin the completely equal application of all laws to all persons under all circumstances. Thus, non-citizens may be debarred from certain professions of special trust open to citizens, such as medicine or law, and corporations may be taxed more heavily than individuals or partnerships. What, then, is the essential inquiry for the Court in those cases in which a denial of equal protection is claimed?

There were three significant cases, in which Justice Hughes wrote the prevailing opinion of the Court, involving as a principal issue the application of the equal protection clause to local legislation. In one, affecting the taxing power of the local government, he extended broad latitude to the legislative discretion. In the other two, affecting minorities peculiarly subject to discrimination and oppression, he found the laws objectionable.

In *Toyota* v. *Hawaii* [17] he upheld, for the entire Court, the constitutionality of a law of the Territory of Hawaii which provided for an annual license fee of $600 for those selling goods at auction in the district of Honolulu and only $15 in every other district. This gross discrimination he found to be within the legislative discretion, for, he said, "it must be assumed" that the legislature took into consideration pertinent factors, such as varying conditions, the amount of business transacted and the corresponding value of such licenses. "Necessarily," he said, "the power of classification 'must have a wide range of discretion.' It is not reviewable 'unless palpably arbitrary.' "

In thus sustaining the legislation even in the case of an apparently gross discrimination, Justice Hughes was deciding the specific issue consistently with the general trend of the Court's decisions that particularly in matters of taxation considerable range of discretion must be given the legislative judgment.

Discrimination against minorities on account of color, or other irrelevant factors, presented issues, however, of a very different nature.

No group in our community has had more frequent occasion to

appeal to the safeguard of equal protection of the laws than members of the Negro race who have been the chief victims of persistent palpable discrimination.[18] That discrimination has taken many forms. The particular form of discrimination before the Court in *McCabe* v. *Atchison, T.&S.F.R.R.*[19] lay in the provisions of a state law authorizing *intrastate* carriers to provide sleeping cars, dining cars and chair cars for white persons only. Speaking for a bare majority of the Court, Justice Hughes stated that the legislation constituted a denial of equal protection of the laws.

While he agreed that the question could no longer be considered an open one that it was not an infraction of the Fourteenth Amendment for a state to require "separate" accommodations for the white and black races on intrastate carriers, it did not follow that it could dispense with "equal" accommodations. He dismissed, "as without merit," the argument that the lack of substantial demand for these special accommodations for Negroes justified the state law.

It makes the constitutional right depend upon the number of persons who may be discriminated against, whereas the essence of the constitutional right is that it is a personal one. Whether or not particular facilities should be provided may doubtless be conditioned upon there being a reasonable demand therefor, but, if facilities are provided, substantial equality of treatment of persons traveling under like conditions cannot be refused.

However, the specific relief sought in this case, that is, to enjoin the companies from making any distinction in service on account of race, was denied on technical grounds because of the failure of the complainant to show any personal injury.[20]

Another group, frequently singled out for discriminatory treatment, particularly in regard to employment, is the alien. This discrimination arises in part out of the fact that aliens, distinguished by color or speech, are frequently willing or compelled to accept employment at wages lower than those customarily paid white Americans. To protect the latter from such competition, Arizona enacted legislation requiring employers of more than five workers within the state to employ not less than 80 per cent qualified electors or native-born citizens of the United States.

In *Truax* v. *Raich,*[21] the statute was held unconstitutional and its enforcement was enjoined. Pointing out that the equal protection clause extended to aliens but did not debar the state from making "reasonable classifications in legislation," Justice Hughes added,

> But this admitted authority, with the broad range of legislative discretion that it implies, does not go so far as to make it possible for the State to deny to lawful inhabitants, because of their race or nationality, the ordinary means of earning a livelihood. It requires no argument to show that the right to work for a living in the common occupations of the community is of the very essence of the personal freedom and opportunity that it was the purpose of the Amendment to secure.

He was not content to rest his decision on the ground of denial of equal protection alone, however, and reasoned that the legitimate interests of the state cannot "be so broadly conceived as to bring them into hostility to exclusive Federal power," that is, to admit or exclude aliens. Yet, he maintained, assertion of the authority to deny to aliens the opportunity to earn a livelihood "would be tantamount to the assertion of the right to deny them entrance and abode, for in ordinary cases they cannot live where they cannot work." [22]

SUMMARY STATEMENT

It should be observed that the Court has consistently affirmed that the legislature enjoys wide discretion in the exercise of the police power to classify "according to general considerations and with regard to prevailing conditions," and to "degrees of harm." [23] But what is the basis upon which it is determined that in particular cases the legislature has exceeded its discretion? Justice Brandeis sought to supply the rationale of the Court's decisions when he wrote that "the equality clause requires merely that the classification shall be *reasonable*. We call that action reasonable which an informed, intelligent, *just-minded*, civilized man could rationally favor [my italics]." [24]

The ultimate test of constitutionality under the equal protection as under the due process clause is, therefore, reasonableness and justice. The process by which these are determined in relation to specific legislation, as we have seen, is necessarily a largely subjective one, despite Justice Brandeis' attempt to give it an objective base. And since there are no fixed and unalterable criteria available for a determination of justice and reasonableness, considerable scope is given judicial discretion. That discretion is influenced by a variety of considerations, some of which may be obvious and some of which may be subtle and imponderable. Among the more obvious influences are the past precedents of the Court by which Justices, out of regard for stability, may deem themselves bound, whatever their personal preferences. But, in this connection, it must be recognized that stare decisis has only limited application to the constitutional decisions of the Court and that many statutes under consideration present novel questions. Another fairly obvious consideration, which forms one of the principal bases for distinguishing Justices, is the extent to which Justices, without regard to their own views, attach weight to the legislative determination of fairness and reasonableness implicit in the very passage of the legislation. Finally, among the more subtle but indubitable influences, however masked in constitutional formulae, are the predilections and biases of the Justices upon which their rationalizations are frequently unconsciously built.[25]

So far as Justice Hughes was concerned his value system led him to evince considerable willingness to accept the legislative restrictions imposed upon the relatively few privileged and propertied individuals in what he deemed the interests of the many as in accord with due process. In terms of legal formulae, it took the form, however, of according considerable discretion to the legislative judgment in matters of policy and a refusal to upset legislation unless clearly arbitrary or not reasonably adapted to achieve legitimate social ends. With respect to equal protection, on the other hand, he showed little hesitancy in striking down legislative restrictions imposed upon the relatively few underprivileged, peculiarly subject to discrimination, in what he deemed the interests of justice.

CHAPTER 4

PUBLIC CONTRACTS, THE CONTRACT CLAUSE AND THE POLICE POWER

GENESIS OF DOCTRINE

During the nineteenth century, no constitutional limitation brought a greater number of issues to the Supreme Court than that contained in Article 1, Section 10, forbidding a state to pass any "law impairing the obligation of contracts." [1] While, in the twentieth century, the due process limitation proved a more fruitful source of constitutional litigation, the contract clause continued to retain considerable vitality.

It is established that the contract clause relates only to a *law* of a *state* and affects only *preexisting* contracts, both *public* and *private*. Limitations upon the making of future contracts by law, as distinguished from the impairment of preexisting contracts, raise a due process question, into which the concept of "freedom of contract," as we have seen, has been articulated.

Although during Mr. Hughes' tenure as Chief Justice he had the occasion to write several opinions of fundamental constitutional significance involving the application of the contract clause to the alleged impairment of *private* contract rights, his decisions in that regard during his first period of service were of little or no importance. It was in connection with the restrictions imposed by the contract clause upon the power of the states in relation to their own contracts, that is, *public* contracts, that Justice Hughes wrote several important decisions and found himself most often in disagreement with other members of the Court.

There is considerable doubt whether it was the intention of the Framers to embrace within the protection of the contract clause purely public, as distinguished from private, contracts. [2] A foremost authority says that there was no direct discussion of this question at the Convention but it was "significant" that several members of the Convention assumed that the contract clause did not affect public contracts. He adds,

Only Henry and Galloway seem to have thought that it could or would be given a broader meaning, and they did so in discussing the problem of depreciated paper currency. Moreover, their interpretations were denied by members of the Convention, and the denials were not challenged.[3]

Be that as it may, the Supreme Court, in a series of famed decisions by Chief Justice Marshall, established the reach of the contracts clause to embrace public contracts and elaborated their scope. In *Fletcher* v. *Peck*,[4] Chief Justice Marshall ruled that sales by a state of public lands, pursuant to law, constituted the making of contracts within the meaning of this clause, and the attempted repeal of the authorizing law an impairment of their obligation. The words of the clause, he wrote, "are general and are applicable to contracts of every description." [5]

Having established that benefits derived through a sale authorized by legislation confer contract rights, Chief Justice Marshall, only two years later, expanded the scope of the contract clause, even beyond the expressed theories of its most ardent supporters,[6] and, in *New Jersey* v. *Wilson*,[7] invalidated a state law which sought to tax lands purchased from the Indians to whom an earlier act of the Colonial legislature had granted a perpetual immunity from taxation. The exemption, he held, ran with the land and was not personal. This doctrine, that the power of taxation may be alienated by one legislature in a manner binding upon subsequent legislatures, although frequently criticized by members of the Court, has never been repudiated.[8] The process of expansion culminated with the decision of Chief Justice Marshall, in *Dartmouth College* v. *Woodward*,[9] that a charter was a contract.[10]

The period of tenure of Roger B. Taney, as Chief Justice, following Marshall, while involving no break with the Marshall tradition in regard to contracts, but simply consolidation and application of its principles, in one significant respect attenuated the full rigor implicit in Marshall's doctrine concerning state franchises as contracts. In *Charles River Bridge* v. *Warren Bridge* [11] Chief Justice Taney, speaking for the Court, held that grants contained in public franchises must be strictly construed so that nothing may be claimed "that is not clearly given . . . by the Act." As a consequence, the grant of a charter to construct a bridge was not considered exclusive, precluding the authorization for the erection of another and competing bridge nearby.[12]

Such, in brief, were the root developments, in regard to the meaning and scope of the contract clause, as applied to public contracts, when Justice Hughes became a member of the Court.

The limitations of the contract clause posed special difficulties, unanticipated by its Framers and early interpreters, in the control of public utilities. The invention of the telephone and of artificial means of lighting, and the development of the railroad and other means of rapid transportation, led, in the nineteenth and early twentieth centuries, to the bestowing, often with reckless abandon, of great privileges to private corporate interests by public authorities, frequently with little or no financial return to the state and with little or no reserved power of control. The services rendered by these utilities were vital to the entire community, and the abuses perpetrated by them in many instances were so rampant, that the demand for government regulation, in the public interest, became insistent. The chief constitutional provision upon which the utilities relied in seeking to thwart or limit such regulation was the contract clause.

While, during the period of service of Justice Hughes, none of the established principles relating to public contracts was repudiated by the Court, there was considerable controversy over the degree and extent to which grants to public utilities were to be liberally or strictly construed in regard to general privileges conferred, rate regulation and tax immunity.

FORFEITURE OR REPEAL OF GRANTS

In *Grand Trunk Western R.R.* v. *South Bend* [13] the issue before the Court was whether a city, which had not reserved its right to repeal or alter a franchise grant, might, under the exigencies that had developed with the years following the grant, in the exercise of its police power, repeal so much of the grant as had not been availed of.

The facts were these. An ordinance of South Bend, Indiana, of 1861 granted the right to a railway company to lay a double track through one of its streets. This was utilized by the company only as to part of the available distance when the city, in 1901, repealed so much of the ordinance as related to the double track. No power to alter or repeal the grant had been reserved by the city. It argued, however, that the partial repeal constituted a reasonable exercise of power in view of the growth of the city and the congestion it had brought in its wake. A majority of the Court, through Justice Lamar, rejected this argument on the ground that not regulation but destruction of the contract was being attempted "which, as it contemplated permanent and not temporary structures, granted a permanent and not a revocable franchise."

Only Justices Hughes and Pitney dissented from the decision of the Court, and without opinion. The fair inference, however, would appear to be that these Justices believed that the franchise grant carried with it, by necessary implication, the requirement that it be fully utilized within a reasonable time, or, to the extent of non-use, be forfeited; or, more broadly stated, that the grant could not, after a lapse of years and partial non-use, be set up against the paramount authority of the state to govern in the interests of the community.

The view that "use" was a limitation implicit in any franchise grant was explicitly stated by Justice Hughes, in a unanimous decision of the Supreme Court, the following year, in *New York Electric Lines Co.* v. *Empire City Subway System.*[14] The city of New York had given permission to New York Electric Lines Co., in 1883, to lay electrical conductors in the city's streets. The permission had never been availed of and was formally revoked in 1906.

"While the grant becomes effective when made and accepted in accordance with the statute and the grantee is thus protected in starting the enterprise," said Justice Hughes,

it has always been recognized that, as the franchise is given in order that it may be exercised for the public benefit, the failure to exercise it as contemplated is ground for revocation or withdrawal. . . . It is a tacit condition annexed to grants of franchises that they may be lost by mis-user or non-user.

This condition, he wrote, "inheres in the nature of the grant."

The difference in the Court suggested by its decisions in the GRAND TRUNK and NEW YORK ELECTRIC LINES cases is that while the whole Court agreed that complete failure to use a granted privilege within a reasonable time might work a forfeiture of the privilege, only Justices Hughes and Pitney were prepared to extend this principle to a partial failure to do so.

Even this statement, however, is subject to the qualification that the entire Court acquiesced in the position, expressed by Justice Hughes in *Russell* v. *Sebastian*,[15] that forfeiture would not operate for partial non-use under circumstances in which the grantee had already made substantial expenditures in anticipation of an extension of its facilities and had changed its position beyond recall.

EXACTING COMPENSATION

However, even when substantial investments had been made in the construction of a public utility, under authorization of law, Justice Hughes evinced a determination to construe reservations of power to the lawmaking authority so broadly as to permit compensation to the municipality for the privileges granted, as distinguished from forfeiture for non-use. The case in point was *Owensboro* v. *Cumberland Telephone and Telegraph Company*.[16] The city of Owensboro, by ordinance passed in 1889, authorized a telephone company to place telephone poles and wires on the city streets. A subsequent ordinance of the city, passed in 1909, required the Company to remove all of its poles and wires unless it purchased from the city a franchise authorizing it to maintain such poles and wires.

Justice Lurton, speaking for a bare majority of the Court which included Justice Holmes, held the later ordinance an impairment of the obligation of contract. Finding three reservation clauses inapplicable, it was the view of the Court that the grant was one in perpetuity. "This conclusion," said the Court, "finds support from a consideration of the public and permanent character of the business such companies conduct and the large investment which is generally contemplated."

Insisting that it is "well settled" that "legislative grants of municipal authority shall be construed most favorably to the public and against persons claiming thereunder," four Justices dissented. The opinion with which Justice Hughes concurred was written by Justice Day who pointed out that the same law which gave the city the power to grant the franchise, that is, the power to "regulate" streets, alleys and sidewalks and all repairs thereof was "limited by the express reservation that it shall be exercised subject to the power of the city to amend and repeal any ordinance so enacted." The large investment involved, in the view of the minority, was no bar to the later ordinance since

the grantee is conclusively presumed to be aware of this limitation and to make his investments subject to the exercise of the reserved right. . . . Moreover, if limited grants are to be construed into perpetuities then the control over the streets for railway, telephone and other kindred enterprises of enormous value are granted to private corporations without compensation for the use of such valuable rights which belong to the municipality.

RATE-MAKING

In the heyday of the period during which public franchises were granted, the rates to be levied were sometimes directly fixed by the legislative authority making the grant, or frequently left to the discretion of the utilities, subject only to the power of courts, under the common law, to decline to enforce those that were excessive or unreasonable. These techniques of rate-making proved unsatisfactory, since they imposed tremendous burdens upon legislatures and common law courts and generally left consumers, who could not defray the expenses of contests, at the mercy of the utilities. As a consequence, the practice developed of setting up special commissions with the expertise necessary to govern rates. As governor, Mr. Hughes had played a leading part in this development. These public agencies were frequently confronted by either general or specific grants of power in enabling Acts or charters authorizing utilities to fix their own rates and these were claimed as contract rights against the regulatory power of the state. As an Associate Justice of the Supreme Court Mr. Hughes construed these grants to the utilities strictly, or construed reservations to the public power broadly to uphold, whenever possible, regulation against the claim of vested right.

Thus, in *Southern Pacific Co.* v. *Campbell*,[17] for example, Justice Hughes, asserting that a provision contained in a general incorporation act of a state, which authorized a common carrier "to collect and receive such tolls or freight for transportation of persons or property . . . as it may prescribe," raised the question whether the judgment of the carrier in fixing rates for transportation shall be supervised and regulated by the judgment of the state exercised through a railroad commission, or remain as it was at common law, within the exclusive power of the carrier, subject only to the power of the courts, upon judicial inquiry, to decline to enforce excessive and unreasonable rates, answered that

it is well established that a general charter provision . . . giving power to charge and collect tolls, necessarily implies that the charges shall be reasonable and does not detract from the power of the State through its legislature, or the agency lawfully constituted thereby, to prescribe reasonable rates to be observed by the carrier.

And in *Louisville & Nashville R.R.* v. *Garrett* [18] Justice Hughes held for the Court that, although by its charter a railway company was authorized to charge specified maximum rates, it was not an unconstitutional impairment of the obligation of contract for a railroad commission to fix lower rates under circumstances in which the company subsequently subjected itself to the operation of an amendment to the state constitution that "every grant of a franchise privilege or exemption, shall remain subject to revocation, alteration or amendment," because "upon the filing of the resolution, the charter provision as to the maximum rates therein specified ceased to be an obstacle, if it has been such before, to the exercise by the State of its rate-making power."

Immunity from Taxation

The Supreme Court, it has been noted, never repudiated the doctrine established by Chief Justice Marshall that a state legislature might grant immunity from taxation which conferred contract rights binding upon subsequent legislatures. Such grants, as in the case of rate-making power, designed to encourage substantial investment of capital in the public interest, were often given to utilities with little regard to future consequences. That Justice Hughes, without seeking to overturn precedent, was disposed to a strict interpretation of tax immunity so as to confer no more than was actually given and to resolve all doubts in favor of the exercise of the taxing power, was made evident by his dissents in two important cases. In *Wright* v. *Louisville & Nashville R.R.*[19] Justice Holmes, speaking for the majority of a divided Court, held that the fact that owners of a railroad, who were exempted by statute from paying a greater tax than a specified per cent on the income thereof, leased the entire road to another company did not open the right to the state to tax such lessees on the fee of the property and that betterments and improvements, made by the lessees of the type that the lessor naturally would have made to meet the necessities of an enlarging business, stood on the same footing as the original road and were similarly exempt. Justice Hughes joined Justices Pitney and McReynolds in dissenting, without opinion.

Justice Hughes took the occasion, however, to express the grounds for his dissent in another case, *Wright* v. *Central of Georgia R.R.*,[20] similarly involving the immunity from taxation of a lessee of railroad properties. The Augusta & Savannah and the Southwestern railroads were both constructed under special charters, admitted to constitute irrepealable contracts, by the terms of which these properties were not to be subject to be taxed higher than one half of one per cent upon their annual incomes. The companies to which the immunities from general taxation had been granted, as authorized by the charters and specific state laws, especially enacted when the roads encountered financial difficulties, leased their respective roads and franchises under agreements, the last of which was executed in 1895 to run for one hundred and one years, subject to renewal for like periods, upon the same terms, forever. The rental provided for the payment of a fixed sum.

For nearly fifty years, notwithstanding these leases, the State of Georgia had been content to collect taxes limited to those authorized by the charter provisions. This suit arose, however, out of the attempt of the Comptroller General of the state to collect from the lessee of the properties on the general tax basis provided by state law, that is, ad valorem on the real estate and franchise values of the roads, after crediting one half of one per cent of the net income of the properties. This action was based upon the view that the property, while nominally under lease, had actually become the property of the lessees, in fee.

A bare majority of the Court, in an opinion by Justice Holmes, ruled that the immunity extended to the properties in the hands of the lessee. In support of this ruling, Justice Holmes pointed out that this immunity from general taxation was granted in a period when the state was encouraging the development of pioneer enterprises involving large capital investment. While Justice Holmes was not prepared to say that the property was exempted from general taxation, "into whosoever hands it might come," the specific transaction, which was "permitted and encouraged" by Acts of the state legislature, was regarded as making the fee exempt from taxation other than that provided for, in favor of the lessee as well as the lessor. In this connection, he thought that "the practical construction given to the law for nearly half a century" was strong evidence that the lessee's claim of immunity was valid. Under the circumstances of this case Justice Holmes did not deem it material to determine whether the properties were held under lease, that might, but not necessarily, be renewed in perpetuity, or in fee, subject to a rent charge, for, he said, "the disregard of technical distinctions is in the interest of substantial justice, not for the purpose of enabling the State to escape from a binding bargain."

Justice Hughes, with the concurrence of Justice Pitney, vigorously dissented.[21] Dealing with the argument that the exemption extended to the lessee because the state had authorized the leasing, he insisted upon the principle that, because of the extreme importance of the taxing power, grants of immunity must be strictly and narrowly construed.

It has repeatedly been declared by this court to be settled law that tax exemptions, or tax limitations, are personal to the grantee, that is, are non-transferable and do not run with the property unless the legislature has explicitly provided otherwise. It has been held not to be enough that the grantee is authorized to make a conveyance of all its property, estate, privileges and franchises. . . . The controlling principle of these decisions is that, in view of the supreme importance of the taxing power of the State, every doubt must be resolved in favor of its continuance.

He saw no reason, he asserted, why a lessee should be in a better position to claim tax exemption than a mortgagee, or a purchaser at a foreclosure sale, who, under legal authority, takes all the property, franchises and privileges of the mortgagor.

Having set forth the applicable general principles which barred any presumption of immunity on grounds of some general or specific authorization to lease property, Justice Hughes inquired whether the lessee could claim any immunity of its own, and this, he said, is answered, "when it is found that it has no contract of its own and no stipulation for a transfer to it of the immunity of others."

Moreover, argued Justice Hughes, in this instance, under what is termed a lease, the "lessee" took the entire property to hold, if it pleased, in perpetuity, subject only to an annual charge. In substance, however this interest may be technically described, it is ownership. Surely, he reasoned, the constitutional limitation imposed by the contract clause is not concerned with mere technicalities of tenure. These, the state is left free to abolish.

SUMMARY STATEMENT

The limitations imposed upon the impairment of public contracts are, as we have seen, largely the product of judge-made, rather than constitution-made, law. Even within the framework of acceptance of the doctrines established by the Court over which Chief Justice Marshall presided, the Justices remained free, as the decisions during Justice Hughes' tenure on the bench revealed, to forfeit or not to forfeit grants for non-use, to recognize or not to recognize the right of states to require compensation for grants made, to permit or not to permit rate regulation of utility charges, to limit or not to limit the grant of tax immunity. No Justice in this period was prepared to go further in circumscribing the limitations of the contract clause, in what he deemed the public interest, than Justice Hughes.[22] It was out of a like regard for, if a different view of, the public interest that Justices, such as Justice Holmes, sought to maintain the sanctity of contract obligations against the governing power.

CHAPTER 5

THE CONTROL OF COMMERCE: NATIONAL AND STATE POWER

The Nature of the Problem and the Genesis of Doctrine

One of the principal grounds of dissatisfaction on the part of the financial and commercial interests of the country with the Articles of Confederation was their failure to place control of commerce among the states in the central government. Under the Articles, the states often imposed taxes on goods in transit through their territories and sometimes dealt more harshly with the commerce of one another than with that of a foreign power. The primary means through which the Framers of the Constitution sought to eliminate or control these evils was to vest in Congress the power "to regulate commerce with foreign nations, and among the several States." [1]

This affirmative grant of power to the central government has engendered serious conflict among competing interests within the community and between the nation and the states. Involved has been a determination of the meaning and scope of the grant under challenge that power was being exercised in conflict with the specific limitations imposed upon the federal government particularly by the due process clause. And since the Constitution enjoins a sundering of commerce which in practice is conducted without regard to state lines, involved, also, has been the difficult problem of determining which commerce falls under exclusively national or exclusively state control, and which may be the concurrent concern of both. A collateral question, not without difficulty, is when the interstate commerce and the national power end, and the power of the state begins. In the resolution of these conflicts, the Supreme Court has played the vital role of arbiter or umpire of our federal system.

The basic doctrines upon which the Court built, and sometimes altered, were those laid down by Chief Justice Marshall. It was not until 1824 that the Chief Justice found an opportunity for a careful exposition of the meaning and scope of the interstate commerce clause. The case in point, *Gibbons* v. *Ogden*,[2] raised the question of whether New York might constitutionally require a license to be obtained for the operation of a steamboat between New York and New Jersey. Speaking for the Court, Chief Justice Marshall refused to construe the grant of power to Congress strictly and defined "commerce" in the broadest possible terms, not only to embrace traffic but "intercourse," including navigation. The power to regulate, he said, was the power "to prescribe the rule by which commerce is to be governed." And this he held to be a completely plenary power, subject only to the prescribed limitations of the Constitution. As for the reach of this power, he wrote:

The genius and character of the whole government seem to be, that its action is to be applied to all the external concerns of the nation, and to those internal concerns which affect the states generally; but not to those which are completely within a particular state, which do not affect other states, and with which it is not necessary to interfere, for the purpose of executing some of the general powers of the government. The completely internal commerce of a state, then, may be considered as reserved for the state itself.

For many years, it was the negative implications of this broad definition of federal interstate commerce power, that is to say, the limitations thereby impliedly imposed upon the states, rather than the affirmative nature of the grant, which preoccupied the Court. This was necessarily the case since Congress, until 1887, made no substantial effort to use its commerce power affirmatively in the regulation of the national economy. The practical result was that the doctrine of exclusive federal power, so long as it held sway, was not a means of enhancing the exercise of federal power but a means of defeating any regulation. Many interests which were the strongest proponents of *exclusive* federal power, under the interstate commerce clause, were to become, when such power threatened their interests, the staunchest opponents of *any* federal power, under the guise of states' rights. When that situation developed, however, they were to derive little comfort from some of the general expressions of John Marshall which readily yielded to a broad view of federal prerogative under the interstate commerce clause.

The first significant exercise by Congress of its power under the commerce clause was its enactment of the Interstate Commerce Act of 1887. A series of Congressional laws followed, but these, until 1903, were almost exclusively confined to the regulation of intoxicating liquors, common carriers and trusts.[3] In the twentieth century Congress continued its regulations in these areas and began to extend its power to govern many other phases of the economy. Despite the assertions of John Marshall respecting the plenary nature of this power, these enactments were frequently challenged as in excess of the interstate commerce power of Congress. They were also frequently assailed as deprivations of liberty or of property without due process of law. The considerations which guide the Court in deciding whether due process has been violated have been the subject of prior discussion. What are the considerations which enable it to fix the line between the legitimate exercise of national and state power over commerce?

INTERSTATE COMMERCE: NATIONAL POWER

There were three cases of some importance in which Associate Justice Hughes wrote the opinion of the Court in regard to the constitutionality of Congressional legislation under the commerce power, and in each of these he gave a very broad interpretation of the permissible scope of federal authority.

Hours of Labor of Railway Employees.   On March 4, 1907, Congress enacted legislation regulating the hours of labor of railway employees engaged in interstate commerce. This act was challenged as in excess of the delegated power of Congress to regulate interstate commerce and as a deprivation of liberty without due process of law contrary to the Fifth Amendment.

Justice Hughes, with the concurrence of the entire Court, in *Baltimore & Ohio R.R.* v. *Interstate Commerce Commission*,[4] sustained the constitutionality of the Act. A restriction upon the hours of labor of employees connected with the movement of trains in interstate commerce, he said, was clearly within the interstate commerce power of Congress. He reasoned: first, that viewed broadly, the length of hours of service has "direct relation to the efficiency of the human agencies upon which protection to life and property necessarily depends"; and, second, that it was competent for Congress to consider, and seek to reduce, the dangers to the employees incident to the strain of excessive hours of duty. There can be no question, therefore, he said, as to the existence of the *power* of Congress to control hours of labor in the regulation of interstate commerce.

Having established the legitimacy of the end sought as within the scope of the commerce power, the inquiry whether the Act arbitrarily interfered with freedom to contract for longer hours, related to the means and raised a due process question. But since the restrictions imposed had a reasonable relation to the end, there was no deprivation of liberty without due process of law, Justice Hughes concluded.

One further aspect of this case is of some importance. One of the arguments advanced by the carrier in opposition to the validity of the legislation was that it was utterly impractical for it to divide its employees in relation to interstate and purely intrastate activities. To this Justice Hughes replied that, the power of Congress being recognized, its exercise of such power may not be defeated "by the commingling of duties relating to interstate and intrastate operations." The doctrine that intrastate activities could be subjected to federal control when necessary to assure the effective exercise of the interstate commerce power of Congress was to receive its definitive formulation, at the hands of Justice Hughes, in one of the STATE RATE CASES.[5]

Employers' Liability. By the provisions of the so-called "Employers' Liability" Acts, passed in 1906 and 1908, Congress had abrogated the fellow servant rule which had barred recovery by interstate railway employees for injury resulting from the negligence of fellow employees, and had also outlawed the enforcement of contracts of immunity which made the acceptance of relief benefits a bar to recovery under the provisions of the Acts. The constitutionality of this legislation had been sustained by a unanimous Supreme Court, in an opinion by Justice Van Devanter, in *Second Employers' Liability Cases.*[6] The primary question before the Court, in *Phil., Balt., & Wash. R.R.* v. *Schubert,*[7] was whether these provisions were retroactively applicable, that is, to the enforcement of contracts made before the act was passed. It was argued by the carrier that as so applied the act would constitute a deprivation of liberty (of contract) without due process of law contrary to the provision of the Fifth Amendment. Rejecting this contention, Justice Hughes, again speaking for the entire Court, maintained that the power of Congress, in its regulation of interstate commerce, was not fettered by the necessity for maintaining existing contractual arrangements which would conflict with the execution of its policy. He continued,

To subordinate the exercise of the Federal authority to the continuing operation of previous contracts, would be to place, to this extent, the regulation of interstate commerce in the hands of private individuals and to withdraw from the control of Congress so much of the field as they might choose by prophetic discernment to bring within the range of their agreements. The Constitution recognizes no such limitation. It is of the essence of the delegated power of regulation that, within its sphere, Congress should be able to establish uniform rules, immediately obligatory, which as to future action should transcend all inconsistent provisions. Prior arrangements were necessarily subject to this paramount authority.

An interesting feature of this decision is that while, in the specific instance, the Act of Congress was sustained although made retroactively applicable to contracts, the Court did not deny that the constitutionality of an Act of Congress might be challenged, in appropriate cases, on this ground, as a denial of due process of law. This is significant because while Article 1, Section 10, denies to the states authority to impair the obligation of contracts, no comparable provision limits the exercise of federal power.

Federal "Police Power." The issue, in *Seven Cases* v. *United States*,[8] concerned the constitutional validity of the so-called "Sherley Amendment" of 1912 to the Pure Food and Drugs Act of 1906 which provided that drugs transported in interstate commerce should be deemed misbranded if the package or label contained any false or fraudulent statement regarding their *curative* effects. This amendment was an almost direct result of an earlier dissenting opinion of Justice Hughes in *United States* v. *Johnson* [9] in which a majority of the Court, in a decision delivered by Justice Holmes, had held that the term "misbranded" contained in the Food and Drugs Act could not be construed as applicable to all false statements on a package or label but only to such as related to the *identity* of the article, possibly including its strength, quality and purity. In dissenting from that decision Justice Hughes had argued that the term "misbranded" should be interpreted as extending to false and misleading statements of fact relative to *curative* properties as well as *identity*. The JOHNSON case had involved simply a difference in interpretation among members of the Court. With the specific extension by Congress of the meaning of misbranded to include false statements regarding curative effects, the issue, in SEVEN CASES, related to the constitutional validity of the enactment. In sustaining its validity, Justice Hughes spoke for the entire Court, except for a non-participating Justice, and reaffirmed two fundamental principles established by the Court: first, that, in its exercise of its constitutional authority under the commerce clause, Congress may adopt means not only necessary but "convenient" to its effectuation; and second, that Congressional action cannot be defeated because it had the quality of police regulations.

Summary Statement. In upholding the constitutionality of the three Acts of Congress cited, the last of which bore no direct relation to the facilities of transportation, the whole Court, at least in the period from 1910 to 1916, appeared to accept the view of Marshall, expressed in the GIBBONS case, that the power over commerce "among the several states, is vested in Congress as absolutely as it would be in a single government, having in its constitution the same restrictions on the exercise of the power as are found in the constitution of the United States." And within these restrictions which included the requirement of due process, it is clear it was not suggested that the mere existence of the states, or the reservation of power to the states provided by the Tenth Amendment, were active principles of limitation.

INTERSTATE COMMERCE: STATE POWER

In what respects and to what extent does the interstate commerce clause, by its own force, in the absence of Congressional legislation, deprive the states of power over the regulation of *interstate* commerce affecting vital interests of the states? In the GIBBONS case, Marshall had implied, without actually ruling, that the mere existence of the interstate commerce delegation barred the exercise of any concurrent regulatory power by the state, even in the absence of any conflict with national law, when he rejected the analogy between the regulation of commerce and taxation, and said that there was "great force" in the argument that the interstate commerce power was exclusive and "the court is not satisfied that it has been refuted." However, since he found that the New York Act was in "direct collision" with an Act of Congress, he preferred to actually rest his decision upon this ground alone.

Only three years later, however, in *Brown* v. *Maryland*,[10] he held, for the Court, that the power vested in Congress to regulate commerce, even in the absence of any federal legislation, built a total immunity against any attempt upon the part of a state to tax, even moderately, foreign, and by implication, interstate commerce, until such commerce had been brought to an end.

It was not until *Cooley* v. *Board of Wardens*,[11] decided in 1851, involving a regulation of pilots, that a majority of the Court accepted the view that the interstate commerce power, in its dormant state, did not constitute a grant of completely exclusive power to Congress. Historically, since the regulation of pilots presented a special case for concurrent state action, the real retreat from the doctrine of exclusiveness of the interstate commerce power, even unexercised, did not occur, however, until 1890, in *Leisy* v. *Hardin*,[12] when a narrow majority of the Court predicated immunity from state regulation not upon the bar of the Constitution but upon practical consideration of the nature of the commerce and the implied intention of Congress, dependent upon whether the subject matter required uniformity or admitted of diversity of regulation. This rule, of course, opened the door to some state action which under the principle of exclusiveness enunciated by Marshall would have been completely shut. But how wide was the door opened? The answer, of course, could not be found in the general phrases of the Constitution nor, in any real sense, in the silence of Congress, since that silence might be invoked both to permit and to deny the exercise of state power. What were then the nature and bases of decisions?

Licensing. The problem is illustrated in *Adams Express Co.* v. *New York*[13] in which the question raised was whether the conduct of an interstate business utilizing municipal facilities could be conditioned upon grant of a local license. And even in the absence of any conflicting federal legislation (which had been found to exist in the GIBBONS case), the entire Court held that a municipal ordinance requiring a party to take out a license for the carrying on of an interstate express business was an unconstitutional burden on interstate commerce.

The police power, said Justice Hughes in speaking for the Court, "does not justify the imposition of a direct burden upon interstate commerce." While a local ordinance may extend "incidentally to the operations of a carrier in its interstate business," this is true "provided it does not subject that business to unreasonable demands" and is confined to matters "which are appropriately of local concern." "Local police regulations cannot go so far as to deny the right to engage in interstate commerce, or to treat it as a local privilege and prohibit its exercise in the absence of a local license."

To the same effect was the ruling of the Court in *City of Sault Ste. Marie* v. *International Transit Co.*[14] when, in an opinion delivered by Justice Hughes, it held that the action of a city in requiring a company to take out a license, and to pay a license fee, for the privilege of operating its ferry from a wharf located in the city, was beyond the power of the state or any of its subdivisions. "One otherwise enjoying full capacity," said Justice Hughes, "cannot be compelled to take out a local license for the mere privilege of carrying on interstate or foreign commerce."

Rate-making. Granting that a company rendering a vital and quasi-public service to the community was engaged in interstate commerce, might the state undertake to regulate rates to assure their reasonableness when the federal government had not done so? This was the serious constitutional question that confronted the Court in two cases in which Justice Hughes delivered the opinion of the Court. In *Port Richmond Ferry* v. *Hudson County* [15] he ruled, with the concurrence of the entire Court, that in the absence of federal regulation a state, or its local subdivision, could constitutionally fix ferry rates to be charged for transportation from a terminus within the state although the company affected was chartered by a neighboring state.

While recognizing that the fixing of rates in this case constituted a clear regulation of interstate commerce, such regulation was not excluded, said Justice Hughes, under the established principle that with respect to

those subjects which require a general system or uniformity of regulation the power of Congress is exclusive; that, in other matters, admitting of diversity of treatment according to the special requirements of local conditions, the States may act within their respective jurisdictions until Congress sees fit to act; and that, when Congress does act, the exercise of its authority overrides all conflicting state legislation.

Accordingly, in view of the character of the subject and the variety of regulation required in fixing rates, there is no "inherent necessity for a single regulatory power over these numerous ferries across boundary streams."

Had the decision been rested solely upon this reasoning, it would be difficult to quarrel with its clarity. Obfuscation, however, was the result of the further argument of Justice Hughes that the burden being imposed upon interstate commerce in this case was "indirect" which, he said, followed from the fact that the nature of the subject did not require the control of one authority and freedom from restriction except as governed by that authority.

It is pertinent to inquire whether Justice Hughes is not confusing inconvenience and impracticality with indirectness of burden. Was the burden imposed upon interstate commerce by rate-making, vitally affecting as it does the profitability of its conduct, any less "direct" because dictated by the complexity of special and varying local conditions?

The rule of the PORT RICHMOND case was reaffirmed by the Court in another decision penned by Justice Hughes, in *Wilmington Transportation Co.* v. *California R.R. Commission*,[16] in which it was held that the mere existence of the federal power to regulate interstate commerce, while dormant, did not preclude the exercise of state authority to prevent exorbitant charges with respect to traffic upon the high seas between two points having their origin and termination within the limits of a state. Such regulation, it was suggested, falls within the class of "matters which are distinctively local in character although embraced within the Federal authority" in relation to which "the rule recognizes the propriety of the reasonable exercise of the power of the states in order to meet the needs of suitable local protection until Congress intervenes."

Intrastate Commerce: State and National Power

The Port Richmond and Wilmington Transportation cases concerned the rate-making power of the *states* in relation to certain public service corporations engaged in clearly *interstate* business of local character. By all odds, the most important and far-reaching of Justice Hughes' decisions during his almost six years upon the Supreme bench related to the nature and extent of *federal and state* power in fixing rates for the purely *intrastate* operations of public service enterprises under circumstances in which those rates bore upon and vitally affected charges for comparable services in *interstate* commerce. It was these "epochal series of controversies" known as the State Rate Cases which, according to William Ransom, "subjected our dual system of State and National sovereignty to the most severe strain and test since the Civil War." [17] The issues at stake were no less than whether federal power over purely intrastate commerce was to be deemed adequate to bring order and uniformity out of the chaos and diversity of competing national and state regulation of railroad facilities—whether the Court would frustrate or encourage the establishment of a truly integrated national system of railroads.

The Minnesota Rate Cases (*Simpson* v. *Shepard* [18]) involved the constitutional validity of the orders of the Railroad and Warehouse Commission and of legislative acts of the State of Minnesota of 1906 and 1907 providing for a general reduction of *intrastate* freight and passenger rates. It was established that, as applied to cities near the state's boundary, or neighboring cities across the state line, the reduction disturbed the relation previously existing between interstate and intrastate rates with the result that, for parity and for competitive reasons, some carriers were required to reduce many of their *interstate* rates to the level of those charged for *intrastate* transportation. The reductions thus necessitated were substantial. It was further established that in the case of each of the companies affected by the reduction, the greater part of the traffic carried was interstate, and that the movement of interstate and local traffic took place at the same time, on the same rails, with the same employees, and largely by means of the same trains and cars, and that a separation would have been impracticable.

Suit was brought by stockholders of the carriers to restrain the enforcement of the Minnesota rates and prevent their maintenance by the carriers. The primary constitutional objections advanced were that the Minnesota rates amounted to an unconstitutional interference with interstate commerce and were in conflict with paramount federal authority exerted under the Act to Regulate Commerce.

The cases were argued before the Court for four days ending April 12, 1912. The closely reasoned opinion delivered by Justice Hughes more than a year later, with the concurrence of the entire Court except for Justice McKenna, who concurred only in the result, covers nearly 100 pages in the official report and reflects herculean labor.

Assuming the rates fixed under state authority to be reasonable so far as *intrastate* traffic was concerned, the first vital constitutional question raised by Justice Hughes was whether the action of the state imposed "a direct burden upon *interstate* commerce." In that event, he said, it must be unconstitutional even in the absence of federal legislation. Secondly, he asked, whether the action taken by the state was in conflict with the Congressional Act to Regulate Commerce and thus at variance with a specific assertion of paramount federal authority.

Each of these questions he answered negatively but in a manner which suggested, in unmistakable terms, that Congress had the authority, if it wished to exercise it, to subject the purely intrastate railroad traffic of a state that impinged upon and had become interwoven with the interstate railroad traffic of the nation to its control.

The general principle is, he wrote, that the power of Congress to regulate interstate commerce "is supreme and plenary," and that "the full control by Congress of the subjects committed to its regulation is not to be denied or thwarted by the commingling of interstate and intrastate operations." This did not mean, he said, that the nation might deal with the internal concerns of the state, as such, but it did mean that the execution by Congress of its constitutional power to regulate interstate commerce was not limited by the fact "that intrastate transactions may have become so interwoven therewith that the effective government of the former incidentally controls the latter."

The crucial distinction, he maintained, was as to those subjects which required a general system or uniformity of regulation, in which case the power of Congress was exclusive, and those subjects admitting diversity of treatment according to special requirements of local conditions, in which case the states may act within their respective jurisdictions until Congress saw fit to act; but, when Congress did act, the exercise of its authority overrode all conflicting state legislation. "The principle," he continued, "which determines this classification, underlies the doctrine that the States cannot under any guise impose direct burdens upon interstate commerce."

Again, it may be suggested, as in the PORT RICHMOND case, that differentiation in terms of "direct" and "indirect" tends to confuse rather than clarify, for obviously Justice Hughes is simply asserting that when uniformity of regulation is practically required any regulation by the state will be viewed as imposing a "direct" burden, but when diversity is admissible such action will be regarded as imposing an "indirect" burden upon interstate commerce. That is but to make a decision first in terms of practical considerations and then to label undesirable state action as "direct" and desirable or necessary state action as "indirect." [19]

Continuing his discussion, Justice Hughes asserted that a direct burden is imposed upon interstate commerce if states seek to tax interstate commerce, or to prohibit interstate trade in legitimate articles of commerce, or to prescribe interstate rates.[20] But within the limitations excluding direct burdens upon interstate commerce, until Congress acts, there remained to the states a wide range for the exercise of power appropriate to their territorial jurisdiction although interstate commerce may be affected. This discretion related to local matters, as in this specific instance, of such a nature that it is impossible to assume that the mere grant to Congress was intended to bar state action pending federal intervention.

The first inquiry having been disposed of in favor of the exercise of the state rate-making power, that brought him squarely to the second—had Congress exercised its paramount authority to exclude state action? He pointed out that when Congress, in 1887, enacted the Act to Regulate Commerce it was acquainted with the course of the development of railroad transportation and with the exercise by the states of the rate-making power and that, having defined the scope of its regulation, it expressly provided that it was not to extend to purely intrastate traffic. Later amendments specifically exempted such traffic. It must be concluded, therefore, that

If the situation has become such, by reason of the interblending of the interstate and intrastate operations of interstate carriers, that adequate regulation of their interstate rates cannot be maintained without imposing requirements with respect to their intrastate rates which substantially affect the former, it is for Congress to determine, within the limits of its constitutional authority over interstate commerce and its instruments the measure of the regulation it should supply.

Thus, while the immediate authority of the state was upheld, the paramountcy of federal power was clearly affirmed, and in this sense, the decision of Justice Hughes in the MINNESOTA RATE CASES was correctly characterized as constituting "the first important step in the evolution of federal power over intrastate rates." [21]

The pressing practical problems involved appeared, however, to have been left unsolved and removed from the judicial to the political forum, and this aroused concern in some quarters. John Bauer, long concerned with utility rate regulation, fearful of the consequences ensuing before the paramount authority of Congress might be exercised, if ever, wrote:

Apparently, as a result of the decision, hereafter in its rate orders, the [Interstate Commerce] Commission must have clear regard for the various state regulations, while, rationally, it should pay no attention to state lines, aiming always and everywhere only at reasonableness and the elimination of discrimination. State borders do not furnish adequate grounds for differing rates.[22]

And, in the *Harvard Law Review* the comment was made that,

If the state railroad commissions as a whole should undertake to use their freshly defined powers in a radical and drastic spirit, and in such a way as to disjoint the interstate system of rates as a whole, a more comprehensive and far-reaching interstate commerce act, occupying the entire domain of federal power as defined by the court, might suddenly become a national necessity.[23]

These fears, however, proved illusory because the question of whether discrimination affecting the relationship between intrastate and interstate rates might be validly engendered by state regulation was resolved in favor of the authority of the Interstate Commerce Commission to bar such discrimination *without the enactment of additional federal legislation.*

The issue was settled in the SHREVEPORT CASE (*Houston, E. and W. Texas R.R.* v. *United States* [24]) decided precisely one year after the decision of the Court in the MINNESOTA RATE CASES. In this instance almost eight months elapsed between the argument of counsel and the decision of the Court.

The SHREVEPORT CASE arose out of the following facts. The Interstate Commerce Commission had found that the *interstate* rates out of Shreveport, Louisiana, to named Texas points were unreasonable and it established maximum rates for such traffic. It also had found that the rates so fixed were higher than the *intrastate* traffic rates in force from one part of Texas to such other named Texas points under substantially similar conditions and circumstances. This, in the view of the Commission, involved discrimination against Shreveport, and it ordered the carriers to desist from charging higher rates for interstate transportation from Shreveport to Texas than were charged for equal distances wholly within the state for commodities moving toward Shreveport. The effect of this order was to require the carriers, in given instances, to ignore rates fixed under state authority and adjust and increase them to the rates fixed for interstate transportation.

Suit was brought by certain railroad carriers to set aside the order of the Commission upon the grounds, first, that Congress lacked the power to control the intrastate charges of interstate carriers even to the extent necessary to prevent discrimination against interstate traffic, and, second, that even if it be assumed that Congress has this power, it had not been exercised by Congress or delegated to the Interstate Commerce Commission.

Speaking for a majority of the Court,[25] Justice Hughes again made reference to the "complete and paramount" character of the interstate commerce power of Congress. Its purpose, he said, was to make impossible the evils which had overwhelmed the Confederation. It had not left interstate trade to be destroyed or impeded by the rivalries of local governments. Citing a series of precedents, the last of which was the MINNESOTA RATE CASES, he insisted that

The fact that carriers are instruments of intrastate commerce, as well as of interstate commerce, does not derogate from the complete and paramount authority of Congress over the latter or preclude the Federal power from being exerted to prevent the intrastate operations of such carriers from being made a means of injury to that which has been confided to Federal care. Wherever the interstate and intrastate transactions of carriers are so related that the government of the one involves the control of the other, it is Congress, and not the State, that is entitled to prescribe the final and dominant rule, for otherwise Congress would be denied the exercise of its constitutional authority and the State, and not the Nation, would be supreme within the national field. . . .

Congress in the exercise of its paramount power may prevent the common instrumentality of interstate and intrastate commercial intercourse from being used in their intrastate operations to the injury of interstate commerce. . . . It is immaterial, so far as the protecting power of Congress is concerned, that the discrimination arises from intrastate rates as compared with interstate rates. The use of the instrument of interstate commerce in a discriminatory manner so as to inflict injury upon that commerce, or some part thereof, furnishes abundant ground for Federal intervention.

He was not unmindful, he continued, of the gravity of the question that it presented when state and federal views conflict. But, "it was recognized at the beginning that the Nation could not prosper if interstate and foreign trade were governed by many masters, and, where the interests of the freedom of interstate commerce are involved, the judgment of Congress and of the agencies it lawfully establishes must prevail."

In the light of his statement in the MINNESOTA RATE CASES that Congress had "expressly provided" that the scope of its regulation should not extend to purely intrastate traffic, the question of whether it had in fact attempted to govern such traffic presented some difficulty. This difficulty was resolved by reference to a section of the old Interstate Commerce Act of 1887 which made it unlawful, in the broadest terms, for any carrier to give any undue or unreasonable preference to any person or locality, or to subject any person or locality to any undue or unreasonable prejudice or disadvantage. And the Interstate Commerce Commission had, of course, been vested with enforcing power.[26] Accordingly, the authority of the Interstate Commerce Commission to require carriers to adjust their intrastate rates to bar discrimination against interstate commerce was upheld.

The far-reaching consequences of the decisions of Justice Hughes in the STATE RATE CASES upon the development of constitutional law can hardly be exaggerated. The immediate and tremendous importance lay in their recognition of federal authority adequate to the molding of an integrated system of transportation without regard to state boundaries which had little practical reality in the actual conduct of the commerce of the nation. Commenting upon the significance of the SHREVEPORT decision, a leading authority, I. L. Sharfman, wrote:

While the holding was adversely criticized at the time in some quarters as an unwarranted invasion of state authority, the principles by which it was guided have now been recognized as indispensable to the maintenance of the freedom of interstate commerce, unhampered by the rivalry of the states in seeking to further their local interests.[27]

This comment was underscored by another authority, who stated,

This decision was perhaps the most far-reaching in its implications of any rendered in the period discussed because it laid the foundation for the radical extension of federal power to intrastate transportation embodied in the Transportation Act of 1920.[28]

But the importance of these decisions goes far beyond their vital effect upon our national transportation system. It relates to the function of the Court in the whole area of nation-state conflicts of power. "In the history of the Supreme Court," Mr. (now Mr. Justice) Frankfurter wrote, "no single quality more differentiates judges than the acuteness of their realization that practical considerations, however screened by doctrine, underlie resolution of conflicts between state and national power." [29] And it may be said precisely of the decisions of Justice Hughes in the STATE RATE CASES that he contributed greatly to fostering a recognition by the Court that the conflicts between national and state power, with regard to the regulation of the commerce of the nation, could be resolved only in terms of practical effect. It was such a consideration, rather than loyalty to an abstract conception of a rigid division of powers enjoined by our system of dual sovereignty, whatever the rationalizations used, that alone gives meaning to the decisions.

That Justice Hughes was acutely aware of the practical nature of the problem was made clear in an address he delivered before the New York State Bar Association on January 14, 1916, near the close of his period of service, when he said that

interstate commerce is a department of practical affairs which as a rule is segregated only in legal theory. It has no separate existence in economics and is not separately maintained by transportation companies or by those engaged in trade. . . . It is a problem of many governments, within one nation, dealing with portions of an activity which has economic unity.[30]

It may also be said that the implications of these decisions extended beyond the immediate issues involved for yet another reason. If it is recognized that intrastate transportation *rates* may, for practical reasons, be controlled by federal authority in so far as they vitally affect interstate commerce, does it not follow that intrastate *production* may for similar reasons be constitutionally controlled by the federal government in so far as it may vitally affect interstate commerce? That, in any event, ultimately proved to be the primary basis upon which considerable power over the processes of local production was accorded to the federal government in the case of *National Labor Relations Board* v. *Jones & Laughlin Steel Corp.*[31] in a decision that Chief Justice Hughes was to deliver.

Nor is that all. It had sometimes been suggested in and out of the Court that the delegated powers of Congress were checked by and had to be reconciled with the reserve sovereign powers of the state to which recognition is accorded by the Tenth Amendment. The decisions of Justice Hughes could not be reconciled with the view that dual federalism, by its very nature and existence, provided a check upon the exercise of a delegated power of Congress. This was clearly affirmed by Justice Hughes, when in his Bar Association address, with specific reference to the meaning of his decisions in the STATE RATE CASES, he said,

Within its sphere as defined by the Constitution, the Nation is supreme. The question is simply of the Federal power as granted; where there is authorized exercise of that power, there is no reserved power to nullify it,—a principle obviously essential to our national integrity, yet continually calling for new applications.[32]

This too was the interpretation of Edward S. Corwin when, in 1934, he wrote that "the Shreveport case brusquely dismissed dual federalism as having no longer any pertinence to the question of railway rate legislation," [33] and predicted, prematurely, the demise of the doctrine.

Finally, it must be suggested, that in demarcating the boundaries of national and state power in relation to the regulation of commerce, since in this area as in other areas, the intention of the Framers and the Constitution, *per se*, supply little guide to the Court, conceptions of the practical and the beneficial, unconscious or avowed, rather than abstract doctrine furnish the surest explanation of the disagreements of the Justices. Thus, Mr. Frankfurter has recognized that while the questions raised have been decided "at least in part, within legal habituations and past utterances," the Court has "inescapably" been implicated in the making of legislative policy designed to effect an accommodation of interest, "however diverse the legal devices by which different judges may make these accommodations." [34]

CHAPTER 6

A SUMMARY EVALUATION

The period of six years, from 1910 to 1916, during which Mr. Hughes was a member of the Supreme Court, in marked contrast with the eleven years, from 1930 to 1941, when he served as Chief Justice of the United States, was not characterized by many far-reaching innovations or reversals nor by sharp and fundamental cleavage within the Court. It was, with some exceptions, a period of clarification, application and extension of established doctrine to the exigencies of governing a vast, growing and complex industrial civilization. And in that process, Justice Hughes played a leading role. Although probably exaggerated, it is not without significance that the author of an analysis of Mr. Hughes' record, made shortly after he left the bench, concluded that his opinions "rank among the most important and able pronouncements upon the principles of constitutional law that have come from the Supreme Court during its entire history." [1]

The philosophy of government which Mr. Hughes brought to the bench had emphasized, in the legislative process, a belief in social progress based upon a "fair" balance of public and private interest. That balance, he believed, the Constitution protected particularly by its clauses designed to secure life, liberty and property. A clear formulation of his own mature conception of the role of the Court in enforcing those clauses against governmental power was presented in the address he delivered before the New York State Bar Association in his final year of service upon the bench. It was manifest, he then said, that these prohibitions were not intended to permit the Court to override legislative action because of the views of the Judges as to its wisdom. "What was thus sought," he continued,

was not a privilege to deny the legislative authority to enact reasonable measures for the promotion of the safety, health, morals, and welfare of the people, not to make improvement or rational experimentation impossible, but to preserve and enforce the primary and fundamental conceptions of justice which demand proper notice and opportunity to be heard before a competent tribunal in advance of condemnation, immunity from the confiscation of property, and, with respect to every department of government, freedom from the exercise of purely arbitrary power.[2]

In striking a balance between public interest and private right, in the judicial process, Justice Hughes voted to sustain exercises of governmental power designed to enable railroad employees to recover adequate compensation for injuries, to make enforcement of child labor limitations effective, to permit the self-organization of employees free from employer interference, and to limit the hours of labor of women and railroad employees. In general, he sought to construe public franchises and grants strictly and to sustain the regulatory and taxing powers of the state against the claim of contract impairment. On the other hand, he cast his vote, as a member of the Court, to deny the authority of governmental power to enact a peonage statute, to limit the rights of aliens to ordinary employment, to foster or permit unequal accommodations for Negroes in intrastate commerce, or to attach to the trial of a Negro under conditions of mob domination and hysteria the concept of due process.[3]

Another fundamental tenet of the philosophy of Mr. Hughes, to which he had given expression as governor of New York State, was his belief in federal power, adequate to coping with problems requiring national regulation, but compatible with the preservation of the independence and existence of the states. In his 1916 address he asserted that he remained convinced of the necessity of autonomous local governments and that an overcentralized government would break down of its own weight. The task of the Court in relation to the federal system was, he said,

To preserve the essential elements of this system—without permitting necessary local autonomy to be destroyed by the unwarranted assertion of Federal power, and without allowing State action to throw out of gear the requisite machinery for unity of control in national concerns.[4]

As a Justice of the Court, it was largely in the interpretation of the authority granted and the limitations imposed by the interstate commerce clause that he sought to effect an appropriate reconciliation between national and state power. In that connection he gave a plenary interpretation to the power of Congress to regulate the instrumentalities of interstate commerce and to control the conditions of such commerce. Accordingly, he sustained legislation limiting the hours of labor of interstate railroad employees and an extension of the Pure Food and Drugs Act, partaking of the quality of a police power regulation. And the paramount nature of the interstate commerce power he deemed sufficient to justify federal regulation of intrastate rates when required to prevent discrimination against interstate commerce. On the other hand, his plenary view of national power which denied force to the Tenth Amendment as a source of limitation did not lead him to exclude the exercise of state power to control rates of interstate instrumentalities serving special and local needs and beyond the practical control of the federal power.

In general he revealed an awareness that the reconciliation had to be effected not in terms of abstract theory but in terms of just such practical considerations applied to "a problem of many governments, within one nation, dealing with portions of an activity which has economic unity." [5]

Basic, too, to the philosophy of Charles Evans Hughes was his belief in the role of the Supreme Court as the final arbiter of all constitutional questions. "I like to think of the Courts," he said in 1916, "as in the truest sense the expert agents of democracy,—expressing deliberate judgment under conditions essential to stability, and therefore in their proper action the necessary instrumentalities of progress." [6] It was the high task of the Court "to preserve and enforce the primary and fundamental conceptions of justice" and "the essentials of liberty." [7] That judicial scrutiny gave greater assurance of the realization of these great values than uncontrolled legislative power derived from his conviction that "a judicial tribunal as far removed as possible from the passion and prejudice of partisan controversy" would "observe the traditional requirements of reasoned judgment in applying to the decisions of controversies the supreme law." [8]

It is apparent, therefore, that to Justice Hughes the great ends subserved by judicial review are the maintenance of the essential duality of our federal system, the assurance of greater justice and reasonableness in the enactment and administration of our laws, and the preservation of individual liberty. Upon the validity of this judgment rests the case for judicial review.[9]

The attempt is frequently made to appraise the record of Justices in terms of liberalism. How "liberal" were the opinions of Justice Hughes? The concept of liberalism, like that of democracy, obviously admits of a variety of meanings. It differs in content when used, on the one hand, by Adam Smith, T. H. Green or Walter Lippmann, and on the other, by L. T. Hobhouse, Harold Laski or John Dewey. In terms, however, of the general, if somewhat indefinite, criteria which have identified such Justices as Holmes, Brandeis and Cardozo as liberals, Justice Hughes qualifies as one of the foremost, if not the foremost, liberal member of the Court during his initial period of service.[10]

In any event, the record of Mr. Hughes' opinions led Ernest Sutherland Bates to conclude that had Mr. Hughes continued on the bench it is possible that he would have gone down in history "as a great liberal Justice," [11] and led the *Nation* to comment, some years later, although it then regarded the liberalism of Mr. Hughes as tarnished, that

His decisions during his first term on the bench, though they do not rank with those of the Olympian Holmes, showed more knowledge of the business world and greater insight than those of the philosopher from Massachusetts. There are a number of cases involving problems of business regulation and at least one in the field of Southern circumvention of peonage laws in which Hughes stirs admiration where Holmes evokes indulgence. This is achievement enough for any judge.[12]

III. The Years Between

CHAPTER 7

PRIVATE CITIZEN AND PUBLIC SERVANT

PRESIDENTIAL CANDIDATE

The record that Mr. Hughes had written across the pages of American history in his investigations of utilities, as reform governor of the most populous and, from the standpoint of electoral success, strategically the most important state in the Union, and as an outstandingly liberal Justice of the Supreme Court, made him, in many ways, the natural and logical choice of the Republican party seeking a nominee for the presidency to defeat the disciple of the New Freedom, Woodrow Wilson.

As early as 1908 Hughes' availability for the presidency had been suggested.[1] Again in 1912, there had been speculation about the possibility of his nomination. At that time, however, according to a New York *Times* report, he expressed unwillingness to be considered. He confirmed a report that he had telephoned his friends in New York and telegraphed others in Chicago that "he would not under any circumstances permit his name to be used." "He would not permit," he said, "the Supreme Court to be brought into politics," and he further declared that "he would not accept the nomination if it were offered to him." [2]

In 1916, although it is generally acknowledged that he made no effort to obtain the nomination, he was unwilling to oppose it, and at the Republican National Convention held in Chicago he was named, on June 7, as its candidate for the presidency.[3] The reception which greeted his resignation from the bench to become a candidate for political office varied. Nearly all agreed upon his excellent character and splendid abilities but many were dismayed by the spectacle of a Supreme Court Justice discarding a high judicial post to become enmeshed in a partisan political contest. The New York *Evening World* commented tartly:

The celerity with which Charles Evans Hughes has ceased to be the Supreme Court Justice and become Busy Charlie the Candidate is bewildering to the country and, in the view of many, far from pleasing.

The nation has grown to think of its highest judicial tribune as something stable and permanent, wherein men sat as with a final dignity befitting ultimate honor. The new view is something of a shock. Not all of us will get used to it—or even wish to.[4]

The New York *Times* praised his qualities which however it found "inferior in capacity and experience" to those of Wilson, and added,

Mr. Hughes will not be elected. His defeat is to be desired, among many other reasons, for this good and sufficient reason that the invasion of the Supreme Court's chamber by needy politicians in search of a leader, now for the first time in American history successfully accomplished, may be rebuked and made a precedent too dangerous for following.[5]

The *New Republic*, in deploring the nomination of a Supreme Court Justice for the presidency, found the "only redeeming feature" in the "personal qualities and character of its nominee" who, it stated, "is a man of unimpeachable moral independence and austere personal integrity." It affirmed,

If he is elected the country can trust absolutely in his good faith. He will not be the creature of any political faction or machine, the servant of any special interests or the accomplice of stronger-willed associates. There is no man in American public life who combines so much character with so much ability.[6]

The *Nation* sought to counter the criticism directed at Hughes' acceptance of a political nomination by pointing out that he "uttered no word and took no step to promote his political fortunes, and . . . stuck quietly to his work until the Convention knocked at his door." It then went on to say, "It is not a bad sign for democracy when it shows confidence in a man of solid rather than showy qualities. . . . The country will look forward to a Presidential campaign almost unexampled for the high intellectual tone which the two candidates will give to it." [7]

In his formal address accepting the Republican nomination for the presidency, delivered at Carnegie Hall in New York City on July

31, 1916, Mr. Hughes revealed the essential bases upon which he rested his claim for support.[8] He announced his belief in "America first and America efficient." He attacked the Administration's conduct of foreign affairs as displaying weakness, inexpertness and lack of firmness. It had involved the "inexcusable yielding of national interest to partisan expediency," and a vacillating, inconsistent and humiliating policy in dealing with Mexico which had won us neither friendship nor the protection of the lives and property of our citizens, nor the security of our borders from depredations.

With regard to the European war, then in its third year, Mr. Hughes stood "for the unflinching maintenance of all American rights on land and sea" which the Administration had not secured "because of its impaired credit and the manifest lack of disposition to back words with action." The Administration had been remiss, he charged, in protecting American property and commerce and had been too content with leisurely discussions. He denied that a firmer course would have drawn us into the war. "Rather, in that course lay the best assurance of peace" and "peace with honor." The Administration had also neglected preparedness, which "is not militarism" but "the essential assurance of security."

In the postwar period Mr. Hughes was to be a strong supporter of American entry into the League of Nations. In his acceptance speech he revealed his sympathy for an international peace organization, avowing that at the end of the war our support must be given to an international organization in order "to provide international justice and to safeguard so far as practicable the peace of the world."

With respect to domestic policy, he asserted that we must anticipate, with the end of the war, the competition of "an energized Europe" which can only be met by the Republican party which stands for the principle of protection. Our prosperity and social justice rest "upon the condition that there shall be a stable basis for honest enterprise." While monopolistic practices must be "cut out, root and branch," this must be accomplished "without hobbling enterprise or narrowing the scope of legitimate achievement."

He would conserve, he continued, the "just interests of labor," and seek to promote health, to protect women and children in industry and to provide greater educational opportunities, with the watchword of "cooperation not exploitation." Specifically, he urged the enactment of a federal workmen's compensation law. In the interests of agriculture he proposed an "effective system of rural credits" and "wise conservation of our natural resources."

Mr. Hughes unequivocally endorsed the statement in the platform favoring woman suffrage. He demanded greater administrative efficiency, fidelity to the principles of our civil service laws, and a simple businesslike budget. He concluded, "We have a vision of America prepared and secure; strong and just; equal to her tasks; an exemplar of the capacity and efficiency of a free people."

These declarations were for the most part general and platitudinous and the campaign which followed was largely conducted upon the same level. Sharp differences were avoided to the advantage of President Wilson who, after all, had "kept America out of war." Nevertheless, the result was close and but for a probably inadvertent slight to Senator Hiram Johnson by Mr. Hughes he probably would have been elected President. Mr. Hughes, in fact, retired on the night of November 6 believing he was President-elect. Late returns from California, Senator Johnson's home state, brought victory to President Wilson.

LAWYER

With his defeat, Mr. Hughes returned to the practice of law in New York City as the senior member of the firm of Hughes, Rounds, Schurman and Dwight. In the years that followed, until his designation as Secretary of State in 1921, the Hughes firm represented some of the leading corporations in the country and Mr. Hughes personally appeared in many cases before his former colleagues on the Supreme Court.

On April 6, 1917, America entered the First World War. In that grave exigency, Congress undertook to draft men and extend its powers over the economy. The power of the federal government to raise an army by conscription, which to that time had not been passed upon by the Supreme Court, became a vital constitutional issue. In an address on "War Powers under the Constitution," delivered by Mr. Hughes before the American Bar Association on September 5, 1917, he maintained that conscription was constitutional.[9] The Framers of the Constitution, he declared, "did not contrive a spectacle of imposing impotency." Specifically, he urged,

"The power to wage war is the power to wage it successfully." And the power given to Congress to raise armies did not enable it simply to call volunteers, "but to raise armies by whatever method Congress deems best, and hence must embrace conscription." Might such an army be used abroad consistently with the Constitution? "The power to use an army," answered Mr. Hughes, "is co-extensive with the power to make war, and the army may be used wherever the war is carried on, here or elsewhere." [10]

Similarly, maintained Mr. Hughes, Congress might constitutionally extend its regulatory power over the economy. He said,

The extraordinary circumstances of war may bring particular businesses and enterprises clearly into the category of those which are affected with a public interest and which demand immediate and thoroughgoing regulation. . . . Reasonable regulation to safeguard the resources upon which we depend for military success must be regarded as being within the powers confided to Congress to enable it to prosecute a successful war.

The address, made by a respected former Justice of the Supreme Court, was widely distributed and was highly influential.

During the war, Mr. Hughes served as chairman of the New York City District Exemption Board and headed an investigation of alleged irregularities in the granting of government aircraft contracts.

The bitterness engendered by the war, the hatred of Socialists who had opposed the war, the fear of revolution induced by the establishment of a Bolshevik state in Russia, led as an aftermath of the war, to violent and often indiscriminate attacks upon radicals and radical sympathizers. The decade following the war witnessed, *inter alia*, the enactment of loyalty oath laws, the raids of Attorney General Palmer, the prosecution of Sacco and Vanzetti, the expulsion of a Socialist from the House of Representatives and the expulsion of five Socialists from the New York State Assembly.

In regard to the last of these incidents, Mr. Hughes played an important, if unsuccessful, role in defense of freedom to differ. Early in 1920, after five Socialist assemblymen had taken their oaths of office in the New York State legislature, suddenly action was taken denying them their seats "pending determination of their qualifications and eligibility to their respective seats." It was charged the Socialist party was an unpatriotic and subversive organization which adhered to the revolutionary forces of Soviet Russia and was pledged to forcible overthrow of all organized government. It was further charged that the party had opposed the war and been connected with a violation of the Espionage Act which by association branded all its members.[11]

The reaction of Mr. Hughes was immediate. He wrote to the Speaker of the Assembly charging that the proceeding was an attempt to indict a political party and deny it representation. "This is not, in my judgment, American government." He angrily continued,

Are Socialists, unconvicted of crime, to be denied the ballot? If Socialists are permitted to vote, are they not permitted to vote for their own candidates? If their candidates are elected and are men against whom, as individuals, charges of disqualifying offenses cannot be laid, are they not entitled to their seats? . . .

I understand that it is said that the Socialists constitute a combination to overthrow the Government. The answer is plain. If public officers or private citizens have any evidence that any individuals, or group of individuals, are plotting revolution and seeking by violent measures to change our Government, let the evidence be laid before the proper authorities and swift action be taken for the protection of the community. Let every resource of inquiry, of pursuit, of prosecution be employed to ferret out and punish the guilty according to our laws. But I count it a most serious mistake to proceed, not against individuals charged with violation, but against masses of our citizens combined for political action, by denying them the only resource of peaceful government; that is, action by the ballot box and through duly elected representatives in legislative bodies.[12]

This statement, in the light of the current campaign to penalize individuals on the basis of association with "subversive" organizations, without regard to personal belief or activity, merits careful restudy.

Although the Judiciary Committee of the Assembly accepted a brief of a special Committee of the Bar Association of the City of New York, of which Mr. Hughes was chairman, it refused to permit the Committee to participate in the proceedings. In this brief it was said, in language suggestive of that to be used by Mr. Hughes as Chief Justice of the United States, "Hyde Park meetings and soap-box oratory constitute the most efficient safety-valve against resort by the discontented to physical force." [13] The Judiciary Committee was unconvinced and recommended expulsion, a step which was carried out by the Assembly.

So disturbed was Mr. Hughes by the attacks being levelled against civil liberties in the postwar period that, in an address at the Harvard Law School, on June 21, 1920, he felt impelled to assert pessimistically,

We have seen the war powers, which are essential to the preservation of the nation in time of war, exercised broadly after the military exigency had passed and in conditions for which they were never intended, and we may well wonder in view of the precedents now established whether constitutional government as heretofore maintained could survive another great war even victoriously waged.[14]

SECRETARY OF STATE

On March 4, 1921, the very day Warren G. Harding assumed the office of President of the United States, he named Charles Evans Hughes as his Secretary of State. In the period of Mr. Hughes' service in that post, between 1921 and 1925, he concerned himself with fostering and safeguarding American private interest abroad, laying the foundation for peace and building good relations with foreign countries, Soviet Russia excluded.

In July of 1921 Congress passed a joint resolution declaring that hostilities had ceased and in August of 1921 separate treaties were signed with Germany, Austria and Hungary which were quickly ratified by the Senate. With respect to Mexico, Mr. Hughes adopted a strong tone in dealing with threats to American interests but was able to effect a compromise solution.[15] Although Mr. Hughes had joined with other prominent Republicans in assuring the nation that Harding's statement that he favored "an association of nations" meant the League of Nations,[16] he made no attempt to press that issue in the face of Harding's declaration in his first message to Congress that the United States would have nothing to do with the League,[17] and later statements that the United States did "not propose to enter now by the side door, or the back door or the cellar door" and that the issue was "as dead as slavery." [18] Hughes did, however, in a letter to President Harding on February 17, 1923, advocate our adherence to the World Court.[19] President Harding transmitted this letter to the Senate with his own recommended approval.[20]

Hughes earnestly sought to create good relations with and destroy the suspicion of South American countries in efforts which continued after he left office. Shortly after the Santiago Conference of 1923 he undertook to redefine the Monroe Doctrine in more acceptable terms.[21] In 1924 he made a good will trip to Rio de Janeiro to open the Brazilian exposition; in 1928, he served, for two months, as chief of the American delegation at the sixth Pan-American Conference in Havana, and, again in 1929, he served at the Pan-American Arbitration Conference which, according to Pearson and Allen, "helped to draft the fairest arbitration and conciliation treaties ever approved by the Senate." [22]

On the other hand, while he was able to elicit a statement from Baron Shidehara pledging evacuation of Eastern Siberia and non-intervention and respect for Russian territorial integrity which was redeemed when the Japanese troops left Vladivostok in October, 1922, he refused to accede in the restoration of formal relations with Soviet Russia, pending "convincing evidence" of a restoration of "private property, the sanctity of contracts and the rights of free labor." He characterized Russia as "a gigantic economic vacuum." [23]

By far the outstanding accomplishment of Mr. Hughes as Secretary of State was his successful stewardship of the Washington Disarmament Conference which opened its first plenary session in November, 1921, with Mr. Hughes as chairman and head of the American delegation. He astounded the delegates by his insistence upon immediate disarmament and his presentation of very concrete proposals for its effectuation down to the naming of specific vessels to be scrapped. His proposals for a ten-year holiday in the construction of capital ships and for the scrapping of specific battleships with a final ratio of 5-5-3-1.75-1.75 for the United States, Great Britain, Japan, France and Italy were finally accepted with some compromises that were largely in deference to Japanese and French security claims. Also, under the "driving leadership of Hughes," a nine-power treaty was concluded by the terms of which the signatories bound themselves to respect the "sovereignty, the independence, and the territorial and administrative integrity of

China," and to recognize the Open Door principle. Senate approval was obtained for the mass of treaties growing out of the Conference.[24]

World opinion, and American opinion particularly, had reached a high point of enthusiasm and hope for peace which was not warranted by the modest achievements of the Conference viewed in the perspective of time. But as one authority puts it:

When both sides are balanced it is clear that the Conference was a landmark in history. It actually did bring about a temporary cessation of frantic naval building, with a consequent improvement of international feeling. In the Far East, where the achievements of the Conference were less dramatic but more important, the Anglo-Japanese Alliance was terminated; the Open Door was given a new lease on life; and the navies of the great Powers in the Pacific were so scaled down that none could hope to attack the other with reasonable prospect of success. The general air-clearing dispelled the fetid international atmosphere, and made possible a more satisfactory recuperation from the World War than would otherwise have been possible.[25]

It is the judgment of two acute newspapermen, largely critical in their judgment of Mr. Hughes, that "compared with his contemporaries, Hughes was an excellent Secretary of State. He was vigorous, forceful, with an amazingly efficient command of all details of his vast office." [26]

The presidential campaign of 1924 gave Mr. Hughes an opportunity to reaffirm his conviction regarding the essential role of the Supreme Court in our constitutional system. The platform of the third party in the campaign, the Progressive party, whose candidate for the presidency was Senator Robert LaFollette, urged the adoption of a constitutional amendment to permit Congress to reenact a statute declared unconstitutional by the Supreme Court and make it effective over judicial nullification. "What would happen if this project succeeded?" Mr. Hughes asked and then replied,

It would mean that Congress could do anything it pleased if it passed an act twice. The States would be subject to the will of Congress. Every power of the President could be overridden by Congress. Anything that Congress saw fit to do would be supreme over all other authority. Could you have anything more revolutionary than that? A majority in Congress could decide upon any system of representation it pleased in order to continue its own power. The right to be secure in your person, in your life, in your property, the right to a fair trial if you were accused, the right to freedom of the press, freedom to worship God according to your own conscience, would be at the mercy of Congress.[27]

On January 10, 1925, Mr. Hughes resigned as Secretary of State, effective March 4, 1925, and returned to the practice of law in order to "recoup his fortune." In the ensuing years until his designation as Chief Justice, Mr. Hughes was the acknowledged leader of the American bar. He represented some of the most important corporate interests in the country and in the normal course of his activities repeatedly appeared before the Supreme Court in defense of those interests.[28] He took several occasions, however, to render important public services as in his special missions to South America. In addition, from 1926 to 1930 he served as a Member of the Permanent Court of Arbitration at The Hague and from 1928 to 1930 as a Judge of the Permanent Court of International Justice.[29]

CHAPTER 8

A HISTORIC DEBATE

Charles Evans Hughes had long been one of the most prominent members of the Republican party. He had served as an outstanding governor, a Justice of the Supreme Court, the candidate of the Republican party for the presidency, and Secretary of State. In each presidential campaign, beginning in 1908 (with the exception of that of 1912), he had been one of the most valued and effective campaigners for the Party. With the resignation of Chief Justice Taft, on February 3, 1930, on account of ill-health, no one could put forward a greater claim to the office than could Mr. Hughes. On that same day he was nominated by President Herbert Hoover to be Chief Justice of the United States. The nomination in due fashion was referred in the Senate to the Committee on the Judiciary headed by the Republican progressive, Senator George Norris.

On February 10, 1930, Senator Norris rose on the floor of the Senate and "by direction of the Committee on the Judiciary" reported favorably the nomination of Charles Evans Hughes to be Chief Justice of the United States.[1] And with this began the most bitter debate over confirmation of a Chief Justice (excepting possibly that with respect to Roger B. Taney) in the history of the United States. The opposition consisted principally of the Senate liberals and the Southern Democrats. Every known aspect of the life of Charles Evans Hughes commanding the slightest public interest or importance was canvassed in the course of this historic debate.

Senator Norris, who as a member of the Judiciary Committee had opposed confirmation, opened the debate with the statement that he was not moved in his opposition "by any personal feeling or any belief in the lack of Mr. Hughes' ability to perform the duties of this high office." There were, he said, two fundamental reasons for his objection: first, because "Mr. Hughes resigned from the Supreme Court to become a candidate for President of the United States," and second, because "no man in public life so exemplifies the influence of powerful combinations in the political and financial world as does Mr. Hughes."

Elaborating on the first reason for opposition, Senator Norris stated that he was not one of those who criticized Mr. Hughes for resigning from the Supreme Court to accept the presidential nomination. "But after he has made the campaign for a higher political office he ought not be, by political power, put back on the bench which he voluntarily left to enter the political world." This would establish a dangerous precedent which might lower the standards of the Supreme Court "to the level of the political machine. . . . Such a procedure must inevitably encourage and stimulate political activity on the part of judges of the Supreme Court" who, in other cases, might "be influenced to disregard justice in rendering their decisions and cater to the wish of politicians in power in the political world."

In support of his second reason for opposing confirmation he stated that there never had been a time in the history of our country when wealth had wielded as great an influence as at the present time. In the face of this fact, he pointed out, Mr. Hughes had, in the past five years, appeared in fifty-four cases before the Supreme Court "almost invariably" representing "corporations of almost untold wealth." There is no doubt, he said, that he had been employed by many of them in the belief that his former membership on the Supreme Court would tend to secure favorable decisions. Association with men of great wealth, and accumulation of a great fortune, were bound to have had their effect, conscious or unconscious, upon the nature of Mr. Hughes and he should not, therefore, "be called upon to sit in final judgment in contests between organized wealth and the ordinary citizen."

By way of illustration, Senator Norris said, among the vital questions coming before the Supreme Court was the dispute between combinations of great wealth and the people over the right to use the air in broadcasting over the radio and it was noteworthy that it was Mr. Hughes who had represented a great radio combination in its claim that the issuance of a license gave a vested right in perpetuity. The evils which would follow, he maintained, if such claim prevailed were beyond human imagination.[2]

The next day, February 11, 1930, Senator Borah rose to the attack. "Bear in mind, Mr. President," he stated,

that at the present time coal and iron, oil and gas, and power, light, transportation, and transmission have all practically gone into the hands of a very few people. The great problem is, how shall the people of the United States be permitted to enjoy these natural resources and these means of transportation, free from extortion and oppression? I can conceive of no more vital question than this which has long divided our Supreme Court.

While "Mr. Hughes was a man of high standing, one of the most distinguished Americans of this day, a man of wide reputation and acknowledged ability" and "integrity," it was a matter of concern that there would be placed upon the Court one whose views on this vital question were known and ought not be incorporated in our law.

What were these views? He made reference to the position of Mr. Hughes in the radio case and said that further indication of the "extreme views" held by Mr. Hughes in defense of property could be gleaned from the nature of the other propertied interests he had represented. In this connection, he noted that Mr. Hughes, on resigning as Secretary of State, became immediately the attorney for vast oil companies of the United States whose interests he had been looking after in Mexico and Persia in discharge of his duties as Secretary of State and for whom, as attorney, he later argued "to the effect that the Government had no power, no means by which to restrain, control or direct the great oil companies in the production of oil." Citing other propertied groups Hughes had represented he asked, "When during the last 16 years has corporate wealth had a contest with the public, when these vast interests claimed advantages which the public rejected, that Mr. Hughes has not appeared for organized wealth against the public?"

One other matter to which Senator Borah alluded was Mr. Hughes' representation of Mr. Truman H. Newberry of Michigan who had been convicted in a trial by jury of having violated the federal Corrupt Practices Act by excessive expenditures in his primary campaign for a Senatorial nomination. Mr. Hughes had carried the case to the Supreme Court, and Senator Borah expressed his unwillingness to give his approval by a vote for confirmation to the contention that Congress had no control over the means by which men seek nomination to a position in the Senate.

"Does not the Senator differentiate between the advocate and the judge?" Senator Shortridge rose to inquire. Senator Borah replied that while he supposed there was a distinction, he could not conceive that in a matter of such supreme importance as that involving the integrity of elections or primaries, Mr. Hughes would have accepted a fee to argue the case unless he actually believed in the position he urged before the Court.[3]

Senator Glass, following Senator Borah, stressed three reasons for opposing confirmation: first, Hughes' "lack of sensibility" in accepting a political nomination and then expressing a willingness to return to the bench; second, his SHREVEPORT decision; and third, Hughes' challenge to the right of the Senate to investigate maladministration in a bureau of the Treasury Department. Specifically, with reference to the SHREVEPORT decision, he argued, that it had "revealed a perfect antipathy to the rights of the States," and had "literally stripped" every right "that a State had possessed of control of interstate traffic."[4] "I have reason to believe," too, asserted Senator Glass, that when five years earlier the President challenged the right of the Senate to investigate alleged maladministration in a bureau of the Treasury, calling it a lawless procedure, that challenge "was formulated" by Mr. Hughes. He added that had that view prevailed in connection with the Teapot Dome investigation, which came after this incident, "very likely Mr. Daugherty would still be the Attorney General of the United States, and very likely other gentlemen of his peculiar type . . . would enjoy their liberties unmolested."[5]

The Senators from New York, both Democrats, spoke briefly in favor of confirmation. Senator Wagner said that Hughes' "fitness" was established by "his high character, the esteem in which the public holds him, and his past record of public service." He alluded to Hughes' "distinguished services as Governor of the State of New York," "the splendid statesmanship which he exhibited as Secretary of State," and "the substantial contribution which he made to the deliberations of the United States Supreme Court" during his earlier term.[6] Senator Copeland added that he had served recently under Mr. Hughes on a commission to reorganize the state government and found him "to be an able, conciliatory, sensible, alert, industrious chairman." He regarded him "as a fine, upstanding, Christian gentleman, one of the model citizens of the great city of New York." [7]

Senator Gillette undertook to deal briefly with the charges made by the opponents of confirmation. As to the first of these, that Mr. Hughes had resigned a judicial post to accept a political nomination, he commented that the nomination had had nothing to do with his service as a Justice of the Supreme Court, in connection with which it could not be claimed that he had catered for public or partisan favor, but came in recognition of the fact that he was a striking national figure and one of the foremost statesmen of the country.

As to the second objection dealing with "the character of service Mr. Hughes has rendered as a lawyer," Senator Gillette stated that such a criticism would bar every great and successful lawyer from the Chief Justiceship. It was true that as a lawyer of extraordinary ability, Mr. Hughes attracted as clients the great business interests of the country. However, it did not follow that his state of mind was so affected thereby that he could not thereafter sit as an impartial judge. An advocate is compelled to present his side of the case with all his talent, but after he is appointed to the bench he exercises his judicial temperament upon the merits of the case.

Ninety-nine out of every one hundred men, he thought, would not only regard Mr. Hughes as the leading lawyer in the United States but a similar proportion would acclaim his appointment as Chief Justice. He concluded, "Mr. Hughes has had a magnificent career as a statesman as well as a lawyer, and he is in every way, in my opinion, peculiarly qualified for the position to which he has been nominated." [8]

On the anniversary of Lincoln's birthday, February 12, the Senate, after a brief eulogy to Lincoln, continued the debate. Senator Dill pointed up the contrast between the lives of Charles Evans Hughes and Lincoln—the first, "the greatest champion of property rights of our time," and the second, "the greatest champion of human rights in the world since Christ." Conceding Mr. Hughes' "quality and great ability," he continued at great length, particularly underscoring the arguments advanced earlier by Senators Norris and

Borah. He expressed his weariness of the doctrine of "a sacrosanct judiciary." "They are men like other men; and as they write their economic views into decisions of the courts that become the basis of the charges for the necessities of life, I can no longer think of them as different from other public officials." The one new objection he interposed was with regard to the wisdom of confirming one of such advanced years, "nearly 70," for the Chief Justiceship.[9]

Senator Shortridge of California interjected to challenge the dichotomy drawn between "property" and "human" rights. "There is no such thing as a 'property' right as a right apart from a person; property has no rights. Men and women have rights to that which we call property," he said.[10]

Senator Glenn, entering the debate, addressed himself first to the argument that Mr. Hughes had represented great corporate wealth. He noted that Lincoln, too, had on occasion represented great power and wealth, argued that "every cause has a right to be heard," and asked,

Can it be true that men, complying with the laws of this country in organizing and conducting corporations are not entitled to employ a lawyer to represent them, and that no lawyer who does represent them can ever after that aspire to the high office of membership on the Supreme Court? If so, how much more force is there, in these times, when we cry out against the lack of law observance, against crime and criminal conduct, in the contention that no man who represents those accused of crime, although their right to be defended in the courts is a constitutional right, can ever expect or hope to reach the high point in his profession?

Senator Glenn further pointed out that Mr. Hughes' position in the NEWBERRY case had won the approval of the Supreme Court, and that the objection of Senator Borah to the confirmation, upon analysis, is "that upon great questions he [Mr. Hughes] is not in accord with the views of the senior Senator from Idaho," and questioned whether the man lived who did not differ with Senator Borah on vital questions.

Then he attacked the criticism of Mr. Hughes as the subservient advocate of public utility corporations. He maintained that Hughes, as governor of New York, "was the first outstanding man in public life in America to advocate the institution of public-utility commissions to regulate the charges, the rates, and the issuance of securities by these corporations." He insisted that labor, too, from time to time, retained Hughes as counsel, as for example, in the dispute between the United Mine Workers of America and the Coronado Mining Company. He called attention to the fact that, two years before it was adopted in Wisconsin, Mr. Hughes first advocated in New York the adoption of a workmen's compensation law. He pointed to the liberal decisions of Mr. Hughes as an Associate Justice, to his record as governor and Hughes' statement in his acceptance speech at Carnegie Hall on July 31, 1916, to support his thesis that Hughes was pro-labor. This record proved Hughes "stood, not for exploitation of human rights, but for their preservation."

He conceded that Hughes had been employed by great corporations, one after another, but added,

but somehow it seems to me in these later days that the old antipathy, the old hostility against corporations, the old idea that every corporation is wrong, that its influence is bad, that it is corrupt, that it seeks to grind down the common people, is disappearing.

We hear no more of this talk of "trust busting." We have come to realize that great mergers and combinations are necessary, so long as they are compelled by strict laws to observe the common interests of the people of this land, and to operate, not with the primary object of gaining great and extortionate profits for themselves but in the interest of all the people of the land.[11]

Senator Wheeler of Montana appealed directly to the members of his own party, the Democratic party, to oppose confirmation, not because Hughes was a Republican, but because of his economic views which while typifying the views of a majority of the Senators upon the other side did not represent the Democratic position.

As to Hughes' record as a liberal governor of New York, Senator Wheeler charged that Hughes had vetoed a bill for equal wages for women teachers, the Coney Island nickel-fare bill, the two cents a mile railroad fare bill and the full crew bill, "and I might go on enumerating bill after bill which he vetoed which was in the interest of the ordinary man and woman of that State." [12]

Senator Blaine of Wisconsin followed Senator Wheeler, reiterated some of the reasons previously urged against confirmation, and added only stinging invective. "I do not believe that the American people for one moment regard the Supreme Court of the United States as a suitable dumping ground for the ebbing life of one of the most zealous defenders and leaders of privilege." [13]

After some inconclusive discussion relative to agreement upon the time for a vote and the need for a night session the Senate recessed until the next day.

When the debate resumed, Senator Nye of North Dakota reasoning that the Senate has the right to consider the environment, training and probable sympathies of nominees for the Supreme Court agreed with Senator Glenn that this should be done on the "record of Charles Evans Hughes and upon that record alone." He proceeded to quote at great length from Gustavus Myers' *History of the Supreme Court*, which, published in 1912, sought to establish Charles Evans Hughes' connection, prior to his earlier appointment to the Court, with the representation of corporate interest seeking special favors against the public interest.[14]

Senator Dill rose to read into the record an editorial that charged that Mr. Hughes had been "squarely in the midst" of the corruption in the Harding cabinet involving Daugherty, Fall and Denby and "gave no indication that he smelled anything. So bad a nose is poor equipment for a Chief Justice of the United States." [15]

Senator LaFollette of Wisconsin believed that "the issues at stake transcend the question of the personal character and ability of the nominee, which are conceded." By tracing the development of judicial review and by quoting from dissenting opinions of Justices Holmes, Moody, Jackson and Harlan in a number of cases, he sought to establish that the Court "not only declared acts unconstitutional when it found them repugnant to some clause of the Constitution but also when, in the opinion of a majority of the judges, the social or economic end which Congress sought to achieve was contrary to their beliefs." Under the circumstances, it was "imperative for every member of this body to weigh the economic and social views of Mr. Hughes before voting to confirm him to the high office of Chief Justice of the Supreme Court." Then alluding to Mr. Hughes' record of advocacy he added,

To contend that Mr. Hughes appealed in the Supreme Court of the United States to his former associates to take a position upon great con-

stitutional questions affecting the rights of the people of this country
when he did not himself believe in it is to make an accusation against his
intellectual integrity.[16]

Senator Norris, in a lengthy, scholarly address, after congratulat-
ing the Senate upon the high order of the debate, conceding that
the motives of the opposition were high-minded, and recognizing
the honesty of Mr. Hughes in support of his views, returned to his
attack. Senator Glenn, he said, made practically the only defense
that could be made of Mr. Hughes and he made it "fairly and elo-
quently," but, significantly, "We all know that the Senator from
Illinois, starting out to defend Mr. Hughes, before he finished was
engaged in a defense of monopoly, of trusts, of combinations—and
that is logical, perfectly logical. That is where it leads."

It was to a great extent true that the people of the United States,
perhaps concluding that they were helpless, were "acquiescing in
this merger march." But he was frightened "at the spectacle that is
presented" and warned his countrymen to rise and insist, before it
was too late, "that the highest court of the land shall not be controlled by the elements that believe that wealth and money should
rule the world."

Ability in a nominee was not enough. Conceding, for the sake of
argument, as Senator Gillette had contended, that Hughes was the
greatest lawyer in the United States, the jails in the United States
were filled with able lawyers "and if they are not found there that is
no reason why some of them should not be there." As for Mr.
Hughes, it has taken clients with big money to employ him, he has
been associated with them and that relationship has been a part of
his life, and "I am not willing to say that that kind of man, regardless of his ability, should go on the Supreme Bench."

Acknowledging that the other side had the votes to win, he
prophetically stated, "the record we have made will be read by
liberty loving citizens who shall be here after we are all dead." [17]

Mr. Ransdell, the Senator from Louisiana, because of the many
references to the SHREVEPORT CASE, believed it necessary to correct
mistaken impressions. He pointed out that under conditions prevailing prior to the decision Shreveport had been discriminated
against so that in a typical case railroads serving both Texas and
Louisiana charged anywhere from one and one-half to six times as

much per mile to carry goods from Shreveport, Louisiana, to Marshall, Texas (42 miles), as from Dallas, Texas, to Marshall, Texas
(147.7 miles). It was a *state* authority, the Louisiana Railroad Commission, which in 1911 appealed to the Interstate Commerce Commission for relief. The Commission required the railroads not to
continue the discrimination and this decision was affirmed by the
United States Supreme Court. Far from destroying the rights of
states, "there never has been a decision in our Republic which did
more to protect the rights of our States in the important matter of
rates." Senator Brookhart of Iowa replied that the decision had been
in direct conflict with a provision of the Act of Congress excluding
control over traffic "wholly within one State." Furthermore, he
queried whether the result would not have been better had the
Supreme Court and the Interstate Commerce Commission reduced
the Louisiana rate to the level of the Texas rate.[18]

At nearly 6 o'clock Senator Norris moved that the Senate recess
until the next day. That motion was defeated by a vote of 35 yeas
and 45 nays.[19]

The end was not yet. Senator Walsh of Montana read into the
record a charge that Mr. Hughes, appointed by President Wilson
as a special investigator into alleged fraud in the handling of wartime
plane contracts, "reported on November 1, 1918, just before the
critical congressional elections of that year" asking that the principal representative of the Government be court-martialed, quoting
in particular against him four telegrams. The War Department board
of review thereafter found that Mr. Hughes had omitted a fifth
telegram, which, if published, would have established his innocence
and negatived "the implications raised by Mr. Hughes."

Senator Walsh added that, though he had voted in the Committee
to report favorably the nomination, he had changed his mind. He
referred, in support of this position, particularly to the undesirability
of promoting one who had resigned judicial office to accept a
presidential nomination and to the fact that he found it difficult to
understand how Hughes, as Secretary of State, could have been
"entirely oblivious of the riot of corruption that was about him."
But even more "inexplicable" was Hughes' failure "to utter one
word of condemnation." [20]

Senator McKellar of Tennessee cited several reasons for opposing confirmation of Mr. Hughes. Among these were "his age," his bias toward the rich, and "because in 1922, as chairman of President Harding's Disarmament Conference, as it was probably improperly called, he [Hughes] agreed to sink the greatest battleship fleet that America ever had, without regard to the best interests of America." [21]

Senator McKellar having concluded, Senator Norris moved that the nomination be referred back to the Committee on the Judiciary. The motion was defeated—yeas 31, nays 49. The Vice-President then put the question, "Shall the Senate advise and consent to the nomination?" The debate was over, the vote was taken—yeas 52, nays 26. And the record contains the memorandum, "So the Senate advised and consented to the nomination of Charles Evans Hughes to be Chief Justice of the United States." [22]

The debate in Congress was paralleled by a debate in the press of the nation. The New York *Herald Tribune* was outraged by the position taken by the opposition to Hughes' confirmation: "That twenty-six Senators should vote to reject so admirable a nomination as that of Mr. Hughes to be Chief Justice of the United States is a symptom of aggravated degeneracy in a body now habituated to disesteem and decadence."

It is "a ridiculous approach" to an examination of Hughes' fitness to regard "certain political and economic leanings attributed to him" as more important than his "integrity, wide experience, capacity and intellectual independence." In any event it is "nonsensical" to impute to him "the opinions of various clients who had employed him," for a lawyer is not responsible for the views of his clients. "He protects the client's legal rights. . . . His political and economic opinions are his own." [23]

The New York *Times*, recognizing the "fine ability" and the "eminent fitness" of Mr. Hughes to be Chief Justice, was not surprised at the attack upon him as one "who for years has been an unswerving partisan." It was all "written in our democratic stars." [24]

The *Wall Street Journal*, while pleased with the appointment, conceded that "It is perfectly true that Presidents choose men for the Supreme Court with an eye to their known attitudes or leanings on great pending issues." [25]

Granting that Mr. Hughes is an able lawyer, the *Nation* regarded him as displaying "a narrowness of understanding, an unteachable stubbornness, and an arid self-righteousness that disqualify him for high judicial service." It castigated Hughes for having "dragged in the dust the court's proud tradition of aloofness from political ambition," for having sat in the Harding cabinet "with his lips sealed" during the infamy and disgrace of Albert B. Fall and the Ohio gang. "His conduct of our foreign affairs was marked by a narrow and uncomprehending insistence at all costs on the most extreme interpretation of American property rights, notably in our oil diplomacy and our relations with Mexico and Russia." It concluded that his appointment "is little less than a public disaster." [26]

In light of the fact that on the great economic and social questions coming before the Court, the decisions of the Justices "are determined not so much by what is explicit in the Constitution as by their personal likes, dislikes, and prejudices," the *New Republic* reasoned that "there is no wonder that an outcry arose against Mr. Hughes, who in his law practice has been so closely associated with great corporations who have had and will have favors to seek at the hands of the Court, in view of some recent appointments." [27]

It may be said of the debate in Congress, which was accompanied by a debate in the nation, that its outcome was a foregone conclusion. The proponents of Senate approval, many of whom had been elected upon the tide of President Hoover's victory, had the votes to win, as Senator Norris conceded, and simply waited for the opposition to spend itself. This, undoubtedly, was one reason why so little, relatively speaking, was said in support of confirmation as against it. But the importance of the debate, from the point of view of the Senate liberals, lay not in the hope of immediate success in blocking the confirmation but in the educational value in expounding to the Senate and to the nation the nature of the issues being decided by the Court and the considerations which controlled its decisions. These issues, the liberals insisted, were largely economic, and the considerations which decided them were fundamentally based not upon the law of the Constitution but the preferences of the Justices. It was this educational effect that Senator Norris no doubt envisaged when he said that "the record we have made will be read by liberty-loving citizens who shall be here after we are all dead."

However, it was not very long before the efforts expended by the liberals obtained concrete results. With the death of Justice Sanford on March 8, 1930, President Hoover, still smarting from the stinging attack upon his designation of Mr. Hughes, waited more than two weeks before submitting the name of Judge John J. Parker to succeed Justice Sanford. The record disclosed that Judge Parker had, as a United States Circuit Court judge, upheld the constitutional validity of a so-called "yellow dog" contract. It was also charged that in the course of a campaign in North Carolina, as the Republican candidate for governor, he had made some derogatory remarks about Negroes. Although his decision had followed precedent established by the Supreme Court and the remarks, if made, were fugitive expressions, his nomination was rejected, on May 7, by a vote of 41 to 39.[28] The position of the liberals that the decisions of Justices were not rendered simply in obedience to the Constitution and, accordingly, that the economic and social views of nominees were pertinent considerations in the process of Senatorial approval or rejection thus found vindication.

In the place of his defeated nominee, President Hoover sent in the name of Owen J. Roberts, who had not been very active politically and whose economic and social views were not well known. His nomination was approved by the Senate.

When, on January 12, 1932, Justice Oliver Wendell Holmes, Jr. resigned from the Court, President Hoover named an outstanding liberal Democratic Justice, Benjamin N. Cardozo, to succeed him. It is probable that apart from the high esteem which Mr. Cardozo commanded from the bar, one of the principal reasons for his designation was the salutary effect that the debates over the confirmation of Mr. Hughes and Mr. Parker had had upon the nation in contributing to its awareness of the nature of the judicial process.

Some years later the powers of the Court and the role of the Justices in our system of government were to become the foci of a great controversy arising out of President Roosevelt's Court reorganization plan in which the issues raised in these historic debates, and what was then said, were again to command the attention of the nation.

IV. Chief Justice of the United States

CHAPTER 9

THE SETTING

The nearly universal acclaim that had greeted Mr. Hughes' designation as an Associate Justice was, as we have seen, conspicuously lacking with his assumption of the high office of Chief Justice of the United States on February 24, 1930, a position he was to hold until his retirement on July 1, 1941.

On June 2, 1930, shortly after the Chief Justice took his seat, Owen J. Roberts, who had been a successful corporation lawyer, had taught at the University of Pennsylvania Law School and had served the government in the Teapot Dome cases, became a member of the Court. Less than two years later, on January 12, 1932, Oliver Wendell Holmes, the sage jurist and philosopher, with a conservative bent of mind and a liberal judicial philosophy, brought to a close thirty years of service upon the bench. He did not, therefore, participate in the decision of the New Deal cases. He was succeeded by Benjamin N. Cardozo on March 14 upon designation of President Hoover.

Between March of 1932 and June of 1937, including the critical years when the Court was to pass upon the constitutionality of the National Industrial Recovery Act, the Agricultural Adjustment Act, the National Labor Relations Act, the Social Security Law, and other vital social legislation, the composition of the Court remained unchanged. Before these issues came before the Court, two of the Justices had already established a reputation as liberals by their willingness, generally speaking, to extend considerable latitude, under the Constitution, to the exercise of federal and state power in the regulation of the economy. They were, first, Louis D. Brandeis, a skillful, crusading reformer, author of the famed "economic brief," whose designation in 1916 by President Wilson had occasioned a bitter contest in the Senate. Second, in point of service, was Harlan F. Stone, whose career as Columbia Law School Dean, corporation lawyer, and Attorney General in the administration of Calvin Coolidge prior to his elevation to the bench in 1925, had given little promise of the tough-minded liberal to follow. Of him Charles Beard wrote that he had "a zest for the facts of life surrounding any case at law." These two outstanding liberals were joined by a third with the appointment of the scholarly, literary and ascetic Benjamin N. Cardozo, who came to the Court directly after many years of service, with nearly universally recognized distinction, as Chief Judge of New York State's highest court where he had given broad scope to governmental power of experimentation.

Four of the Justices, on the other hand, were commonly regarded as conservatives because of their generally expressed opposition to extensions of governmental power over the economy. Willis Van Devanter, stolid and unimaginative, had been Chief Justice of the Wyoming Supreme Court, an Assistant Attorney General of the United States and a United States Circuit judge before being named to the Supreme Court by President Taft in 1910. James C. Mc-Reynolds, Democrat from Tennessee, had been a trust-busting Attorney General under President Wilson, with a liberal reputation, but after his appointment in 1914 "had gradually become more conservative and finally emerged as a die-hard reactionary." [1] Wilson came to regard that appointment as a great mistake.[2] The remaining two conservatives, both designees of President Harding in 1922, were: George Sutherland, who had served in both houses of Congress, had been a president of the American Bar Association and a leading corporation lawyer, and who was equipped with a good mind, considerable legal ability and facility of expression; and Pierce Butler, who had been a prominent railroad attorney and expert in railroad law and was, as a member of the Court, to continue to share the economic philosophy of his quondam employers.

In the light of this division in the Court, the crucial inquiry was to become: where would Chief Justice Hughes and Mr. Justice Roberts stand in relation to legislation designed to ameliorate the bitter distress induced by what one Justice called "an emergency more serious than war"? [3]

In November of 1928 Mr. Herbert Hoover had been swept into office upon the tide of a general wave of prosperity that gave little or no sign of receding. In October of 1929, however, came the Wall Street debacle. The debate over the nomination of Mr. Hughes as Chief Justice of the United States in February, 1930, had proceeded as the debacle gathered momentum and engulfed the nation in catastrophic depression. In the years that followed the depression deepened.

With the collapse of the stock market in October, 1929, a spiral of deflation set in. The depression took on catastrophic proportions. National income declined from $81,100,000,000 in 1929 to $40,000,000,000 in 1932, salaries and wages paid fell from $49,200,000,000 to $29,941,-000,000, dividend payments from $6,000,000,000 to $2,700,000,000, gross farm income from $12,000,000,000 to $5,300,000,000. The index of physical volume of production dropped from 125 in June, 1929, to 59 in March, 1933. Foreign commerce was reduced from slightly less than $5,500,000,000 to approximately $1,750,000,000 in the same period. As a result, many businesses and banks went to the wall, thirteen to fifteen million persons became unemployed, homes and savings were lost, thousands of farmers lost their farms through foreclosures, and other thousands were threatened with foreclosure.[4]

So devastating was this depression that despite some efforts under President Hoover and herculean efforts under President Roosevelt, it was not until America began serious preparation for entry into the Second World War that the nation was restored to a level of full employment and productivity comparable with that of 1929 preceding the crash.

This great and continuing crisis which divided the nation into bitterly opposed camps of opinion was reflected within the Court. Unlike the relative harmony and general agreement which had prevailed in the Court during Mr. Hughes' first tenure, the Court was soon rent by bitter internal strife in the second. Unlike the relative lack of departure from established precedent in the first period, the second was characterized by startling innovations and precedent-shattering reversals and brought with it an attack upon the fundamental prerogatives of the Court itself. To preside over the

most controversial and most bitterly divided Court in our entire
history in a period of deep national crisis was the task that befell
Chief Justice Hughes and taxed his skill and ingenuity to the full.

While the Chief Justice has only one vote, he enjoys considerable
opportunity for leadership.[5] At the conference, the Chief Justice,
unless he prefers not to do so, states his opinion first and votes last.
When a decision has been reached, if the Chief Justice is part of
the majority, he assigns the case for opinion. If the Chief Justice is
with the minority, the senior Associate Justice with the majority
assigns the case for such opinion while the Chief Justice decides on
the author of the minority opinion. Within this limitation, the Chief
Justice may retain any cases for himself, and make such assignments
to others, as he pleases and "his assignments are never questioned." [6]

In the process of making such assignments, Chief Justice Hughes
assumed a heavy share of the burden for himself and wrote the
opinion of the Court in 283 cases and dissented in 23 cases, frequently with opinion.[7] Although the Chief Justice will ordinarily
seek to distribute the cases so that each Justice will have a fair
share of work in relation to importance as well as burden, he nevertheless retains considerable range of choice and it is understandable,
therefore, that as Chief Justice of the United States, Mr. Hughes
assumed the privilege of writing the opinion of the Court, or the
dissenting opinion, in many of the leading cases to come before the
Court. As a consequence, the record of his tenure as Chief Justice
is unquestionably a record of opinions which in importance may
be rivalled only by those of Chief Justice Marshall.[8]

CHAPTER 10

PROCEDURAL DUE PROCESS AND GOVERNMENTAL POWER

In the long reach of Anglo-Saxon history, due process has imposed limitations upon the procedure through which government has sought to deprive persons of life, liberty or property.[1] But the due process clauses which stay both the national and state governments are couched in general terms which contain no description of the procedures necessary to accord with the requirements imposed. In the course of its decisions, the Court has ruled that the procedures embraced within the due process rubric may vary greatly depending not only upon specific mandates of the Constitution and historic usage but also upon what it deems to accord with justice in the light of the nature and importance of the interests affected and the practical exigencies of governing. Obviously the Court has enjoyed a wide ambit of choice. How that choice was exercised by Chief Justice Hughes is the subject of consideration in the pages that follow.

CRIMINAL PROCEEDINGS

When the Constitution mandates a certain mode of procedure in federal criminal proceedings but makes no reference to such mode in relation to the criminal proceedings of a state, it would seem that a state is free to adopt or refuse to adopt such practice. For a great number of years this was precisely the view of the Court which asserted that when an explicit procedure was prescribed by a provision of the Constitution other than due process for use by the federal government that procedure was thereby excluded from the requirements of due process affecting the states. This proceeded on the reasonable and logical assumption, supported by a well-recognized canon of construction, that to hold otherwise was to assume redundancy and superfluity of language in our fundamental law.[2]

Before, however, Mr. Hughes had become Chief Justice of the United States, the Court had retreated from the full rigor of the logic implicit in this doctrine and held that when fundamental principles of liberty and justice were deemed to require a particular mode of proceeding, such mode was embraced within the protection of due process affecting states even though it was the subject of specific provision affecting the federal government under a clause other than due process.[3] The manner in which this doctrine was applied is illustrated by the decision of the Court in *Powell* v. *Alabama*.[4] In this case the Chief Justice joined in an opinion of Justice Sutherland in holding that it was a denial of *due process* for the trial court of a state to fail to assign counsel for the defense, whether requested or not, in a capital case when the defendant (a Negro) was unable to employ counsel and was incapable adequately of making his own defense. The right to counsel, it should be observed, is guaranteed in all criminal prosecutions of the *federal government* by *specific* provision in the *Sixth Amendment* and if earlier principle had been adhered to would have been excluded from the requirement of due process.

While this result which imposed upon the states *some* of the requirements of "just" procedure specifically mandated for use by the federal government may be considered desirable, especially when as here it was effected in aid of a group frequently subjected to the wanton disregard of elementary procedures of fairness, it had the odd effect of giving broader restrictive scope to the due process clause of the Fourteenth Amendment than that encompassed within the identically worded clause of the Fifth Amendment and served to demonstrate, too, the flexibility enjoyed by the Court in due process interpretations.

That the really fundamental consideration underlying procedural due process is the demand of justice was clearly revealed by two decisions of the Court in 1935 and 1936. In *Mooney* v. *Holohan* [5] the Court, in a *per curiam* opinion, while denying leave without prejudice to the petitioner, of Mooney-Billings fame, to file an original petition for a writ of habeas corpus in the Supreme Court and instructing him to first exhaust his state remedies, nevertheless expressed its agreement with the view urged by the petitioner, long after normal processes of appeal had been exhausted, that due process was violated if his conviction had been procured by the state "through a deliberate deception of court and jury by the presentation of testimony known to be perjured." "Due process," said the Court, "in safeguarding the liberty of the citizen against deprivation through the action of the State, embodies the fundamental conceptions of justice which lie at the base of our civil and political institutions."

Again, in *Brown* v. *Mississippi*,[6] the Court waved aside technical rules of procedure historically accepted in order to achieve a just result. In upsetting a conviction for crime which rested solely upon confessions shown to have been extorted by brutality and violence as a denial of due process, the Chief Justice said for a unanimous Court that because a state may exercise discretion in regulating the forms of trial, it did not follow "that it may substitute trial by ordeal. The rack and torture chamber may not be substituted for the witness stand." The contention of the state that counsel for the defendant had waived the right to reversal of the conviction by failing to move for the exclusion of the confessions was based on a misconception, said the Chief Justice. "The complaint is not of the commission of mere error, but of a wrong so fundamental that it made the whole proceeding a mere pretense of a trial and rendered the conviction and sentence wholly void."

The decision of the Court in this, as in the MOONEY case, in spirit, if not in precise fact, was inconsistent with that of *Frank* v. *Mangum* decided in 1915 and vindicated the position Justice Hughes had then joined in taking by way of dissent. The Court, in effect, announced that the disregard of the requirements of justice in criminal proceedings would not be countenanced despite historic modes of procedure and technical rules of practice. It is in this area and particularly in relation to the states that judicial review finds strong moral appeal.

ADMINISTRATIVE PROCEEDINGS

At no time in the Court's history did the question of the procedure appropriate to the process of administration within the conception of due process assume such importance as during the tenure of Chief Justice Hughes. This was true, of course, because of the proliferation of New Deal agencies which were vested with wide authority to control many aspects of the economy and to use more summary procedures than had generally theretofore prevailed when vital economic interests were affected.

As governor of the State of New York Mr. Hughes had taken the lead in proposing the establishment of administrative agencies to regulate utility rates and had supported their authority free from hampering restrictions. As the years went by and increasingly resort was had to the administrative process for the regulation of vital economic interests, his fears were apparently aroused that the process had been carried to the point where fundamental rights of liberty and property were being subjected to arbitrary control. In the summer of 1924, speaking in historic Westminster Hall, he took the occasion to say,

The spirit of the common law is opposed to those insidious encroachments upon liberty which take the form of an uncontrolled administrative authority—the modern guise of an ancient tyranny, not more welcome to intelligent free men because it may bear the label of democracy.[7]

His growing fear of the new and nostalgia for the old ways of the law were clearly voiced when Chief Justice Hughes addressed the Federal Bar Association in 1931 and said,

A host of controversies as to provisional rights are no longer decided in courts. Administrative authority, within a constantly widening sphere of action, and subject only to the limitation of certain broad principles, establishes particular rules, finds the facts, and decides as to particular rights. The power of administrative bodies to make findings of fact which may be treated as conclusive, if there is evidence both ways, is a power of enormous consequence. An unscrupulous administrator might be tempted to say, "Let me find the facts for the people of my country, and I care little who lays down the general principles." We all recognize that this development has been to a great extent a necessary one. . . . Experience, expertness and continuity of supervision, which could only be had by administrative agencies in a particular field, have come to be imperatively needed. But these new methods put us to new tests, and the serious question of the future is whether we have enough of the old spirit which gave us our institutions to save them from being overwhelmed.[8]

One year later, in *Crowell* v. *Benson*,[9] the Chief Justice converted his fears into a hampering restriction on the administrative process. It had long been established that due process required in most instances that final determination of questions of law be left to courts. Per contra, it had generally been held that finality could be validly attached, conformably to due process, to administrative determinations of fact if supported by evidence. The decision in this case seriously disturbed that principle.

The case arose out of a suit brought in the District Court to enjoin the enforcement of an award made under the Longshoremen's and Harbor Workers' Compensation Act of 1927 which rested upon the finding of the deputy commissioner that one Knudsen was injured in the course of his employment while performing service upon the navigable waters of the United States. In opposing recovery, it was denied that an employer-employee relationship had existed at the time of injury. The case turned upon the validity of the procedure used in determining the correctness of this denial. That procedure was challenged as unconstitutional under the due process clause of the Fifth Amendment and the provisions of Article 3 of the Constitution with respect to the judicial power of the United States.

Chief Justice Hughes, writing for a majority of the Court, upheld the constitutional validity of the statute upon finding that it did not purport to attach finality to administrative determination of questions of law and authorized the court below, in proceedings to set aside an order as not in accordance with law, to make "its own examination and determination of facts whenever that is deemed to be necessary to enforce a constitutional right properly asserted."

Apart from questions of law and "constitutional facts," said the Chief Justice, the attaching of finality to rulings of the commissioner upon questions of fact, assuming due notice, proper opportunity to be heard, and findings based upon evidence, was "easily within the principle of the decisions sustaining similar procedure against objections under the due process clauses of the Fifth and Fourteenth Amendments."

Whether the statutory procedure was in conflict with Article 3 of the Constitution, which provides that the judicial power of the United States extends "to all Cases of admiralty and maritime Jurisdiction," presented, he said, "a distinct question." That question related only to determinations of *fact* since final determination of legal questions was in all cases reserved to the court. There is "no requirement," he conceded, that "in order to maintain the essential attributes of judicial power," that *all* "determinations of fact in constitutional courts shall be made by judges." Juries, he pointed out, frequently make determinations of fact in federal constitutional courts. So, too, the method of permitting determinations of ordinary fact, which arise in the routine of making compensation awards to employees by the commissioner, was necessary to effective enforcement and constitutional.

But, he continued, a different requirement lies with respect to the determination of "fundamental" or "jurisdictional" facts, in the sense that their existence is a "condition precedent to the operation of the statutory scheme." What were these facts? They related to the provisions of the statute that injury must occur upon the navigable waters of the United States and that the relation of master and servant must exist. The very power of Congress to enact the legislation turned upon the existence of these conditions, he reasoned, because unless injuries occur upon navigable waters and unless an employer-employee relationship exists there could be no liability under the Constitution. In regard to these "basic facts" it is "a question of the appropriate maintenance of the federal judicial power in requiring the observance of constitutional restrictions."

It is the question whether the Congress may substitute for constitutional courts, in which the judicial power of the United States is vested, an administrative agency—in this instance a single deputy commissioner —for the final determination of the existence of the facts upon which the enforcement of the constitutional rights of the citizen depend. The recognition of the utility and convenience of administrative agencies for the investigation and finding of facts within their proper province, and the support of their authorized action, does not require the conclusion that there is no limitation of their use, and that the Congress could completely oust the courts of all determinations of fact by vesting the authority to make them with finality in its own instrumentalities or in the executive department. That would be to sap the judicial power as it exists under the Federal Constitution, and to establish a government of a bureaucratic character alien to our system, wherever fundamental rights depend, as not infrequently they do depend, upon the facts, and finality as to facts becomes in effect finality in law.

After rejecting as irrelevant citations of state cases since separation of powers is not enjoined under the federal Constitution for the distribution of state powers, and also finding inapposite decisions with respect to determinations of fact "made by administrative agencies which have been created to aid in the performance of governmental functions," he flatly asserted, "In cases brought to enforce constitutional rights, the judicial power of the United States necessarily extends to the independent determination of all questions, both of fact and law, necessary to the performance of that supreme function." [10]

The question remained—upon what record was it constitutionally required that the determination of such facts be made? To this he gave the answer: "We think that the essential independence of the exercise of the judicial power of the United States, in the enforcement of constitutional rights, requires that the federal court should determine such an issue upon its own record and the facts elicited before it."

Had these mandates imposed by Article 3 of the Constitution been violated by the legislation or the proceedings in this case? The negative answers given by Chief Justice Hughes were derived, first, from his construction of the *Act* as authorizing the Court to determine for itself the "jurisdictional" or "fundamental" facts upon which liability proceeded and, second, from the fact that the District Court had permitted a trial *de novo* on the issue of employment.[11]

In an extremely vigorous dissent, in which Justices Stone and Roberts joined, Justice Brandeis argued as follows: First, the Act did not authorize a trial *de novo* on the existence of an employer-employee relation as the Chief Justice had found because the use of similar language in analogous statutes with a different construction rendered that view untenable. Second, there was no basis for a construction that a right of trial *de novo*, conceded by the majority to have been denied by Congress as to most issues of fact, was intended in respect to the issue of employer-employee relationship. It must be recognized, he contended, that the absence of the employer-employee relation was only one of many grounds for non-liability under the statute. If the denial of this right rendered the statute unconstitutional, then it must be so held since to read this right into the act was to remake rather than construe it. Third, trial *de novo* was not required by due process since that clause does not even require that parties shall be permitted to have a judicial tribunal pass upon the weight of the evidence introduced before administrative bodies. Fourth, the view that trial *de novo* was required by Article 3 of the Constitution could not be reconciled with the ruling of the Court holding it compatible with the grant of power to deny a trial *de novo* as to most of the facts; the exception made with respect to the employer-employee relation was not well founded since the existence of that relation "is a question going to the applicability of the substantive law, not to the jurisdiction of the tribunal." Fifth, the cases cited by the Court in support of its conclusion that the statute would be invalid unless construed to permit trial *de novo* of so-called "jurisdictional facts" related to tribunals "generally different" from that involved here and the doctrine should not be extended. Such a doctrine "logically applied" would "seriously impair the entire administrative process." Sixth, even assuming an independent determination as to "jurisdictional" facts was required, no good reason was suggested why it could not proceed on the record before the Commissioner and why a retrial must be permitted imposing unnecessary and burdensome expenses and crippling the effective administration of the Act.

It requires no extended analysis to recognize that reason and precedent in relation to the legal and constitutional issues in this case were with the dissenters. But such an analysis would be largely irrelevant. For, while the argument between the Chief Justice and Justice Brandeis dealt with the construction and constitutionality of a specific Act of Congress, the essential debate, underlying the decision, and only occasionally intimated, was concerned with the fundamental issue of the role of administrative agencies in our constitutional system and more narrowly with the degree of finality to be attached to their determinations. The key to the decision lies, I believe, not in the involved and labored reasoning of the Chief Justice but in his apprehension that to vest authority in administrative agencies to make final determinations on all questions of fact would be "to establish a government of a bureaucratic character alien to our system." It was a fear which he had voiced a year earlier in his address before the Federal Bar Association.

This decision, in short, was an attempt, dictated by the growth of administrative agencies, (soon to burst forth in even greater abundance), to retain for the courts a measure of their ancient power. In the circumstances of this case it was a singularly unfortunate attempt because of the impeding effect it was bound to have on the administration of workmen's compensation legislation where speed was often essential to relief.[12] But its implications went beyond its immediate effect and contributed a fundamental threat to the whole administrative process.[13]

It was not long, however, before the doctrine of the CROWELL case which broadened the scope of judicial determination in cases involving so-called "fundamental, constitutional or jurisdictional facts" began to be severely restricted by the Court and perhaps overruled, *sub silentio*. Interestingly enough, the Chief Justice himself wrote the opinions in some of these cases.

In *Voehl* v. *Indemnity Insurance Co.*,[14] for example, where the issue was whether injury for which compensation was sought under the Longshoremen's and Harbor Workers' Compensation Act arose out of and in the course of employment, the relation of master and servant admittedly existing, the Chief Justice said,

We think that there can be no doubt of the power of Congress to invest the deputy commissioner, as it has invested him, with authority to determine these questions after proper hearing and upon sufficient evidence. And when the deputy commissioner, following the course prescribed by the statute, makes such a determination, his findings of fact supported by evidence must be deemed to be conclusive.

It is true that the issue in this case related to whether injury had occurred in the *course* of employment rather than, as in the CROWELL case, to the *fact* of employment itself. But the difference is at most only one of degree, not of kind, and if the existence of the employer-employee relationship generally is necessary to the constitutional authority of Congress, why is not the existence of that relationship specifically at the time of injury similarly requisite? [15]

Fear of the growing power of administrative agencies by the Court suggested by the CROWELL decision was made palpable in *Jones* v. *Securities and Exchange Commission* [16] in which Chief Justice Hughes found it possible to concur in an intemperate opinion by Justice Sutherland. The immediate issue hardly merited the "denunciatory fervor" aroused. It involved interpretation of an Act of Congress under which the Commission sought to continue its investigation of a registration statement, attacked as misleading or fraudulent, after the statement had been suddenly withdrawn.

To continue the investigation after withdrawal struck Justice Sutherland as in the nature of a "fishing expedition" which "finds no support in right principle or in law. It is wholly unreasonable and arbitrary." "The fear that some malefactors may go unwhipped of justice," said Justice Sutherland, "weighs as nothing against . . . just and strong condemnation of a practice so odious." He likened the procedure to that of "the Star Chamber."

Justice Cardozo, with whom Justices Brandeis and Stone joined in dissent, argued that "recklessness and deceit do not automatically excuse themselves by notice of repentance." With regard to the analogy with Star Chamber proceedings, he commented wryly, "historians may find hyperbole in the sanguinary simile."

Whatever may be said of the technical issue, which raised no question of constitutionality, as to whether Congress had intended to permit withdrawal of a misleading or fraudulent statement submitted to the Commission to bar further proceedings, it is difficult to quarrel with the comment of Robert Jackson that,

Seizing a case in which the Securities and Exchange Commission had, at the worst perhaps, misunderstood the law, though three of the most respected Justices insisted that the Commission had not even done that, the majority used the occasion to write an opinion which did all that a court's opinion could do to discredit the Commission, its motives, its methods, and its existence.[17]

The requirement of the CROWELL case that opportunity for an independent determination by courts of so-called "constitutional, jurisdictional and fundamental facts" must be accorded in conformity with *Article 3* of the Constitution bore a close relationship to that imposed, as early as 1920, in *Ohio Valley Water Co.* v. *Ben Avon Borough* [18] which made it a prerequisite to *due process* in rate-making proceedings that provision be made for courts "to determine the question of confiscation according to their own independent judgment." The same month as the Court excoriated an administrative practice in the *Jones* v. *Securities and Exchange Commission* case, it reaffirmed and buttressed its decision in the OHIO VALLEY WATER Co. case.

In *St. Joseph Stock Yards Co.* v. *United States*,[19] suit was brought by the company to restrain enforcement of an order of the Secretary of Agriculture (made under the authority of the Packers and Stock-yards Act of 1921) fixing maximum rates for the company's services. It was claimed that these rates were so low as to be a confiscatory deprivation of property without due process of law. In the hearing before the District Court no additional evidence was introduced. That court, however, made an independent determination of the facts as well as the law. The primary question in this case related to the scope of judicial review which the court below was required to provide to accord with due process.

Chief Justice Hughes for the Court took some pains to point out that the question was not one of fixing a reasonable charge for a mere personal service subject to regulation under the commerce power and involving but little capital. "Here, a large capital investment is involved and the main issue is as to the alleged confiscation of that investment."

The power to fix rates, he said, is a legislative function which may be performed either by the legislature directly or by its administrative agent. But, when declarations or findings of the legislature itself are challenged as a deprivation of property without due process of law, they are "necessarily subject to independent judicial review upon the facts and the law by courts of competent jurisdiction to the end that the Constitution as the Supreme Law of the land may be maintained." So, too, for legislative agencies:

[To] say that their findings of fact may be made conclusive where constitutional rights of liberty and property are involved, although the evidence clearly establishes that the findings are wrong and constitutional rights have been invaded, is to place those rights at the mercy of administrative officials and seriously to impair the security inherent in our judicial safeguards. That prospect, with our multiplication of administrative agencies, is not one to be lightly regarded.

This did not mean, he said, that the Court must disregard findings made upon hearing and evidence by the administrative agent. In fact there was a strong presumption in favor of its conclusion. In this case, since the District Court had passed upon the evidence, making findings of its own and adopting findings of the Secretary, adequate and appropriate judicial determination had been granted. An analysis of the evidence and findings failed to establish confiscation and the decree of the District Court was affirmed.[20]

Justice Brandeis agreed with the conclusion of the Court but "on a different ground." He reiterated many of the arguments he had advanced in dissenting in the Crowell case. He saw no reason for expanding the scope of permissible judicial review of facts bearing upon "a constitutional right" beyond that accorded in other cases involving issues of fact. He denied that, under the decisions of the Court, due process required that a decision made by an appropriate tribunal shall be reviewable by another. It is true, he said, that so highly is liberty of the person prized that in certain instances it had been held that due process requires an opportunity for a judicial determination of the facts. "But a multitude of decisions tells us that when dealing with property a much more liberal rule applies." He cited cases involving condemnation proceedings, taxation, tariff act valuations and others in support of this proposition.

These cases show that in deciding when, and to what extent, finality must be given to an administrative finding of fact involving the taking of property, the Court has refused to be governed by a rigid rule. It has weighed the relative values of constitutional rights, the essentials of power conferred, and the need of protecting both.

After pointing to the herculean task the Court takes upon itself in seeking to provide an independent determination of the facts, he insisted that a pertinent consideration was the effect of the transfer upon the agencies affected. He said,

Responsibility is the great developer of men. May it not tend to emasculate or demoralize the rate-making body if ultimate responsibility is transferred to others? To the capacity of men there is a limit. May it not impair the quality of the work of the courts if this heavy task of reviewing questions of fact is assumed?

It was pertinent to consider, too, he added, that

Congress concluded that a wealthy and litigious utility might practically nullify rate regulation if the correctness of findings by the regulating body of the facts as to value and income were made subject to judicial review. For that conclusion experience affords ample basis. I cannot believe that the Constitution, which confers upon Congress the power of rate-regulation, denies to it power to adopt measures indispensable to its effective exercise.

Justices Stone and Cardozo, while convinced that Justice Brandeis had stated "the law as it ought to be," appreciated "the weight of precedent that has now accumulated against it." Therefore, if the majority had been content to do no more than accept those precedents and follow them "we might be moved to acquiesce." What was objectionable, however, was to base a finding that the rule was "firm and true" upon a reexamination. On such a broad basis of reconsideration approval could not be given.[21]

In speaking for the majority, Chief Justice Hughes denied that greater latitude by courts in making independent determinations of fact in cases affecting personal liberty, as distinguished from those affecting property, was justified. "The principle," he said, "applies when rights either of person or of property are protected by constitutional restrictions. . . . This is the purport of the decisions . . . with respect to the exercise of an independent judicial judgment upon the facts where confiscation is alleged."

In the light of the decision of the Court in the OHIO VALLEY WATER Co. case it is true that precedent supported Chief Justice Hughes. It must be added, however, that the Constitution itself offers no suggestion that questions of confiscation, raised under due process, necessarily require exceptional procedures. The basic rationale supporting this position is, therefore, the conviction that the interests affected are too substantial, as the Chief Justice suggested, to place them "at the mercy of administrative officials and seriously to impair the security inherent in our judicial safeguards."

Nor, on the other hand, could Justice Brandeis maintain that the Constitution, *per se*, required broader latitude for the Court in reviewing fact determinations in cases affecting liberty of the person than the rights of property. It was a value judgment, as he freely conceded, which led him to the conclusion that the former merited greater protection than the latter. And this value judgment was supported by his belief that the public interest required expeditious administrative procedures relatively free from opportunities of abuse by "wealthy and litigious" utilities. Again, it may be said, that different conceptions of social utility and justice rather than the Constitution were responsible for differing views.

In 1940, the Supreme Court retreated from its position that an independent determination of fact by a Court was required, under the due process clause, in cases involving the regulation of substantial property interests under claim of confiscation. The case of *Railroad Commission* v. *Rowan & Nichols Oil Co.*[22] brought a challenge, under the due process clause, to an oil proration order promulgated by the Railroad Commission of Texas affecting the property of the company. The company claimed that the order operated in such a way as to permit the draining away of its reserves and was confiscatory. The District Court on a *de novo* hearing reached the conclusion that the order was confiscatory. The Circuit Court of Appeals approved and adopted the findings and conclusions of the District Court. Reinstating the order of the Commission, Mr. Justice Frankfurter for the Court said,

Certainly in a domain of knowledge [oil regulation] still shifting and growing and in a field where judgment is therefore necessarily beset by the necessity of inferences bordering on conjecture . . . it would be presumptuous for courts, on the basis of conflicting expert testimony, to deem the view of the administrative tribunal, acting under legislative authority, offensive to the Fourteenth Amendment.

Pointing to the value of entrusting the regulatory task to "the day-to-day exertions of a body especially entrusted with the task because presumably competent to deal with it," he added, "It is not for the federal courts to supplant the Commission's judgment even in the face of convincing proof that a different result would have been better."

The Chief Justice and Justice McReynolds joined in the dissent of Mr. Justice Roberts who, noting that the order was challenged as confiscatory, reasoned that although the problem of proration presented technical and difficult questions, that could not justify the court in "abdicating its jurisdiction to test the Commission's order." He approved the granting of a *de novo* hearing by the District Court and lamented that "the opinion of this court, in my judgment, announces principles with respect to the review of administrative action challenged under the due process clause directly contrary to those which have been established."

While the cited case does not directly relate to utility rate regulation in the usual sense, the reasoning of the majority certainly supports the view that even in such cases, although confiscation is alleged, finality will be attached to determinations of fact made by administrative agencies if supported by evidence. By 1940, it should be observed, there had been many changes in the personnel of the Court. Still another established doctrine appears to have fallen when a change in men brought different conceptions of the public interest to the Court.

Returning, however, to 1936, within a month of its decision in the ST. JOSEPH STOCK YARDS Co. case, the Court came to grips with another phase of the problem of assuring "fair" hearings in administrative proceedings. In the first of four companion cases, the Court was able to rest its decision on statutory requirements. In *Morgan* v. *United States*,[23] after testimony had been heard and a rehearing held before an examiner, the Secretary of Agriculture, on June 14, 1933, found the rates charged by market agencies for buying and selling livestock at the Kansas City stock yards to be excessive and fixed maximum charges pursuant to the Packers and Stockyards Act of 1921. The brokers affected brought suit in the District Court to restrain enforcement of the order. They attacked the order as invalid, among other reasons, allegedly because they had not received the "full hearing" required by the statute. The District Court struck out the allegations respecting improper procedure by the Secretary of Agriculture and decided the case on its merits.

Chief Justice Hughes, for a unanimous Court, ruled that error had not been committed by the District Court in striking *some* of the allegations relating to procedure. Specifically the Chief Justice said that the failure to hear the complainants separately was not an abuse of discretion. So, also,

while it would have been good practice to have the examiner prepare a report and submit it to the Secretary and the parties, and to permit exceptions and arguments addressed to the points thus presented,—a practice found to be of great value in proceedings before the Interstate Commerce Commission—we cannot say that that particular type of procedure was essential to the validity of the hearing.

Nor would any question of fair hearing have arisen if the Assistant Secretary who had heard the argument had thereafter made the decision.[24]

However, *if* it was true, as alleged—and an opportunity should be given to prove the allegation—that the Assistant Secretary who had heard the argument assumed no responsibility for the findings or the order and that the Secretary of Agriculture had made the rate order without having heard or read any of the evidence, oral arguments or briefs and had relied solely upon consultation with employees of the Department, "full hearing" in the statutory sense had not been granted.

The rate-making duty prescribed by Congress in this case, said the Chief Justice, "is widely different from ordinary executive action. It is a duty which carries with it fundamental procedural requirements. There must be a full hearing. There must be evidence adequate to support pertinent and necessary findings of fact. . . . Findings based on the evidence must embrace the basic facts which are needed to sustain the order." The "full hearing" mandated by the statute "has obvious reference to the tradition of judicial proceedings in which evidence is received and weighed by the trier of the facts." "The 'hearing' is the hearing of evidence and argument. If the one who determines the facts which underlie the order has not considered evidence or argument, it is manifest that the hearing has not been given." That duty is not an impersonal obligation. "It is a duty akin to that of a judge. The one who decides must hear." Accordingly, he ruled the District Court had erred in striking the allegation relating to this aspect of the hearing and the cause was remanded to that Court for further proceedings consistent with this decision.

Precisely what was necessarily encompassed in a "full hearing" required by the statute might easily be a matter of dispute. In reading the statute to require the one who decides to hear evidence or argument, the Chief Justice was obviously attempting to "judicialize" administrative proceedings, to assure that administrators charged with the responsibility for making decisions did so at the very least with a summary view of the arguments on both sides and not simply on the basis of informal consultation with subordinate employees. If the exigencies of modern life made resort to administrative agencies more and more inevitable and ousted the courts more and more from the sphere of economic regulation, then the Court must at least insist upon fair procedures. Of course, in this case, the Court was able to read the requirements of fair procedure into the statutory prescription of a "full hearing," thus avoiding any constitutional conflict. But the question remained—assuming the procedure followed in the case had been clearly authorized by the statute, would it then have constituted a denial of due process of law violative of the Constitution?

Upon remand, the District Court in the MORGAN case confined itself to the one issue which the Supreme Court had apparently held warranted further inquiry which was whether the Secretary of Agriculture who had decided upon the order fixing maximum charges had in fact personally considered the evidence and argument. The District Court received testimony bearing on this question and concluded that the Secretary had done so. It reaffirmed its earlier order. On appeal to the Supreme Court, in the second MORGAN case,[25] it was again contended that the Secretary's order was made without the "full hearing" required by the statute.

The reading by the Secretary of the summary presented in the briefs of those affected by the order and his conferences with his subordinates who had sifted and analyzed the evidence were, somewhat reluctantly, deemed by the Supreme Court to meet the objection which had been the basis of its decision in the first MORGAN case. "But," now added the Supreme Court, for the first time, per its Chief Justice,

a "full hearing"—a fair and open hearing—requires more than that. The right to a hearing embraces not only the right to present evidence but also a reasonable opportunity to know the claims of the opposing party and to meet them. The right to submit argument implies that opportunity; otherwise the right may be but a barren one. Those who are brought into contest with the Government in a quasi-judicial proceeding aimed at the control of their activities are entitled to be fairly advised of what the Government proposes and to be heard upon its proposals before it issues its final command.

What of the statement in the earlier MORGAN case that the submission of a tentative report, while recommended, was not essential to the validity of the hearing? That, said the Chief Justice, related to proceedings in which the Secretary himself heard the evidence and the contentions of both parties and made his findings on the spot, or to a case in which the evidence having been taken before another, the

Secretary received the proposed findings of both parties, each having been notified of the proposals of the other, heard argument thereon and made his own findings. However,

what would not be essential to the adequacy of the hearing if the Secretary himself makes the findings is not a criterion for a case in which the Secretary accepts and makes as his own the findings which have been prepared by the active prosecutors for the Government, after an *ex parte* discussion with them and without according any reasonable opportunity to the respondents in the proceeding to know the claims thus presented and to contest them. That is more than irregularity in practice; it is a vital defect.

This requirement, added the Chief Justice, was not designed to hobble the administrative function.

On the contrary, it is in their manifest interest. For, as we said at the outset, if these multiplying agencies deemed to be necessary in our complex society are to serve the purposes for which they are created and endowed with vast powers, they must accredit themselves by acting in accordance with the cherished judicial tradition embodying the basic concepts of fair play.

This time the hearing was held "fatally defective" and the order of the Secretary "invalid." Accordingly no opinion was expressed upon the merits. The protracted and costly proceedings were a nullity.[26]

The requirement imposed in the second MORGAN case obviously has much to commend it in further "judicializing" administrative procedure. However, the explanation proffered by the Chief Justice that his statement in the first MORGAN case that a tentative report by the examiner was not essential to full hearing related only to a proceeding in which the findings were made directly by the Secretary can hardly be reconciled with the fact that this was said precisely in a case in which, to the knowledge of the Chief Justice, it was being charged that such findings had not been made by the Secretary. Link this inconsistency with the bitter attack of the press upon the absence of "fair play" in New Deal administration, and one can readily appreciate the indignation of the Secretary of Agriculture, Henry A. Wallace. Three days after the opinion he discussed the case over the radio [27] and expressed the hope that the courts would not only guard against "the evils of hasty and inadequate procedure but also against legalistic, destructive and expensive delay." Writing to the New York *Times*, shortly thereafter, he commented that "the Court's cloudy phraseology was made necessary by the fact that two years previously the Chief Justice in this same case had taken a different stand and there was necessary a careful job of legal reconciliation which confused the clarity of thought." [28]

A few days later, the Chief Justice delivered an address before the American Law Institute which many newspapers headlined as a warning to the New Deal. In the course of this address, he took the occasion to say:

The multiplication of administrative agencies is the outstanding characteristic of our time. The controversies within the range of administrative action may be different and extremely important, and they may call for a particular type of experience and special methods of inquiry, but the spirit which should animate that action, if the administrative authority is to be properly exercised, must be the spirit of the just judge.[29]

As might have been anticipated, Solicitor General (now Associate Justice) Robert A. Jackson filed a petition for reargument. He bluntly asserted that "the decision of the Court is directly contrary to the law of the case as established by the Court's decision in the same case at the 1935 Term." On May 31, 1938, the Court, in a *per curiam* opinion, quite unusual in denying a petition for rehearing, heatedly defended its consistency.[30]

Twice more the issues of the MORGAN case required decisions of the Supreme Court before they could be finally adjudicated. One immediate problem related to the disposition of several hundred thousand dollars collected by the brokers from farmers at rates higher than those fixed by the Secretary of Agriculture and paid into the District Court pending final decision on the merits. The District Court, guided by the ruling in the second MORGAN case that the procedure had been fatally defective and the order of the Secretary invalid, ordered the money paid to the brokers. The Government appealed contending that the impounded fund should not be turned over to the brokers as a result of a procedural error and in the face of an earlier finding of the District Court "upon its own independent consideration of the evidence" that the lower charges fixed by the

Secretary were fair and reasonable. The Court, surprisingly enough with the concurrence of the Chief Justice, in an opinion by Justice Stone, found a way out of its dilemma by holding that the procedural error might still be corrected by the Secretary of Agriculture "proceeding with due expedition" to a final order during which time repayment of the impounded fund might be withheld. As if admonishing its own earlier petulance, the Court added that it was a "cardinal principle" that

In construing a statute setting up an administrative agency and providing for judicial review of its actions, court and agency are not to be regarded as wholly independent and unrelated instrumentalities of justice, each acting in the performance of its prescribed statutory duty without regard to the appropriate function of the other in securing the plainly indicated objects of the statute. . . . Neither body should repeat in this day the mistake made by the courts of law when equity was struggling for recognition as an ameliorating system of justice; neither can rightly be regarded by the other as an alien intruder, to be tolerated if must be, but never to be encouraged or aided by the other in the attainment of the common aim.[31]

Finally, the Secretary of Agriculture having conformed with the procedures laid down by the Supreme Court in the MORGAN cases and having issued a new order fixing rates, the order was upheld in May, 1941 by the Supreme Court in a decision of Mr. Justice Frankfurter, with only Mr. Justice Roberts dissenting.[32] At the same time the Court rejected the claim that the proceedings were defective because the Secretary of Agriculture had failed to disqualify himself for bias, allegedly reflected in his letter to the New York *Times* criticizing the decision of the Court in the second MORGAN case. That letter, said the Court, had not prejudged the rates to be fixed, but expressed concern about the disposition of the impounded fund. Furthermore, the Secretary had indicated that he might have disqualified himself "as a matter of expediency" except for the fact while disqualification was being urged, it was being simultaneously contended that none other than the Secretary had legal authority to make the order. "But," added the Court, "intrinsically, the letter did not require the Secretary's dignified denial of bias."

That he not merely held but expressed strong views on matters believed by him to have been in issue, did not unfit him for exercising his duty in subsequent proceedings ordered by this Court. . . . Cabinet officers charged by Congress with adjudicatory functions are not assumed to be flabby creatures any more than judges are.

Thus ended the MORGAN cases!

SUMMARY STATEMENT

In the entire area of procedural due process, it has been made obvious that but for some deference to historic practice and earlier precedents, the Court has been engaged in the process of seeking to reconcile the practical exigencies of governing with its conception of the fundamental requirements of justice. This is what serves to explain its incorporation, during the tenure of Chief Justice Hughes, of the right to counsel within the protection of due process, its denunciation of the use of extorted confession or perjured testimony as the basis of conviction for crime, its refusal to attach finality to determinations of fact by administrative agencies when involved were so-called "jurisdictional, constitutional or fundamental facts" or the claim of confiscation, and also its later emasculation of these requirements, and finally its attempt to judicialize administrative proceedings in cases involving important interests and complex issues of fact to assure a full and fair hearing.

This aspect of the supervisory power of the Court has, on the whole, been subjected to little criticism since it affects not the ends of legislative policy but only the means, and there is a deep-rooted and widely held belief that in connection with any taking of life, liberty or property there should be some assurance that the procedures utilized do not entail wanton and arbitrary disregard of private right and interest. Nevertheless, it must be recognized that what may strike some Justices as unreasonable and unjust may strike others as eminently reasonable and just. In the field of administrative due process, for example, we have seen that certain procedures deemed necessary by some members of the Court to prevent arbitrary rule over important economic interests were considered by other members of the Court to impose unwarranted burdens upon the administrative process to the advantage of wealthy and litigious interests. The fundamental question remains, therefore, whether in regard to procedural due process the advantages of judicial review outweigh its disadvantages to the community.

CHAPTER 11

DUE PROCESS AFFECTING
ECONOMIC INTERESTS

GENESIS OF DOCTRINE

The due process clauses have had their greatest significance and effect not in relation to matters of procedure but in relation to matters of substance. No other clauses of the Constitution have afforded the Court greater opportunities for the review of the content of legislation than that offered by the due process clauses. Yet, interestingly enough, the Constitution as it emerged from the hands of the Framers contained no "due process" clause. It first appeared as part of the Bill of Rights as a limitation upon the power of the federal government (Article V of the Amendments, ratified in 1791) and was thereafter adopted as a limitation upon state power (Article XIV of the Amendments, ratified in 1868).

What were the historic origins and meaning of this limitation? It derived from "the law of the land" clause in the Magna Carta and found its earliest expression in its present form in the English Statute of Westminster of 1354. From the fourteenth to nearly the end of the nineteenth centuries, in English and American jurisprudence, except for a few fugitive or abortive attempts, it was interpreted as imposing limitation upon the *procedure or method* by which persons were deprived of life, liberty or property and not upon the substance of legislation.[1] With reference to American experience with this limitation, Professor Robert E. Cushman has said,

For a hundred years due process was held to be a limitation upon governmental procedure and not upon the substance or content of legislative policy. It required notice and hearing and a fair trial, but it did not forbid the legislature to regulate a social or economic problem.[2]

While scholars are in general agreement with Professor Cushman, Mr. Hughes in his lectures on the Supreme Court, delivered in 1927, raised his voice in dissent from this historic conception. He said,

If the legislature was not to be permitted by any law to dispense with the essentials of a just course of judicial procedure, was the legislature none the less to be free to enact laws which would operate to deprive one of life, liberty or property by an arbitrary fiat? It would be difficult to maintain such a hypothesis, and at the same time to do justice to the temper and dominant thought of the builders of our constitutions. . . . The phrase "due process of law" was vague, its meaning was unsettled, but it was not meaningless nor was it limited by anything short of the general purpose to afford immunity from any violation of fundamental right.[3]

Justice Brandeis, however, that same year, found the arguments that the Fourteenth Amendment was intended to apply only to matters of procedure "persuasive." [4] And Professor Corwin has insisted that due process was transformed "from a guaranty to accused persons of a certain mode of trial into a bulwark of the *laissez-faire* conception of governmental function." [5]

It must be added that the rights of property were not wholly defenseless against the legislative power before substantive content was breathed into the due process limitation. In addition to the curb imposed by the contract clause, in the early history of the Court there had been rather tenuously assimilated into the law what Edward S. Corwin calls the doctrine of "vested right" as a limitation upon the exercise of governmental power.[6] This embraced certain "higher law" concepts based upon the commonly accepted view of Locke that the rights of property were anterior to government and protected by natural law and by the social compact through which government was formed. It found expression, for example, in the statement that property was protected against arbitrary acts of government by "the nature of society and of government." [7] The vested rights theory, however, proved an unsatisfactory basis upon which to predicate judicial supervision over legislative power in the face of increasing rationalism and the development of the doctrines of popular sovereignty and the police power.[8] The due process clause with its constitutional basis but sufficiently vague contours offered a more useful instrumentality for judicial intervention.

At first, however, the Supreme Court, concerned about preserving the balance of our federal system, declined to give to the Fourteenth Amendment any efficacy as a limitation upon the exercise of state power except possibly in the interest of racial equality.[9] It was not until late in the nineteenth century that the Court was persuaded to encompass within the concept of due process the substantive limitations of vested rights. It is probable that the motive force back of this expanded conception lay in the search by the bar and the Court, thoroughly imbued with the philosophy of *laissez-faire*, for an appropriate instrument with which to curb the legislative march which had produced, in the late nineteenth century, a host of ameliorative measures to cope with the problems arising from a rapidly developing industrial society.

Obviously, however, even under the expanded concept, not every taking of life, liberty or property by governmental authority is excluded. Illustrations are legion of such deprivations which are clearly within the power of government, such as punishment for crime, the taxing of property, zoning and prohibition laws. The fact is that virtually every piece of legislation limits liberty or restricts the possession or use of property in some degree. Objection lies, therefore, only when in the view of the Court the deprivation is "without due process of law." What is the test of such a deprivation? The Constitution does not define due process and its historic limitations, as we have seen, have not been accepted by the Court. Nor, under its expanded conception of the due process limitation, has the Court attempted a definitive formulation. Instead it has preferred to employ a process of "inclusion and exclusion." [10] Nevertheless, the criteria repeatedly reaffirmed by the Court are those of justice, fairness and reasonableness. And since important legislation represents the legislative process of conciliation of economic and social conflict within society, implicit in the determination is the judgment of the Court as to the manner and extent to which rival interests may be adversely affected and benefited. How these criteria were applied by the Court over which Chief Justice Hughes presided for eleven years, in a period of great upsurge of social legislation, viewed in the historic perspective of the development of doctrine, provides an excellent case study of the virtues and defects of judicial review.

MARTIAL LAW

A significant illustration of the use to which the power of the Supreme Court might be put to prevent the allegedly arbitrary use of state power affecting vital economic interests occurred fairly soon after Mr. Hughes became Chief Justice. It arose out of the fact that vast oil deposits were discovered in East Texas at a time when because of world-wide depression the oil industry was already over-developed and disorganized. By 1931 the East Texas area alone was producing about a million barrels of oil a day as prices continued to drop. The Texas legislature, on August 12, 1931, passed an oil conservation Act authorizing the State Railroad Commission to prorate and limit production. Before any such order was made by the Commission, however, on August 16, Governor Sterling issued a proclamation reciting that in certain counties in East Texas a group of oil producers were in "a state of insurrection, tumult, riot, and a breach of the peace" against the conservation laws, that physical waste was resulting from reckless production, and that as a result of the state of public feeling acts of violence were to be anticipated. He therefore declared martial law in the territory and directed General Walters to assume command. Troops were brought in and the wells were closed. On September 2, 1931, the Railroad Commission issued its order fixing the amount which might be produced at any well in the territory. The governor permitted the wells to be reopened but limited production to the maxima then and thereafter to be fixed by the Commission.

On October 13, Constantin and others, with oil interests in the territory, brought suit in the United States District Court. A federal District Court judge thereafter issued a temporary order restraining the Commission and others from limiting production at the maxima fixed pending a hearing for a preliminary injunction. The governor, learning that the orders of the Commission could no longer be enforced, ordered military authority to maintain the limits previously fixed by the Commission which he himself now set. The governor was then made a party to the suit in an amended bill. The authority of the governor under a declaration of martial law, and not the authority of the Commission, was now squarely before the Court in *Sterling* v. *Constantin*.[11]

The District Court found that at no time had there been any actual riot, tumult or insurrection in the territory and that at no time had the civil authorities or courts been interfered with or their processes made impotent. At most, that Court said, if the anticipated conditions had come to pass, they would have resulted merely in breaches of the peace to be suppressed by the militia as a civil force and not in a condition even remotely resembling a state of war.

Whether the governor was vested with the power to *declare* martial law was deemed, by the Supreme Court, to be a matter of local law as to which the courts of the state had the final word. The crucial question, then, was whether the Court could control by injunction the *means* of enforcing martial law. To this the Court, per Chief Justice Hughes, answered,

When there is a substantial showing that the exertion of state power has overridden private rights secured by that [federal] Constitution, the subject is necessarily one for judicial inquiry in an appropriate proceeding directed against the individuals charged with the transgression. To such a case the Federal judicial power extends (Art. III, sec. 2) and, so extending, the court has all the authority appropriate to its exercise.

Nor, in such circumstances, he said, was the Court bound by the determinations of fact made under state authority because "when questions of law and fact are so intermingled as to make it necessary, in order to pass upon the Federal question, the court may, and should, analyze the facts."

It was true, he continued, that by virtue of his duty to "cause the laws to be faithfully executed," the executive was vested with discretion to determine whether military aid to that end was necessary and his decision to that effect was conclusive. The nature of the power also implied that there was a permitted range of judgment, if exercised in good faith, in the face of an emergency and directly related to the quelling of disorder. But he added:

It does not follow from the fact that the Executive has this range of discretion, deemed to be a necessary incident of his power to suppress disorder, that every action the Governor may take, no matter how unjustified by the exigency or subversive of private right and the jurisdiction of the courts, otherwise available, is conclusively supported by executive fiat. The contrary is well established. What are the allowable limits of military discretion, and whether or not they have been overstepped in a particular case, are judicial questions.

In the instant case the evidence, he held, supported the findings that there was no military necessity which could justify the governor's limiting production in the face of a Court order to the contrary. Assuming the governor was entitled to declare a state of insurrection and to bring military force to the aid of Civil authority, "the proper use of that power in this instance was to maintain the Federal court in the exercise of its jurisdiction and not to attempt to override it."

The decision in *Sterling* v. *Constantin* imposed for the first time a clear and significant limit upon the powers of governors exercised under declarations of martial law. As Charles Fairman points out martial law had become almost a "household remedy." [12] In Texas alone it had been used seven times in the previous fourteen years. It had served a variety of purposes: to curb strike violence, to open an interstate bridge, to cope with forest fires suspected of being incendiary in origin, to enforce a state tuberculin test of cattle, and (by Huey Long) to prevent a lieutenant-governor from assuming gubernatorial office.

Only once before since the adoption of the Fourteenth Amendment had the measures taken under a declaration of martial law been brought before the Supreme Court. In that case, *Moyer* v. *Peabody*,[13] action for damages had been brought by a union leader against a former governor and militia officers for illegal detention for seventy-six days, during the suppression of an "insurrection," while the courts continued open. The Court then held that "the Governor's declaration that a state of insurrection existed is conclusive of that fact," and added, "So long as such arrests are made in good faith and in the honest belief that they are needed in order to head the insurrection off, the Governor is the final judge and cannot be submitted to an action after he is out of office on the ground that he had not reasonable ground for his belief." Furthermore, it was said that "when it comes to a decision by the head of the State upon a matter involving its life, the ordinary rights of individuals must yield to what he deems the necessities of the moment. Public danger warrants the substitution of executive process for judicial process."

On the basis of this decision and a number of others in federal District and state Supreme Courts, it had been generally assumed that a governor might, on his own finding of emergency, proclaim martial law and be the sole judge of necessary measures to be taken. The decision of the Chief Justice, to be sure, imposed no limitation upon the *declaration* of martial law, but it subjected the *measures* taken thereunder not only to possible ultimate recovery in damage suits but to immediate restraint. In this connection, it should be noted, however, that the Chief Justice did not follow the court below in ruling that the governor was limited, in suppressing insurrection, to the powers of a police officer. He spoke instead of a permitted range of judgment in the face of an emergency and directly related to the quelling of disorder. This supplies broader latitude to the governor than to a police officer but not so broad as that of a general in the field in time of war. The matter of degree is significant.

Back of the decision lay the necessity for striking a balance between the powers of government in serious emergencies threatening insurrection or chaos and the preservation of important economic interests from arbitrary destruction or impairment. This decision attempted to strike such a balance recognizing, on the one hand, that the state must sometimes intervene in economic or other conflicts to maintain respect for its laws and prevent violent and irreparable injury. But, on the other hand, the decision served notice that

it is neither an expedient nor a lawful course to call the conflict an insurrection and then force one party into line by the use of troops. . . . The interests involved are too important for their evaluation to be left to the rough empiricism of a single executive officer.[14]

"AFFECTED WITH A PUBLIC INTEREST"

In 1877, in *Munn* v. *Illinois*,[15] Chief Justice Waite, borrowing a phrase written about 1670 by Lord Chief Justice Hale, held for the Court that businesses "affected with a public interest" were peculiarly subject to the regulatory power of the state. Accordingly, regulation of the charges of grain elevators and of insurance companies was sustained.[16]

In 1923, however, the Court unanimously invalidated a Kansas compulsory arbitration act as applied to the packing industry. It was in the course of that decision that Chief Justice Taft undertook to define the general criteria by which the Court would determine whether businesses were "affected with a public interest." These businesses were of three types, said the Chief Justice: first, those conducted under a public franchise or grant, for example, public utilities; second, those traditionally subject to regulation, for example, public inns; and third, those "which though not public at their inception may be said to have risen to be such." [17] The first two criteria offer a fairly clear guide to the legislature. The third, it is apparent, lacked concreteness and admitted of varying opinions. That variance of opinion was resolved by the Court against the legislative judgment in three decisions of the Court in the years immediately preceding Mr. Hughes' designation as Chief Justice. In 1927 the Court struck down a New York act prohibiting the resale of theatre tickets at an advance of more than fifty cents per ticket; [18] in 1928 a New Jersey law requiring licenses for the conduct of employment agencies and regulating their fees was declared unconstitutional; [19] and in 1929 a Tennessee act regulating the price of gasoline was also found to offend the Constitution.[20]

In the first year of Mr. Hughes' tenure the Court by the narrow margin of one vote, in a decision in which the Chief Justice concurred, upheld the constitutionality of state legislation regulating the amount of commissions to be paid to fire insurance agents. It did not appear, wrote Justice Brandeis for the majority, "that in New Jersey evils did not exist in the business of fire insurance for which this statutory provision was an appropriate remedy." [21]

The insurance business was one of those regarded as traditionally subject to government regulation. A more difficult problem for the Court arose, therefore, in connection with the attempts of state legislatures, in the wake of unprecedented depression, to regulate a number of businesses which had theretofore been largely exempt from such regulation.

The following year, the Court was called upon to consider the constitutionality of an Oklahoma statute which had undertaken to require a license for the business of manufacturing and selling ice because of chaotic conditions in the industry. In *New State Ice Co.* v. *Liebmann* [22] the Chief Justice joined in an opinion of Justice Sutherland invalidating the statute. With respect to the nature of the business involved Justice Sutherland, for a majority of the Court,[23] wrote,

It is a business as essentially private in its nature as the business of the grocer, the dairyman, the butcher, the baker, the shoemaker, or the tailor. . . . And this Court has definitely said that the production or sale of food or clothing cannot be subjected to legislative regulation on the basis of a public use.

In dissent, Justice Brandeis argued that the notion of a distinct category of businesses affected with a public interest rested upon historical error and the "true principle is that the state's power extends to every regulation of any business reasonably required and appropriate for the public protection." Regard, he said, must be had for the facts of depression, "an emergency more serious than war." He deplored the denial by the majority of "one of the happy incidents of the federal system that a single courageous State may, if the citizens choose, serve as a laboratory; and try novel social and economic experiments without risk to the rest of the country."

Two years later, in *Nebbia* v. *New York*,[24] a majority of the Court was brought over to the essential position of Justice Brandeis. By a vote of five to four, in an opinion by Mr. Justice Roberts in which the Chief Justice concurred, the Court upheld the validity of a New York statute fixing maximum and minimum prices for the sale of milk and affecting precisely "the grocer" and the "dairyman." The minority of the four conservatives, in dissent, quite reasonably argued that the precedents of the Court and particularly that of the NEW STATE ICE case sustained the proposition that the state regulatory power could not be invoked to deal with a business of this character, "essentially private in nature." Mr. Justice Roberts, on the other hand, for the majority, called attention to the importance of milk in the human diet, the paramount nature of the industry and the critical conditions prevailing in the industry as a result of the depression, and added,

It is clear that there is no closed class or category of businesses affected with a public interest. . . . The phrase "affected with a public interest" can, in the nature of things, mean no more than that an industry, for adequate reason, is subject to control for the public good.

Again the Court found itself yielding to the practical demands of governing under conditions of acute depression. This, to be sure, was accomplished only by the narrowest of possible margins when Chief Justice Hughes and Mr. Justice Roberts, exercising a balance of power in the Court, shifted from the logic of the position they had accepted in the New State Ice case. It was erroneous to assume, however, as soon became apparent, that the discarding of "affected with a public interest" as a phrase having any efficacy in limiting public regulation involved an abandonment of the supervisory role of the Court over police power legislation. The inquiry had simply been disencumbered and was now restricted to the essential due process inquiry of reasonableness and justice.

Immediately, however, the decision in the Nebbia case when linked with the Court's decision that same year in *Home Building & Loan Association* v. *Blaisdell*,[25] which appeared to have discarded the contract clause as, *per se*, imposing any limitation upon the police power of the states,[26] gave substantial grounding for the hope, soon to be dissipated, that the Court had come to take heed of "an emergency more serious than war" and was prepared to give elastic scope to the powers of government in support of the innovations induced by depression. Mr. Robert Jackson expressed the situation which then prevailed as follows:

The year 1934 came to a close with little awareness of the impending struggle. New Deal experiments were under way and economic improvement noticeable. The election returned an overwhelming New Deal majority to the Congress. Most people, in and out of the Administration, were confident that all was well. . . . But the Court was poised between two worlds. The older world of *laissez-faire* was recognized everywhere outside the Court to be dead. Would the Court then hold any other world powerless to be born? [27]

Minimum Wages for Women

That the Court had not abandoned the *laissez-faire* philosophy which beneath verbal rationalizations was used to strike down social legislation was demonstrated in *Morehead* v. *People ex rel. Tipaldo*,[28] involving the constitutionality of legislation designed to guarantee a minimum wage for women. No clearer illustration of the scope for judicial lawmaking appears than in the history of the vicissitudes of such legislation before the courts.

In *Stettler* v. *O'Hara* [29] an Oregon Act of 1913 fixing minimum wages for women and children was sustained as constitutional by an evenly divided Court when Justice Brandeis, who had helped prepare the brief in defense of the Act and obviously thought it constitutional, disqualified himself. Only six years later, after some changes in the Court, in *Adkins* v. *Children's Hospital*,[30] a similar law enacted by Congress in 1918 for the District of Columbia was invalidated by a vote of five to three.

It is in the nature of a commentary upon the judicial role in constitutional cases that apart from the substantive scope incorporated into the due process limitation, the notion of a free labor contract was in reality a "historical myth." "There never was a time," wrote Professor Morris Raphael Cohen, "when the relation between master and servant was not the subject of governmental regulations except that formerly they were almost invariably and openly in the interests of the employers." [31] It is a further commentary upon the flexibility of the judicial process that by actual count including the vote in the ADKINS case, thirty-two judges of the highest state and federal courts had thought minimum wage for women legislation constitutional and only nine had not done so.[32] But the judgment of the nine prevailed. It is interesting to observe, too, how fortuitous were the circumstances that led to invalidation in the ADKINS case. But for the fact that Justice Brandeis had been of counsel in the case before his appointment to the bench, the Court, in 1917, in the STETTLER case would have stood five to four, instead of four to four, for constitutionality, and the issue might not have been raised thereafter. Or again, but for a strange incident in the Court of Appeals in the District of Columbia, which led it to reverse itself in the ADKINS case some seventeen months after its original decision, the case would probably have reached and been decided by the Supreme Court at a time when, because of its composition the legislation would have been held constitutional. This has led Professor Powell to conclude that "the unconstitutionality of minimum-wage legislation has been dictated by the calendar rather than by the Constitution." [33]

In 1925 and again in 1927, without opinion, and on the authority of the ADKINS case the Court declared similar Arizona and Arkansas statutes unconstitutional.[34]

Such was the history of decisions in the minimum wage cases when in 1936 the New York State minimum wage law came before the Court in the MOREHEAD case. The Act made it punishable for any employer to employ any woman at an oppressive or unreasonable wage, defined as one which was "both less than the fair and reasonable value of the services rendered and less than sufficient to meet the minimum cost of living necessary for health." Procedures were set up by the Act for the determination of such minimum wage.

A majority of the Court, consisting of Justice Butler, who wrote the opinion, and Justices Van Devanter, McReynolds, Sutherland and Roberts who concurred, held the Act repugnant to due process on the authority of the ADKINS case. Asserting that no application had been made for reconsideration of the constitutional question then decided, the Court dealt with the contention that the statutes were distinguishable. In the ADKINS case the standard fixed by the Act had been a wage adequate "to supply the necessary cost of living to . . . women workers to maintain them in good health and protect their morals." In this case the statute imposed the further standard that the wage fixed must not exceed "the fair and reasonable value of the services rendered." It had been implied in the ADKINS decision that such a provision might make a difference. The additional standard, the majority ruled, however, was not material. It said:

The dominant issue in the *Adkins* case was whether Congress had power to establish minimum wages for adult women workers in the District of Columbia. The opinion directly answers in the negative. The ruling that defects in the prescribed standard stamped that Act as arbitrary and invalid was an additional ground of subordinate consequence.

While technically the decision of the majority was rested on an inability to distinguish the present from the ADKINS case, the reasoning of the Court revealed marked sympathy with the philosophy expressed in the ADKINS opinion thirteen years earlier. This was reflected in the statement in the MOREHEAD decision, for example, that "any measure that deprives employers and adult women of freedom to agree upon wages, leaving employers and men employees free so to do is necessarily arbitrary," and in the support found not only in the ruling in the earlier case but also in "the reasoning upon which it rests" that "the State is without power by any form of legislation to prohibit, change or nullify contracts between employers and adult women workers as to the amount of wages to be paid." This sympathy is hardly surprising in the light of the fact that four of the five justices who participated in the majority opinion in both cases were the same, that is, Justices Van Devanter, McReynolds,

Sutherland and Butler. The additional member of the majority was Mr. Justice Roberts, who had been appointed by President Hoover in 1930.

Chief Justice Hughes dissented.[35] The Chief Justice said that he could find nothing in the federal Constitution "which denies to the State the power to protect women from being exploited by over-working employers through the refusal of a fair wage as defined in the New York statute and ascertained in a reasonable manner by competent authority." The inclusion of the "fair wage" standard did, in the view of the Chief Justice, provide a material basis of distinction from the standard and reasoning of the ADKINS case. "That opinion," he said, "contained a broad discussion of state power, but it singled out as an adequate ground for the finding of invalidity that the statute gave no regard to the situation of the employer and to the reasonable value of the service for which the wage was paid." Since the New York Act was free from that defect "the question comes before us in a new aspect." Furthermore the close divisions in the previous decisions of the Court "point to the desirability of fresh consideration when there are material differences in the cases presented."

Since liberty of contract was not an absolute right, it was necessary, he wrote, to apply "the test of reasonableness in the circumstances disclosed." These circumstances warranted the exercise of the police power to fix minimum wages for women since it was a legitimate concern of the state that women were not as a class upon a level of equality in bargaining power with their employers in regard to fair minimum standards; that as to them freedom of contract was illusory; that they were peculiarly subject to the over-reaching of employers; that the payment of less than a minimum wage by some employers constituted unfair competition with others, threatened the stability of industry and threw a burden on taxpayers to supplement wages with relief; and that such legislation was of interest to the community at large in maintaining health and preventing deterioration of the race.

But "granted" that these considerations would not justify placing the burden of the support of women who did not receive a living wage upon employers who paid the equivalent of the service they obtained, there was no reason, he thought, "why the burden caused by the failure to pay that equivalent should not be placed upon those who create it." He concluded: "In the statute before us, no unreasonableness appears. The end is legitimate and the means appropriate. I think the act should be upheld."

In addition to concurring in the dissent of the Chief Justice, Justice Stone wrote a separate dissenting opinion [36] in which he said that he would not make the differences between the present statute and that involved in the ADKINS case the "sole" basis of decision, and added,

I attach little importance to the fact that the earlier statute was aimed only at a starvation wage and that the present one does not prohibit such a wage unless it is also less than the reasonable value of the service. Since neither statute compels employment at any wage, I do not assume that employers in one case, more than in the other, would pay the minimum wage if the service were worth less.

Denying that the due process clause supplied a mechanical formula and pointing out that wage regulation was found by Congress and the legislatures of seventeen states and twenty-one foreign countries to be "an appropriate corrective for serious social and economic maladjustments," Justice Stone could not see how it could be said "it is a remedy beyond the bounds of reason," and caustically commented,

It is difficult to imagine any grounds, other than our own personal economic predilections, for saying that the contract of employment is any the less an appropriate subject of legislation than are scores of others, in dealing with which this Court has held that legislatures may curtail individual freedom in the public interest.

The ADKINS case, he thought, was in conflict with sound law and with later decisions of the Court, especially the NEBBIA case, and should be overruled rather than distinguished. As for the contention that reconsideration of the ADKINS decision had not been requested, the arguments advanced in support of an application for certiorari did not, in his view, restrict the Court to a choice between conflicting precedents. The real question was whether the New York law contravened the due process clause. But, in any event, the petition, he said, *had* requested "reconsideration of the ADKINS case in the light of the New York act and conditions aimed to be remedied thereby."

Furthermore, he insisted, "Unless we are now to construe and apply the Fourteenth Amendment without regard to our decisions since the ADKINS case, we could not rightly avoid its reconsideration even if it were not asked."

The opinion of the majority in the final analysis was based, we have seen, upon the technical ground that reconsideration of its decision in the ADKINS case had not been requested. It is of some interest, therefore, to note that had the Court so desired it could have dealt squarely with the issue of constitutionality when presented with a petition to rehear the New York case in October, 1936. This it declined to do.[37]

Furthermore, the principle implied if not expressed by the majority that it must render a decision in a constitutional case which might be unsound simply because it had not been specifically requested to abandon an earlier precedent was one that the Court had never regarded as binding and which it soon demonstrated had little force when it reversed a century-old precedent without even hearing argument on the point.[38]

On the larger issues, it is clear that as late as 1936 a majority of the Court, consisting of the four conservatives and Mr. Justice Roberts, showed great sympathy with the force of reasoning that made minimum wage legislation for women unconstitutional. Three Justices, Stone, Brandeis and Cardozo, while concurring in Chief Justice Hughes' opinion differentiating the ADKINS and MOREHEAD statutes, believed the distinction to be of "little importance," and were prepared to categorically overrule the ADKINS case as erroneous. The Chief Justice stood alone in regarding the distinction as material and sufficient to support the validity of the New York act without necessitating the abandonment of the precedent of the ADKINS case. This furnishes yet another illustration of the reluctance of the Chief Justice, presumably out of regard for stability and the prestige of the Court, to overturn precedent if an adequate result might be obtained by other and less drastic means.

Within nine months however the Chief Justice was to be faced with the necessity of reconsidering the precedent of the ADKINS case *unsupported by the distinction available in the* MOREHEAD *case.* In *West Coast Hotel Co.* v. *Parrish* [39] the Court had before it a statute of the State of Washington providing a minimum wage for women adequate for their maintenance and the protection of their health and morals. The standard was comparable to that in the ADKINS case and *did not include the element of a "fair" wage* which the Chief Justice had said distinguished the MOREHEAD from the ADKINS statutes.

The Court, by a five to four decision, in an opinion delivered by the Chief Justice on March 29, 1937, sustained the constitutionality of the Washington statute and specifically overruled the ADKINS case. The composition of the Court had not changed since the MORE-HEAD decision rendered on June 1, 1936. What had intervened, however, was the reelection of President Franklin D. Roosevelt by a tremendous plurality which gave him the electoral votes of every state in the Union but two. Even more significantly, what had also intervened was a proposal by the President made in February, 1937, and then pending before Congress to reorganize the Court.

It may reasonably be conjectured that these developments were of some importance in inducing a reversal in the Court. Reversal presented no problem for Justices Stone, Brandeis and Cardozo, who had earlier sought to discard the ADKINS precedent. It presented only a minor obstacle in consistency to Chief Justice Hughes, who while he had attempted to distinguish the ADKINS and MOREHEAD standards had refrained from expressing any sympathy for the reasoning in the ADKINS case, and contrariwise, made some statements which reflected antipathy to that reasoning. No difficulty was encountered by the four conservatives, who simply dissented from the decision of the Court and reiterated the reasoning of the ADKINS decision. The problem was most acute for Mr. Justice Roberts, who was induced to cast the decisive vote for constitutionality. This difficulty was not lessened by the fact that one year earlier Mr. Justice Roberts, in his opinion in the case invalidating the Agricultural Adjustment Act, had insisted, presumably in anticipation of criticism, that the process of judicial review was largely mechanical. He then wrote:

When an act of Congress is appropriately challenged in the Courts as not conforming to the constitutional mandate the judicial branch of the Government has only one duty—to lay the article of the Constitution which is invoked beside the statute which is challenged and to decide whether the latter squares with the former.[40]

Nor was it lessened by the fact that in the MOREHEAD case Mr. Justice Roberts had revealed great sympathy with the reasoning that had prevailed in the ADKINS case. It was true, however, that the technical basis for decision in the MOREHEAD case had been the alleged failure of counsel to request reconsideration of the ADKINS precedent and this was seized upon as a face-saving device to bring Mr. Justice Roberts over to the other side. In writing for the majority in the WEST COAST HOTEL case, Chief Justice Hughes explained that while no application for reconsideration of the principles upon which the ADKINS case rested had been made in the MOREHEAD case, per contra, in this case, the state court had refused to regard the decision in the ADKINS case as determinative in the light of decisions of the Supreme Court both before and after that in the ADKINS case. He made reference, too, to the importance of the question which concerned many states with similar laws, the close division in the ADKINS case, and "the economic conditions which have supervened," all of which made it "imperative" that the subject receive fresh consideration.

The basis of attack upon the legislation, the Chief Justice pointed out, was that it was a deprivation of freedom of contract barred by the due process clause of the Fourteenth Amendment. "What is this freedom?" he inquired, and said,

The Constitution does not speak of freedom of contract. It speaks of liberty and prohibits the deprivation of liberty without due process of law. In prohibiting that deprivation the Constitution does not recognize an absolute and uncontrollable liberty. Liberty in each of its phases has its history and connotation. But the liberty safeguarded is liberty in a social organization which requires the protection of law against the evils which menace the health, safety, morals and welfare of the people. Liberty under the Constitution is thus necessarily subject to the restraints of due process, and regulation which is reasonable in relation to its subject and is adopted in the interests of the community is due process.

The Court, he noted, had repeatedly sustained restrictions on freedom of contract in limiting hours of labor of miners and women, in upholding workmen's compensation laws, and in other cases. The argument that adult employees should be deemed competent to make their own contracts had not been accepted by the Court when the parties had not stood upon an equality of bargaining power or where the public health demanded that a party to the contract be protected against himself. This, he said, was "peculiarly applicable" in relation to women in whose protection the state has a special interest for the variety of reasons he had previously urged in the MOREHEAD case.

As for the contention that this statute, as in the ADKINS case, in fixing minima, took no account of the value of the services rendered, he said, "It may be assumed that the minimum wage is fixed in consideration of the services that are performed in particular occupations under normal conditions." Furthermore, and here the Chief Justice adopted the argument which he had ignored in the MORE- HEAD case, but which had been urged by Justice Stone in that case, and earlier by Justice Holmes in the ADKINS case: "It is safe to assume that women will not be employed at even the lowest wages allowed unless they earn them, or unless the employer's business can sustain the burden."

The dissenting opinion of Justice Sutherland,[41] who had written the prevailing opinion in the ADKINS case some fourteen years earlier, was largely a reiteration of the views then set forth. First, however, he challenged the suggestion that fresh consideration of the decision in the ADKINS case was justified because of "the economic conditions which have supervened." "The meaning of the Constitution," he insisted, "does not change with the ebb and flow of economic events." And it was not the judicial function to amend the Constitution under the guise of interpretation.

While it was true, he said, that freedom of contract was subject to restraints, freedom was the rule and restraint the exception justified only by exceptional circumstances. A limitation upon freedom of contract for adult women legally capable of contracting for themselves to assure a minimum wage was not such a circumstance. Furthermore, the statute here, as in the ADKINS case, from which he found it indistinguishable, was clearly arbitrary because it treated the question of the minimum necessary for health and morals as a composite rather than an individual question. It failed, too, to take account of the necessities of the employer and exacted from him a wage without regard to the value of the service rendered. "In principle, there can be no difference between the case of selling labor and the case of selling goods." Also the statute denied to women the right to compete with men for work paying lower than minimum wages which men might be willing to accept. "And it is an arbitrary exercise of the legislative power to do so."

The persistence of the minority of the court in a process of reasoning so thoroughly impregnated with Spencerian *laissez-faire* in 1937, in the light of all that had occurred in the years of devastating depression, strikes one as little less than a startling anachronism. What it is pertinent to note, but the Chief Justice failed to point out, is that the reasoning of the minority could serve to defeat virtually every piece of social legislation ever devised by the wit of man. For example, state legislation curbing child labor, it could as easily be argued, presents an individual and not a composite question and fails to take account of the needs of the marginal employer. It would not be difficult to establish that *some* children laboring under the most adverse conditions for long hours emerge healthy and sound nor that some employers compelled to employ adults instead of children might be driven out of business. The legislature has the right to consider, however, that whatever may be true in exceptional instances, in the generality of cases, labor by children of tender years is bound to have a debilitating effect upon their health, and that most employers equally affected by a social regulation will be able to adjust to it. So, too, while the minimum wage fixed under the Washington statute might not have been necessary for some women who contributed nothing to their upkeep at home or who practiced "cooperative economies," it is only common sense to suggest that most women working at less than a subsistence wage were bound to suffer in their health. As for the relation of wages to morals, it may be true that some women would prefer to starve than resort to prostitution. It is, however, equally true and palpably obvious that the *incidence* of prostitution is bound to be unusually high among women earning less than enough for purposes of mere subsistence.

The decision of the Chief Justice in the WEST COAST HOTEL case foreshadowed a change in the Court's attitude toward legislation challenged as deprivations of liberty or property without due process of law. Apart from the decisions of the Court dealing with alleged invasions of civil liberties, which are the subject of separate consideration in this volume, between March, 1937, and June, 1941 (when the Chief Justice retired from the bench), there were only fourteen cases in which state legislation was invalidated and only two of these held unconstitutional statutes interfering with the rights of property. In this same period not a single Act of Congress was declared invalid by the Court although many were subjected to challenge.[42] In this latter connection, it is a striking fact that the Court which experienced such great difficulty in sustaining *subsistence* wages for *women*, who presented a special and more favorable case against due process challenge, and did so finally in 1937 only by the narrowest of margins, found it possible in 1941 to uphold *minimum* wages for *men*, above the subsistence level, as consistent with due process, by unanimous vote.[43]

Summary Statement

An attempt to appraise judicial review, in relation to the due process power of the Court, must proceed from the recognition that the authority of the Court to interpret definitively the Constitution enabled it to enhance its power by giving a meaning and scope to this limitation that went far beyond its historic connotations. In that process it developed a series of tests upon which the constitutionality of legislation challenged as a denial of due process was made to depend. Basic, however, was the requirement that the legislation accord with justice and reasonableness. These criteria, however, defy objective application and by their very nature require subjective judgments which inevitably implicate the Court in legislative policy-making. As a consequence, when Justices have been inclined to little self-restraint, they could find warrant in the demands of due process for the nullification of legislation that did not accord with their personal predilections which, for a considerable period of time, were thoroughly impregnated with the philosophy of *laissez-faire*. So far in fact had this process of judicial nullification been motivated, consciously or otherwise, by adherence to that philosophy that as early as 1905 Justice Holmes was led to complain that "the Fourteenth Amendment does not enact Mr. Herbert Spencer's Social Statics." [44] And by 1930, in the year that Mr. Hughes became Chief Justice of the Court, Justice Holmes was impelled to add,

I have not yet adequately expressed the more than anxiety that I feel at the ever-increasing scope given to the fourteenth amendment in cutting down what I believe to be the constitutional rights if they happen to strike a majority of this Court as for any reason undesirable.[45]

The early Hughes Court represented an uneasy compromise between the *laissez-faire* and the social welfare conceptions of the state. By the end of the 1940 term, however, when the Chief Justice retired, the latter had apparently become dominant and the Court showed a marked and increasing disposition to attach considerable weight to legislative determinations of reasonableness and justice as against purely personal conceptions. Another significant departure effected in this period was the disencumbering of due process from the special and additional limitation which had denied that business might be closely regulated unless "affected with a public interest."

It would be erroneous to think that these developments suggest that the Court has abandoned its supervisory role. They mean simply that the Court is presently disposed to accord considerable discretion, short of finality, to legislative determinations of reasonableness and justice divorced from additional hampering restrictions imposed by special doctrine. But the ultimate inquiry is whether the role of the Court, even thus limited, offers greater assurance of the realization of these great ends than the uncontrolled legislative judgment.

CHAPTER 12

INTELLECTUAL LIBERTY
UNDER THE CONSTITUTION

THE NATURE OF THE PROBLEM
AND THE GENESIS OF DOCTRINE

The reconciliation of liberty and authority has commanded the attention of philosophers and rulers throughout the ages and has related to all forms and activities of government at all times. It has posed, however, certain unique problems for democracies, particularly in regard to the intellectual freedoms of speech, press, assembly and religion. For here, democracies confront a dilemma. On the one hand, great latitude to intellectual freedom is essential to support the very foundation of the democratic process and to realize the social and individual values which inhere in that process.[1] On the other hand, some curbs upon intellectual freedom may be considered essential to prevent that freedom from encompassing the destruction of democracy, or in a lesser degree, from disturbing the peace and good order of society.

In democracies other than our own, the problem is resolved by legislative authority subject to the control of popular opinion. In our democracy the task of striking an appropriate balance involves the participation of the Supreme Court. Writing in 1927, Mr. Hughes said, "It is the function of the Supreme Court to maintain this balance between the constitutional guarantees of liberty and legislative requirements in the interest of the social order."[2] And this authority resides in the Court to be exercised against the exertion of legislative power, national and state, and against the will of popular majorities. Its historic bases and the manner of its exercise are important to any just appraisal of judicial review.

The Constitution of the United States as originally drafted contained no general guarantees of religious or intellectual freedom. In the process of ratification considerable dissatisfaction was manifested with the absence of such guarantees and their adoption was made almost a condition of entry into the Union by four states.[3] The very first Congress meeting in 1789 proposed a Bill of Rights which was ratified in 1791. In 1833 it was established, however, that this Bill of Rights gave security only against federal action.[4] For protection against state attempts at curtailment of civil liberties reliance was put upon the provisions of state constitutions. With the conclusion of the Civil War, however, the conviction existed that state constitutions and laws could not be relied upon to extend equal justice to the newly freed and enfranchised Negroes and a deliberate attempt was made to extend the protections afforded against federal action by the Bill of Rights to the action of states. The nationalization of the protection of civil liberties, effecting a far-reaching change in our constitutional system, was deliberately sought to be accomplished by the radical Republican leadership through *the privileges and immunities* clause of the Fourteenth Amendment.[5] That attempt was frustrated, however, by the Supreme Court in the SLAUGHTER-HOUSE CASES,[6] when, in effect, it virtually read the privileges and immunities clause out of the Constitution. But, the Supreme Court which had rendered that attempt nugatory, many years later undertook to read back into the *due process* clause *some* of the protection against state invasions of liberty it had read out of the Constitution. This process began with *Gitlow* v. *New York*,[7] when the Court held that the word "liberty" in the due process clause of the Fourteenth Amendment included protection of the right of freedom of speech. Later decisions of the Court incorporated within the scope of the due process clause, as affecting states, the primary freedoms of press, assembly and religion.

These freedoms, however, are not unlimited. Nor in the nature of the case could they be. No competent person, as the distinguished libertarian Justice Holmes has said, could ever suppose that it would be an unconstitutional interference with free speech to make it criminal to counsel murder or falsely shout fire in a theatre.[8] And obviously constitutional guarantees afford no protection against prosecution for obscenity, personal libel or the disclosure of military information vital to the security of the nation. The fundamental constitutional inquiry, therefore, is at what point and under what circumstances the line is to be drawn between permissible and non-permissible freedom. The decisions of the Court before 1917 offer practically no guidance for they "did little more than place obvious cases in this or that side of the line" and "were too few, too varied in their character, and often too easily solved to develop any definite boundary between lawful and unlawful speech." [9] The two leading post World War I decisions which dealt with the question of freedom of speech were *Schenck* v. *United States* and *Gitlow* v. *New York*. In the first, a unanimous Court in fixing the limits of freedom said that "the question in every case is whether the words used are used in such circumstances and are of such a nature as to create a clear and present danger that they will bring about the substantive evils that Congress has a right to prevent." In the other, a divided Court adopted the so-called "bad tendency" test when it stated that "a State may penalize utterances which openly advocate the overthrow of government of the United States and the several States, by violence or other unlawful means." Such utterances were held by "their very nature" to involve danger to the public peace and to the security of the state.

The Right of Symbolic Expression

For a year after Chief Justice Hughes assumed his position no civil liberties case came before the Court for decision. On May 18, 1931, however, he decided, for the Court, the case of *Stromberg* v. *California*.[10] The essential facts were these. Yetta Stromberg, nineteen years of age, and a member of the Young Communist League affiliated with the Communist party of the United States, participated in a daily ceremony at a summer camp for children during which a red flag was raised and the children recited a pledge of allegiance "to the worker's red flag, and the cause for which it stands; one aim throughout our lives, freedom for the working class." In addition, Miss Stromberg taught the children class consciousness and the theory that the workers of the world were brothers. The camp library included books and articles containing incitements to violence and armed uprisings. There was no evidence, however, that any of this literature was brought to the attention of the children or that the suggestion of violence or anarchism or sedition was employed in her teaching.

Miss Stromberg was convicted under a California statute which provided:

Any person who displays a red flag, banner or badge or any flag, badge, banner, or device of any color or form whatever, in any public place or in any meeting place or public assembly, or from or on any house, building or window [1] as a sign, symbol or emblem of opposition to organized government or [2] as an invitation or stimulus to anarchistic action or [3] as an aid to propaganda that is of a seditious character is guilty of a felony.

The highest state Court had held the clauses to be separable. But, under the instructions given to the jury it was impossible, in the view of the Chief Justice, to say under which of the three conviction had been obtained. He concluded, therefore, that if *any one* of the three was invalid, the conviction must be set aside.

That invalidity he found in the first clause which made it a criminal offense to display a flag "as a sign, symbol or emblem of opposition to organized government." Since as construed by the state Court it might serve to proscribe peaceful and orderly opposition to government by legal means and within constitutional limitations, it was, he said, upon its face, repugnant to the Constitution. "A statute which upon its face, and as authoritatively construed, is so vague and indefinite as to permit the punishment of the fair use of this opportunity is repugnant to the guaranty of liberty contained in the Fourteenth Amendment."

This derived from the fact, affirmed the Chief Justice, that

The maintenance of the opportunity for free political discussion to the end that government may be responsive to the will of the people and that changes may be obtained by lawful means, an opportunity essential to the security of the Republic, is a fundamental principle of our constitutional system.[11]

The significance of the decision in the STROMBERG case was not confined to the precise issue involved. For one thing, it cast some doubt upon the constitutional validity of many criminal anarchy statutes which were vaguely and inconclusively phrased to proscribe "subversive" activity.[12] It was also significant that the indefinite reach of the statute was judged on its face by its phrasing rather than by its specific application to Miss Stromberg. The decision represented, too, an extension of the free speech guarantee beyond utterance by word of mouth to symbolic expression. Finally, it is noteworthy that Chief Justice Hughes again took the occasion to express his deeply held conviction that broad tolerance of dissident opinion was essential to the very safety of the Republic.[13]

It may be regretted, however, that the Chief Justice failed to judge the constitutional validity of the legislation by a return to the test of whether the utterance created a clear and present danger of consummating an evil the state might seek to prevent. On the contrary, while refusing to pass on the validity of the second and third clauses, he asserted, "There is no question but that the State may thus provide for the punishment of those who indulge in utterances which incite to violence and crime and threaten the overthrow of organized government by unlawful means." And this assertion was made without regard to whether the danger was clear or obscure, imminent or remote.

CITIZENSHIP AND THE CONSCIENTIOUS OBJECTOR

Within exactly one week the Court was again called upon to consider the scope of freedom under the Constitution and laws of the United States in the case of *United States* v. *Macintosh*.[14] Macintosh was a Baptist minister who had been born in the Dominion of Canada. He came to the United States in 1916 and in 1925 declared his intention to become a citizen. At the time he was a professor of theology at Yale University. His application was denied since he would not promise in advance to bear arms in defense of the United States without regard to whether he believed the war morally justified. He could not, he said, put allegiance to the government of any country before allegiance to the will of God.

Under Act of Congress the applicant was required to take oath that he would "support and defend the Constitution and laws of the United States against all enemies, foreign and domestic, and bear true faith and allegiance to the same." It was also required to be shown that the applicant was "attached to the principles of the Constitution of the United States, and well disposed to the good order and happiness of the same."

Justice Sutherland delivered the opinion of the Court.[15] Naturalization, he said, was a privilege, to be given, qualified or withheld as

Congress may determine. The case, he added, was ruled in principle by *United States* v. *Schwimmer*.[16] The duty of citizens to bear arms whenever the necessity arose, he continued, "is a fundamental principle of the Constitution," which contemplates the possibility of war and empowers Congress to declare and wage war. Having thus ambiguously made reference to a constitutional duty, he concluded that the refusal to bear arms also conflicted with numerous statutes which contemplated such defense and required a disposition on the part of the applicant for citizenship to promote the "good order and happiness" of the United States.

Chief Justice Hughes wrote the dissenting opinion.[17] He took some pains to define the narrow scope of the issue as he saw it. It was not whether Congress *might* exact a promise to bear arms as a condition of its grant of naturalization. It was simply whether Congress *had* exacted such a promise. Neither literally nor historically could the exaction, he thought, be derived from the general words in the Act of Congress. If such a promise was demanded, Congress might have been expected to do so in unequivocal terms.

That the language of the oath did not imply a promise to bear arms notwithstanding religious or conscientious scruples was apparent from a consideration of its history, he said. The oath was the same in substance as that which had been required by Act of Congress of civil officers generally for over sixty years. When one considered the history of the struggle for religious liberty, the large number of citizens who from the very beginning had been conscientiously opposed to war, it was impossible to conclude, he believed, that it was the intention of Congress to disqualify such persons from public office because of the requirement of the oath. "I think," he added, "that the requirement of the oath of office should be read in the light of our regard from the beginning for freedom of conscience." And when Congress reproduced the historic words of the oath of office in the naturalization oath, he reasoned, it could be supposed that, according to familiar rules of interpretation, they were intended to carry the same significance.

Furthermore, while it was true that the proper interpretation of the requirements of the oath was distinct from the legislative policy in regard to military service, "the long-established practice of excusing from military service those whose religious convictions oppose it confirms the view that the Congress in the terms of the oath did not intend to require a promise to give such service." The policy of granting exemptions in such cases, he pointed out, went back to colonial times and was found in Acts of Congress.

Government, he recognized, could enforce obedience to laws regardless of scruples. But consideration must be had for the fact that

The battle for religious liberty has been fought and won with respect to religious beliefs and practices, which are not in conflict with good order, upon the very ground of the supremacy of conscience within its proper field. What that field is, under our system of government, presents in part a question of constitutional law and also, in part, one of legislative policy in avoiding unnecessary clashes with the dictates of conscience. There is abundant room for enforcing the requisite authority of law as it is enacted and requires obedience, and for maintaining the conception of the supremacy of law as essential to orderly government, without demanding that either citizens or applicants for citizenship shall assume by oath an obligation to regard allegiance to God as subordinate to allegiance to civil power.

In the light of these considerations, said the Chief Justice, it would require strong evidence that Congress had intended a reversal of its policy in prescribing the general terms of the naturalization oath. No such evidence appeared.

Nor did he regard it as sufficient reason to exclude Macintosh from citizenship that his scruples related not to all wars but to wars believed unjust because if objection to all war was not a bar to citizenship, he could discern no basis upon which religious or conscientious objection to participation in wars believed to be unjust should constitute such a disqualification.

Apart from the oath the requirement of "attachment to the principles of the Constitution" was, he said, in general terms "which should be construed, not in opposition to, but in accord with, the theory and practice of our Government in relation to freedom of conscience." As for the SCHWIMMER decision, it "stands upon the special facts of that case, but I do not regard it as requiring a reversal of the judgment here."

Several observations appear pertinent. With regard to the technical issues involved, the Chief Justice rightly insisted upon the narrow scope of the inquiry. While the opinion of the majority in the final analysis appeared to recognize that the basic question related to the intention of Congress in prescribing the oath, it sometimes reasoned as if it believed that the Constitution, of its own force, required an affirmation by aliens seeking citizenship of a willingness to bear arms. Nor did the majority make any effective answer to the argument of the Chief Justice, which he based upon history and analogy, that it was not the intention of Congress to require aliens, as a condition of naturalization, to take an oath to bear arms contrary to conscientious scruples.

More fundamental, however, was the fact that in regard to the necessity for accommodation of liberty and authority in relation to religious scruples, the statements of the Chief Justice represented a lofty libertarian conception rarely excelled in judicial opinions.

It must, however, I think, be recognized that the Hughes opinion could not be reconciled with the decision in the SCHWIMMER case despite the statement that that case stood upon its "special facts." His own reasoning supported the view that conscientious opposition to all war was as readily compatible with the requirements of the oath as opposition to unjust wars. Candor would have required the Chief Justice to suggest that the SCHWIMMER decision should have been overruled.[18]

FREEDOM OF THE PRESS

Again within one week the Chief Justice read another opinion in a civil liberties case, this time, however, for a narrow majority of the Court, in a case involving freedom of the press. The case in point was *Near* v. *Minnesota*.[19]

The facts which were the bases upon which the state had sought to enjoin the publication of a newspaper were as follows: A Minnesota newspaper in 1927 published nine articles charging in substance that a Jewish gangster was in control of gambling, bootlegging and racketeering in Minneapolis and that local public officials, and particularly the Chief of Police, were guilty of gross neglect of duty, illicit relations with gangsters and participation in graft. The county attorney was accused of knowing the conditions and failing to take measures to remedy them. The mayor was taxed with inefficiency and dereliction of duty.

Section 1(*b*) of the pertinent Minnesota statute provided for the abatement, as a public nuisance, of a "malicious, scandalous and de-famatory newspaper, magazine or other periodical." (Section 1(a) permitted similar action against an obscene publication.) Under other provisions of the Act truth was made a defense, only however, if publication had been "with good motives and for justifiable ends." A temporary injunction enjoining perpetually the further com-mission of such nuisance might be granted by a court "upon such evidence as the court shall deem sufficient." And after more formal hearing a permanent injunction might be granted enjoining con-tinued violation of the Act and "in and by such judgment, such nuisance may be wholly abated." Violation of the injunction was punishable by imprisonment for contempt.

A judgment was handed down by the District Court based upon the only evidence submitted—the nine articles themselves—adjudg-ing the publication to be a public nuisance and perpetually enjoining its future publication of any malicious, scandalous or defamatory ma-terial as defined by law and "from further conducting said nuisance" under its existing name or any other name. This judgment was chal-lenged as repugnant to the due process clause of the Fourteenth Amendment.

Pointing out that "it is no longer open to doubt" that the liberty of the press was within the protection of the due process clause of the Fourteenth Amendment, the Chief Justice proceeded with a critical analysis of the meaning and scope of the statute. The statute, he said, was not designed to redress individual or private wrongs as in the case of libel laws. It was aimed, instead, at the distribution of defamatory matter regarded as detrimental to the general welfare. The object of the statute was, he maintained, not punishment, in the ordinary sense, but suppression and effective censorship. The operation and effect of the statute were such that

public authorities may bring the owner or publisher of a newspaper or periodical before a judge upon a charge of conducting a business of pub-lishing scandalous and defamatory matter—in particular that the matter consists of charges against public officers of official dereliction—and un-less the owner or publisher is able and disposed to bring competent evidence to satisfy the judge that the charges are true and are published with good motives and for justifiable ends, his newspaper or periodical is suppressed and further publication is made punishable as a contempt.

This, said the Chief Justice, "is of the essence of censorship." He proceeded then on the scores of history and social advantage to condemn the statute.

Citing Blackstone and Cooley and the renunciation by Parliament of the power of censorship of the press, such a statute as this, imposing previous restraints, he contended, was not consistent with liberty of the press as historically conceived and guaranteed.

It was true, he conceded, that immunity from previous restraint might in some cases be denied. But this was so only "in exceptional cases," such as actual obstruction to recruitment or the disclosure of military information or incitements to violence or overthrow of government by force or to maintain the primary requirements of decency. But these limitations were not applicable here. In fact, the exceptional nature of the recognized limitations "places in a strong light the general conception that liberty of the press, historically considered and taken up by the Federal constitution, has meant, principally although not exclusively, immunity from previous restraints or censorship."

Referring to the struggle beginning with colonial times which "led to the guaranties of liberty of the press," he thought that the fact that for approximately one hundred and fifty years there had been almost an entire absence of attempts to impose previous restraints upon publications relating to the malfeasance of public officers was significant of the deep-seated conviction that such restraints would violate constitutional right. This view, he pointed out, found support in many decisions under state constitutions.

Nor was this immunity from previous restraint simply a matter of historical interest and importance. With keen appreciation for the continuing value of an uncensored press, he said,

The administration of government has become more complex, the opportunities for malfeasance and corruption have multiplied, crime has grown to most serious proportions, and the danger of its protection by unfaithful officials and of the impairment of the fundamental security of life and property by criminal alliances and official neglect, emphasize the primary need of a vigilant and courageous press, especially in great cities. The fact that the liberty of the press may be abused by miscreant purveyors of scandal does not make any the less necessary the immunity of the press from previous restraints in dealing with official misconduct. Subsequent punishment for such abuses as may exist is the appropriate remedy, consistent with constitutional privilege.

The statute, he thought, could not be defended on the score that the publisher might avoid penalty by showing truth *and* publication with good motives for justifiable ends. "The preliminary freedom, by virtue of the very reason for its existence, does not depend . . . on proof of truth." And since in addition to truth justifiable ends must be shown what would prevent the legislature from determining, in the complete exercise of its discretion, what are justifiable ends and restrain publication accordingly?

Neither, in his view, could the fact that the statute was designed to prevent the circulation of scandal which tended to disturb the public peace and provoke the commission of crime serve as a defense of its validity.

Charges of reprehensible conduct, and in particular of official malfeasance, unquestionably create a public scandal, but the theory of the constitutional guaranty is that even a more serious public evil would be caused by authority to prevent publication. . . . The danger of violent reactions becomes greater with effective organization of defiant groups resenting exposure, and if this consideration warranted legislative interference with the initial freedom of publication, the constitutional protection would be reduced to a mere form of words.

The dissenting opinion of Justice Butler emphasized the vicious character of the charges, and insisted that there was no basis for the suggestion that the defendants might not, under the statute, have negatived the charge of malice by showing that the publication was made in good faith "in belief of its truth" or that it constituted fair comment on public affairs. Furthermore, he argued, the actual criminal actions that surrounded the publication, including blackmail and assault, revealed the kind of conditions, in respect of the business of publishing scandalous periodicals, by which the state legislature presumably was moved in seeking to prevent abuses of the liberty of the press.

Justice Butler quoted from Justice Story's monumental work on the Constitution in support of the proposition that the First Amendment imported no more than that "every man shall be at liberty to publish what is true, with good motives and for justifiable ends."

He denied, too, that in any proper meaning of the phrase, did the Minnesota statute operate as a previous restraint on publications. "It does not authorize administrative control in advance such as was formerly exercised by the licensers and censors but prescribes a remedy to be enforced by a suit in equity. . . . The restraint authorized is only in respect of continuing to do what has been duly adjudged to constitute a nuisance."

This phase of the argument of Justice Butler was, I believe, in the nature of a quibble for the fact was that while restraint was conceived of as a penalty for past offenses under the statute, its inevitable consequence was to bar future publication. But, even if the proceedings were viewed simply as a punishment for past conduct, they might within any broad conception of freedom of the press, have been held unconstitutional as imposing unreasonable restraint upon free discussion of public affairs.[20]

The majority opinion, Justice Butler continued, seemed to concede that an obscene publication might be enjoined as a nuisance under clause (a) of the statute and he found it difficult to perceive any distinction, having any relation to constitutionality, between clause (a) and clause (b) under which this action was brought. "Both nuisances are offensive to morals, order and good government."

Justice Butler concluded with an emphasis upon the practical social need for such legislation.

It is well known . . . that existing libel laws are inadequate effectively to suppress evils resulting from the kind of business and publications that are shown in this case. The doctrine that measures such as the one before us are invalid because they operate as previous restraints to infringe freedom of press exposes the peace and good order of every community and the business and private affairs of every individual to the constant and protracted false and malicious assaults of any insolvent publisher who may have purpose and sufficient capacity to contrive and put into effect a scheme or program for oppression, blackmail or extortion.

In this first case in which the Supreme Court had been required to pass upon the constitutional validity of a statute imposing "previous restraint" on publication, qualified though it was, to imposition only after initial offensive publication, the whole Court, it should be observed, agreed upon two propositions: first, that the due process clause protected freedom of the press against state impairment, and second, that freedom of the press was not unlimited even as against previous restraints. The inquiry, then, as to whether *this statute* constituted a deprivation of liberty without due process of law proceeded largely on two bases, that is, a study of past history including the comment of constitutional authorities, and rationalizations of the Justices in regard to the public interest. Since history and particularly authority could be summoned to support either view and the language of the Constitution gave no greater support to previous restraints upon obscene publications than scandalous ones, it is perhaps fair to assert that, in the final analysis, the differing positions of the members of the Court may be ascribed to differing conceptions of the public interest. It would be difficult, otherwise, to explain why the four more or less consistent conservatives should arrive at one conclusion as to the lessons of history and the five more or less liberal members of the Court should arrive at another. Furthermore, the usual division characterizing conservative and liberal members of the Court was not reflected in this decision. Ordinarily it has been the liberals who have sought to give broad and expansive power to the exercise of federal delegated or state reserve power. The contrary was, of course, true here.

What, then, were the differing conceptions of the public interest that underlay the division? The Chief Justice while cognizant of the dangers of tolerating "reckless assaults upon public men" emphasized "the primary need of a vigilant and courageous press especially in great cities" in the face of the increase of crime and opportunities for corruption with their "impairment of the fundamental security of life and property." Justice Butler, on the other hand, expressed concern over the inadequacy of libel laws to cope with publications which may expose "the peace and good order of every community and the business and private affairs of every individual" to a program of oppression, blackmail or extortion.

Broadly viewed, the decision had far-reaching implications. It discouraged passage of similar statutes. Furthermore, it has been suggested by Professor Chafee that "its strong hostility to previous restraints against the expression of ideas may conceivably be applied to quite different forms of censorship, affecting other media of communication besides the press." [21] While Professor Chafee's anticipations have not as yet been substantially realized, it is true that the NEAR case has served as a landmark in attempts to batter down the restrictions of previous restraint and may yet play a part in curbing censorship in related fields.

Finally, it may be suggested that much of the force of the Chief Justice's "tract of political liberalism" lay in the fact that his pronouncement came in defense of a particularly odious type of publication. This was editorially recognized by the New York *Herald Tribune* in its comment that "the very fact that the exercise of liberty of the press in this momentous case came before the Supreme Court in the least favorable light adds a buttress of steel to the constitutional guaranty." [22]

REVOLUTIONARY AGITATION

In 1937 freedom of assembly, guilt by association and revolutionary advocacy came under the scrutiny of the Court in two cases involving avowed members of the Communist party. The first of these, *De Jonge* v. *Oregon*,[23] arose out of the following facts. In July of 1934 the Communist party organized a public meeting in Portland as a protest against illegal raids on workers' halls and homes and the shooting of striking longshoremen by police. It was estimated that not over 15 per cent of those in attendance were Communist party members. De Jonge and other speakers dealt with the subject of the protest meeting except for making an appeal for party membership and urging the purchase of certain communist literature. The meeting was orderly. The literature distributed or sold at the meeting was not shown to advocate criminal syndicalism or any unlawful conduct. While the meeting was in progress it was raided by the police.

De Jonge was indicted, convicted and sentenced to imprisonment for seven years under the specific provision of the Criminal Syndicalism law of Oregon making it a criminal offense to *assist in the conduct of a meeting* called by any organization advocating criminal syndicalism or sabotage. The Communist party, it was alleged, was such an organization.

Limiting himself to the particular offense charged and "with the validity of the statute in this particular application," the Chief Justice, speaking for the Court,[24] pointed out that:

The broad reach of the statute as thus applied is plain. While defendant was a member of the Communist Party, that membership was not necessary to conviction on such a charge. A like fate might have attended any speaker, although not a member who "assisted in the conduct" of the meeting. However innocuous the object of the meeting, however lawful the subjects and tenor of the addresses, however reasonable and timely the discussion, all those assisting in the conduct of the meeting would be subject to imprisonment as felons if the meeting were held by the Communist Party.

The right of peaceable assembly, the Chief Justice continued, cannot be denied without violating "those fundamental principles of liberty and justice which lie at the base of all civil and political institutions,—principles which the Fourteenth Amendment embodies in the general terms of its due process clause." The question of whether the Communist party advocated criminal syndicalism was deemed immaterial for present purposes. Whatever its objectives, the defendant was entitled to free speech and to take part in a peaceable assembly having a lawful purpose, although called by the Communist party. The Oregon statute was, accordingly, "as applied to the particular charge as defined by the state court" held repugnant to due process.

The most obviously significant fact about the decision of the Chief Justice lay in its extension of the range of protection of "liberty" under the due process clause to include "peaceable assembly." Characteristically, this was accomplished by the Chief Justice without reference to the decision of the Court in *Presser* v. *Illinois*,[25] decided in 1886, although by implication, if not forthrightly, that case was overruled. It had then been held that the right to assemble peaceably was not protected from state impairment by the due process clause of the Fourteenth Amendment.[26]

It is unfortunate that the Chief Justice did not accompany his stirring defense of freedom of assembly with a flat invalidation of the offending section of the law but contented himself with holding the law invalid as applied in the narrow context of this case. The very indefiniteness and reach of the provision might have been deemed abhorrent to the requirements of due process. Possibly, his failure to do so was the price expediency in winning support paid to principle.

It must be noted, too, that again the Chief Justice did not take the occasion to repudiate the test of validity of criminal syndicalism acts laid down in the GITLOW case although, by indirection, he cast some doubts upon it. That test, it will be recalled, made conviction possible even in the absence of a showing of any clear and present danger of substantive evil arising out of the actions of the accused. Conceivably, the Chief Justice might have predicated his decision in the DE JONGE case on the absence of such a danger.[27]

Whatever the limitations in the scope of the decision it would be carping, indeed, to ignore the tremendous value to the struggle for freedom, first, in the incorporation of freedom of assembly into due process protection of the Fourteenth Amendment, second, in the implication of rejection of guilt by association, and finally in the stirring declaration of the Chief Justice that

The greater the importance of safeguarding the community from incitements to the overthrow of our institutions by force and violence, the more imperative is the need to preserve inviolate the constitutional rights of free speech, free press and free assembly in order to maintain the opportunity for free political discussion, to the end that government may be responsive to the will of the people and that changes, if desired, may be obtained by peaceful means. Therein lies the security of the Republic, the very foundation of constitutional government.

In an age when many men continue to believe that the best way to prevent revolutionary change is to still the voice of revolutionary utterance, statements such as these which find safety in freedom of expression are not without their beacon value to the community.

In the second case, *Herndon* v. *Lowry*,[28] the Court, in an opinion of Mr. Justice Roberts,[29] came close to a specific reaffirmation of the "clear and present danger" test. Herndon, a Negro, and a paid organizer for the Communist party, was convicted under a pre-Civil War Georgia statute for attempting to incite insurrection, largely on the basis of his enrolling activities and possession of a booklet urging "Self-Determination for the Black Belt." This booklet advocated a revolutionary struggle for power "even if the situation does not yet warrant the raising of the question of uprising."

Rejecting the view of the highest state court that a "dangerous tendency" might be made the standard of guilt, the Supreme Court held that "penalizing even of utterances of a defined character must find its justification in a reasonable apprehension of danger to organized government." The statute, in this instance, was "so vague and indeterminate" affording no standard for appraising utterances and conduct to determine the existence of "a clear and present danger of forcible obstruction of a particular state function" that it "necessarily violates the guarantees of liberty embodied in the Fourteenth Amendment." [30]

FREEDOM OF RELIGION

Within the next few years the Court was to deal with a number of cases arising out of the activities of Jehovah's Witnesses, a sect marked by great religious and proselytizing zeal. The first of these cases, *Lovell* v. *Griffin*,[31] arose out of the distribution by Lovell, a member of this sect, of a pamphlet and a magazine setting forth the gospel of the Kingdom of Jehovah. Lovell was convicted of violating an ordinance of the city of Griffin, Georgia, which forbade the distribution, "either by hand or otherwise" of "literature of any kind" within the limits of the city "without first obtaining written permission from the City Manager." Violation was declared to be punishable as a nuisance. The ordinance was defended by counsel for the city of Griffin as a police measure warranted in coping with the sanitary problems of the city.

Chief Justice Hughes [32] analyzed the broad sweep of the statute and found that by its terms it prohibited the distribution of literature of any kind, at any time, at any place, and in any manner without a permit from the City Manager. Such an ordinance, he said,

is invalid on its face. Whatever the motive which induced its adoption, its character is such that it strikes at the very foundation of the freedom of the press by subjecting it to license and censorship. The struggle for the freedom of the press was primarily directed against the power of the licensor. . . . Legislation of the type of the ordinance in question would restore the system of license and censorship in its baldest form. The liberty of the press is not confined to newspapers and periodicals. It necessarily embraces pamphlets and leaflets.

The fact that the ordinance related to circulation and not to publication was deemed immaterial since without circulation, publication would be of little value.

The decision in this case was predicated on the broad and unlimited reach of the statute. It did not go so far as to suggest that curbs upon distribution under all circumstances were impermissible. On the contrary, Chief Justice Hughes made a point of noting that the particular ordinance was "not limited to ways which might be regarded as inconsistent with the maintenance of public order, or as involving disorderly conduct, the molestation of inhabitants, or the misuse or littering of the streets." Nevertheless, this case "marked a sharp turning-point in the law, and checked the use of permits for activities concerned with speech." Prior to this decision numerous state courts had upheld requirements of special permits for various types of handbill distribution.[33] In essence, of course, this decision rested upon the conviction that the social interest in "freedom of speech" transcended in importance the social interest in clean streets.

In *Cantwell* v. *Connecticut* [34] disciples of Jehovah's Witnesses were again before the Court, this time for soliciting contributions for religious and charitable purposes without the approval of a public welfare official. Solicitation was carried on in predominantly Catholic neighborhoods in a manner many regarded as particularly offensive. "Witnesses" first asked permission to play a record, without disclosing its nature. The record attacked the Catholic Church. The "witnesses" then sought to sell a publication or obtain a contribution. The Chief Justice acquiesced in a decision by Mr. Justice Roberts holding the statute, as to solicitations for religious purposes, violative of the freedom of religion as well as free speech guarantees of the due process clause. The Court, by its decision in this case, completed its incorporation of the guarantees of the First Amendment into the concept of "liberty" under the due process clause of the Fourteenth Amendment.

Within less than a month, however, a unanimous Court, except for the vigorously protesting Justice Stone, in an opinion by Mr. Justice Frankfurter, sustained a statute requiring children attending public school to salute the flag on pain of expulsion. Members of Jehovah's Witnesses had objected that this law violated their religious scruples and deprived them of freedom of religion and speech.[35]

The last Jehovah's Witnesses case with which Chief Justice Hughes was concerned was that of *Cox* v. *New Hampshire* [36] in which members of this sect were convicted for violating a state statute prohibiting a "parade or procession" upon a public street without a special license. They had walked in groups of from fifteen to twenty persons in single file through the business district of Manchester each carrying a sign. Some of these read "Religion is a Snare and a Racket."

Chief Justice Hughes, writing for a unanimous Court, found that there was no evidence that the statute had been administered in other than a fair and non-discriminatory manner. Rejecting the contention that denial of liberties protected by the due process clause was involved in the statute or its application, he said,

Civil liberties, as guaranteed by the Constitution, imply the existence of an organized society maintaining public order without which liberty itself would be lost in the excesses of unrestrained abuses. The authority of a municipality to impose regulations in order to assure the safety and convenience of the people in the use of public highways has never been regarded as inconsistent with civil liberties but rather as one of the means of safeguarding the good order upon which they ultimately depend. The control of travel on the streets of cities is the most familiar illustration of this recognition of social need. Where a restriction of the use of highways in that relation is designed to promote the public convenience in the interest of all, it cannot be disregarded by the attempted exercise of some civil right which in other circumstances would be entitled to protection.

The exaction of a fee, reasonable in amount, required for a license as incident to the administration of the Act and to the maintenance of public order was held not to be contrary to the Constitution.

It is obvious that upon a balance of social interest the Chief Justice concluded in this case that restriction rather than freedom was warranted.

Freedom of Labor

Where did the Chief Justice stand in relation to other important cases, specifically with respect to a greatly expanded concept of freedom for labor organization? In *Senn* v. *Tile Layers Protective Union* [37] he joined in a narrow majority of the Court which upheld a state law prohibiting the use of injunctions against peaceful picketing.[38] In *Lauf* v. *Shinner & Co.*[39] and *New Negro Alliance* v. *Sanitary Grocery Co.*[40] he was with the majority in sustaining the general scope and the validity of the procedural requirements of the Norris-LaGuardia Act regulating and limiting the issuance of injunctions in labor disputes.[41]

In *Hague* v. *Committee for Industrial Organization* [42] a majority of the Court, including the Chief Justice, agreed upon a decree invalidating and enjoining the enforcement of an ordinance of Jersey City prohibiting assemblies "in or upon the public streets, highways, public parks or public buildings" without a permit from the Director of Public Safety. Among other things, the Court found that officials of Jersey City had adopted a deliberate policy of forbidding the Committee for Industrial Organization from communicating its views respecting the National Labor Relations Act to citizens of Jersey City by holding meetings or assemblies in the open air and at public places.

The basis of the ruling in this case was the subject of disagreement. Justices Roberts and Black believed the ordinance "void upon its face" as an abridgment of "a privilege inherent in citizenship of the United States" which the Fourteenth Amendment protects. Justices Stone and Reed denied the applicability of the privileges and immunities clause and sought to predicate the decision on the guarantees of due process. The crucial difference is that the former clause protects only citizens, the latter aliens as well. In a separate and brief concurring opinion, Chief Justice Hughes agreed with "what is said in the opinion of Mr. Justice Roberts as to the right to discuss the National Labor Relations Act being a privilege of a citizen of the United States." On technical grounds, however, he did not think the record supported resting jurisdiction of the Court upon that ground.[43]

In *Thornhill* v. *Alabama* [44] and *Carlson* v. *California* [45] the Chief Justice concurred in two opinions of Justice Murphy for the Court, which brought the right of peaceful picketing and the display of signs or banners by the picketers within the scope of "liberty" protected against invasion by the due process clause.[46]

In *Milk Wagon Drivers Union* v. *Meadowmoor Dairies, Inc.,*[47] however, the Chief Justice agreed with a majority of the Court, speaking through Mr. Justice Frankfurter, that peaceful picketing may be enjoined when enmeshed with contemporaneously violent conduct.[48] And in *American Federation of Labor* v. *Swing* [49] the Chief Justice aligned himself with the opinion of Mr. Justice Roberts in dissenting from a decision of the majority of the Court, delivered by Mr. Justice Frankfurter, which held that peaceful picketing, under the common law, could not be enjoined even when it was part of an attempt to "organize" a business in which none of the employees was or wished to become a member of the union and no employer-employee dispute in that sense existed.

SUMMARY STATEMENT

In the whole process of striking a balance between freedom and restraint in the individual and social interest in the area of intellectual liberties presumably the Court acted under the guidance of the Constitution. But since the protection of such liberties finds expression in general clauses with undefined and malleable limits which must be reconciled with grants of power, like the war power, and with reservations of power, like the police power, in practice, the preferences and philosophical rationalizations of the Justices inevitably played a decisive role.

Those preferences and rationalizations were utilized by the Court, over which Chief Justice Hughes presided, to accomplish the progressive incorporation of the great intellectual freedoms of the First Amendment within the concept of due process as limitations upon the exercise of state power. In that process, the Chief Justice played the leading role.

Shortly before the Chief Justice retired from the bench, the Court began to reassert the test of constitutionality, which while never specifically repudiated had been largely ignored for some years following its pronouncement, that restraint upon intellectual freedom would not be countenanced by the Court unless it could be shown that a clear and present danger existed that some substantive evil the state might seek to proscribe would otherwise accrue from tolerance. Shortly after the Chief Justice left the Court, that test was not only made the very cornerstone of constitutionality but to it was added the doctrine, first urged by Justice Stone, that in civil liberties cases, as distinguished from those affecting property, the legislation must be subjected to a "more searching judicial inquiry" amounting to virtually a presumption against constitutionality.[50] To this development, by the logic of his decisions, if not by formal expression, the Chief Justice must be credited with a substantial contribution despite his affirmation in the St. Joseph Stockyards case that there was no constitutional warrant for differentiating between personal liberty and property rights in requiring an independent judicial determination of certain facts in issue.

More significant perhaps than the precise issues settled by his decisions were the great libertarian ideals to which the Chief Justice gave vocal expression which had their undoubted educational effect upon the nation and the Court. Particularly noteworthy was his emphasis upon the value of free expression both as a means of making government responsive to the people, upon which the security of our democracy, he discerned, ultimately rested, and as a "safety-valve" to draw off discontent. And these stirring defenses of the value of freedom to democracy, it will be recalled, antedated his accession to the Court.

In the light of this record, it is understandable that Joseph Percival Pollard should have written as early as 1934 that Chief Justice Hughes displays a "greater fondness for the Bill of Rights than any Chief Justice this country ever had," [51] and that on the occasion of his retirement from the bench, Attorney General Robert Jackson should have said, "In the numerous cases dealing with civil liberties he has been a consistent and forthright champion of the American freedoms." [52] To this may be added the comment of a severe critic of many of Chief Justice Hughes' economic opinions that "as a jurist, Charles Evans Hughes will be best remembered as a friend of civil liberties and the rights of minorities, particularly that minority which has most needed protection, the Negro." [53]

CHAPTER 13

EQUALITY BEFORE THE LAW
AND THE POLICE POWER

Among the more difficult and persistent problems with which the
Court has had to deal are those affecting a tenth of the American
people whose skin is tinged with varying degrees of black pigmen-
tation. These problems have assumed their most acute form in the
South, complicated by the dependency of that section on a mass of
cheap and, in the view of many, preferably servile labor, by a determination to maintain a social pattern no longer fully commanding
the support of law, and by bitter memories of civil strife and reconstruction.

In the period that Charles Evans Hughes presided over the deliberations of the Supreme Court, three phases of the problem—in
essence one of discrimination—commanded the attention of the
Court. The first concerned the protection of Negroes in criminal
proceedings, the second related to equality in the exercise of the
franchise and the third involved discrimination in access to facilities
provided by or closely controlled by the state. Most of these issues
raised questions regarding the scope of the protection given by
that portion of the Fourteenth Amendment which provides that no
state shall "deny to any person within its jurisdiction the equal protection of the laws."

THE SCOTTSBORO CASES

In 1931 a group of Negroes was removed from a train and
charged with that most heinous of offenses for Negroes in the
South—rape. They were quickly brought to mass trial and convicted
after a vague and inadequate designation of counsel who failed to
interview the clients and made no investigation of the facts about
which it later developed there was considerable basis for dispute.
In 1932, in the first of the so-called "Scottsboro cases," a majority of

the Court had held that an effective designation of counsel was, under the circumstances, requisite to due process.[1]

This, however, was only the first of a series of cases. Upon retrial and conviction, counsel challenged the result upon the ground that the systematic exclusion of Negroes from jury service constituted a denial of equal protection of the laws.

In *Norris* v. *Alabama* [2] the Supreme Court unanimously held, in an opinion by Chief Justice Hughes, that the exclusion from jury duty, grand or petit, of all Negroes whether effected through legislation or by the courts or executive or administrative officers of a state, solely because of their race or color, constituted a denial of equal protection of the laws contrary to the Fourteenth Amendment.[3] And it is noteworthy that even in the absence of concrete evidence of deliberate exclusion, it was concluded that discrimination had in fact been practiced when it was shown that there were large numbers of eligible Negroes in the county none of whom had ever been called upon to serve.

The determination of the Supreme Court to prevent technical rules of procedure from defeating the ends of justice, in the cases affecting the Scottsboro defendants, was made palpable in the case of *Patterson* v. *Alabama*.[4] The question of long-continued, systematic and arbitrary exclusion of qualified Negroes from jury service, solely by reason of their race and color, was raised in this as in the Norris case.[5] However, the evidence submitted in support of such exclusion was not considered by the Supreme Court of the state on the technical ground that the defendant's bill of exceptions had not been presented in time as required by state law. It was argued that the Supreme Court of the United States, therefore, had no jurisdiction since the decision of the state court had been rested entirely upon a question of state appellate procedure which raised no federal question.

Normally, the determination of the highest state court on the requirements of its appellate procedure is regarded as involving a non-federal question and having the effect of finality. But, said the Chief Justice,[6] while regard must be had to the ruling of the state in the matter of its procedure, "we cannot ignore the exceptional features of the present case." He pointed out that while the Patterson case had come up on a separate appeal and a separate record from that in the NORRIS case, decisions in both cases had been announced by the court below the same day. If that court had known what the determination of constitutional right would have been in the NORRIS case, "we are not satisfied," he said, that it would have struck the bill of exceptions in the PATTERSON case, involving as it did a judgment of death in a case in which the same constitutional issue of exclusion was raised. "At least the state court should have an opportunity to examine its powers in the light of the situation which has now developed." The judgment was vacated and the case remanded to the state court for further proceedings.

Clearly the basic motivating consideration in this opinion was the awful contemplation that for a technical defect in procedure a human being might be sent to his death. With a little ingenuity in reasoning, the technical requirements of the law were subordinated to the ends of justice.

THE RIGHT TO VOTE

Determined to maintain "white supremacy," many of the Southern states resorted to a variety of means designed to debar Negroes from voting in elections. One of the more flagrant attempts had been the adoption by a state of the so-called "grandfather test" which had provided that only persons might vote in elections in that state who had been legal voters at a date preceding the adoption of the Fifteenth Amendment. That amendment, enacted at the end of the Civil War, provides that the right of citizens to vote shall not be abridged on account of color. This statute had been declared unconstitutional in 1915 in *Guinn* v. *United States*.[7]

In a deliberate attempt at circumvention, Oklahoma enacted a statute requiring registration within twelve days of all who had not voted in 1914, before the invalidation of the "grandfather clause," with perpetual disenfranchisement to follow a failure to do so. This, in the opinion of Mr. Justice Frankfurter, in which the Chief Justice joined in *Lane* v. *Wilson*,[8] ran counter to the Fifteenth Amendment. Even in this palpable case of a violation of a constitutional amendment Justices McReynolds and Butler found reasons for dissent.

In most Southern states, selection in the primary of the Democratic party makes ultimate election at the polls a foregone conclusion.

Several of these states conjectured, therefore, that since they could not constitutionally bar Negroes from voting in actual elections, it might prove as effective, practically, to exclude them simply from voting in Democratic party primaries. Two important cases dealing with this issue were decided during the tenure of the Chief Justice.

In the first of these, *Nixon* v. *Condon*,[9] he concurred in a decision by Justice Cardozo invalidating a Texas statute under which Negroes were barred from voting in Democratic party primaries. The statute had authorized the executive committees of political parties in the state to determine who should be qualified to vote in their primaries.[10] The statute was deemed unconstitutional as a denial of equal protection of the laws under the Fourteenth Amendment.

Subsequently, however, the whole Court, in an opinion of Mr. Justice Roberts, found that when this statute was repealed and the Democratic party state convention, acting without authorization of state law, thereafter excluded Negroes from participating in party primaries, no basis existed for invalidating this action. This ruling was rested on the assumption that the action taken was private and not public, the Court stating, "We are not prepared to hold that in Texas the state convention of a party has become a mere instrumentality or agency for expressing the voice or will of the State." [11] Some doubt was cast upon this precedent when in 1941, in the case of *United States* v. *Classic*,[12] the Supreme Court upheld the application of a federal penal law against persons guilty of altering and falsely counting ballots in a Louisiana Democratic party primary contest involving the nomination of a candidate for a seat in Congress. The Chief Justice, however, took no part in the consideration or decision of this case.[13]

"Equal but Separate"

In 1883 the Supreme Court, in the Civil Rights Cases,[14] ruled that the prohibitions of the Fourteenth Amendment were applicable only to the states and that legislation by Congress to protect Negroes against discrimination practiced by private persons or groups was beyond its constitutional power.

And even with respect to action which was clearly that of a state, beginning in 1896 with its decision in *Plessy* v. *Ferguson*,[15] the Supreme Court gave approval to legislation requiring segregation of Negroes and whites on the theory that segregation, as such, did not constitute a denial of equal protection of the laws provided only that "equal" facilities were provided.

Late in 1938 the Supreme Court had occasion to consider the requirements of "equal protection of the laws" in relation to this established principle in the case of *Missouri ex rel. Gaines* v. *Canada*.[16] Lloyd Gaines, a Negro citizen of Missouri, who met the requirements of scholarship, was denied admission, because of his color, to the law school of the University of Missouri, an institution maintained by the state. State law made provision for defraying the tuition of Negroes at a law school in a neighboring state "pending the full development" of such facilities within the state.

Chief Justice Hughes, speaking for a majority of the Court, ruled that the failure of the state to furnish Gaines "within its borders facilities for legal education substantially equal to those which the State there afforded for persons of the white race" constituted a denial of equal protection.

The argument that the declaration of intention by the state to provide legal facilities for Negroes met its constitutional obligation was rejected by the Chief Justice with the statement that "it cannot be said that a mere declaration of purpose, still unfulfilled, is enough." As for the provision for legal education for Negroes outside the state,

The basic consideration is not as to what sort of opportunities other States provide, or whether they are as good as those in Missouri, but as to what opportunities Missouri itself furnishes to white students and denies to Negroes solely upon the ground of color. . . . It is an obligation the burden of which cannot be cast by one State upon another, and no State can be excused from performance by what another State may do or fail to do.

Nor, he ruled, may the absence of sufficient demand by Negroes for legal education serve to excuse the discrimination. Whether particular facilities shall be provided may be conditioned on demand, but, if facilities are provided, substantial equality of treatment cannot be refused. The right to equal protection of the laws is not based on race. It is "a personal one."

Justice McReynolds dissented.[17] Missouri, he said, believes that the best interests of her people are served by segregation in schools.

In the light of the prevailing opinion she will be required to either abandon her law school, disadvantaging her white citizens without improving the opportunities for legal education of Negroes, or "break down the settled practice concerning separate schools and thereby, as indicated by experience, damnify both races."

With overt irony he pointed out that the state had offered to provide the Negro petitioner—"if perchance that is the thing really desired"—with legal education in a neighboring state which was a "fair effort" to solve a difficult problem. "The State," he added, "should not be unduly hampered through theorization inadequately restrained by experience."

The decision of the Chief Justice, while it did not directly challenge the formula of "separate but equal" facilities, a formula more frequently honored in the breach than in the observance, at least constituted an attempt to breathe substance into the formula. But what can be said of the opinion of the dissenting Justices of the Supreme Court of the nation who, in language reminiscent of the Dred Scott decision, dismissed a demand for equality in facilities provided by public funds as based on "theorization inadequately restrained by experience" and equality itself, the denial of which is totally alien to elementary principles of ethnology, democracy and social justice, as calculated to "damnify both races"?

A case which presented a similar issue in different legal form, however, was that of *Mitchell* v. *United States*.[18] Mitchell, a Negro Congressman, having paid a railway company a first-class fare for the trip from Chicago to Hot Springs, Arkansas, and having offered to pay the charge for an available seat in the Pullman car for the trip from Memphis, Tennessee, to Hot Springs, was nevertheless compelled upon reaching Arkansas to leave the first-class car and ride in a second-class car which did not provide many of the conveniences afforded first-class passengers. This was done in purported compliance with an Arkansas statute requiring segregation of colored from white persons. Mitchell filed a complaint with the Interstate Commerce Commission alleging an unjust discrimination in violation of the Interstate Commerce Act.

Chief Justice Hughes, writing for a unanimous Court, said that the issue raised no question in regard to segregation but only in regard to equality of treatment which pertained to individuals and not to races. The Interstate Commerce Act, he pointed out, explicitly made it unlawful for any common carrier under the Act "to subject any particular person . . . to any undue or unreasonable prejudice or disadvantage in any respect whatsoever." The discrimination shown in this case "was palpably unjust and forbidden by the Act." But he was not content to rest the decision on legislative grounds alone. With specific reference to *McCabe* v. *Atchison, T.&S.F.R.R.*[19] and *Missouri ex rel. Gaines* v. *Canada*, in both of which he had written the opinion of the Court, he asserted that denial of equality of accommodations because of race "would be an invasion of a fundamental individual right which is guaranteed against state action by the Fourteenth Amendment" and added that "in view of the nature of the right and of our constitutional policy it cannot be maintained that the discrimination as it was alleged was not essentially unjust."

The very last comment of the Chief Justice appears to intimate that discrimination of the type here involved if attempted under federal law would be found to violate the federal Constitution. Since no equal protection clause limits federal action reference is presumably intended to the due process clause of the Fifth Amendment.

Summary Statement

Generally speaking, the action of the Supreme Court, with respect to legislation of certain of the states, reveals the Court in the position of safeguarding the Negro against the intense bias and discrimination that characterize the attitude of many Southern legislators determined to maintain the Negro in a position of inferiority and servility. In this regard, at least among those who regard discrimination based upon color as odious, judicial review finds strong social justification. That is not to say that the record of the Court with respect to acts of the states is not without its shortcomings. As already shown, it emasculated the privileges and immunities clause principally designed as protection to Negroes, and limited the applicability of the Fourteenth Amendment to the action of states. It may be said, furthermore, that in its formulation and adherence to the doctrine accepting segregation in the use of state facilities, the Court placed a restricted scope on the meaning of the equal protection clause of the Fourteenth Amendment and lent its moral support to the process of branding Negroes with the badge of inferiority. Its insistence that facilities must be equal though segregated was hardly an adequate equivalent, for, practically speaking, there will be no equality unless segregation is ended. Commenting on the theory and practice involved, the President's Committee on Civil Rights recently said,

Theoretically this system simply duplicates educational, recreational and other public services, according facilities to the two races which are "separate but equal." In the Committee's opinion this is one of the outstanding myths of American history for it is almost always true that while indeed separate, these facilities are far from equal. Throughout the segregated public institutions, Negroes have been denied an equal share of tax supported services and facilities.[20]

It is heartening to observe, however, that the Supreme Court, shortly before this book went to press, took a long step forward, in a trio of cases decided June 5, 1950, in dooming segregation. One of the decisions was "largely controlled by that in the MITCHELL case," above, and requires no additional comment.[21] In the second [22] a unanimous Court ruled that to admit a Negro to a state graduate school at the University of Oklahoma but require him to sit in a classroom in a row specified for colored students, and to use only a designated table in the library and the cafeteria, "impair and inhibit his ability to study, to engage in discussions and exchange views with other students, and, in general, to learn his profession," and concluded that "state-imposed restrictions which produce such inequalities cannot be sustained." Finally, the entire Court concurred in holding that to bar a Negro from admission to the University of Texas Law School and require him to attend, if at all, a newly created law school for Negroes which was inferior in number of faculty, variety of courses, opportunity for specialization, size of student body, availability of law review and similar activities, and other "qualities which are incapable of objective measurement but make for greatness in a law school," and for success at the bar, did not afford him "substantially equal" education.[23]

The Court, to be sure, did not go so far as to accept the argument, which had been urged by the Attorney General of the United States, that "separate" facilities could not be made to conform with the "equal" protection clause because, *inter alia*, the very practice of segregation is intended "to signify that each member of the colored race is not equal to any member of the white race." [24] And the Court specifically refused the invitation to overrule its 1896 precedent of *Plessy* v. *Ferguson*. Nevertheless, given the criteria the Court set up, in relation not only to physical facilities but to such intangibles as prestige, reputation, personal contacts, etc., it is doubtful whether any segregated school will hereafter be able to meet the requirement of equality under the Fourteenth Amendment.

CHAPTER 14

PRIVATE CONTRACTS, THE CONTRACT CLAUSE AND THE POLICE POWER

GENESIS OF DOCTRINE

The decision of Chief Justice Hughes in *Home Building and Loan Ass'n* v. *Blaisdell*,[1] written in 1934, which sustained the constitutional validity of the Minnesota Mortgage Moratorium Law, is unquestionably one of the great constitutional landmarks the importance and implications of which have probably not been fully appreciated despite voluminous comment.[2]

An understanding of the true significance of the decision in this case requires some reference back to the intentions of the Framers and the earlier decisions of the Court. Whatever doubt may have existed as to whether the limitation contained in Article 1, Section 10, which debars the states from passing any "law impairing the obligation of contracts" was intended by the constitutional Fathers to curb the exercise of state power affecting its own contracts, that is, public contracts, there is no doubt that it was intended as a curb upon state power affecting private contracts.[3]

It is true that the actual proceedings and debates of the Constitutional Convention shed little light on the meaning and scope attached to the obligation of contracts clause. No mention of any desire to secure contracts against impairment by state legislatures was made at the Convention until three months had passed and then only briefly and inconclusively.[4] But, two weeks later, such a clause appeared in the report of the Committee on Style and was accepted without discussion or debate.[5]

It is clear, however, that among the principal causes of dissatisfaction on the part of the propertied and commercial classes, who largely dominated the proceedings of the Constitutional Convention, with the Articles of Confederation were the variety of measures passed by state legislatures to relieve the burden of necessitous debtors. These measures took the form of inflationary paper money laws, stay laws, which permitted postponement of the repayment of debts or extended the period for the redemption of property beyond that fixed by the terms of the mortgage contract or by pre-existing law, laws permitting repayment of debts in installments when no such provision was made in the contract, laws permitting repayment of debts with commodities instead of money, and bankruptcy laws.[6]

The great concern of the creditor class with debtor relief legislation found expression in the enactment of Congress under the Articles of Confederation, even after the Convention had assembled, of the Ordinance for the Northwest Territory, providing "that no law ought ever to be made or have force in the said territory, that shall, in any manner whatever, interfere with or affect private contracts, or engagements *bona fide*, and without fraud previously formed." [7]

The opposition to currency inflation met general support at the Convention and was embodied in specific provisions forbidding the states to emit bills of credit, coin money, or make anything but gold or silver legal tender.[8] The intention to bar all other devices to relieve debtors, except bankruptcy, was written into the contract clause.[9]

The *Federalist*, written in support of the new Constitution during the contest over ratification, probably accurately reflects the dominant view among the Framers that the contract clause was essential to protect creditors against the denigration of their contract rights within states and to moderate hostility between states. Thus Madison wrote: "Laws impairing the obligation of contracts, are contrary to the first principles of the social compact, and to every principle of sound legislation. . . . Some thorough reform is wanting, which will banish speculations on public measures, inspire a general prudence and industry, and give a regular course to the business of society." [10]

And Hamilton, in arguing that the states would have many inducements, if disunited, to make war upon one another, regarded "laws in violation of private contracts" as one source of danger because of the "disposition to retaliation," as in the instance of Connecticut, "in consequence of the enormities perpetrated by the Legislature of Rhode Island." [11]

The conclusion that may, I believe, rightly be drawn from the foregoing is that while the contract clause excited relatively little debate either in the Convention or in the process of ratification, it was clearly designed to inhibit state interference, in any substantial degree, with private contracts and prevent, *inter alia*, the passage of stay or moratoria laws adverse to the rights and remedies of creditors under contracts and preexisting laws. That, in any event, is the conclusion of an authority who has made an exhaustive study of the available material. He states that "there is reason to believe that the contract clause was intended to prevent the enactment of statutes which would make private contractual obligations of less value, or in some way postpone the necessity for their payment." [12]

It was not until Mr. Taney became Chief Justice, however, that the Supreme Court had occasion to pass upon the validity of legislation of a type clearly intended to be proscribed by the contract clause. The hope that the Taney Court, 1835–1864, reflecting the triumph of Jacksonian democracy, would prove sympathetic to state legislation designed to relieve the plight of debtors proved ephemeral.

In 1843, in the classic case of *Bronson* v. *Kinzie*,[13] Chief Justice Taney declared invalid two laws designed to aid mortgage debtors. The first gave mortgagors the right to redeem mortgaged premises sold by decree of the court within twelve months from the date of sale by repaying the principal debt with interest at the rate of 10 per cent. The other provided that property should not be offered for sale upon execution unless two-thirds of its value should be bid for the property. Such laws as applied to mortgage debts contracted before their passage were invalid, said the Chief Justice. The first, he maintained, gave the mortgagor an equitable estate in the premises in conflict with the interest the mortgagee had acquired when the mortgage contract was made, and the second deprived the mortgagee of his preexisting rights in regard to foreclosure. While, he said, "Whatever belongs merely to the remedy may be altered according to the will of the state," that is true "provided the alteration does not impair the obligation of the contract. But if that effect is produced, it is immaterial whether it is done by acting on the remedy or directly on the contract itself. In either case it is prohibited by the Constitution." [14]

The decision in the BRONSON case was reaffirmed the following year in *McCracken* v. *Hayward*.[15] Speaking for the Court, Justice Baldwin then stated that "any law, which in its operation amounts to a denial or obstruction of the rights accruing by a contract, though professing to act only on the remedy, is directly obnoxious to the prohibition of the Constitution." [16]

In essence these cases established the principle that any change in remedy after a contract was made which substantially impaired the preexisting rights of the creditor constituted as to him an impairment of the obligation of the contract and was therefore invalid.[17]

Later decisions of the Supreme Court repeatedly invoked the principle of the BRONSON case, under a variety of circumstances.[18] In *Edwards* v. *Kearzey*, for example, the Court flatly declared that "stay laws are void, because they are in conflict with the national Constitution."

The one important exception to the uniformity with which the Court struck down any change in law directly and substantially impairing rights given by contract, and the law in effect when the contract was executed, occurred in a series of cases affecting the lessor-lessee relationship as distinguished from the creditor-debtor relationship. During the period of scarcity of housing facilities following the first world war, federal legislation (governing the District of Columbia) and state legislation were enacted, declaring that a public emergency existed and depriving the owners of certain dwellings, for a stated period, of all possessory remedies without regard to the term of preexisting contracts of lease. This was made subject to the requirement that tenants continue paying reasonable rentals. The claims that the federal act violated due process and that the state legislation in addition constituted an impairment of the obligation of contracts were rejected by the Supreme Court by the narrow margin of a single vote.[19]

THE MINNESOTA MORTGAGE MORATORIUM ACT

Such then was the historic development of doctrine when in 1933 the State of Minnesota passed a Mortgage Moratorium Act. The Act was directly induced by the critical position of agriculture in the catastrophic depression which began at the end of 1929. By 1932, gross farm income throughout the nation had dropped from $12,000,000,000 to $5,300,000,000.[20] Agriculture suffered more intensely than industry because of the relative flexibility of its prices so that while its production declined only 6 per cent its prices fell 63 per cent.[21]

The specific situation which prevailed in Minnesota is presented in a law review article by William L. Prosser, who suggested the constitutional theory to support proposed moratoria legislation. He states that

approximately one-half of the land in the State was subject to mortgages; the greater part of which had been incurred when the general price level was about twice, and the level of farm prices nearly four times, as high as at the close of 1932. The increase in the value of the dollar, together with the almost complete collapse of farm prices, which had fallen below the cost of production, made it inevitable that these mortgages should be in default when payment fell due. The result was a constantly mounting wave of foreclosures and forced sales, which flooded the market and drove land values abruptly down. . . . It was apparent that a substantial number of land-owners of the State were confronted with the loss of their homes and their only means of support. In isolated instances mobs of farmers took the law into their own hands and prevented foreclosure sales by force. . . . When the legislature assembled, a caravan of two or three thousand farmers descended upon St. Paul . . . making demands and threats and uttering dire predictions.

Thereafter the governor threatened to invoke martial law in aid of the farmers and actually issued an executive order directing all sheriffs to refrain from conducting foreclosure sales until after the legislative session.[22]

It was under these circumstances that in April of 1933 the State of Minnesota passed a Mortgage Moratorium Act by the terms of which, during the emergency declared to exist but in *no event beyond May 1, 1935*, foreclosures of mortgages and execution sales thereunder might be postponed and periods of redemption extended "for such additional time as the court may deem just and equitable." This result could only be effected, however, *upon application to the court*, on notice, for an order determining the reasonable value of the income, or, if it produced no income, then the reasonable rental value of the property, and directing the mortgagor, while he continued in possession, to pay all or a reasonable part of such income or rental value toward meeting the taxes, insurance, interest and principal "at such times and in such manner" as the court determined.

The constitutionality of this statute was sustained by the margin of a single vote in a decision written by Chief Justice Hughes with the concurrence of Justices Brandeis, Stone, Roberts and Cardozo. Justices Van Devanter, McReynolds and Butler joined in the dissenting opinion of Justice Sutherland. The point of departure of the Chief Justice was his emphasis upon the "temporary and conditional" nature of the relief granted under the statute. The decision then continued with a discussion of the effect of emergency upon constitutional power, the historic meaning and scope attached to the contract clause limitation, and the course of judicial interpretation in regard to the distinction between remedy and obligation of contracts and the police power of the states.

What is the relation, asked the Chief Justice, of emergency to constitutional power. "Emergency," he stated,

does not create power. Emergency does not increase granted power or remove or diminish the restriction upon power granted or reserved. The Constitution was adopted in a period of grave emergency. Its grants of power to the Federal Government and its limitations of the power of the States were determined in the light of emergency and they are not altered by emergency.

Having stated this proposition, which the dissenting minority found unexceptional, he proceeded,

While emergency does not create power, emergency may furnish the occasion for the exercise of power. . . . The constitutional question presented in the light of an emergency is whether the power possessed embraces the particular exercise of it in response to particular conditions. Thus, the war power of the Federal Government is not created by the emergency of war, but it is a power given to meet that emergency.

Some prohibitions, to be sure, are "specific" and "particularized" in nature, not affected by emergency—for example, states are limited to two Senators in Congress and are forbidden to coin money or to make anything but gold and silver legal tender. But the contract limitation is set forth in a "general" clause which affords only a "broad outline" and makes construction "to fill in the details" essential.

While the Chief Justice does not unequivocally say so, the essential point apparently made is that while some limitations on state power are absolute in nature, unaffected by emergency, the contract clause is not and may be affected by emergency.

Justice Sutherland had little difficulty in revealing the logical inadequacy of the peculiarly contradictory reasoning of the Chief Justice in regard to emergency power. He stated,

> The opinion concedes that emergency does not create power, or increase granted power, or remove or diminish restrictions upon power granted or reserved. It then proceeds to say, however, that while emergency does not create power, it may furnish the occasion for the exercise of power. I can only interpret what is said on that subject as meaning that while an emergency does not diminish a restriction upon power it furnishes an occasion for diminishing it; and this, as it seems to me, is merely to say the same thing by the use of another set of words, with the effect of affirming that which has just been denied.[23]

The analogy drawn by the Chief Justice between the emergency war powers of the nation and those that states might exercise under their police powers was also summarily dealt with by Justice Sutherland who pointed out that the Constitution contemplated that emergency would furnish the occasion for the exercise of war powers, "since they cannot be exercised upon any other occasion." But in dealing with the state police power, as distinguished from a granted power, the question is

> whether an emergency furnishes an occasion for the relaxation of the restrictions upon the power imposed by the contract impairment clause; and the difficulty is that the contract impairment clause forbids state action under any circumstances, if it have the effect of impairing the obligation of contracts.

The Chief Justice, having suggested that emergency might justify the exercise of state power notwithstanding the contract clause, faced the difficult problem of reconciling this doctrine with the fact that the contract clause was itself a product of emergency intended by the Framers to prohibit legislation of the precise character in issue. He agreed, he said, that "the reasons which led to the adoption of that clause . . . are not left in doubt." He described the motivating situation as follows:

The widespread distress following the revolutionary period and the plight of debtors had called forth in the States an ignoble array of legislative schemes for the defeat of creditors and the invasion of contractual obligations. Legislative interferences had been so numerous and extreme that the confidence essential to prosperous trade had been undermined and the utter destruction of credit was threatened.

But, continued the Chief Justice, "full recognition of the occasion and the general purpose of the clause does not suffice to fix its precise scope." That scope, he said, was fixed by "the course of judicial decisions in its application." This, of course, does not quite amount to saying that the original intention of the Framers must be subordinated to judicial interpretation inconsistent with that intention. At a later point, however, Chief Justice Hughes came close to saying so when he wrote that it may not be insisted that

what the provision of the Constitution meant to the vision of that day it must mean to the vision of our time. If by the statement that what the Constitution meant at the time of its adoption it means to-day, it is intended to say that the great clauses of the constitution must be confined to the interpretation which the framers, with the conditions and outlook of their time, would have placed upon them, the statement carries its own refutation.

Justice Sutherland, in dissenting, found it difficult to reconcile these statements of the Chief Justice. There could be no mistaking the intention of the Framers, he insisted.

A candid consideration of the history and circumstances which led up to and accompanied the framing and adoption of this clause will demonstrate conclusively that it was framed and adopted with the specific and studied purpose of preventing legislation designed to relieve debtors *especially* in time of financial distress.[24]

How, then, he questioned, could it be said that the clause admits of an opposite interpretation? It cannot be urged, he contended, that "conditions which produced the rule may now be invoked to destroy it."

But assuming that the intention of the Framers must yield to interpretations of the Court, what support could the Chief Justice in fact derive from the "course of judicial decisions"? That support, he purported to find, in the first instance, in the decisions of the Court which had recognized the authority of the state to modify the remedy provided no substantial rights secured by the contract were thereby impaired. And no substantial impairment was effected in this instance, he wrote, because of the "temporary and conditional" nature of the relief granted. "The statute," he said, "does not impair the integrity of the mortgage indebtedness. The obligation for interest remains." If the mortgagor fails to redeem within the extended period "the validity of the sale or the right of the mortgagee-purchaser to title in fee, or his right to obtain a deficiency judgment" are not affected. And, he added, "While the mortgagee-purchaser is debarred from actual possession he has, so far as rental value is concerned, the equivalent of possession."

On this basis, he insisted, was it possible to distinguish the BRONSON from the present case, because in the former, "extension of the period of redemption was unconditional, and there was no provision, as in the instant case, to secure the mortgagee the rental value of the property during the extended period."

The implication that relief being temporary and conditional and involving the payment of rental value it could therefore not be deemed to constitute a *substantial* impairment of rights formerly secured by the contract was effectively dealt with by Justice Sutherland. Assuming, he said, that a statute extending the period of redemption may be upheld if something of commensurate value be given the creditor, the conclusion that that was done in this instance "is purely gratuitous." He then pointed out that the effect of the statute was to extend the period of redemption absolutely for a period of sixteen days [25] and conditionally for a period of two years. For that entire period the creditor was deprived of ownership and all its attributes which included the rights to occupy, sell, or rent the property to whomsoever he pleased. In essence, maintained Justice Sutherland, the statute, therefore, simply allowed the creditor to retain a small part of what he might otherwise have enjoyed, that is, the rental value of the property, but only on condition that he give up the rest, the other attributes of ownership. This, in the view of Justice Sutherland, which would appear to be supported by common sense, affected a "material and injurious change in the obligation," and could not be dismissed as insubstantial even if temporary and conditional. [26]

Justice Sutherland might, with justice, have added that the significance attached by Chief Justice Hughes to the *temporary* nature of the relief as a basis for constitutionality was unwarranted for yet another reason. The Court has always retained its prerogative of nullifying legislation previously sustained as justified by emergency when in its judgment the emergency has ended. Thus, Justice Holmes, who had delivered the opinion for the Court sustaining constitutionality in the two primary housing cases, wrote in 1924 that "a law depending upon the existence of an emergency or other certain state of facts to uphold it may cease to operate if the emergency ceases or the facts change, even though valid when passed." [27]

Dictated, perhaps, in part, by an awareness of the tenuousness of resting his decision on the ground that the contract clause is "qualified by the measure of control the State retains over remedial processes," the Chief Justice sought a more substantial basis for his decision. He found that basis in the police power of the state and asserted that "the State also continues to possess authority to safeguard the vital interests of its people" even if it " 'has the result of modifying or abrogating contracts already in effect.' " He continued,

Not only are existing laws read into contracts as a postulate of the legal order, but the reservation of essential attributes of sovereign power is also read into contracts as a postulate of the legal order. The policy of protecting contracts against impairment presupposes the maintenance of a government by virtue of which contractual relations are worth while, —a government which retains adequate authority to secure the peace and good order of society.

This principle, he maintained, had won progressive recognition in the decisions of the Court, and he cited in support a whole series of cases in which legislation forbidding a lottery, controlling the sale of intoxicating liquors, protecting public health and safety, regulating utility rates and promoting important economic interests, had been sustained as constitutional exercises of police power notwithstanding their interference with contracts. And, he inquired, if state power existed to afford temporary relief from the strict enforcement of contracts in the presence of physical causes such as fire or flood, how can it be said to be absent when "the urgent public need demanding such relief is produced by other and economic causes"?

The reply offered by Justice Sutherland to the general police power argument was that the Chief Justice was confusing two essentially different things. It was true, he said, that a state, by virtue of its reserved power, might protect public welfare although its action might have the *indirect effect* of absolutely destroying private contracts previously made in contemplation of a continuance of legality. That involved, however, not appropriation of the contract but frustration and was a very different thing, he argued, from the situation, as in this case, in which the contract was legal when made and continued legal and might be fully executed as made, but by action of the state and at the option of one of the parties might be postponed in regard to enforcement.

The Chief Justice, in turn, denied the pertinence of the distinction relating to indirect effect. "The question," he said, "is not whether the legislative action affects contracts incidentally, or directly or indirectly, but whether the legislation is addressed to a legitimate end and the measures taken are reasonable and appropriate to that end."

Only as the argument neared its end did the Chief Justice produce the major weapon in his arsenal. Whatever doubt, he said, might have existed as to the power of the state to directly prevent the immediate and literal enforcement of contractual obligations, by a temporary and conditional restraint, was removed by the decisions in the housing cases which upheld legislation depriving landlords of possessory remedies for a period of years even after leases had expired provided the tenants continued payment of reasonable rentals. In the housing cases, the Chief Justice pointed out, as here, the relief given had been justified by emergency conditions, had been temporary and had been conditioned upon reasonable compensation to the landlord during the period he was prevented from regaining possession.

Justice Sutherland was hard put to it to find a suitable reply to this phase of the Chief Justice's argument. These cases, he said, had dealt with "an exigent situation due to a period of scarcity of housing caused by war," had later been characterized by the writer of the opinions in the first two cases as having gone "to the verge of the law," and concluded that decisions which narrowly escaped unconstitutionality "should be applied toward the solution of a doubtful question arising in a different field with a very high degree of caution." This is hardly in the nature of a satisfactory answer since to accept the housing legislation as warranted by "an exigent situation" would conflict with the tenor of his argument that emergency did not justify any substantial impairment of contract rights. What he might have said with better reason was that the nature of the emergency in the BLAISDELL case was precisely of the type that the Framers had sought to protect against in the adoption of the contract clause while that in the housing cases was unknown to the Framers and presumably not within their contemplation.

Notwithstanding that fact, there is little room for doubt that the housing cases were in conflict with the principles established in the BRONSON case and offered substantial support for the decision of Chief Justice Hughes in the BLAISDELL case. Had he chosen to predicate his decision on that basis without seeking both to reconcile it with and distinguish it from the BRONSON case there would have been little opportunity for objection. He sought, however, to give a broad constitutional foundation to the exercise of police power in derogation of contract rights. This he made palpably clear by some of his statements defining what he conceived to be the course of the decisions of the Court and the reasons that had impelled them. "It is manifest from . . . our decisions," he wrote, "that there has been a growing appreciation of public needs and of the necessity of finding ground for a rational compromise between individual rights and public welfare." He continued,

The settlement and consequent contraction of the public domain, the pressure of a constantly increasing density of population, the interrelation of the activities of our people and the complexity of our economic interests, have inevitably led to an increased use of the organization of society in order to protect the very bases of individual opportunity. Where, in earlier days, it was thought that only the concerns of individuals or of classes were involved, and that those of the State itself were touched only remotely, it has later been found that the fundamental interests of the State are directly affected; and that the question is no longer merely that of one party to a contract as against another, but of the use of reasonable means to safeguard the economic structure upon which the good of all depends.

The ultimate meaning of the "principle of this development," he concluded, "is . . . that the reservation of the reasonable exercise of the protective power of the State is read into all contracts."

If one discards some of the circuity and ambiguity of the reasoning of the Chief Justice, the BLAISDELL case appears to establish the proposition that the test of constitutionality in contract impairment cases is substantially identical with that of due process, in a word, reasonableness. It will be recalled, in this connection, that the Chief Justice, in language plainly borrowed from due process cases, said, "The question is not whether the legislative action affects contracts incidentally, or directly or indirectly, but whether the legislation is addressed to a legitimate end and the measures taken are reasonable and appropriate to that end." [28]

While the essential test is thus made the same as in due process cases, it should be added that the existence of private contracts, whose literal enforcement may be interfered with by the legislation, is presumably one of the factors to be weighed by the Court in determining reasonableness. And this would appear to apply also to the factors of emergency and the nature of the safeguards and limitations written into the legislation. Thus, an emergency may make the derogation of contract obligations appear reasonable to the Court when otherwise they might seem arbitrary. And a statute carefully drawn, as clearly was true in this instance, limiting the duration of interference with contract rights and providing some measure of compensation to the creditor will, on a balance of private and public interest, have a greater chance to survive the test of reasonableness.

There is, however, presumably another factor to be given consideration in determining reasonableness. In justifying the use of the police power in denigration of contract rights, Chief Justice Hughes, it will be remembered, said that "the policy of protecting contracts against impairment presupposes the maintenance of a government by virtue of which contractual relations are worthwhile,—a government which retains adequate authority to secure the peace and good order of society."

Doubtless this statement was made with reference to the violence and lawlessness evoked by widespread foreclosures of farm properties before the passage of the Minnesota statute. Whatever its inspiration, if it means what it seems to say, it announces a doctrine of stark and startling simplicity and importance for it suggests that limitations of the Constitution may be put aside provided only that to enforce them would bring such a degree of violence and lawlessness as to place in jeopardy the authority of government to maintain peace and good order. This doctrine would appear to bring into our system of government, under and presumably limited by a written Constitution, the theory, theretofore thought to be attached only to uncontrolled sovereign powers, that the first law of the state is survival.

The test of reasonableness, to be sure, when viewed in the light of the intention of the Framers and the BRONSON and related cases, substantially altered the nature of the judicial inquiry in contract cases. This development was inevitable, in a sense, if the Court was to continue to preserve the fiction that the Constitution as written is adequate to all the exigencies of governing. The dilemma of the Court was either to affirm that it had no authority to amend the Constitution in the guise of interpretation and deny relief sorely needed and socially warranted, or to rationalize "a constitutional limitation to subserve what it deems the requirements of an increasingly complex economic structure." [29] It preferred the latter course. However much one may approve the immediate effects of the decision, it is pertinent to inquire whether an easier and more desirable method of amending the Constitution should not be found than one which either depends upon Article V of the Constitution which is virtually inoperable when an important economic minority is adversely affected, or, which depends upon the consent of a majority of nine non-elected Justices.

The optimism engendered for the successful weathering of constitutionality by the New Deal program as a result of the apparent willingness of the Court to ascribe reasonableness to legislation designed to cope with the problems of economic crisis was understandable. Thus Professor Corwin commented that "the emergency concept is important as illustrating the inherent ability of governmental power under the Constitution to expand to meet new necessities. . . . It is not unreasonable to think that the BLAISDELL decision has broad significance, particularly for the New Deal." [30] "As it stands," wrote T. R. B. from Washington, "the decision has created the popular impression that the Supreme Court sees no unconstitutionality in the Roosevelt program." [31]

This optimistic view was further encouraged by the decision in the same year of the Court in the NEBBIA case which discarded the concept of "affected with a public interest" as a principle of limitation and similarly made reasonableness the criterion of constitutionality. This optimism, however, took insufficient account of the fact that reasonableness, on a balance of public interest and private right, involved the subjective judgment of nine fallible human beings.

Little more than four months after the decision in the BLAISDELL case the meaning and scope of that decision were redefined and limited. In *W. B. Worthen Co.* v. *Thomas* [32] the Court was dealing with a law of Arkansas which provided that life, accident, sickness and disability insurance should be exempt from liability or seizure under judicial process. Chief Justice Hughes, for a unanimous Court, held the exemption, as applied in the case of debts owing before its creation, an unconstitutional impairment of the obligation of contracts.

Defining the meaning of the Court's decision in the BLAISDELL case, the Chief Justice said that it had avowed that the contract clause "did not make it impossible for the State, in the exercise of its essential reserved power, to protect the vital interests of its people." But, he added, that case had also held that the essential reserved power of the state must be construed in harmony with the fair intent of the constitutional limitation.

The Chief Justice pointed out that the exemption in this case, unlike that in the BLAISDELL case, was permanent and unconditional, made no discrimination on the basis of need, and would enable debtors who invested the profits of a business in insurance to withdraw them from the pursuit of creditors to whatever extent desired. The argument that the state might alter the forms of remedy was rejected, as retroactively applied, because the statute altered "substantial rights." Similarly, the Chief Justice dismissed the contention that the exemption was justified by the emergency which the legislature found to exist because "the legislation was not limited to the emergency and set up no conditions apposite to emergency relief."

Justice Sutherland regarded the decision as a vindication of the position he had taken in the BLAISDELL case and with the concurrence of the same Justices who had joined in his quondam dissent he now concurred in a separate opinion. While agreeing "unreservedly" in the judgment of the Court, he was unable to agree, wrote Justice Sutherland, that the differences between the Minnesota and Arkansas statutes were material, and he added,

We were unable then, as we are now, to concur in the view that an emergency can ever justify, or what is really the same thing, can ever furnish an occasion for justifying, a nullification of the constitutional restriction upon state power in respect of the impairment of contractual obligations. . . . We reject as unsound and dangerous doctrine, threatening the stability of the deliberately framed and wise provisions of the Constitution, the notion that violations of those provisions may be measured by the length of time they are to continue or the extent of the infraction. . . . The power of this court is not to amend but only to expound the Constitution.

In April, 1935, the Court again found occasion to distinguish the BLAISDELL decision. In *W. B. Worthen Co.* v. *Kavanaugh* [33] Justice Cardozo, with the agreement of the entire Court, invalidated an Arkansas statute which modified the procedure relative to defaulted mortgage obligations given to secure payment of improvement benefit assessments. In addition to omitting costs and attorney's fees and reducing the penalty, the statute substantially extended the period of possession of a delinquent owner from a minimum of sixty-five days to six and one-half years during which period no effective means was provided the mortgagee to enforce payment of principal or interest.

Justice Cardozo characterized the statute as reflecting "studied indifference" to the interests of the mortgagee. Refuting arguments based on the BLAISDELL case, he pointed out that the relief granted was neither temporary nor conditioned upon payment of interest, taxes, rental value or even the inability of the debtor to pay, and said, "Not even changes of the remedy may be pressed so far as to cut down the security of a mortgage without moderation or reason or in a spirit of oppression. Even when the public welfare is invoked as an excuse, these bounds must be respected."

One other case in which the BLAISDELL decision was mentioned remains to be discussed. In *Richmond Mortgage and Loan Corp.* v. *Wachovia Bank and Trust Co.*[34] the Court, unanimously, per Mr. Justice Roberts, upheld as constitutional a North Carolina statute which provided that, when a mortgagee became the purchaser of foreclosed property for a sum less than the amount of the debt, the mortgagor might show, in defense or offset, the fair worth of the property and thereby defeat or reduce the recovery.

Since this legislation was not emergency in nature, the principle of the BLAISDELL case was not directly applicable. The decision turned instead upon the distinction between an alteration of remedy and obligation. Important, too, was the fact that the law tended merely to make the procedure conform, in effect, to that prevailing under equitable foreclosure. In sustaining the act, the Court said, "The contract contemplated that the lender should make itself whole, if necessary, out of the security, but not that it should be enriched at the expense of the borrower or realize more than would repay the loan with interest."

This decision was reaffirmed by the Court in an opinion by Chief Justice Hughes in *Honeyman* v. *Jacobs* [35] sustaining the validity of a New York Act that provided that a mortgagee of real estate should be denied a deficiency judgment in a foreclosure suit when the state court found that the value of the property purchased by the mortgagee at the foreclosure sale was equal in value to the debt secured by the mortgage.

In the light of the later decisions of the Court applying and limiting the principles of the BLAISDELL case, what may be said with regard to the meaning and scope of that decision? Fundamentally, its far-reaching significance, never repudiated, lay in the establishment of the general principle that the "reasonable" exercise of the police power of the state in the public interest will be sustained even when it has the effect of *directly* impairing private contractual obligations. Legislation has a better chance of surviving the test of reasonableness, however, if it meets the following criteria: (1) it does not go so far in impairing substantive rights under the contract as to evoke the conviction of the Court that eminent domain and just compensation are requisite; [36] (2) it is limited to the period of emergency when called forth by emergency; (3) it makes relief contingent upon payment of rental value or other consideration reasonably equivalent to the possessory value, and, contrariwise, it refrains from oppression and a studied indifference to the rights of the creditors; (4) it differentiates among debtors on the basis of need; (5) it gives to courts control over the procedures and some discretion in relation to the differing circumstances of each case.

CHAPTER 15

THE FEDERAL SYSTEM: TAX IMMUNITY OF GOVERNMENTAL INSTRUMENTALITIES

THE NATURE OF THE PROBLEM AND THE GENESIS OF DOCTRINE

Our federal Constitution, giving recognition to historic associations and loyalties, established a system of dual sovereignty. Under that charter powers were distributed and limited. Within that scheme it has been recognized that certain powers essential to the existence of both federal and state governments might be concurrently exercised by both and this has included the power to tax. With two governments exercising the same power over the same persons within the confines of the same territory conflicts were bound to arise. One of the areas of most acute and persistent conflict has related to the power of one government to tax the instrumentalities of the other.

In *McCulloch* v. *Maryland* [1] Chief Justice Marshall laid down the proposition that the nature of the federal system and the supremacy of federal law *constitutionally* divested the states of the right to tax "the means employed by the government of the Union, for the execution of its powers." The right, he said, "never existed, and the question whether it has been surrendered cannot arise." Its exercise constituted a "usurpation of power." The power to tax, he added, "involves the power to destroy," incompatible with the power of the federal government to create instrumentalities to effectuate its delegated powers. In establishing the grandiose principle of a total want of power, Marshall, of course, ruled out any consideration of the practical burden imposed by the specific tax upon the operations of a federal instrumentality.

Whether the arguments advanced in support of his decision would sustain the reciprocal immunity of state instrumentalities from taxation by the federal government, it was not necessary to decide. However, Marshall pointed out "the two cases are not on the same reason," and added,

The people of all the States have created the general government, and have conferred upon it the general power of taxation. The people of all the States, and the States themselves, are represented in Congress, and, by their representatives, exercise this power. When they tax the chartered institutions of the States, they tax their constituents; and these taxes must be uniform. But, when a State taxes the operations of the government of the United States, it acts upon institutions created, not by their own constituents, but by people over whom they claim no control. It acts upon the measures of a government created by others as well as themselves, for the benefit of others in common with themselves.

Notwithstanding the distinction suggested by Marshall, the Supreme Court, in 1871, in *Collector* v. *Day*,[2] extended the doctrine of immunity to exempt state instrumentalities from federal taxation. A federal income tax on the salary of a judge of a state court was barred as incompatible with the sovereignty and self-preservation of the state.

In time, as Mr. Justice Frankfurter pointed out, the principle established by these decisions, and extended by later decisions, "withdrew from the taxing power of the States and Nation a very considerable range of wealth without regard to the actual workings of our federalism, and this, too, when the financial needs of all governments began steadily to mount." [3]

The difficult, tortuous process by which the doctrine of immunity came to be drastically reshaped was largely the product of the Court presided over by Chief Justice Hughes, although earlier attacks had challenged some of the force of the reasoning in the Marshall and Day opinions,[4] and Justice Holmes had sought to destroy a substantial prop of the immunity doctrine with his famous statement: "The power to tax is not the power to destroy while this Court sits." [5] The Court, too, earlier had revealed some resistance to an indiscriminate extension of this doctrine and Justice Stone had taken the lead in seeking to place the doctrine of immunity upon a pragmatic basis tested by the effect of the tax on the actual functioning of government.[6]

GOVERNMENTAL SECURITIES

A keystone of the arch of intergovernmental tax immunity has been the exemption from taxation of government securities. The theory is that such immunity is essential to induce persons to risk capital in support of the financial needs of government. With the tremendous increase in government borrowing and taxation, which were concomitant developments of the past several decades, the result was that private owners of wealth, who possessed government securities, found themselves exempted, to that extent, from the burden of supporting government common to the citizenry.

Two decisions of the Hughes Court suggested both the sweep and limitations of the immunity. In the first of these, *Missouri ex rel. Missouri Insurance Co.* v. *Gehner*,[7] a majority of the Court, in an opinion by Justice Butler, held that *ownership* of government securities might not be taxed by indirection. Accordingly, a state law taxing the assets of insurance companies was ruled unconstitutional in so far as it provided that allowable deductions should be decreased by the proportion that the value of non-taxable United States bonds bore to total assets. "A state," said Justice Butler, "may not subject one to a greater burden upon his taxable property merely because he owns tax-exempt government securities. Neither ingenuity in calculation nor form of words in state enactments can deprive the owner of the tax exemption established for the benefit of the United States." The Chief Justice concurred separately "on the ground that this case is governed by *National Life Insurance Co.* v. *United States*, 277 U.S. 508."

The minority, composed of Justices Stone, Holmes and Brandeis in an opinion by Justice Stone, dissented. Justice Stone expressed his belief that the majority opinion opened "a new and hitherto unsuspected field of operation for the immunity from taxation" enjoyed by the owners of national and state securities which had been restricted by the Court "as to relieve only from the burden of taxation imposed on such securities or their income." He did not regard the case cited by the Chief Justice as warranting a different conclusion since that case related to the exercise of power by the *national* government and was, he said, distinguishable on other counts.

It was characteristic of the Chief Justice that in upholding immunity he did so on the strength of precedent and was unwilling either to acquiesce in the reasoning of the majority which reaffirmed the sweep of the doctrine or to acquiesce in the reasoning of the minority which sought to limit that sweep.

The following year, however, Chief Justice Hughes, with the support of the entire Court, imposed an important limitation upon the immunity doctrine when, in *Willcuts* v. *Bunn*,[8] he ruled that a federal law in so far as it taxed the *profits* realized upon the sale of state or municipal bonds laid no unconstitutional burden upon the instrumentalities of states.

While recognizing the historic immunity, Chief Justice Hughes stated,

The power to tax is no less essential than the power to borrow money, and, in preserving the latter, it is not necessary to cripple the former by extending the constitutional exemption from taxation to those subjects which fall within the general application of non-discriminatory laws, and where no direct burden is laid upon the governmental instrumentality, and there is only a remote, if any, influence upon the exercise of the functions of government.

Chief Justice Hughes reasoned that because the tax on the interest of such bonds was deemed a tax on the bonds it did not follow

that the Congress cannot impose a non-discriminatory excise tax upon the profits derived from the sale of such bonds. The sale of the bonds by their owners, after they have been issued by the State or municipality, is a transaction distinct from the contracts made by the government in the bonds themselves, and the profits on such sales are in a different category of income from that of the interest payable on the bonds.

The important consideration, Chief Justice Hughes believed, was that in practice such a tax had not imposed and would not impose a substantial burden upon borrowing power.

These two decisions point up the fundamental problem presented to the Court in accommodating the demands for revenue through the taxing and borrowing powers of government. Purchasers of government securities, in the first instance, anticipate receiving interest but many, no doubt, anticipate the possibility of resale at a profit. Both presumably increase the marketability of such securities. To deprive either, therefore, of tax immunity might, in strict constitutional theory, be deemed to impose a burden upon the functioning of government. To characterize the first as direct and the second as indirect is simply to use labels to suggest that it is the degree and not the essential nature of the burden which is to be considered controlling. The fact, therefore, that income was granted immunity denied to profits suggests that the inquiry of the Court was shifting but had not yet been overtly converted from one of abstract constitutional theory to the more practical basis of measuring the extent and locus of burden.

PROPERTY OR INCOME DERIVED FROM GOVERNMENT

The extremes to which the doctrine of immunity had been carried and the retreat that was under way are well illustrated by four decisions of Chief Justice Hughes. In *Fox Film Corp.* v. *Doyal* [9] copyrights were held not to be exempt from state taxation upon the ground that such taxation imposed only an indirect burden upon a governmental instrumentality and had only a remote, if any, influence upon the exercise of functions of government. The argument that a copyright was in the nature of a franchise or privilege bestowed by the government was met with the reply that it was not "exercised on behalf of the Government or in performing a function of the Government." It is significant, too, that this was one of the few cases, decided before 1937 and the Court reorganization fight, in which the Chief Justice deemed it necessary to overrule rather than distinguish or ignore earlier incompatible precedent.

In the second, *Indian Territory Illuminating Oil Co.* v. *Board of Equalization,* [10] the Court ruled that oil produced from restricted Indian lands under lease approved by the Secretary of the Interior might be subjected to a non-discriminatory ad valorem state *property* tax under circumstances in which the Indians had been paid and the oil had been commingled with the lessee's oil from unrestricted properties. The Court distinguished this case from one in which it had upheld immunity when the Indians had not been paid and the product had not been commingled.

To this ruling, some years later, the Court added the limitation that the *income* derived from such lease was not exempt from a non-discriminatory tax upon the theory that the effect of such tax upon the Government was "indirect and remote." [11] To accomplish this result it was likewise necessary to overrule two precedents of the Court. [12]

Finally, in *James* v. *Dravo Contracting Co.* [13] Chief Justice Hughes, speaking for a narrow majority of the Court, upheld the constitutional validity of a non-discriminatory tax imposed by a state upon the gross receipts of a general contractor although made in part applicable to receipts realized under contracts with the United States for the construction of locks and dams in navigable streams. The tax, he said, did not "interfere in any substantial way with the performance of federal functions and is a valid exaction." He pointed out that the tax was not laid upon the contract itself. He distinguished between the immunity applicable to earnings from government bonds and from contracts with the government; the former, he said, involving questions of the ability of government to maintain its credit, and the latter being analogous to taxing property used by contractors in performing services which long had been exempted from immunity. He regarded the METCALF & EDDY decision as a "pivotal" decision which constituted "a definite refusal to extend the doctrine of cases relating to government securities, and to the instrumentalities of government, to earnings under contracts for labor."

Mr. Justice Roberts, for the minority, asserting that "the judgment seems to me to override, *sub silentio,* a century of precedents, and to leave the application of the rule uncertain and unpredictable," maintained that the Court had "repeatedly held that a tax nominally upon one who contracts with the government was in effect and in fact imposed upon the operations of the latter." He rejected the distinction between government bonds and contracts, reasoning that "the federal power to contract for supplies and services is as necessary and as fundamental as the power to borrow money." Nor could he see any distinction between a sales tax on goods sold to the federal government, proscribed in *Panhandle Oil Co.* v. *Mississippi,*[14] and a gross receipts tax upon the furnishing of goods and services under a contract with the government. So, too, he deemed it irrelevant that the tax was non-discriminatory and "not so burdensome as seriously to interfere with governmental functions." Since the McCULLOCH case "the court has consistently held that the question is not one of quantum, not one of the weight of the burden, but one of power." [15]

SALARIES OF GOVERNMENT EMPLOYEES

The doctrine of reciprocal immunity of federal and state instrumentalities from taxation had no more sweeping importance than in relation to the salaries of employees, federal and state, who found themselves exempted from taxation by one government or the other. The principle that supported this exemption was that these employees were necessary instrumentalities of government without which it was powerless to function, and that a tax upon their salaries laid a direct burden upon the operations of government incompatible with its sovereign authority. This principle confronted, however, the urgent demands of government for revenue at a time when governmental functions were expanding and government employees were numbered in the millions.

The relaxation of the immunity doctrine was in part made possible by reference to the distinction between governmental and non-governmental functions. This was the basis upon which, in *Helvering v. Powers,*[16] it was held that the compensation of members of a public authority, set up under state law to operate a railway company, was not constitutionally exempt from federal income tax.

Immunity, where it exists, Chief Justice Hughes stated, is predicated upon "the necessary protection of the independence of the national and state governments within their respective spheres under our constitutional system." He continued,

The principle of immunity thus has inherent limitations. And one of these limitations is that the State cannot withdraw sources of revenue from the federal taxing power by engaging in businesses which constitute a departure from usual governmental functions and to which, by reason of their nature, the federal taxing power would normally extend.

It followed that if the business itself was not immune neither was the compensation of its employees.

The federal government exercises only "governmental" functions, however, and early in 1937 the entire Court in *New York ex rel. Rogers v. Graves,*[17] with the exception of Justice Stone, who took no part in the consideration or decision of the case, acquiesced in a decision by Justice Sutherland, in which it was ruled that the Panama Railroad Company owned by the United States Government as an auxiliary to the Panama Canal was immune from state taxation as an instrumentality of the national government and that it "necessarily results that fixed salaries and compensation paid to its officers and employees in their capacity as such are likewise immune."

This decision was in effect reaffirmed when later that year, in *Brush* v. *Commissioner*,[18] Justice Sutherland again spoke for the Court in holding that the salary of the Chief Engineer of the Bureau of Water Supply of the City of New York was exempt from federal income taxation upon the ground that the "water system of the city was created and is conducted in the exercise of the city's governmental functions." [19]

As late as March, 1937, therefore, when the BRUSH case was decided, apparently the entire Court, notwithstanding some expressions relative to a possible need for revision, and the emphasis in other areas upon the "directness" of burden, was agreed in upholding the immunity of federal employees from state income taxation and of state employees from federal income taxation provided only the latter were engaged in clearly "governmental" activities.

Within little more than a year, however, the Supreme Court, in the case of *Helvering* v. *Gerhardt*,[20] struck a decisive blow at the whole doctrine of tax immunity as applied to salaries of government employees when it held that the salaries of a construction engineer and assistant general managers of the Port of New York Authority were not exempt from federal income tax. Waving aside consideration of whether or not the agency was engaged in the performance of so-called "governmental" as distinguished from "proprietary" or "corporate" functions, the majority of the Court in an opinion by Justice Stone, in which the Chief Justice concurred, based its decision upon the fact that in its view "the present tax neither precludes nor threatens unreasonably to obstruct any function essential to the continued existence of the state government."

With that single stroke, the Court rid the law of tax immunity from the frequently nebulous and confusing distinction between governmental and non-governmental functions and made the test of immunity of state instrumentalities the very narrow and practical one of obstruction of functions "essential to the continued existence of the state government," a test which the salaries of employees could not meet.

But the decision went far beyond these rulings. Justice Stone returned to an emphasis upon the political distinction between the immunity of federal instrumentalities from state taxation and of state instrumentalities from federal taxation first suggested in *McCulloch* v. *Maryland* but ignored in *Collector* v. *Day*. This distinction arises not only out of the supremacy clause, said Justice Stone, but out of the fact that

in laying a federal tax on state instrumentalities the people of the states, acting through their representatives, are laying a tax on their own institutions and consequently are subject to political restraints which can be counted on to prevent abuse. State taxation of national instrumentalities is subject to no such restraint, for the people outside the state have no representatives who participate in the legislation; and in a real sense, as to them, the taxation is without representation.

Having laid the basis for limiting state immunity in political terms, Justice Stone proceeded to define the basis for limiting federal immunity in constitutional terms. To accomplish this, he reinterpreted Marshall's decision in *McCulloch* v. *Maryland* as if the immunity of a federal instrumentality from state taxation was predicated in that case, not upon a conflict between the state law and the Constitution itself making state taxation "a usurpation of power," but upon a conflict between such law and an Act of Congress, namely,

It was held that Congress, having power to establish a bank by laws which, when enacted under the Constitution, are supreme, also had power to protect the bank by striking down state action impeding its operations; and it was thought that the state tax in question was . . . inconsistent with Congress's constitutional action in establishing the bank.

In a footnote, directly following, he added that Congress might, if it wished, curtail immunity of its instrumentalities.[21]

What Justice Stone said, however, in the GERHARDT case respecting the immunity of federal instrumentalities was in the nature of dicta. The opportunity to convert dicta into the rule of the Court came within less than a year when the Court was confronted with the question of whether the imposition by the State of New York of an income tax on the salary of an employee of the Home Owners' Loan Corporation, a federal agency, placed an unconstitutional burden upon the federal government.

Speaking for a majority of the Court in *Graves* v. *New York ex rel. O'Keefe* [22] Justice Stone gave recognition to the fact that the federal government is solely a government of delegated powers and hence "its every action within its constitutional power is governmental action." However, he maintained,

Silence of Congress implies immunity no more than does the silence of the Constitution. It follows that when exemption from state taxation is claimed on the ground that the federal government is burdened by the tax, and Congress has disclosed no intention with respect to the claimed immunity, it is in order to consider the nature and effect of the alleged burden, and if it appears that there is no ground for implying a constitutional immunity there is equally a want of any ground for assuming any purpose on the part of Congress to create an immunity.

In this case, he could find no "basis for the assumption that any such tangible or certain economic burden is imposed upon the government . . . as would justify a court's declaring that the taxpayer is clothed with the implied constitutional tax immunity of the government by which he is employed."

He specifically overruled *Collector* v. *Day* and *New York ex rel. Rogers* v. *Graves* "so far as they recognize an implied constitutional immunity from income taxation of the salaries of officers or employees of the national or a state government or their instrumentalities."

Chief Justice Hughes concurred in the result. This apparently again reflected the painful dilemma of the Chief Justice who deemed it desirable to go along with the change but found himself either disturbed by some expressions of the Court or by the necessity of overturning one very old and one very recent precedent of the Court.

Justices Butler and McReynolds dissented in reliance upon established precedent and warned that "surely it may be said that presently marked for destruction is the doctrine of reciprocal immunity that by recent decisions here has been so much impaired."

SUMMARY STATEMENT

The early Hughes Court was characterized by an unwillingness to extend the doctrine of reciprocal tax immunity beyond the scope it had already obtained and by some minor departures and fugitive expressions suggesting a need for reorientation in terms of weighing the directness and immediacy of burden. For all that as late as 1937, as exemplified in the BRUSH case, the fundamental doctrines established by the McCULLOCH, *Collector* v. *Day* and related cases remained essentially undisturbed. Although Justice Stone, as early as 1926,[23] had suggested the need for a more pragmatic basis of inquiry, and thereafter played the major role in the formulation of new doctrine severely limiting the immunity of federal and state agencies, the first significant indication of a break with the past came in the decision of the Chief Justice in the JAMES case on December 6, 1937, to be followed by sweeping and extensive revisions of doctrine.

While it is true that earlier many members of the Court displayed a growing appreciation for the revenue needs of government, it is pertinent to mention that in the interim between the reaffirmation of the primary immunity doctrines and decision in the later cases, the criticism of the Court had reached its apogee and had led to the attempt to reorganize the Court. By December, 1937, too, there had been a change in the personnel of the Court and by the time of the GERHARDT and O'KEEFE decisions changes in personnel had been extensive.

In a concurring opinion in the second of these cases Mr. Justice Frankfurter took the occasion to say,

The judicial history of this doctrine of immunity is a striking illustration of an occasional tendency to encrust unwarranted interpretations upon the Constitution and thereafter to consider merely what has been judicially said about the Constitution, rather than to be primarily controlled by a fair conception of the Constitution. Judicial exegesis is unavoidable with reference to an organic act like our Constitution, drawn in many particulars with purposed vagueness so as to leave room for the unfolding future. But the ultimate touchstone of constitutionality is the Constitution itself and not what we have said about it.[24]

It would be difficult to deny that the history of the developments in regard to the doctrine of reciprocal tax immunity affords a particularly good illustration of complications and logical inconsistencies which may derive from particular applications of "judicial exegesis." To assume, however, that these difficulties might have been avoided by reference to "a fair conception of the Constitution" is to oversimplify the judicial task. The Constitution offers virtually no guidance to the determination of whether and the extent to which the instrumentalities of one government are exempt from taxation by the other.

The Hughes Court, it has been seen, finally predicated tax immunity essentially upon a factual determination of the practical effect of the tax burden. In the case of the state, if the economic burden is uncertain or intangible, it will not be deemed to impair the exercise of any function "vital to its existence." In the case of the federal government, while it may obtain immunity without regard to effect, by legislative fiat, absent such fiat, if the economic burden is uncertain or intangible it will be assumed from the silence of Congress that it did not intend immunity. The ultimate touchstone of constitutionality, even after radical alterations of doctrine, is thus not the Constitution itself, but the conceptions of the Justices in regard to the degree of burden. This gives greater latitude for governmental taxation than had been the case theretofore, but has little connection with any mandate of the Constitution.

It is pertinent to suggest, finally, that while the distinction with respect to the difference in political process first formulated by Marshall was used by Justice Stone to support relatively greater scrutiny of state than federal legislation in the area of intergovernmental tax immunity, it might be invoked, with equal logic, to bring into question the desirability of judicial review over federal legislation in any case. Specifically, however, it may be queried whether the practical process of weighing the economic burden of *federal* taxation upon state instrumentalities should be left to the judgment of the political branches of the government, that is, Congress and the President, or continue to remain the ultimate responsibility of the judiciary.

V. Chief Justice of the United States: the Constitution, "Road or Gate?"

CHAPTER 16

SOME IMPORTANT FEDERAL LEGISLATION

THE NATURE OF THE PROBLEM

Throughout the world, as the depression deepened and assumed both in range and depth a form unprecedented in the history of modern times, came an increasing acceptance of a new conception of the role of the state in the economy. That conception rejected the anarchic principles of Adam Smith and substituted a belief in the social welfare function of the state. In America, at first, it was widely believed to be the responsibility of the states and municipalities to bring economic assistance to the suffering and to attempt to restore prosperity and stability. But when the governmental and financial resources of the states proved inadequate to cope with the near disaster engulfing the nation, the necessity for large-scale national action won increasing recognition. The crucial constitutional inquiry then became whether the Constitution, as interpreted by the Court, would provide sufficient scope for the exercise of Congressional power in accord with the new conception of the state and more immediately to meet the exigencies of debilitating depression.

DEBTOR AND FARM RELIEF

One of the most serious problems confronting the nation was the plight of farm mortgage debtors who, unable to meet their obligations as prices for their commodities catastrophically declined, were threatened with foreclosure of their properties. So far, in fact, had foreclosures already gone that individual ownership of land, and the American way of life, were threatened with extinction. In aid of these debtors, Congress invoked its delegated bankruptcy power and enacted the Frazier-Lemke Act which provided that a mortgagor might submit to the mortgagee a plan of purchase of the mortgaged property and, if the mortgagee refused his consent to such plan, the bankruptcy court must stay all proceedings for a period of five years during which the bankrupt retained possession of the property, under control of the court, provided he paid a reasonable rental annually. At the end of the five-year period, or sooner, the debtor could be discharged of his obligation by paying into court, for the benefit of the mortgagee, the appraised value of the property. Since the obligation of contracts clause is inapplicable to federal legislation, the attack upon the constitutionality of this law was based upon the due process clause of the Fifth Amendment.

In June, 1935, a unanimous Court, per Justice Brandeis, in *Louisville Joint Stock Land Bank* v. *Radford*,[1] upset its constitutionality. In essence, ruled Justice Brandeis, the test of constitutionality in regard to mortgage relief legislation, whether national or state, was whether "substantive rights of mortgagees were being impaired." While under the specifically granted bankruptcy power, Congress might discharge the debtor's personal obligation, it could not, said the Justice, take away substantive rights in specific property acquired prior to the passage of the relief statute.

BLAISDELL was distinguished on the ground that, in that case, relief was limited to an emergency period at the close of which the mortgagee was free to apply the mortgaged property to the satisfaction of the debt, while here, "the option and the possession would continue although the emergency which is relied upon as justifying the Act ended" before the expiration of the five-year period. However great the need, concluded Justice Brandeis, if substantive rights in property are taken by government, "resort must be had to proceedings by eminent domain; so that, through taxation, the burden of relief afforded in the public interest may be borne by the public."

This case had a dual significance. First, it affirmed that any far-reaching impairment of contract rights would not be countenanced by the Court, notwithstanding the BLAISDELL case. Secondly, it achieved virtually the same limitation upon federal interference with private contract rights under due process that existed against state interference under the contract clause, which led Benjamin F. Wright to comment, "Evidently the obligation of contracts clause is now almost, if not quite, superfluous." [2]

In a further attempt to aid agriculture, Congress, in 1933, enacted the Agricultural Adjustment Act, which the President later wrote had been designed "to help the farmers protect themselves by co-operative action against the accumulation of farm surpluses which had brought about disastrous farm prices and left agriculture practically prostrate throughout the country." [3] The Act had been predicated upon the taxing power of the United States, and, although it actually produced millions of dollars in revenue, it was held, in effect, in *United States* v. *Butler* [4] not to levy a tax at all, but to constitute an expropriation of money from one group for the benefit of another and an invasion of the reserved powers of the states. Five members of the Court, including Chief Justice Hughes, concurred in the prevailing opinion of Mr. Justice Roberts. Justice Stone, joined in dissent by Justices Brandeis and Cardozo, charged the majority with a "tortured construction of the Constitution."

The nation-wide depression dried up tax sources and among the principal victims were municipalities. Hemmed in by constitutional and legislative restrictions, they lacked the flexibility possessed by the national government, and to a lesser extent by the states, in adjusting to crisis conditions. By January, 1934, it was estimated that several thousand municipalities, and other local subdivisions of state government, were in default in their obligations, in the amount of $2,800,000,000. Cities in forty-one of the forty-eight states were affected. By and large the states were powerless to afford relief, not only because of their own precarious financial position, but because the contract impairment clause made attempts at adjustment of debts of doubtful validity. Both the debtor and creditor interests clamored for action. [5] On May 24, 1934, acting under its bankruptcy power, Congress authorized municipal corporations, unable to pay their debts, to resort to federal bankruptcy courts for re-adjustment of their obligations. These courts were authorized to scale down debts with the consent of creditors holding sixty-six and two-thirds per cent of the indebtedness despite the opposition of the balance of the creditors. No municipality was permitted to apply for relief unless consented to by appropriate state authority.

In May, 1936, in *Ashton* v. *Cameron County District* [6] the Supreme Court, by a vote of five to four, with Justice McReynolds as spokesman for the majority, invalidated the Act as in excess of granted federal bankruptcy power and as in derogation of the sovereign power of the state to control its own fiscal affairs. In this connection, the Court took pains to assert that "neither consent nor submission by the states can enlarge the powers of Congress; none can exist except those which are granted."

Justice Cardozo, with the concurrence of three members of the Court, including the Chief Justice, voiced dissent. The legislation, he thought, constituted an appropriate exercise of federal bankruptcy power. Emphasizing the permissive nature of the act, he pointed out that it could not be invoked unless authorized by the state and he could not see, therefore, how it could be said to invade the sovereign power of the state.

Few issues brought before the Supreme Court in its entire history were as pregnant with importance to the economy of the nation as those relating to the action of Congress, taken on June 5, 1933, abrogating gold clause provisions in contracts, public and private. The action of Congress was the product of crisis conditions which had affected the entire world. [7] In September, 1931, England was compelled to suspend redemption of its obligations in gold. Sixteen countries followed suit the same year and these and many others placed some kind of restriction on the export of gold.

The problem in America became increasingly acute. By 1933 domestic prices had declined to the point at which a dollar commanded, on average, one and one-half times the purchasing power of the dollar for the period 1921–1929. It is estimated that in 1933 there were seventy-five billions of dollars in outstanding gold obligations in private contracts and twenty-five billions in public contracts, federal and state. The total gold reserves of the country were only about four billions of dollars. Fear of devaluation created a tremendous demand for gold, and in the period from February 1, 1933, to March 6, of that year, $476,100,000 in gold was withdrawn from depositaries for export, earmarking or domestic hoarding— threatening to create panic conditions. The Emergency Banking Act of March 9, 1933 conferred authority on the President to halt the export and hoarding of gold.

The control over the free market in gold became vital to the economy for another reason. In May of 1933, to halt the terrible spiral of deflation which had gripped the country, Congress authorized the President to devalue the dollar, a power he exercised by decreasing the gold value of the dollar by 40.94 per cent. If under gold clauses, creditors might insist, as their contracts provided, upon repayment in gold or the equivalent it commanded in current legal tender, then relief to the debtor class would have been, in large part, rendered nugatory. In fact, it would have a contrary effect and might well encompass its ruin. This affected not only small debtors, but many railroads and utilities who had been heavy borrowers.

In the light of these conditions Congress, on June 5, 1933, passed a joint resolution declaring that "every provision contained in or made with respect to any obligation which purports to give the obligee a right to require payment in gold or a particular kind of coin or currency, or in an amount in money of the United States measured thereby" was "against public policy" and void. "This policy," President Roosevelt was later to explain, "was, to a great extent, the basis of the recovery program—the means used to bring order out of chaos in foreign exchange and domestic currency, and to remove the unfair debt structure then in existence." [8]

With regard to this legislation, three decisions were delivered by Chief Justice Hughes on February 18, 1935, in each of which, by the slim margin of a single vote, recovery was denied, although any other result would have had the most appalling effect upon the economy of the nation after almost two years of operation under the legislation.

In the first case, *Norman* v. *Baltimore & Ohio R.R.,*[9] a holder of a railroad bond bearing an interest coupon payable in gold of face value of $22.50 demanded its equivalent in current dollars, or $38.10. Chief Justice Hughes, speaking for a majority of the Court including Justices Brandeis, Stone, Roberts and Cardozo, sustained the validity of the gold clause resolution as applied to *private* contracts and to those made by *states* or their political subdivisions. Contracts for payment in gold, he held, were not commodity contracts but, in essence, called for payment in money. With respect to such payments, he asserted, delegations contained in Article 1, Section 8, of the Constitution gave Congress the power to establish a monetary system and "broad and comprehensive national authority over the subjects of revenue, finance and currency." The power of Congress being established, it follows that contracts of private parties or of the states, however expressed, cannot fetter its constitutionally given authority.

Contracts may create rights of property, but when contracts deal with a subject matter which lies within the control of the Congress, they have a congenital infirmity. Parties cannot remove their transactions from the reach of dominant constitutional power by making contracts about them. . . . There is no constitutional ground for denying to the Congress the power expressly to prohibit and invalidate contracts previously made, and valid when made, when they interfere with the carrying out of the policy it is free to adopt.

The Court, of course, as in any due process case, retained the power to decide whether the action was arbitrary or bore a reasonable relation to a legitimate end. But in this connection the Chief Justice added, "If it is an appropriate means to such an end, the decisions of the Congress as to the final degree of the necessity for the adoption of that means, is final."

This did not quite dispose of the controversy over the gold clause law because, as the Chief Justice said, "The Government's contracts—the obligations of the United States—are in a distinct category and demand separate consideration." That consideration was given in the two other cases decided that day.

The first of these, *Nortz* v. *United States*,[10] while involving a gold clause obligation of the United States, was disposed of in a brief opinion on highly technical grounds of slight importance. It was the decision in the last case which, despite its denial of recovery, evoked not only the bitter criticism of the minority who dissented from the decisions in all three cases but also the criticism of Justice Stone who concurred in the result. The issue in *Perry* v. *United States* [11] was whether plaintiff who held an obligation of the United States which provided that "the principal and interest hereof are payable in United States gold coin *of the present standard of value* [my italics]" was entitled to recover from the United States either gold coin or its equivalent in current dollars for gold of equal weight and fineness. The difference to the plaintiff in relation to the obligation in face amount of $10,000 was almost $7,000. In general, however, the difference in terms of national debt ran into billions of dollars.

Chief Justice Hughes, speaking for the Court, said that the obligation for a " '*present* standard of value' stood in contradistinction to a *lower* standard of value," and obviously was intended to afford protection against loss. By a truly amazing process of legal legerdemain the Chief Justice then proceeded to reason that while the obligation was binding on the moral conscience of the sovereign and beyond its legal power of repudiation, it could not be enforced because damage could not be shown. How this result was accomplished merits analysis.

There is no question, said the Chief Justice, as to the power of Congress to determine the currency of the country. The question is whether Congress can use that power so as to invalidate the terms of obligations which the Government has issued pursuant to another power, its power to borrow money on the credit of the United States.

The argument that an earlier Congress could not restrict the continuing constitutional powers of later Congresses to establish a monetary system, said the Chief Justice, "necessarily imports that the Congress can disregard the obligations of the Government at its discretion and that, when the Government borrows money, the credit of the United States is an illusory pledge." To insist upon the faithful performance of such obligations is not in derogation of sovereignty, he continued, because "the right to make binding obligations is a competence attaching to sovereignty." As for the fact that the United States could not be sued without its consent, that "is a matter of procedure which does not affect the legal and binding character of its contracts." Not only does the contractual obligation remain "binding upon the conscience of the sovereign," but the Joint Resolution of June 5, 1933, in so far as it attempted to override the obligation, "went beyond congressional power." [12]

The question of damages, however, was held to be "a distinct question." The actual loss, said the Chief Justice, cannot be fairly determined "without considering the economic situation at the time the Government offered to pay him the $10,000, the face of his bond, in legal tender currency." In this connection it must be recognized that gold coin was no longer in circulation. Considering, therefore, legal limitations, the question of value must have regard for the purchasing power of the dollars received. In relation to buying power, the plaintiff sustained no loss. On the contrary, to pay him the amount he demands, in view of the adjustments in the economy, "would appear to constitute not a recoupment of loss in any proper sense but an unjustified enrichment."

It is a permissible conclusion to draw from the opinion of the Chief Justice that, although he was not prepared to permit a recovery that would wreak havoc upon the economy, he was determined to deliver a lecture to the New Deal on what he regarded as its cavalier manner of repudiating obligations. Justice Cardozo, who concurred in the result, felt impelled to quarrel with that part of the opinion which went beyond the needs of the case and appeared to set up some indefinable obligation. He wrote that he could not

join in so much of the opinion as may be taken to suggest that the exercise of the sovereign power to borrow money on credit, which does not override the sovereign immunity to suit, may nevertheless preclude or impede the exercise of another sovereign power, to regulate the value of money; or to suggest that although there is and can be no present cause of action upon the repudiated gold clause, its obligation is, nevertheless, in some manner and to some extent, not stated, superior to the power to regulate the currency which we now hold to be superior to the obligation of the bonds.

A single dissenting opinion was delivered by Justice McReynolds, with the concurrence of Justices Van Devanter, Sutherland and Butler, in the three gold clause cases. He characterized the actions of the Government as "repudiation and spoliation of citizens by their sovereign," denied that such power was ever delegated to the federal government and said that "loss of reputation for honorable dealing will bring us unending humiliation; the impending legal and moral chaos is appalling." In his oral opinion Justice McReynolds had gone even further and at one point exclaimed, "this is Nero at his worst. The Constitution is gone." This language proved too vitriolic for the formal record and was excised.[13]

A pertinent question raised for the nation by the debtor and farm relief cases is whether out of concern for the preservation of private rights it could afford to make vital public measures ultimately depend for their validity upon the judgment of a majority of nine judges, however learned in the law and however conscientious in the performance of their responsibilities.

THE TENNESSEE VALLEY AUTHORITY

In the Tennessee Valley, the federal government, under the authority of the National Defense Act of June, 1916, had undertaken a huge project in flood control and navigation improvement with the added intention of assuring an abundant supply of electric energy for the manufacture of munitions as a defense measure. This project in time brought cheap electricity and other manifold benefits to millions in the Valley. One of the great dams erected pursuant to Congressional authority was the Wilson Dam at Muscle Shoals. Beginning in 1925 the Alabama Power Company had bought power generated at the Wilson Dam from the Government and resold it at a profit. Having determined to sell power directly, and presumably at lower price, to a number of communities in the vicinity, the Tennessee Valley Authority on January 4, 1934, entered into a contract with the Alabama Power Company providing for (1) the purchase by the Authority from the Company of certain transmission lines, substations and auxiliary properties for $1,000,000, (2) the purchase by the Authority from the Company of certain real property for $150,000, (3) an interchange of hydro-electric energy and the sale by the Authority to the Company of its "surplus power" on stated terms, and (4) mutual restrictions as to the areas to be served in the sale of power. The transmission lines to be purchased by the Authority extended from the Government's Wilson Dam in northern Alabama into seven counties in that state.

The plaintiffs were holders of preferred stock of the Alabama Power Company who, believing the contract to be injurious to the corporation and beyond the constitutional power of the federal government, demanded that the Board of Directors take steps to have the contract annulled. The Board refused. The plaintiffs thereupon brought suit to have the invalidity of the contract determined and its performance enjoined. They sought also to restrain other activities of the Authority.

Three opinions were written in this case, *Ashwander* v. *Tennessee*

Valley Authority.[14] The prevailing opinion of Chief Justice Hughes was concurred in by Justices Van Devanter, Sutherland and Butler. The opinion by Justice Brandeis, which was joined in by Justices Stone, Roberts and Cardozo, in part concurred in and in part dissented from the opinion of the Chief Justice. The opinion of Justice McReynolds similarly concurred in and dissented from parts of the prevailing opinion.

At the outset the Court confronted the question of the capacity of stockholders to bring suit in the right of the Alabama Power Company. Commenting on the problem, Robert Jackson later wrote:

To entertain the suit would be to ignore the tradition that a court will not interfere with corporate management on far-fetched suppositions of minority stockholders. And if historic practice counted for anything, the Court would not review such an act of corporate management when to do so would also require it to review an act of Congress.[15]

The view that the suit should not have been entertained met with the support of a minority of the Justices, who, in the opinion of Justice Brandeis, reasoned that while, within limits, stockholders may invoke judicial aid to enjoin acts of management which threaten their property interest, they cannot secure the assistance of a court to correct what they regard as "mistakes of judgment" on management's part, even where the mistake "is due to error . . . of law" or "the mistake alleged is the refusal to assert a seemingly clear cause of action, or the compromise of it." Nor, in his judgment had the stockholders sustained their burden of showing the danger of irreparable injury which is requisite if equitable relief is to be granted by a court.

A majority of the Justices disagreed and affirmed the right to sue. In the opinion of Chief Justice Hughes, when stockholders challenge a contract not only as injurious to the interests of the corporation but also as illegal as contravening the Constitution, "to entitle the complainants to equitable relief, in the absence of an adequate legal remedy, it is enough for them to show the breach of trust or duty involved in the injurious and illegal action." Nor is it necessary, he said, to show that the contract was beyond the power of the corporation to make.

The illegality may be found in the lack of lawful authority on the part of those with whom the corporation is attemping to deal. Thus, the breach of duty may consist in yielding, without appropriate resistance, to governmental demands which are without warrant of law or are in violation of constitutional restrictions.[16]

The capacity of the plaintiffs to sue having been determined, another issue related to the scope of the inquiry to be pursued by the Court. If Justice McReynolds had had his way, consideration would not have been limited to the specific contract of January 4, 1934. "We must give attention," he wrote, "to the whole transaction—its antecedents, purpose and effect—as well as to the terms employed."

But in this view Justice McReynolds stood alone. It was the opinion of the Chief Justice that the scope of the inquiry should not be extended beyond the precise issue of the effect and validity of the contract of January 4, 1934.[17] To go further was to seek to extend the judicial power "to the determination of abstract questions."

And as the transmission lines were to run from the Wilson Dam and the current generated was sufficient to meet all the requirements of the contract, the Court further limited itself in regard to the contract "to the constitutional authority for the construction of the Wilson Dam and for the disposition, as provided in the contract, of the electric energy there generated."

Thus limited, the case posed several questions relative to the authority of the United States—first, to construct the dam; secondly, in general, to dispose of the current generated; and, third, as to the precise manner of disposition.

With respect to the right of construction, the entire Court concurred in the position taken by Chief Justice Hughes that construction constituted an appropriate exercise of the war and commerce powers of the United States. So, also, the whole Court agreed with the Chief Justice that the Government had the right to convert water power incident to construction into electrical energy, and that the electric energy produced constituted property belonging to the United States which it might constitutionally dispose of under Article IV, Section 3, of the Constitution. The contention that the authority of Congress to dispose of the energy was limited to the extent it was surplus necessarily created in the course of making munitions of war or operating the works for navigation purposes was rejected by the Court.

What limitations were there, if any, with regard to the *method of disposal* of surplus energy? It was at this point that Justice Mc-Reynolds found himself in sharpest dissent from the decision of the Court. Believing that inquiry should not be limited to the precise contract at issue and after giving detailed consideration to the "whole transaction," it showed, he maintained, that "the primary purpose was to put the Federal Government into the business of distributing and selling electric power throughout certain large districts, to expel the power companies which had long serviced them, and to control the market therein." This threatened the property of the stockholders with complete destruction. Nothing, he said, suggests that this contract was necessary or designed "solely to obtain solvent customers willing to pay full value for all surplus power generated at Wilson Dam"; and he concluded,

If under the thin mask of disposing of property the United States can enter the business of generating, transmitting and selling power as, when and wherever some board may specify, with the definite design to accomplish ends wholly beyond the sphere marked out for them by the Constitution, an easy way has been found for breaking down the limitations heretofore supposed to guarantee protection against aggression.

It was his view, therefore, that the trial court had reached the correct conclusion in annulling the January 4 contract and enjoining the Alabama Power Company from performing it.

The Chief Justice, in carefully balanced phrases, agreed that there were limitations upon the method of disposal. He wrote:

That method, of course, must be an appropriate means of disposition according to the nature of the property, it must be one adopted in the public interest as distinguished from private or personal ends, and we may assume that it must be consistent with the foundation principles of our dual system of government and must not be contrived to govern the concerns reserved to the States.

Confining himself, however, to the disposition effected by the particular contract at issue, he found it constitutional. Pointing out that the method of disposal took the form of sale, interchange of energy, and the purchase of certain transmission lines, he reasoned that the right to sell is provided for by the constitutional authority to dispose, that interchange presented no questions which differ essentially from those pertinent to sales, and that the transmission lines did no more than provide a means of distributing to a large population the electrical energy generated at the dam. With obvious reference to those interests whose motivations were more financial than constitutional, he said that the Alabama Power Company had no constitutional right to insist that it be the sole purchaser of the energy generated at the Wilson Dam.

The claim that the Government could not make its ownership of energy "a means of carrying on competitive commercial enterprises and thus drawing to the Federal Government the conduct and management of business having no relation to the purposes for which the Federal Government was established" he deemed "irrelevant to the issue here, since the Government is not using the water power at the Wilson Dam to establish any industry or business. . . . The question here is simply as to the acquisition of the transmission lines as a facility for the disposal of that energy." [18]

Several aspects of this decision are worthy of comment. It is significant that Justice McReynolds supplied the one added vote necessary to enable the Court to accept jurisdiction of the suit at the behest of stockholders, when his failing to do so would have avoided a declaration sustaining the constitutional validity of the contract at issue, a declaration with which he disagreed. Whether this served the interests of the Government, however, is, at least, debatable. It was apparently part of the strategy of the Government to avoid a determination of constitutionality, presumably in the hope that no way would be found to raise a justiciable issue before the Court. It must be observed, too, that the victory scored by the Government in this case, while of major importance, was severely circumscribed. "There was gratification in Administration circles," wrote Robert Jackson, "that the threatened annihilation of its power policy had been at least postponed." "But," he added, "there was no assurance of the future of projects other than the Wilson Dam, and every transaction by a corporation with the Government was now subject to the risk of a lawsuit by a stockholder, whether as a stalking horse or otherwise." [19]

More fundamentally, the decision in this case brings into question the adequacy of the scheme by which federal power is made to depend upon delegations made in 1787, rather than the felt needs of the time, and the desirability of a judicial determination of vital public policy in which considerations of bias and interest, however unconscious, must inevitably play a part.

CHAPTER 17

THE DELEGATION OF LEGISLATIVE POWER

THE NATURE OF THE PROBLEM
AND THE GENESIS OF DOCTRINE

In seeking to ameliorate the distress produced by depression, Congress found itself compelled to deal with problems affecting many industries in their almost infinite variety and aspects. Increasingly, therefore, it placed reliance upon general regulatory statutes involving the delegation of considerable discretion to the Chief Executive and administrative agencies. In several important cases to come before the Hughes Court, these delegations confronted the separation of powers principle written into our Constitution.

This principle has ancient roots. Aristotle, for example, wrote that well-ordered constitutions have three elements, one which deliberates about public affairs, another, the officers of the state, and the third, the judicial department.[1]

Much more important, however, in influence upon the Framers of our Constitution were the books of Locke and particularly of Montesquieu. Writing in defense of the English Revolution of 1688, Locke maintained that if the legislative and executive powers were in the same hands, they might suit the making and execution of laws to private advantage. "And thus the legislative and executive power come often to be separated." Nor, he insisted, might the legislative power voluntarily transfer the lawmaking power to any other hands, "for it being but a delegated power from the people, they who have it cannot pass it over to others." *Delegata potestas non potest delegari.*[2]

The primary fountainhead of the separation of powers doctrine was Montesquieu. In his classic *Esprit de Lois* he wrote:

When the legislative and executive powers are united in the same person, or in the same body of magistrates, there can be no liberty;

because apprehensions may arise, lest the same monarch or senate should enact tyrannical laws, to execute them in a tyrannical manner.

Again, there is no liberty, if the judiciary power be not separated from the legislative and executive. Were it joined with the legislative, the life and liberty of the subject would be exposed to arbitrary control; for the judge would then be the legislator. Were it joined to the executive power, the judge might behave with violence and oppression.

There would be an end of everything, were the same man, or the same body, whether of the nobles or of the people, to exercise those three powers, that of enacting laws, that of executing the public resolutions, and of trying the causes of individuals.[3]

The greatness of the British Constitution he ascribed, in great measure, to its separation of powers. And this was true, oddly enough, in the face of the growing omnipotence of Parliament.[4]

Jefferson gave his support to this doctrine and in his *Notes on Virginia* wrote in 1781 that the concentration of all powers of government "in the same hands is precisely the definition of despotic government," and this applied to "an elective despotism" as to any other.[5]

Having won nearly universal acceptance in America, in 1787, the doctrine found expression in the Constitution, as a limitation upon the federal government, in the opening phrases of Articles 1, 2 and 3 as follows:

(1) All legislative powers herein granted shall be vested in a Congress of the United States. . . . (2) The executive power shall be vested in a President of the United States. . . . (3) The judicial power of the United States shall be vested in one Supreme Court, and in such inferior Courts as the Congress may from time to time ordain and establish.[6]

In the struggle over ratification of the Constitution, it is interesting that both sides frequently appealed to the authority of Montesquieu and that Madison found it necessary to defend the Constitution against the charge that it failed adequately to provide for separation of powers. He cited Montesquieu approvingly but argued that while the sense in which the preservation of liberty requires that the three great departments of power should be separate and distinct excluded the exercise of the whole power of one department by another it did not require "that these departments ought to have no *partial agency* in, or no *control* over, the acts of each other." [7]

It should be added that in the historic development of the separation of powers doctrine its proponents, by and large, saw in it not only a defense of individual liberty in the ordinary sense, but a defense of individual property as well.[8] The implications of this fact, applied to the restrictions of the Constitution, are significant, for while the theories of Locke and Montesquieu were used as focal points of opposition to monarchical absolutism, in the Constitution they served as the basis for curbing popular majorities. Thus J. Allen Smith points out that the doctrine "was built up originally as a means of limiting monarchical and aristocratic power; that it was not designed to make government in any true sense responsible, but to abridge its powers because it was irresponsible"; and he adds,

It is to be observed, then, that what originally commended the system to the people was the fact that it limited the positive power of the king and aristocracy, while the framers of the Constitution adopted it with a view to limiting the power of the people themselves.[9]

And Professor Finer, commenting that it will probably never be known what were "the respective weights of the influence of the anti-democratic and anti-despotic tendencies in the Philadelphia Convention," remarks that, while Montesquieu and the great liberal thinkers were concerned with the power of the state in a period "when governments were still in the coercive and exploitive stages," they had the "bad effect" of "converting all discussion of government into one of despotism, and making freedom from the State, *dissociation*, appear the proper ideal." [10]

Not only has the theory of separation of powers been brought under critical scrutiny, however, but its practice as well, for it has been increasingly recognized that if government is to prove adequate to its modern tasks there must be large delegations to the executive and administrative agencies. As Dean Landis has pointed out, "the administrative process springs from the inadequacy of a simple tripartite form of government to deal with modern problems." [11]

Nevertheless, it would be unwise to assume that this doctrine has no value for the modern world. One need only view the practice of totalitarian states to recognize merit in the statement of Professor Carl J. Friedrich that

Many who today belittle the doctrine in their clamor for governmental and administrative efficiency seem scarcely aware of the fact that the fusion of powers, which is the alternative, leads easily to a one-party dictatorship and therefore threatens constitutional government.[12]

The function of the Court, in relation to the separation of powers principle, has been the delicate and difficult one of attempting to strike a balance between the practical demands of effective government and the preservation of individual liberty and property against arbitrary rule. How has this balance been struck? Despite manifold and sometimes generous delegations of power made by Congress to the President and administrative agencies from the beginning of the Republic until 1935, every delegation was upheld as constitutional despite repeated reiteration of the formal principle that legislative power may not be delegated.[13] This result was achieved, in part, by according recognition to the functions of so-called "quasi-legislative" or "quasi-judicial" bodies as consistent with the Constitution,[14] and, in part, by ruling that when a policy had been declared by Congress and "standards" had been set up to guide the exercise of power by the delegate no real delegation of legislative power had taken place at all.

Illustrative of the latter was the decision in 1932 of the unanimous Court, delivered in an opinion by Chief Justice Hughes, in *New York Central Securities Corp.* v. *United States.*[15] It was then held that a section of the Transportation Act of 1920 which empowered the Interstate Commerce Commission to permit acquisition of control by one carrier of another when "in the public interest" did not involve an invalid delegation of authority by Congress to the Commission as based on an uncertain criterion. Said the Chief Justice, "It is a mistaken assumption that this is a mere general reference to the public welfare without any standard to guide determinations." He added that the term "has direct relation to adequacy of transportation service, to its essential conditions of economy and efficiency, and to appropriate provision and best use of transportation facilities."

THE NATIONAL INDUSTRIAL RECOVERY ACT

The first case in American history in which an Act of Congress was invalidated by the Supreme Court as involving an unconstitutional delegation of legislative power was that of *Panama Refining Co.* v. *Ryan*,[16] affecting a regulation of the oil industry.

The oil industry was in 1933 the third largest in America. In the light of existing purchasing power it was then affected by chronic overproduction and wasteful competition. The wholesale price of gasoline fell at one point to 2½ cents per gallon. The attempt of the states to regulate the industry had failed since they could not agree upon a common policy. Several states appealed for federal aid.

Congress met this appeal in two principal ways under the National Industrial Recovery Act of 1933. First, codes of fair competition were authorized for industry in general and one was thereafter adopted for the oil industry which prescribed quotas for the various states but left to each state the allocation of its quota among its own operators. Secondly, a specific provision was included within the NIRA, Section 9(c), as follows:

The President is authorized to prohibit the transportation in interstate and foreign commerce of petroleum and the products thereof produced or withdrawn from storage in excess of the amount permitted to be produced or withdrawn from storage by any State law or valid regulation or order prescribed thereunder, by any board, commission, officer, or other duly authorized agency of a State.

On July 11, 1933, the President by Executive Order prohibited the transportation of oil in excess of amounts permitted by state action and on July 14 the President authorized the Secretary of the Interior to exercise all the powers vested in him "for the purpose of enforcing" the Act and the Executive Order. Co-plaintiffs, an owner of an oil refining plant and a producer of oil, attacked the validity of Section 9(c) as an unconstitutional delegation to the President of legislative power and as transcending the authority of Congress under the commerce clause.

After disposing of some preliminary questions, Chief Justice Hughes, for a majority of the Court, turned to the claim of unlawful delegation of legislative power. Assuming, he said, without deciding, that Congress had the *authority*, under the interstate commerce clause, to forbid the transportation of the excess oil, the question of whether it should be prohibited "is obviously one of legislative policy." Accordingly, the Court must look to the statute "to see whether the Congress has declared a policy with respect to that subject; whether the Congress has set up a standard for the President's action; whether the Congress has required any finding by the President in the exercise of the authority to enact the prohibition." Thus looking at Section 9(c) he found that none of these things has been done by Congress. On the contrary, "it gives to the President an unlimited authority to determine the policy and to lay down the prohibition, or not to lay it down, as he may see fit. And disobedience to his order is made a crime punishable by fine and imprisonment."

Nor did the Chief Justice find any declaration of policy or a standard of action in any other part of the law. As for Title 1 of the Act, he said, while it speaks in general terms of certain broad objectives, "it is manifest that this broad outline is simply an introduction of the Act, leaving the legislative policy as to particular subjects to be declared and defined, if at all, by the subsequent sections."

The fact that deleterious consequences follow the transportation of "hot oil" did not, he thought, serve to sustain the legislation, since *Congress* had not prohibited that transportation or even said that it was injurious or unfair competition. On the contrary, "Congress left the matter to the President without standard or rule, to be dealt with as he pleased."

Reviewing the pertinent decisions of the Supreme Court, the Chief Justice concluded that in every case "the Court has recognized that there are limits of delegation which there is no constitutional authority to transcend," and added,

We think that section 9(c) goes beyond those limits. As to the transportation of oil production in excess of state permission, the Congress has declared no policy, has established no standard, has laid down no rule. . . . If Section 9(c) were held valid, it would be idle to pretend that anything would be left of limitations upon the power of the Congress to delegate its law-making function.

Chief Justice Hughes found another objection to the validity of the prohibition laid down by the Executive Order of the President under section 9(c) in that it contained "no finding, no statement of the grounds of the President's action in enacting the prohibition." This, he declared, was in notable contrast with historic practice "by which declarations of policy are made by the Congress and delegations are within the framework of that policy and have relation to facts and conditions to be found and stated by the President in the appropriate exercise of the delegated authority." Even if, therefore, one could discern within the compass of the Act a declared policy of Congress authorizing the presidential order under certain circumstances and conditions, "findings by him as to the existence of the required basis of his action would be necessary to sustain that action, for otherwise the case would still be one of an unfettered discretion as the qualification of authority would be ineffectual." It would, in effect, invest him "with an uncontrolled legislative power."

The Executive Order of the President and the Regulations of the Secretary of the Interior issued thereunder were accordingly held unconstitutional.[17]

Justice Cardozo was the sole dissenter. He stated that his point of difference with the majority was "narrow." He agreed that to uphold the delegation "there is need to discover in the terms of the act a standard reasonably clear whereby discretion must be governed." He denied, however, that such a standard was lacking when the Act with all its reasonable implications was considered as a whole. The nature of the standard was, then, the "pivotal inquiry."

The act the President was authorized to perform, he said, was definite beyond the possibility of challenge. He might prohibit the transportation in interstate and foreign commerce of a particular commodity when produced or withdrawn from storage in contravention of state law. He was given choice, within limits, of the occasion but none whatever as to the means, that is, prohibition.

The means being clear and definite, what standard was provided the President by Congress? Justice Cardozo conceded that it could not be found in Section 9(c) alone, but thought it might be gleaned from "the declared policies of the act,—not merely his own conception of its policies, undirected by an extrinsic guide, but the policies announced by section 1 in the forefront of the statute as an index to the meaning of everything that follows."

The "policies" declared by Title 1, which Chief Justice Hughes regarded as only an introduction to the act which left policies to be declared, if at all, by subsequent sections, were cited by Justice Cardozo as (1) "to eliminate unfair competitive practices," (2) "to conserve natural resources," (3) "to promote the fullest possible utilization of the present productive capacity of industries," and

(4) "except as may be temporarily required" to "avoid undue restriction of production."

The argument that affording the President a choice between one standard and another, in effect, amounted to setting up no standard at all was rejected by the Justice who conceived the mandate to the President as follows:

What he does is to inquire into the industrial facts as they exist from time to time. These being ascertained, he is not to prefer one standard to another in any subjective attitude of mind, in any personal or wilful way. He is to study the facts objectively, the violation of a standard impelling him to action or inaction according to its observed effect upon industrial recovery,—the ultimate end, as appears by the very heading of the title, to which all the other ends are tributary and mediate.

Nor, viewed in long-range terms, was there any essential conflict among the standards. Restriction upon shipment in interstate commerce "in its immediacy may in its ultimate and larger consequences be expansion and development."

Thus linked with the policy of Congress, as defined in the whole Act, Justice Cardozo was persuaded, the standard was sufficiently defined to make the statute valid. "Discretion," he said, "is not unconfined and vagrant. It is canalized within banks that keep it from overflowing." Separation of powers, he continued,

is not a doctrinaire concept to be made use of with pedantic rigor. There must be sensible approximation, there must be elasticity of adjustment, in response to the practical necessities of government, which cannot foresee today the developments of tomorrow in their nearly infinite variety. . . . There is no fear that the nation will drift from its ancient moorings as the result of the narrow delegation of power permitted by this section.

Justice Cardozo then turned to the necessity for "findings" by the President to support the exercise of delegated power. The President, he said, was not required by the Constitution or by statute to state the reasons for his exercise of the granted power.

It is enough that the grant of power had been made and that pursuant to that grant he had signified the will to act. The will to act being declared, the law presumes that the declaration was preceded by due inquiry and that it was rooted in sufficient grounds. Such, for a hundred years and more, has been the doctrine of this Court.

That is not to say that any action of the President may not be challenged as arbitrary. But there can be no challenge "unless the possibility of a rational nexus [between the order and the standard] is lacking altogether." A distinction must be drawn, too, between an administrative agency which may be required by reviewing courts to express its decision in formal and explicit findings so that review may be intelligent and the Chief Executive, exercising a power committed to him by Congress, and subject, in respect of his acts, to the restrictions accompanying the grant and not to any others.

The entire Court, it should be observed, agreed that a valid delegation of legislative power to the President required a declaration of *policy* and the setting up of a *standard* by Congress as a guide to the President's action. Whether policy and standard were sufficiently explicit in this instance was the basic issue in dispute. That this admitted of two differing and rationally defensible conclusions is apparent from the foregoing discussion. But on the issue of lesser importance concerning the necessity for *findings* by the President, it is significant that while Chief Justice Hughes could cite not a single directly pertinent precedent, Justice Cardozo could summon quite a number in support of his position. Authority would therefore seem to support the view that precedents of long standing were upturned by the majority in extending the necessity for express findings from administrative agencies and quasi-judicial officers to the President himself when acting in the exercise of a delegated power.

The agreement of the Court on the necessity for a declaration of policy and standard to support legislative delegation raised an immediate question for the Administration—if the limited and circumscribed delegation under Section 9(c) of the NIRA was unconstitutional, what might be said by the Court of the more sweeping delegations made by Congress to the President under the general provisions of the NIRA authorizing him to approve general codes to govern industries with the force of law?

The answer came within a few months when, in *Schechter Poultry Corp.* v. *United States*,[18] the basic provisions of the National Industrial Recovery Act were held invalid as involving unconstitutional delegation by Congress to the President of its lawmaking power.

In this case, the Schechter brothers and certain corporations organized by them were indicted for conspiracy to violate and for violations of the Code of Fair Competition, governing the Live Poultry Industry, approved by the President under authority vested in him by the NIRA.

The "Live Poultry Code" was promulgated under Section 3 of the NIRA which authorized the President to approve "codes of fair competition" upon application of a trade association or group under certain limitations designed to assure that the group was representative, monopoly and oppression were not promoted, and the policies of Title 1 of the Act would tend to be effectuated.[10] As a condition for his approval, the President might impose such requirements "in furtherance of the public interest, and may provide such exceptions to and exemptions from the provisions of such code as the President in his discretion deems necessary to effectuate the policy herein declared." Where such a code had not been approved, the President could prescribe one. In either event, whether approved or prescribed, violation of any provision of a code "in any transaction in or affecting interstate or foreign commerce" was made a misdemeanor.

Speaking for the Court, Chief Justice Hughes, after pointing out that the Constitution provides that "all legislative powers herein granted shall be vested in a Congress" (Article 1, Section 1) and that Congress is authorized "to make all laws which shall be necessary and proper to carry into execution" the delegated powers, categorically asserted, "The Congress is not permitted to abdicate or to transfer to others the essential legislative functions with which it is thus vested."

True, legislation must be adapted to complex conditions involving details with which the legislature cannot deal directly. Quoting from his decision in the PANAMA REFINING Co. case, he said that the Constitution has never been regarded as denying to Congress

the necessary resources of flexibility and practicality, which will enable it to perform its function in laying down policies and establishing standards, while leaving to selected instrumentalities the making of subordinate rules within prescribed limits and the determination of facts to which the policy as declared by the legislature is to apply.

But this cannot "be allowed to obscure the limitations of the authority to delegate if our constitutional system is to be maintained."

The problem, therefore, becomes one of discerning whether Congress in authorizing "codes of fair competition" with the force of law has established the standards.

Does the phrase "fair competition" furnish a standard? It does not since the phrase has no reference to a category established by law in the sense that "unfair competition" is so recognized. In its widest range "unfair competition" as so understood does not reach the objectives of the codes. The codes may cover what existing law condemns but they are not thus limited.

Rather, the purpose is clearly disclosed to authorize new and controlling prohibitions through codes of laws which would embrace what the formulators would propose, and what the President would approve, or prescribe, as wise and beneficent measures for the government of trades and industries in order to bring about their rehabilitation, correction and development, according to the general declaration of policy in section one.

That the codes will consist of rules of competition deemed fair by representative members of industry vitally concerned and most familiar with its problems cannot justify the delegation for it cannot be seriously contended "that Congress could delegate its legislative authority to trade or industrial associations or groups so as to empower them to enact the laws they deem to be wise and beneficent for the rehabilitation of their trade or industries." It must be obvious that "such a delegation of legislative power is unknown to our law and is utterly inconsistent with the constitutional prerogatives and duties of Congress."

Nor, for that matter, may Congress "delegate legislative power to the President to exercise an unfettered discretion to make whatever laws he thinks may be needed or advisable for the rehabilitation and expansion of trade or industry." Yet, subject to few restrictions such as the barring of monopolies, the discretion of the President is "virtually unfettered." "We think that the code-making authority thus conferred is an unconstitutional delegation of legislative power."

In seeking to differentiate the delegation here involved from those to the Interstate Commerce Commission, the Federal Radio Commission and to the President under the flexible tariff provision of the Tariff Act of 1922, Chief Justice Hughes emphasized that standards were in those instances prescribed by the Acts of Congress and that to facilitate their application an expert body was provided by Congress.

Justice Cardozo, in concurring in a separate opinion [20] with the Chief Justice, distinguished this case from the PANAMA REFINING Co. case. The delegated power of legislation, he wrote, "which has found expression in this code is not canalized within banks that keep it from overflowing. It is unconfined and vagrant." In the PANAMA REFINING Co. case, he said, choice, within limits, had been given to the President,

as to the occasion, but none whatever as to the means. Here, in the case before us, is an attempted delegation not confined to any single act nor to any class or group of acts identified or described by reference to a standard. Here in effect is a roving commission to inquire into evils and upon discovery correct them.

Here, the President was authorized to do anything Congress might do to plan improvements as well as extirpate abuses in the whole field of industrial regulation. "This is delegation running riot. No such plenitude of power is susceptible of transfer."

Never before in America had such sweeping delegations of legislative power been made to any President as under the general code-making provisions of the NIRA. It would be difficult to quarrel with the view of the unanimous Court that it gave the President almost "unfettered discretion" to make whatever laws he deemed advisable to govern industry and industrial relations. Whatever criticism, therefore, may justly be levelled at the doctrine of non-delegability of legislative power *per se*, and whatever the inconsistency or ambiguity in earlier decisions of the Court, so long as the Court maintains its supervisory role and the doctrine retains a scintilla of value, this would appear to have been an appropriate occasion for its invocation.

Had the Court rested its decision on this ground alone, which it might have done, especially in the light of its action in the PANAMA REFINING Co. case, few could have challenged its judgment, at least on constitutional grounds. But the Court went further and held that Congress had exceeded its interstate commerce power. Standing alone the first obstacle might have been surmounted either by laborious Congressional enactment of Codes or possibly by the establishment of more precise standards to guide the President. The second ground for invalidation struck a mortal blow.[21]

THE BITUMINOUS COAL CONSERVATION ACT

The following year, in *Carter* v. *Carter Coal Co.*,[22] a majority of the Court, in an opinion delivered by Justice Sutherland, invalidated the Bituminous Coal Conservation Act of 1935 designed to bring some measure of stability in the coal mining industry. One of the principal grounds for invalidation [23] was that in the judgment of the Court the Act, in so far as it conferred upon a stated plurality of producers and miners the authority to fix maximum hours of labor and minimum wages subject to the imposition of an excise tax and certain other penalties upon those producers who failed to accept the hours and wages fixed, constituted

legislative delegation in its most obnoxious form; for it is not even delegation to an official or an official body, presumptively disinterested, but to private persons whose interests may be and often are adverse to the interests of others in the same business. . . . And a statute which attempts to confer such power undertakes an intolerable and unconstitutional interference with personal liberty and private property.

The Chief Justice, in a separate opinion, concurred in this phase of the Court's decision. He agreed that a broad delegation of legislative power without standards or limitation was involved. The analogy, urged by the Government in support of constitutionality, to legislation which becomes effective on the happening of a specified event was, he said, being pressed to the point "where the principle would be entirely destroyed" because to accept it would be to

remove all restrictions upon the delegation of legislative power, as the making of laws could thus be referred to any designated officials or private persons whose orders or agreements would be treated as "events," with the result that they would be invested with the force of law having penal sanctions.

Apart from the question of delegation of legislative power, he acquiesced in the majority view that to permit a group of producers and miners, as they thought expedient, to make rules as to hours and wages for other producers and miners who were not parties to the agreement was not in accord with the requirements of due process of law.

SUMMARY STATEMENT

After a history of almost one hundred and fifty years in which not a single Act of Congress had been invalidated as involving an unlawful delegation of legislative power, in quick succession within one year, the Court set aside three vital New Deal measures as offending against this principle. These statutes, to be sure, went far beyond historic delegations. It must be recognized, however, that this was at least in part because of the unprecedented nature of the problems confronting the nation. It is necessary to add, too, that the principles laid down by the Court to support a valid delegation, however clear in theory, are not without their difficulties in application. The requirements that policies must be explicitly stated in the legislation and that findings must be made by the administrative agent are reasonably clear and precise. But what of the additional requirement imposed by the PANAMA REFINING Co. and SCHECHTER cases that Congress must set forth standards to guide the exercise of delegated power? In the very nature of the case, standards must frequently be fairly vague and general if the flexibility requisite to effective regulation without the day-to-day intervention of the legislature is to be secured.

Thus, the Court itself has sustained rather broad and general delegations particularly to so-called "quasi-legislative" bodies. The requirement that rates be "just and reasonable" has been regarded as a sufficient standard to uphold the delegation by the legislature of its rate-making authority. And, as Justice Cardozo pointed out in the PANAMA REFINING Co. case, a "conspicuous illustration" of latitude is that extended by the Court to the Interstate Commerce Commission, "probing the economic situation of the railroads of the country, consolidating them into systems, shaping in numberless ways their capacities and duties, and even making or unmaking the prosperity of great communities." The Court, too, has sustained the standard of the Tariff Act permitting duties to be raised to equalize costs of production at home and abroad. And, however realistic the difference in costs formula may sound, in practice, as Professor Schattschneider has concluded, after thorough study, "it can be made to mean almost anything." [24] So extensive and uncontrolled in fact have been the delegations permitted in fields of accepted Congressional regulation that in 1938 Professor McGowen, for one, maintained that in such fields "almost unlimited delegation is allowable" while in the fields not yet accepted by the Court as proper subjects of Congressional regulation the "delegation is almost inevitably bad." [25]

But assuming that adequate and acceptable standards could be clearly defined by Congress it may at times find itself impaled on the horns of another dilemma. The dilemma of the legislators was thus expressed in the brief of the United States in the case of *Currin* v. *Wallace*.[26]

They are confronted on the one hand with the nebulous requirements of due process. If they pronounce a rigid set of standards, unforeseen cases to which the standards may apply present the danger of unconstitutionality because of caprice or arbitrary application. If, on the other hand, they seek to avoid the danger of capricious and arbitrary application through provision for flexibility in application, the statute is then attacked for undue delegation, an equally nebulous and undefined concept.[27]

Apart from the difficulty of fixing standards at once sufficiently explicit to satisfy the Court and sufficiently vague to be adapted to the demands of flexibility, the principle laid down in the CARTER case posed an additional problem for the Administration. With the complexity of our economy, the form of legislation which enables a majority of a private group to work out detailed provisions of law, subject to general declarations of Congressional policy, and to bind others with the force of law, has been found increasingly useful and perhaps necessary. To some extent this has been accorded recognition by the Court. Thus, for example, it has found no unconstitutionality in the provision of federal law which requires government contractors to pay the "prevailing rate of wages" although this in essence amounts to a delegation to local employers, by their practice, to determine wages to be paid in a locality. And only six months after the CARTER decision, Justice Sutherland, who wrote the opinion in that case, sustained the validity of an Illinois law which granted to manufacturers of trade-marked articles the authority to fix, and invoke the aid of the state to maintain, resale prices,[28] although this, too, involved a delegation of authority to some individuals to restrict the liberty of others.

These, in short, were some of the practical problems facing the Administration as it sought to alleviate the distress caused by the depression. The Court had announced that its efforts had to be made consistent with the constitutional mandate that there could be no large and uncontrolled delegations of power either to the executive or to private groups amounting to an abdication of the legislative function. This announcement was consistent with the principles of Locke and Montesquieu and Jefferson. Was it also consistent with the exigencies of government under conditions of crisis and emergency?

CHAPTER 18

THE CONTROL OF COMMERCE

With few significant exceptions, the Supreme Court beginning with Marshall's famed decision in *Gibbons* v. *Ogden* had given a "plenary" interpretation to the interstate commerce power of Congress.[1] While Congress had recourse, as we have seen, to many of its delegated powers to implement the growing conception that it was legitimate for the nation to intervene in the regulation of the economy in the public interest, it was upon this power that, beginning with the Interstate Commerce Act of 1887, Congress primarily relied.

THE RAILWAY LABOR ACT OF 1926

In the first year of his assumption of the position of Chief Justice, Mr. Hughes, for the Court, in *Texas & New Orleans R.R.* v. *Brotherhood of Railway & Steamship Clerks*,[2] upheld the validity of a Congressional measure passed in 1926 which undertook to protect the right of interstate railway employees to self-organization and to choose their own representatives for purpose of collective bargaining without "interference, influence or coercion" by their employers. And this right was held to embrace railway clerks who had no direct connection with the actual operation of an interstate facility.

Rejecting the contention that the act was unconstitutional "because it seeks to take away an inherent and inalienable right in violation of the First and Fifth Amendments," the Chief Justice reaffirmed the plenary nature of Congressional power over commerce, and said, "Exercising this authority, Congress may facilitate the amicable settlement of disputes which threaten the service of the necessary agencies of interstate transportation."

Pointing out that the right of self-organization of employees had long been recognized, he added, "Congress was not required to ignore this right of the employees but could safeguard it and seek to make their appropriate collective action an instrument of peace rather than of strife."

The reasoning of the Court in the cases of *Adair* v. *United States* and *Coppage* v. *Kansas* [3] might have appeared to present some difficulties. But these were disposed of by the Chief Justice as "inapplicable," since, he said, this Act did not interfere "with the normal exercise of the right of the carrier to select its employees or to discharge them."

While this case was limited to employees of a railway company having direct relation to the facilities of interstate commerce, it is clear that in 1930 the entire Court with the possible exception of Justice McReynolds, who took no part in the decision, was in principle accepting the basis of the National (Wagner) Labor Relations Act in so far as it guaranteed the right of self-organization to employees free from employer interference as a legitimate exercise of the regulatory power of government *as against attack under the due process clause.* The Court, however, had not yet arrived at the position of extending this doctrine to employees of industry whose relation to transportation was less direct. And the question remained, as to such employees, whether such regulation could be encompassed within the interstate commerce power.

RADIO FREQUENCIES

Again, in 1933, the interstate commerce power served to sustain the authority of Congress and of its agencies to reassign radio frequencies. In the case of *Federal Radio Commission* v. *Nelson Bros.,*[4] Chief Justice Hughes pointed out for the Court that since no state lines divided the radio waves, national regulation was not only appropriate but essential to the efficient use of radio facilities. It was not open to question, he said, that Congress might authorize the Commission "to delete stations, in view of the limited radio facilities available and the confusion that would result from interferences." He continued, "Those who operated broadcasting stations had no right superior to the exercise of this power of regulation. They necessarily made their investments and their contracts in the light of, and subject to, paramount authority."

Of course, he added, in making any adjustment, the Commission must consider "the equities" of existing stations. They must not be "the victims of official favoritism." "But the weight of the evidence as to these equities and all other pertinent facts is for the determination of the Commission in exercising its authority to make a 'fair and equitable allocation.' "

While it is difficult to see how any other decision could have been rendered by the Court, it is of interest to note that in the debate over the nomination of Mr. Hughes one of the bases of attack had been the fear that he might follow the position he had taken in a case as counsel for the radio interest and find that the assignment of a wave length to an existing station conferred a vested right.

THE RAILROAD RETIREMENT ACT

No period in American history witnessed the degree of intervention in time of peace in the control of the economy as that which began with the compelling leadership of Franklin D. Roosevelt upon his accession to the presidency. One of the earliest decisions of the 1935 term of the Supreme Court, which struck down several vital New Deal measures, came in the case of legislation which although it had not originated as an Administration measure had commanded its support. In *Railroad Retirement Board* v. *Alton Railroad Co.*,[5] the Court in an opinion by Mr. Justice Roberts, with which the four conservatives concurred, held the Railroad Retirement Act of June 27, 1934, establishing a compulsory retirement and pension system for all carriers subject to the Interstate Commerce Act, unconstitutional. The Act provided for compulsory contributions by employees of a percentage of their compensation and by each carrier of double the total payable by its employees.

Not only was the Act found arbitrary and invalid "because several of its inseparable provisions contravene the due process of law clause of the Fifth Amendment," but far more serious, because placing it beyond the corrective power of Congress, was the ruling "which goes to the heart of the law, even if it could survive the loss of the unconstitutional features," that the "Act is not in purpose or effect a regulation of interstate commerce within the meaning of the Constitution."

To the contention that the Act was an appropriate regulation of interstate commerce since it would improve the efficiency of interstate transportation by enhancing the morale of employees by assurance of security in old age, Mr. Justice Roberts answered that the fostering of a contented mind on the part of employees by legislation of this type was not in any just sense a regulation of interstate commerce. If that were true, he said, Congress might require free medical attendance, housing, food or the education of children as tending to relieve the employee of strain and worry. "Can it fairly be said that the power of Congress to regulate interstate commerce extends to the prescription of any or all of these things? Is it not apparent that they are really and essentially related solely to the social welfare of the worker, and therefore remote from any regulation of commerce as such?"

In a vigorous dissent, with the support of Justices Brandeis, Stone and Cardozo, the Chief Justice pointed to the gravity of the majority decision in placing a barrier against *all* legislative action of the nature involved, argued that the interstate commerce power had been held complete and plenary and pointed out that some years earlier the unanimous Court had said, "To regulate, in the sense intended, is to foster, protect, control and restrain, with appropriate regard for the welfare of those who are immediately concerned and of the public at large." [6] Particularly, the Chief Justice insisted, has the "exercise of the power, thus broadly defined," had "the widest range in dealing with railroads, which are engaged as common carriers in interstate transportation. As their service is vital to the nation, nothing which has a real or substantial relation to the suitable maintenance of that service, or to the discharge of the responsibilities which inhere in it, can be regarded as beyond the power of regulation." It has been recognized that efficiency suffers "from a failure to meet the reasonable demands of justice."

The practice of many of the carriers in providing pension systems was, he believed, an answer to the argument that a pension system is, *per se*, unrelated to ends which Congress is entitled to serve. It must be clear, he added, that the morale of employees does have an important bearing upon the efficiency of the transportation service and that a reasonable pension plan is an appropriate means to that end. Nor did he think that the plan could be removed from the reach of Congressional power by classing it with housing, food, education for children or other conceivable benefits "which have no such close and substantial relation to the terms and conditions of employment." With so many utility and government employees covered by retirement plans it is evident that there is a widespread conviction that a pension plan "is closely and substantially related to the proper conduct of business enterprises."

The imposition of non-contractual incidents for social ends did not, he believed, serve to condemn the Act. He found close analogy in compensation Acts which impose burdens notwithstanding the lack of fault on the employers' part. "The fundamental consideration which supports this type of legislation," he maintained, "is that industry should take care of its human wastage, whether that is due to accident or age."

Recognizing then that the retirement and pension system is a legitimate regulation of interstate commerce, do the particular provisions of the Act violate the requirement of due process, he inquired. The objection that the pooling arrangement which treated all railroads as a single employer and imposed unequal burdens condemned the plan encounters, he said, previous decisions of the Court in sustaining compensation laws and the imposition of assessments on state banks generally in order to create a guaranty fund affecting insolvent banks. But even more directly pertinent, he noted, the Court has sustained the grouping of railroads for the purpose of regulation as in the case of the recapture clause of the Transportation Act of 1920. "The underlying principle is that Congress has the power to treat the transportation system of the country as a unit for the purpose of regulation in the public interest, so long as particular railroad properties are not subjected to confiscation." As to the classes of persons to be covered and other details of the plan, the Chief Justice maintained that all but one were within the discretionary power of Congress. The single provision deemed arbitrary was regarded as coming within the clause as to severability.

It is pertinent to observe that this was the third case in American history in which a Congressional Act regulating railroads under the interstate commerce clause had been held unconstitutional and all three had favored the interests of railroad labor.[7]

It is pertinent to observe, too, that the blow struck by the majority opinion went far beyond the requirements of decision. A cardinal canon of the Court, frequently, to be sure, honored in the breach, is that in constitutional cases it will decide only so much as is necessary to dispose of the case. The majority having reached the conclusion that specific inseparable provisions of the Act offended against due process and that the Act was therefore invalid, there was no legitimate occasion to inquire into the question of whether Congress had exceeded its interstate commerce power. Or, doing so, it might at least have limited its inquiry to whether *this* Act exceeded the interstate commerce power of Congress. It went further however by declaring that the subject matter itself lay beyond the reach of Congressional authority. To do this was not merely to condemn the particular plan before it but any plan that might be offered. The majority, wrote Professor Powell, ventured "upon a sweeping condemnation twice removed from all that is necessary to dispose of the case between the litigants. . . . Lavishly gratuitous was the readiness to declare that a different statute which might or might not later be passed would also fail to be a regulation of interstate commerce." [8]

The extravagant sweep of the majority opinion was also the subject of special comment in the dissenting opinion of the Chief Justice, who stated,

In that view, no matter how suitably limited a pension act for railroad employees might be with respect to the persons to be benefited, or how appropriate the measure of retirement allowances, or how sound actuarily the plan, or how well adjusted the burden, still under this decision Congress would not be at liberty to enact such a measure. That is a conclusion of such serious and far-reaching importance that it overshadows all other questions raised by the Act.

That dissenting opinion was, of course, limited to a consideration of the constitutionality of a pension plan for employees of carriers in relation to which the Chief Justice said the exercise of the interstate commerce power of Congress had the "widest range." Nevertheless, the insistence that such a plan provided a benefit having a "close and substantial relation to the terms and conditions of employment" which fostered a sense of security, met "the reasonable demands of justice" and took care of "human wastage" and thereby promoted the efficiency of interstate carriers suggested the inquiry: Would not a minimum wage and maximum hour law or a collective bargaining law made applicable to employers engaged in interstate commerce likewise provide benefits to labor closely and substantially related to the terms and conditions of employment and by curtailing strikes, meeting the reasonable demands of justice and reducing human wastage promote the efficiency of interstate commerce?

More immediately, however, the prevailing opinion which had given a restricted interpretation to the interstate commerce power, in invalidating the Railroad Retirement Act, foreshadowed difficulties in regard to the constitutional validity of a much more important act shortly to be the subject of judicial decision, the National Industrial Recovery Act.

THE NATIONAL INDUSTRIAL RECOVERY ACT

On May 17, 1933, President Roosevelt, in a message to Congress requesting passage of the National Industrial Recovery Act, said it would provide "the machinery necessary for a great co-operative movement throughout all industry in order to obtain wide re-employment, to shorten the working week, to pay a decent wage for the shorter week, and to prevent unfair competition and disastrous overproduction." In signing the bill, he commented that "history probably will record the National Industrial Recovery Act as the most important and far-reaching legislation ever enacted by the American Congress."

This Act, we have seen, was invalidated on the ground that it involved an unlawful delegation of legislative power to the executive.[9] Far more serious was the second ground of invalidation, which likewise commanded unanimous support in the Court, that the Act was beyond the interstate commerce power of Congress. This made or appeared to make *any* legislation of the type involved impossible.

In the case of *Schechter Poultry Corp.* v. *United States*, it will be recalled, the Schechter brothers and their corporations were indicted for conspiracy to violate and for violations of the Code of Fair Competition for the Live Poultry Industry approved by the President with the declared purpose of effectuating the policies of Title 1 of the NIRA.[10] The Code concerned every person engaged in the business of selling, purchasing for resale, transporting, handling or slaughtering live poultry "from the time such poultry comes into the New York metropolitan area to the time it is first sold in slaughtered form."

With certain exceptions, the Code provided for a forty-hour work week and a minimum wage of 50 cents per hour. It prohibited employment of persons under sixteen years of age, provided for free collective bargaining, and fixed the minimum number of employees on a graduated basis, according to volume of business. It also proscribed various practices as "unfair methods of competition."

The evidence revealed that 96 per cent of the live poultry marketed in New York City came from without New York State. Most of this amount was consigned to commission men who ordinarily sold to slaughterhouse operators. Among these were the Schechter corporations which conducted wholesale poultry slaughterhouse markets in New York City. They ordinarily purchased their poultry from commission men in New York City but occasionally in Philadelphia. After slaughtering they sold the poultry to retail dealers and butchers who sold directly to consumers. They did not sell in interstate commerce.

The indictment charged the defendants with violation of the minimum wage and maximum hour provisions of the Code, permitting selection of chickens in violation of a "trade practice" provision of the Code, the sale of an unfit chicken and other infractions of the Code.

Two preliminary points stressed by the government were initially dealt with in the opinion of the Chief Justice. With respect to the first, that the provision of the Act authorizing the codes should be viewed in the light of the national crisis with which Congress was confronted, the Chief Justice said,

Undoubtedly, the conditions to which power is addressed are always to be considered when the exercise of power is challenged. Extraordinary conditions may call for extraordinary remedies. But the argument necessarily stops short of an attempt to justify action which lies outside the sphere of constitutional authority. Extraordinary conditions do not create or enlarge constitutional power. The Constitution established a national government with powers deemed to be adequate, as they have proved to be both in war and peace, but these powers of the national government are limited by the constitutional grants. Those who act under these grants are not at liberty to transcend the imposed limits because they believe that more or different power is necessary.

The supplementary argument that the crisis demanded the co-operative effort of trade and industry fostered by the codes was likewise rejected by the Chief Justice who pointed out that the statutory plan did not call simply for voluntary effort but involved the coercive exercise of the lawmaking power, binding equally those who did and did not assent.

The circuitous and slightly bewildering reasoning of the Chief Justice in regard to the effect of emergency upon constitutional power justly evoked this comment from Professor Corwin:

Just what meaning these carefully balanced phrases cancel down to is not entirely clear. Certainly, if "extraordinary conditions may call for extraordinary remedies" and this fact has to be considered "when the exercise of power is challenged," then to people unacquainted with legalistic jargon, or not disposed to be unduly impressed thereby, it would seem that "extraordinary conditions" do "enlarge constitutional power." [11]

There is difficulty too in understanding just how this reasoning might be reconciled with that of the Chief Justice in the BLAISDELL case decided only one year earlier. In that case the Chief Justice, while asserting that emergency did not create power, had added that "emergency may furnish the occasion for the exercise of power." He then explained that some grants of power to Congress, like the war power, were designed to cope with emergencies; others, like those providing for two Senators from each state, were specific and particularized and not affected by emergency; and still others were set forth "in general clauses" which required construction "to fill in the details." The contract clause he then held to be of the last type and proceeded to sustain the Act which in the absence of emergency would have been deemed unconstitutional. Might it not with equal validity have been held that the commerce clause belongs in the third category requiring construction "to fill in the details" and thus that the constitutional validity of the NIRA should be judged in the light of emergency?

Certain it is that the extent to which emergency enlarges delegated power was left obscure by the Chief Justice. Perhaps the explanation of the apparent confusion in the emergency doctrine as applied to the delegated powers of Congress and the reserve powers of the state lies, as Professor Thomas Reed Powell has suggested, in what was *not* said in the SCHECHTER case, that is, "that the emergency doctrine belongs only to the mellowing of restrictions in favor of private interest and can never be invoked in aid of determining the line between national and state power." [12]

Having brusquely dismissed emergency as a relevant consideration, the Chief Justice proceeded to hold the NIRA invalid as in excess of the interstate commerce power of Congress. He based this conclusion on the grounds that the transactions sought to be regulated were not "in" interstate commerce and only "indirectly" affected such commerce.

Codes of fair competition, Chief Justice Hughes said, appeared to be authorized without regard to any interstate commerce limitation although penalties provided were confined to violations "in any transaction in or affecting interstate or foreign commerce." Were the particular provisions of the Live Poultry Code, relating to wages and hours and retail sales, which the defendants were convicted for violating, within the interstate commerce power of Congress, he inquired.

Neither the slaughtering nor the sales in this case, he ruled, were "in" interstate commerce. So far as the poultry in question was concerned the flow in interstate commerce had ceased. It had come to permanent rest within the state and was not being held or sold in relation to any further transactions in interstate commerce and was not destined for transportation to other states. "Hence," he added,

decisions which deal with a stream of interstate commerce—where goods come to rest within a State temporarily and are later to go forward in interstate commerce—and with the regulations of transactions involved in that practical continuity of movement, are not applicable here.

The transactions of the defendants were thus deemed purely intrastate. Did they, however, "affect" interstate commerce so as to be subject to federal regulation? In this connection he insisted that in determining how far the federal government may go in controlling intrastate transactions, "there is a necessary and well-established distinction between direct and indirect effects." While the precise line can be drawn only as individual cases arise, the principle is clear for if federal power

were construed to reach all enterprises and transactions which could be said to have an indirect effect upon interstate commerce, the federal authority would embrace practically all the activities of the people and the authority of the State over its domestic concerns would exist only by sufferance of the federal government. Indeed, on such a theory, even the development of the State's commercial facilities would be subject to federal control.

The distinction, the Chief Justice insisted, was "a fundamental one, essential to the maintenance of our constitutional system." Otherwise, there would be virtually "no limit to the federal power and for all practical purposes we should have a completely centralized government."

In predicating constitutional invalidity upon the allegedly "indirect" effects of the transactions in question upon interstate commerce the Chief Justice availed himself of a distinction which has been the subject of much criticism. Some years earlier, in a dissenting opinion, Justice Stone spoke of the formula as "too mechanical, too uncertain in its application, and too remote from actualities, to be of value." The terms, he said, were labels "to describe a result rather than any trustworthy formula by which it is reached." He urged, instead, that the legislation be subjected to a searching factual analysis to determine "the actual effect on the flow of commerce." [13]

It must be recognized that although there is considerable merit in this criticism its importance may easily be exaggerated. The lack of felicity in the language employed should not be permitted to obscure the fact that while a formula measuring "the actual effect on the flow of commerce" may portend a more realistic and workable inquiry than one measuring "direct" and "indirect" effects, both impose limits upon the interstate commerce power and that the considerations which enter into defining those limits are likely, in the final analysis, to be pretty much the same. Either might be easily rationalized to support broad or restricted views of the reach of federal power.

Specifically, it is important to emphasize that in this case, so far as the *principle* involved in the distinction between "direct" and "indirect" effects is concerned, the Chief Justice did not go so far as to suggest that *all* production and local transactions are beyond the reach of the interstate commerce power. He simply said that was true if their effect on interstate commerce was "indirect." He turned then to consider "the provisions here in question in the light of this distinction."

In support of the validity of the legislation and the Code, the Government had contended, first, that hours and wages affect prices and that the paying of low wages or the exaction of long hours enabled operators to lower prices and thereby demoralize the price structure affecting interstate commerce. To this the Chief Justice replied that the persons employed in slaughtering and selling in local trade were not directly employed in interstate commerce and that their hours and wages had no direct relation to interstate commerce. He added that if these could be controlled by the federal government "because of their relation to cost and prices" as affecting interstate commerce, then

similar control might be exerted over other elements of cost, also affecting prices, such as the number of employees, rents, advertising, methods of doing business, etc. . . . If the cost of doing an intrastate business is in itself the permitted object of federal control, the extent of the regulation of cost would be a question of discretion and not of power.

A second contention of the Government had been that Congress might enact its own wage and hour law to govern the country because the establishment of high labor standards by states had been impeded by fear of loss of commerce. "The apparent implication," said the Chief Justice, with respect to this argument,

is that the federal authority under the commerce clause should be deemed to extend to the establishment of rules to govern wages and hours in intrastate trade and industry *generally throughout the country* [my italics], thus overriding the authority of the States to deal with domestic problems arising from labor conditions in their internal commerce.

He declared, "It is not the province of the Court to consider the economic advantages or disadvantages of such a centralized system. It is sufficient to say that the Federal Constitution does not provide for it."

The argument, finally, that economic recovery would generally be stimulated by higher wages met with the rejoinder of the Chief Justice that "without in any way disparaging this motive, it is enough to say that the recuperative efforts of the federal government must be made in a manner consistent with the authority granted by the

Constitution." The Act was accordingly held unconstitutional as in excess of federal regulatory power under the interstate commerce clause.

It was widely assumed that the Chief Justice had laid down the proposition in this case that Congress might not under any circumstances control or regulate local production and local relations intrastate in character. Thus, Professor Corwin, for example, asserted that the decision had revived the formula "which classified as 'indirect' and hence outside the power of Congress under the commerce clause, any effects which might reach commerce from conditions surrounding production, '*however inevitable and whatever the extent*' of such effects." [14]

That sweeping generalization is not supported, I believe, by careful analysis of the opinion of the Chief Justice. Whatever criticism may be levelled at the reasoning which found only "indirect" effect upon interstate commerce here, the fact remains that at no point did the Chief Justice suggest that *all* conditions surrounding production or local trade, *whatever* their effects upon interstate commerce, were exempt from federal control. What the Chief Justice did say was, first, that with respect to employees engaged in *intrastate* activities, the *mere fact* that their wages and hours constituted elements of employers' costs and thus bore upon the price structure affected *interstate* commerce only remotely and as such could not be the subject of regulation under the interstate commerce power of Congress.[15]

It is important to emphasize in this connection that in the view of the Court the Schechters were not engaged in interstate commerce in any phase of their activities. "In this," as Professor Powell points out, "they were fundamentally distinguishable from manufacturers who ship across state lines. Such manufacturers are the major beneficiaries or victims of the Sherman Act." [16]

The additional statements of the Chief Justice, that the federal authority could not be extended to govern wages and hours generally throughout the country because of the inability of states to establish high labor standards for fear of diversion of commerce or because such standards would aid in national recovery, do not sustain the broad generalization of Professor Corwin. They support only the narrower and more limited proposition that Congress may not control wages and hours in *all* local industry and trade *without regard* to the impact of such control upon interstate commerce.

The narrower scope of the ruling in the case is, I think, supported too by an analysis of the concurring opinion of Justice Cardozo,[17] who on the question of the reach of the interstate commerce power of Congress said that "little can be added to the opinion of the Court." That opinion, he thought, was concerned with matters of degree to which the law is not indifferent and affirmed the proposition that "activities local in their immediacy do not become interstate and national because of distant repercussions." Although "what is near and what is distant may at times be uncertain," there "is no penumbra of uncertainty obscuring judgment here. To find immediacy or directness here is to find it almost everywhere," said the concurring Justice. And he, too, sounded the warning that "if centripetal forces are to be isolated to the exclusion of the forces that oppose or counteract them, there will be an end to our federal system."

While possible consideration of expediency may not be ignored, there is little reason, in the light of the analysis made, to question the Chief Justice's own summary view of the scope of the SCHECHTER decision in *National Labor Relations Board* v. *Jones & Laughlin*.[18] He then wrote that

the fact that the employees here concerned were engaged in production is not determinative. The question remains as to the effect upon interstate commerce of the labor practice involved. In the SCHECHTER case, we found that the effect there was so remote as to be beyond the federal power. To find "immediacy or directness" there was to find it "almost everywhere," a result inconsistent with the maintenance of our federal system.

THE BITUMINOUS COAL CONSERVATION ACT

In May of 1936, the Court struck another blow at the New Deal program, this time by invalidating the Bituminous Coal Conservation Act of 1935. This legislation was the result of the chronic ailments afflicting the coal industry. Between 1913 and 1945 there had been nineteen official investigations and hearings affecting the industry. According to then Attorney General Robert Jackson,

These investigations had uniformly revealed a surplus capacity in the industry, cutthroat competition, including price cutting and wage cutting, a breakdown of the machinery of collective bargaining, heavy financial losses for operators, and violence and disorder in mining communities. They also disclosed serious waste of coal resources.[19]

Particularly violent had been several strikes arising from the failure of some operators to grant the right of collective bargaining which had led to bloodshed and martial law. After 1929, these difficulties were intensified.

In 1933, the Supreme Court had refused to rule that the creation of a collective marketing agency by the operators was a violation of the anti-trust law. It had not questioned the interstate character of an industry so vital to the national economy. In fact, the intimate connection between production and commerce had been recognized by the Chief Justice when he said by way of dictum: "The interests of producers and consumers are interlinked. When industry is grievously hurt, when producing concerns fail, when unemployment mounts and communities dependent upon profitable production are prostrated, the wells of commerce go dry." [20]

Under these circumstances, and since the states were powerless to stabilize conditions in this industry, Congress in 1935 enacted the Bituminous Coal Conservation Act. It imposed a tax of 15 per cent of the sale price or market value at the mine of all bituminous coal with provision for a draw-back of 90 per cent to those producers who submitted to the price-fixing and labor provisions of the Act. In addition to establishing procedure for the fixing of minimum and maximum prices, the Act also gave to employees the right to organize and bargain collectively with employers, free from interference, and made certain provisions for the fixing of maximum hours and minimum wages.

In *Carter* v. *Carter Coal Co.* the wage and hour provisions of the Act were, in part, declared invalid, with the concurrence of the Chief Justice, as involving an illegal delegation of legislative power.[21]

Much more significant, however, as placing it beyond the corrective power of Congress, was the decision of the majority, in an opinion by Justice Sutherland, that the Act was not an appropriate exercise of the taxing power and was also in excess of the interstate commerce power of Congress as to certain of its inseparable provisions. Ruling that a stockholder of a corporation might maintain a bill in a court of equity to enjoin that corporation from submitting to legislative exactions and regulations which allegedly would seriously and adversely affect the business of the corporation and were challenged as unconstitutional, Justice Sutherland went on to hold that the tax imposed by the Act to procure enforcement was not a tax but a penalty which could not be sustained under the taxing power of Congress. Nor, he reasoned, might the provisions of the Act for the control of wages, hours and working conditions of miners or guaranteeing the right of collective bargaining be upheld under the interstate commerce power of Congress, since these were local activities with at most a "secondary and indirect" effect upon commerce. Notwithstanding a separability clause in the Act, and without passing upon their separate validity, he concluded that the price-fixing provisions of the Act must also fall because, he said, the conclusion is unavoidable that these provisions "are so related to and dependent upon the labor provisions as conditions, considerations or compensations, as to make it clearly probable that the latter being held bad, the former would not have been passed."

In a "separate opinion" Chief Justice Hughes agreed that the stockholders were entitled to bring their suits; that the suits were not premature; that the so-called "tax" was in reality a penalty; that the constitutional power of the federal government to impose the penalty must rest, if at all, upon the commerce clause; "that production—in this case mining—which precedes commerce, is not itself commerce; and that the power to regulate commerce among the several States is not a power to regulate industry within the State." While, he added, Congress had adequate authority to maintain the orderly conduct of interstate commerce and to provide for the peaceful settlement of disputes which threaten it, it could not, he said,

use this protective authority as a pretext for the exertion of power to regulate activities and relations within the States which affect interstate commerce only indirectly. Otherwise, in view of the multitude of indirect effects, Congress in its discretion could assume control of virtually all the activities of the people to the subversion of the fundamental principle of the Constitution.

In that view, he concluded that the wage and hour section of the Act went "beyond any proper measure of protection of interstate commerce and attempts a broad regulation of industry within the State."

On the question of the validity of the price-fixing provisions of the Act, however, Chief Justice Hughes parted company with the majority of the Court. He pointed out that Congress had set up elaborate machinery for the fixing of prices of bituminous coal sold in interstate commerce; that the provision was being attacked *in limine* since the prices had not yet been fixed; that, if fixed, they could be contested and provision was made in the Act for review of the administrative ruling; that, if due process was violated by arbitrary action or if an attempt was made to fix prices for sales in intrastate commerce, judicial remedy was available. Furthermore, he reasoned, the evidence showed that substantially all the coal mined by the Carter Coal Company was sold f.o.b. mines and transported into other states to bill orders. "Such transactions," he said, "are in interstate commerce."

He dissented also from the conclusion of the Court that the plan for regulation of prices must fall because of its inseparability from the labor provisons, and urged that "the express provisions of the Act preclude such a finding of inseparability." The presumption created by the Congressional declaration must be upheld when it is apparent as here that the marketing and labor provisions "are not so interwoven that they cannot have separate operation and effect." [22]

Again it was widely asserted that the Chief Justice had lent his support to the proposition that *any* regulation of hours and wages in production and specifically in the mining of coal exceeded the interstate commerce power of Congress. That conclusion while understandable in the light of some ambiguous phrasing fails, I believe, upon careful analysis. It must be borne in mind that by the terms of the Act *every* producer of bituminous coal within the United States was brought within its provisions without regard to whether coal produced at individual mines entered the channels of interstate commerce. Furthermore, except for the flat declaration that the production and distribution of such coal bore upon and directly affected interstate commerce, the Act purported, in very general terms, to seek to protect the general public interest and the health

and comfort of the people, to maintain just relations between producers and employees, and to promote the general welfare by controlling nation-wide production and distribution of coal. It was to
the claim of power thus broadly based, which in his view would
convert our national government from a government of limited
and delegated powers to a unitary one, that the Chief Justice countered that "production—in this case mining—which precedes commerce, is not *itself* [my italics] commerce; and that the power to
regulate commerce among the several states is not a power to regulate industry within the State." In essence this amounted to no more
than a declaration by the Chief Justice that the regulation of industry
per se in terms of general welfare was a power denied to Congress.
It left open the question of whether a regulation of industrial employers limited and circumscribed by the impact of their activities
upon the movement of goods in interstate commerce was within
the power of Congress.

That the failure of Congress to tie the regulation of hours and
wages to interstate commerce in a clear and appropriate fashion
lay at the base of his rejection of such provisions is, I think, further
supported by the position the Chief Justice took with respect to the
price-fixing provisions of the Act which he thought should have
been upheld as constitutional. "The Act," he pointed out, "provides
for the regulation of the prices of bituminous coal sold in *interstate*
commerce and prohibits unfair methods of competition in *interstate*
commerce [all italics mine]." "Undoubtedly," he added,

transactions in carrying on interstate commerce are subject to the federal power to regulate that commerce. . . . The Court has repeatedly
stated that the power to regulate interstate commerce among the several
States is supreme and plenary. . . . Whether the policy of fixing prices
of commodities sold in interstate commerce is a sound policy is not for
our consideration.

But whatever may be said of the position of the Chief Justice, the
fact remained that a majority of the Court composed of the four
confirmed conservatives and Mr. Justice Roberts were apparently
committed to the proposition that the labor-management relation in
industry and all its aspects was a purely local relation beyond the
regulatory interstate commerce power of Congress.

The question of whether Congress might regulate the employer-employee relation when clearly connected and limited to those aspects which in the view of Congress burdened or obstructed interstate commerce was to come before the Court in the cases involving the constitutional validity of the National Labor Relations Act. In the interim, however, President Roosevelt with startling suddenness presented to Congress and to the nation a proposal to reorganize the Supreme Court.

CHAPTER 19

THE COURT UNDER ATTACK

THE NEW DEAL "UNDERMINED"

In November, 1936, President Franklin D. Roosevelt was re-elected President of the United States by a plurality of over ten million votes out of a total of forty-five million cast. He obtained the electoral college votes of all of the states in the Union but two. Although the President had given no indication of his intentions in the campaign, it was almost inevitable, in the light of his stunning victory and his belief that the decisions of the Court had "fairly completely undermined" his program, that he should turn his attention to the power of the Supreme Court.[1] Especially was this to be anticipated in the light of the fact that the President was convinced that many of these decisions had not been dictated by the Constitution but by the conservative economic bias of many of the Justices—a view that commanded some support in the Court itself. He was motivated, furthermore, by the conviction that some of the aged Justices of the Court, otherwise anxious to retire, were determined to remain on the bench to the very end in order to thwart his program. "The reactionary members of the Court," later wrote the President, "had apparently determined to remain on the bench as long as life continued—for the sole purpose of blocking any program of reform."[2] In this connection, it must be borne in mind that throughout the entire first term of President Roosevelt no opportunity arose for him to make a single appointment to the Supreme Court although six Justices had passed the retiring age of seventy.

Writing in 1941, when the struggle over the plan to reorganize the Court was consigned to history, President Roosevelt cited twelve decisions of the Hughes Court which, he said, had persuaded him that the New Deal program had been "fairly completely undermined." And "what was worse," he added, "the language and temper of the decisions indicated little hope for the future" at a time when moving up to and yet to come before the Court were such major New Deal measures as the Social Security Act, the National Labor Relations Act and the Public Utility Holding Company Act.[3]

What were these decisions? A chronological résumé may serve to convey a sense of the impact on the President's thinking.[4] In January, 1935, the Court, by a vote of eight to one, invalidated a section of the National Industrial Recovery Act designed to prevent a shipment of "hot oil" across state lines.[5] The following month the Court passed upon the power of the federal government to abrogate gold clause provisions in private and public contracts. While Congressional action was sustained as to private contracts, that result was achieved by the margin of a single vote.[6] At the same time, the Court, with a single dissent, held the abrogation of the gold clauses in public contracts unconstitutional but denied recovery when a narrow majority concluded that actual damage could not be shown.[7] In May, 1935, the Court, again by a five to four vote, invalidated the Railroad Retirement Act providing pensions for retired railroad employees.[8]

Three weeks later the Court handed down three unanimous decisions assailing New Deal actions. The first declared invalid the Frazier-Lemke Act designed to relieve farm mortgage debtors.[9] The second restricted the power of the President to remove members of regulatory commissions whose philosophy of government was at variance with his own.[10] This decision was widely criticized as inconsistent with the scope of the removal power of the President suggested in *Myers* v. *United States*.[11] The third struck down, as unconstitutional, the National Industrial Recovery Act.[12]

In 1936 important New Deal legislation also fell before the Court. Most vital was the decision of the Court in January, 1936, invalidating the Agricultural Adjustment Act by vote of six to three.[13] In February, 1936, while the Court, eight to one, upheld the right of the federal government to develop water power into electric energy at the Wilson Dam and to sell such energy,[14] its decision was based upon the specific and narrow delegations of power to the national government to wage war and to improve navigation, was expressly limited to a single dam and established the right of disaffected stockholders to contest the action of directors when the validity of Congressional action was at issue.

A clear indication of a basic lack of sympathy on the part of a majority of the members of the Court with the practices of administrative agencies in regulating the economy as an aspect of New Deal policy was revealed in April, 1936, when the Court, in a six to two division, brutally excoriated the Securities and Exchange Commission for refusing to permit a registrant to withdraw an allegedly false or misleading statement to escape penalty.[15]

One month later, the Bituminous Coal Conservation Act of 1935 designed "to bring order out of chaos in the bituminous industry," [16] through the regulation of wages and hours of employees and the fixing of prices, was nullified by the Court.[17] Finally, in June, 1936, five Justices upset the New York State minimum wage for women law.[18] While this last decision affected state legislation, the fact that the law was held to constitute a denial of due process, which also limits federal action, seemed to suggest that any federal legislation establishing minimum wages for women, and certainly for men, would meet a similar fate. This created what the President and others characterized as a "no man's land" which placed the regulation of wages, even of the sweatshop variety, beyond the reach of any government, federal or state.[19]

How had the Chief Justice voted in relation to Administration supported program and policy in the twelve cases? In seven he had voted against the Administration and in five he had supported it. He had cast his vote against the New Deal position in the "hot oil," farm mortgage relief, Federal Trade Commission, National Industrial Recovery Act, Agricultural Adjustment Act, Securities and Exchange Commission and bituminous coal cases. He had supported the New Deal position in the private gold clause, public gold clause, railroad pension, Tennessee Valley Authority and minimum wage for women cases.[20]

Throughout the period in question, from January, 1935, until June, 1936, the composition of the Court had remained constant. How had the position of the Chief Justice compared with that of the other members of the Court in the twelve cases considered crucial by President Roosevelt? The Court had been unanimous in ruling against the Administration in three of the cases, farm mortgage relief, Federal Trade Commission and NIRA. In the remaining nine cases the Justices had given their support to the Administration as follows: Justice Cardozo in all nine, Justice Brandeis and Stone in eight each, Chief Justice Hughes in five, Justice Roberts in three, Justices Van Devanter, Sutherland and Butler in one each, and Justice McReynolds in none. Since four of the members of the Court, with a single exception affecting three of the four, had voted against the Administration in all twelve of the cases in question, and three members of the Court had supported the Administration in at least eight of the cases, the crucial balance of power upon which constitutionality had generally depended had been in the hands of the Chief Justice and Mr. Justice Roberts.

THE PRESIDENT'S PLAN TO REORGANIZE THE COURT

For some time before and after his reelection in 1936 President Roosevelt considered alternative proposals for curbing the power of the Supreme Court. The plan which was finally presented was worked out in great secrecy by the President with the assistance of Attorney General Homer S. Cummings and Solicitor General Stanley Reed (now a Justice of the Supreme Court).[21] With regard to the real authors of the plan, Franklin D. Roosevelt wrote: "I discussed the objectives and the issues with many people; but in the final determination of details I was joined by the Attorney General and Solicitor General of the United States, and by nobody else." [22]

On February 5, 1937, the President sent to Congress his Court message accompanied by a letter from the Attorney General and by a bill. These made no reference to the course of judicial decisions and their thwarting of New Deal measures. They dealt, instead, with the effects upon government and private interest of overburdened courts and superannuated judges. The President's message insisted that the Supreme Court had been "forced by the sheer necessity of keeping up with its business to decline, without even an explanation, to hear 87% of the cases presented to it by private litigants" for review. It discussed the infirmities of age of Justices and the need for "a constant and systematic addition of younger blood" to "vitalize the courts." According to a report given by Thomas J. Corcoran to Harry Hopkins, some years after the event, this approach was suggested by Cummings who had "discovered that

McReynolds, our bitterest opponent on the Court, had while Attorney General in the Wilson Administration proposed a scheme to provide substitutes for judges who were disabled." [23]

The message made only one proposal directly affecting the Supreme Court. The President sought authority from Congress to appoint a new Justice to the Supreme Court whenever an incumbent reached the age of seventy and failed to retire on full pay as existing law permitted. A maximum of fifteen judges was suggested. Six Justices, the Chief Justice and Justice Brandeis, Van Devanter, Butler, McReynolds and Sutherland, were then above seventy years of age.[24]

On March 9, 1937, the President spoke to the people in support of his plan and shifted the basis of his attack. "The Courts," he said, "have cast doubts on the ability of the elected Congress to protect us against catastrophe by meeting squarely our modern social and economic conditions." And this, he maintained, was not because of the Constitution, but because the Court has been acting "as a policy-making body" as many of the Justices have themselves charged. Amendment he rejected as impossible "within anything like a reasonable time" in the face of the opposition of "any powerful economic interests or the leaders of any powerful political party." He referred again to the need for a reinvigorated judiciary but made no reference to the inability of the Court to keep up with its work.

There ensued a bitter and protracted struggle within the Congress and the nation. Few sought to justify the trend of Court decisions, but many assailed the method of reform.[25]

The Court whose existence as an independent and coordinate agency of the federal government seemed fundamentally threatened could not fail but be disturbed by the Roosevelt plan. And the dismay of the Court was most acutely felt by its Chief Justice. Yet the traditions of the Court forbade his direct and overt participation in a political controversy before Congress. If the reports of Alsop and Catledge are to be credited, attempts were made to persuade Chief Justice Hughes to testify before the Senate Judiciary Committee but without success. He was persuaded, however, to address himself by letter to the procedural arguments raised in support of the plan.

The leader of the opposition to the Court plan was Senator Burton K. Wheeler of Montana, whose orthodox liberalism seemed at the

time beyond question. On March 22, 1937, as the first of the opposition witnesses, he appeared before the Senate Judiciary Committee to testify against the bill. As a stunning surprise he read to
the Committee a letter addressed to him by Chief Justice Hughes,
who said that his statement had the approval of Justices Van Devanter and Brandeis. While, wrote the Chief Justice, he had not
been able to consult with the members of the Court generally because of lack of time, he added, "I am confident that it is in accord
with the views of the Justices." [26] In the form of responding to
inquiries made by Senator Wheeler, the Chief Justice then pointed
out that "the Supreme Court is fully abreast of its work," that
properly and as contemplated by Act of Congress the Supreme
Court grants review, when not a matter of right, only in cases of
great public interest, and that "no single court of last resort, whatever
the number of judges, could dispose of all the cases which arise
in this vast country and which litigants would seek to bring up if
the right of appeal were unrestricted." The considerations which
guide the Court in granting certiorari were set forth and he noted
that "petitions for certiorari are not apportioned among the Justices." All the Justices participate in the decision. About 60 per cent
of the applications for certiorari, he said, are wholly without merit
and ought never to have been made, about 20 per cent have a degree
of plausibility which fail, however, to survive critical examination,
and the remainder show substantial grounds and are granted. If the
Court errs, he maintained, it is on the side of liberality, and added,

An increase in the number of Justices of the Supreme Court, apart from
any question of policy, which I do not discuss, would not promote the
efficiency of the Court. It is believed that it would impair that efficiency
so long as the court acts as a unit. There would be more judges to hear,
more judges to confer, more judges to discuss, more judges to be convinced and to decide.[27]

As for the suggestion that with more Justices the Court could
hear cases in divisions, aside from its impracticability in light of the
importance of many of the cases heard, he pointed out that the
Constitution vests the judicial power "in one Supreme Court. . . .
The Constitution does not appear to authorize two or more Supreme
Courts or two or more parts of a Supreme Court functioning in effect as separate courts."

The effect of the Hughes letter was to expose as without foundation the claim of the President that the efficiency of the Court had suffered because of the size of the Court or the age of the Justices. And although this approach had already been deemphasized by the Administration, in the public mind it had retained some cogency.

So much of the Chief Justice's statement as dealt with questions of fact in regard to the work of the Court might be regarded, except perhaps for its timing, as a non-political reply to legitimate inquiries. The advisory opinion, however, offered by the Chief Justice that any provision for the Court to hear cases in divisions would be unconstitutional was contrary to the practice of the Justices in passing only upon actual cases and controversies before them. As such its non-political character is open to serious question.[28]

One week later, on March 29, 1937, the struggle for reorganization of the Court was dealt another blow when the Chief Justice, speaking for a narrow majority, rendered an opinion, only nine months after the Court's decision in the MOREHEAD case, upholding a minimum wage for women law enacted by the State of Washington in 1913 and specifically overruling the ADKINS case.[29] The same day the Court unanimously sustained the new Railway Labor Act providing for collective bargaining and mediation in railroad labor disputes [30] and a revised version of the Frazier-Lemke Act for the relief of farm mortgagors previously held unconstitutional.[31] Even more important, as involving in the mind of many a more elastic interpretation of the commerce power of Congress than had prevailed in the SCHECHTER and CARTER cases, on April 12, 1937, the Court handed down a series of decisions sustaining by five to four votes the constitutionality of the National Labor Relations Act as applied to manufacturers of goods—steel,[32] trailers,[33] and men's clothing.[34] Finally, on May 24, 1937, the same Court upheld the constitutional validity of the unemployment and old-age features of the Social Security Act [35] and a state law providing a tax for unemployment insurance.[36]

It would tax credibility to assume that Chief Justice Hughes and Mr. Justice Roberts, who exercised a balance of power in the Court, were unaware and unconcerned about the political significance of these decisions. That is not to say that their motivation was simply to defeat the Court plan. Unlike the four die-hard conservatives,

Hughes and, to a lesser extent, Roberts, had earlier revealed some appreciation for and sympathy with the need for extensions of governmental power over the economy. But, doubtless, they also realized that if the Court continued to block social reform, in the face of an unprecedented political mandate to the Administration, it was the Court and not the New Deal which would ultimately be shorn of power.[37]

Yet one more blow was struck by a Justice of the Court in the struggle over the Bill. At the close of the Court term, in June, Justice Van Devanter resigned. In this connection Robert Jackson commented, "What planning preceded it has never been revealed, but it was so perfectly timed as a strategic move that it seems unlikely to have been accidental." [38]

In June, too, came the adverse report of the Senate Judiciary Committee.[39] And on July 14 Senator Joseph Robinson, the leader of the floor fight for the President's bill, suddenly died. This was the final stroke of ill fortune for the Administration. On August 24, 1937, some minor *lower* court reforms embodied in a Judiciary Act were enacted into law. Singularly perspicacious was the opinion expressed by Robert Jackson: "In politics the black-robed reactionary Justices had won over the master liberal politician of our day. In law the President defeated the recalcitrant Justices in their own Court." [40]

In the course of the historic debate over the President's plan the whole record of the Court was spread before the nation. Its every virtue and weakness, its every contribution and abuse of power was thoroughly explored. Many of the arguments that had been advanced in opposition to the confirmation of Charles Evans Hughes were again reiterated. That the plan failed of acceptance within less than a year after the affirmation of overwhelming support of the President and his general program by the people was no doubt owing in part to the initial indirection of the President, to certain tactical maneuvers and fortuitous events already mentioned, and to the quickened recognition of two Justices of the Court, the Chief Justice and Mr. Justice Roberts, that continuing frustration of economic reforms vital to recovery would bring disaster to the nation or to the Court or to both. Fundamentally, however, failure may, I believe, be attributed to the deeply held conviction of the people, whether amounting to a majority or near-majority, and whether warranted or unwarranted, that an independent judiciary vested with authority to annul legislative acts was essential to the preservation of our democracy and our basic institutions.

THE END OF AN ERA: REEXAMINATION AND RETREAT

The startling and far-reaching reversals of established precedents, some hoary with age and veneration, and the redefinition of the role of the Court in constitutional cases, which began early in 1937, even before the composition of the Court had been altered, signified a recognition that the age of *laissez-faire* was dead. Some of the causes of this belated recognition have been examined. It remains to consider the nature of the changes effected. These changes in so far as they gave expanded scope to the police powers of the states and diminished intergovernmental tax immunity have been the subjects of earlier examination. Reference has been made, too, to some of the Court's decisions which sustained the exercises of federal power while the President's plan was in the balance but these will receive more extended consideration. In January, 1937, however, even before the President presented his proposals to Congress, but after his reelection, came a unanimous decision of the Court which suggested that retreat may already have begun.

Federal "Police Power"

The Court has never deviated from the principle that the federal government may not legislate simply and directly for the purpose of promoting the general welfare of the people of the United States. The sole exceptions recognized by the Court relate to the District of Columbia, in which Congress enjoys general police powers, and in some respects to the conduct of foreign affairs.[1] This principle is based upon the nature of federal power which is delegated and limited under the Constitution.

But granting this limitation upon federal governing power, the issue presented in *Kentucky Whip & Collar Co.* v. *Illinois Central R.R.*[2] was whether Congress might use an admittedly delegated power not to serve some purpose intimately connected with the nature of the specific delegation but in order to foster its own conception of the public good or to aid in the effectuation of the social policy of states.

In sustaining the constitutionality of federal legislation which made it unlawful, subject to fine and forfeiture, to transport in interstate commerce goods made by convict labor into any state where the goods were to be sold or used in violation of its laws, Chief Justice Hughes, for the Court, rejected the contention that the Act was invalid because the articles immediately affected, horse collars and harness, were "useful articles." So, he pointed out, had been the stolen motor vehicles and kidnapped persons whose transportation across state lines had been validly made a federal offense.

Having repudiated any distinction based upon the alleged harmlessness of the articles, he proceeded to sustain the legislation on two general grounds. First, finding support for the belief that the sale of convict-made goods in competition with the products of free labor was an evil in fact and in the legislation of many states, he affirmed that if a state might restrict or prohibit such sales internally, "the Congress may, if it sees fit, put forth its power to regulate interstate commerce so as to prevent that commerce from being used to impede the carrying out of the state policy." This power, he pointed out, had repeatedly been used to prevent the frustration of valid state laws.

Second, and without regard to state action, he insisted that "the Congress in exercising the power confided to it by the Constitution is as free as the States to recognize the fundamental interests of free labor." And, in this connection, he added, the means employed "may have the quality of police regulations." This right, he maintained, derived from the plenary nature of the interstate commerce power which is subject to no limitation other than that which is found in the Constitution itself. The validity of the Act was accordingly upheld.

In view of the reasoning of the Chief Justice, in which the entire Court acquiesced, it might have been anticipated that the Court would find it necessary to overrule its decision in *Hammer* v. *Dagenhart*,[3] in which, by a narrowly divided vote, it had held unconstitutional a federal statute barring the transportation in interstate commerce of certain products of child labor. The Court had then maintained that its precedents permitted the closing of the channels of interstate commerce only when their use was "necessary to the accomplishment of harmful results," and denied that this could be done when the goods shipped were "of themselves harmless." In relation to "ordinary commodities," barring interstate transportation was considered an attempt to interfere with the purely internal affairs of the states. The Court had then also denied that Congress might aid high standard states against unfair competition by closing the channels of interstate transportation to manufacturers in those states where the local laws did not meet what Congress deemed "to be the more just standard of other states."

It is difficult to comprehend how Chief Justice Hughes could repudiate the distinction based upon the harmlessness of the articles, affirm the right of Congress to use its interstate commerce power to aid in the effectuation of state policy or to establish its own policy having the quality of police regulations, and still maintain that the Court's ruling in the HAMMER case in "no way contravenes" the principles enunciated in the instant case. The evil involved in competition of convict with free labor, it would be difficult to argue, is any greater, or presents a different constitutional question, than that involved in the competition of child with adult labor.

Whatever may be said, however, of the labored, if characteristic attempt of the Chief Justice at a non-existent distinction, whether motivated by concern for stability or by expediency, the fact remains that the decision of the unanimous court in the KENTUCKY WHIP & COLLAR Co. case, in the broadest possible terms, affirmed the authority of Congress to close the channels of interstate commerce to the products of local manufacturing on the basis of its own reasonable and non-arbitrary policy with regard to the general welfare. This struck a devastating blow at the doctrine of dual federalism in so far as it suggested that the rights of the states over local production limited the interstate commerce power of Congress and in that sense was inconsistent not only with the reasoning in the HAMMER case but with that of Justice Sutherland in the CARTER case as well.[4]

It was not, however, until the decision of the Court in *United States* v. *Darby*,[5] delivered in 1941, after the composition of the Court had been radically altered, that the HAMMER case was specifically overruled. Sustaining the validity of the Fair Labor Standards Act of 1938 which barred the shipment in interstate commerce of products manufactured by employees engaged in interstate commerce or in the production of goods for interstate commerce whose wages were less than a prescribed minimum or whose weekly hours of labor were greater than a prescribed maximum, Justice Stone, speaking for the Court, with reference to the HAMMER case, said:

The distinction on which the decision was rested that Congressional power to prohibit interstate commerce is limited to articles which in themselves have some harmful or deleterious property—a distinction which was novel when made and unsupported by any provision of the Constitution—has long since been abandoned.

In support of this conclusion he cited, *inter alia*, the KENTUCKY WHIP & COLLAR CO. case. Chief Justice Hughes acquiesced without comment.

THE NATIONAL LABOR RELATIONS ACT

On March 29, 1937, as has already been noted, while the President's court reform proposals were being debated in an atmosphere of strife and bitterness, the Court handed down three decisions, the first sustaining a minimum wage for women law, a second approving an amended version of the Frazier-Lemke Act for the relief of farm mortgagors which had been carefully framed to meet the constitutional objections expressed in the RADFORD case, and a third upholding the Railway Labor Act of 1934. Since the authority of the federal government to protect collective bargaining rights of interstate railway employees had earlier been recognized, the last case in extending that right to so-called "back-shop" employees had a limited importance.[6]

Much more vital was the decision of the Court, announced in April, 1937, in *National Labor Relations Board* v. *Jones & Laughlin Steel Corp.*,[7] declaring valid the National Labor Relations Act of 1935 known as the Wagner Act.

Section 1 of the Act affirmed that the denial of self-organization and collective bargaining rights to employees leads to industrial strife with the intent or effect of burdening or obstructing commerce and declared it to be the policy of the United States to eliminate the causes of obstructions to the free flow of commerce arising out of this denial. Other sections of the Act granted the right of employees to self-organization and to bargain collectively through representatives of their own choosing, defined certain unfair labor practices including interference with these rights, and created a National Labor Relations Board empowered to prevent these unfair labor practices affecting commerce by established procedures. To secure enforcement of its orders the Board was authorized to petition designated courts which were enjoined to regard the findings of the Board, as to the facts, if supported by evidence, as conclusive. The Act did not compel employers to come to agreements with employees but did require them to bargain in good faith.

The Jones & Laughlin Steel Corporation was found by the Board to have violated the Act by engaging in unfair labor practices affecting commerce in discriminating against members of the union with regard to hire and tenure of employment, and in interfering with their self-organization. At issue was the legality of a Board order requiring the corporation to desist from such practices and to reinstate with back pay employees discriminatorily discharged.

A fundamental preliminary inquiry was whether the basic rights given protection by the Act, without regard to the effect of the violation of these rights upon interstate commerce, were an appropriate concern of governmental power within the limitations imposed by the requirements of due process of law. The right of employees to choose their own representatives and bargain collectively free from coercion by the employer, said the Chief Justice, speaking for a narrow majority of the Court,[8] "is a fundamental right" correlative with the right of the employer to organize its own business. "Discrimination and coercion to prevent the free exercise of the right of employees to self-organization and representation is a proper subject for condemnation by competent legislative authority." Restraints for the purposes of preventing an unjust interference with the right of employees to organize, to secure the redress of grievances, and to promote agreements with employers cannot be considered arbitrary or capricious. "The theory of the Act is that free opportunity for negotiation with accredited representatives of employees is likely to promote industrial peace and bring about the adjustments and agreements which the Act in itself does not attempt to compel."

The Act was accordingly sustained against attack as a denial of due process. The difficulty in reconciling this ruling with the Court's decisions in the ADAIR and COPPAGE cases was disposed of by the Chief Justice with the simple assertion that these earlier precedents were "inapplicable to legislation of this character." Just as the Chief Justice had, as an Associate Justice, joined in the dissent of Justice Day in attempting to distinguish the COPPAGE from the earlier ADAIR statute, he now sought to distinguish both from the present one.[9] By what tortuous alchemy these cases may all be reconciled is difficult to discern.

The distinction between the earlier acts and that in this case, said the Chief Justice, lay in the fact that the last did not "interfere with the normal exercise of the right of the employer to select its employees or to discharge them." But what are the "normal" rights of the employer in regard to hire and tenure? In all three statutes there was substantial interference with the freedom of the employer to hire and fire at will and essentially in the same way and for the same reasons. One form of interference, given the concept of a free labor contract, was no more abnormal than another. The distinction attempted by the Chief Justice was thoroughly untenable, and was yet another illustration of the refusal of the Chief Justice to directly overrule precedents in the very process of their emasculation.[10]

Be that as it may, the recognition of the right of self-organization and collective bargaining as a "fundamental right" and its protection as the appropriate concern of legislative power constituted a significant departure by the Court from a mere negative, Hobbesian conception of liberty as simply "an absence of law" upon which reliance had been placed by the Court in many earlier decisions in striking down social legislation. "Liberty" was now conceived of as a balance of rights and liberties with the Court, of course, retaining its ultimate right to determine the imbalance. There was at least the tacit recognition that the denial of the liberty of the employer to hire and fire at will must be weighed against the liberty of his employees to organize and bargain collectively.

The legislation having met the test of due process, the inquiry remained whether and the extent to which the rights given protection might be affirmatively encompassed within the delegated power of Congress to regulate interstate commerce.

Dealing first with the declared scope of the Act, the Chief Justice found that

The grant of authority to the Board does not purport to extend to the relationship between all industrial employees and employers. Its terms do not impose collective bargaining upon all industry regardless of effects upon interstate or foreign commerce. It purports to reach only what may be deemed to burden or obstruct that commerce.

"And thus qualified," he continued,

it must be construed as contemplating the exercise of control within constitutional bounds. It is a familiar principle that acts which directly burden or obstruct interstate or foreign commerce, or its free flow, are within the reach of the congressional power. Acts having that effect are not rendered immune because they grow out of labor disputes. It is the effect upon commerce, not the source of the injury, which is the criterion.

The Act being a valid regulation of interstate commerce in its *declared scope*, the Chief Justice turned to consider, specifically, whether the industrial relations and activities, in the manufacturing department of the corporation, affected such commerce "in such a close and intimate fashion as to be subject to federal control."

The essential facts found by the National Labor Relations Board, in this connection, were that the corporation owned and operated ore, coal and limestone properties, lake and river transportation facilities and terminal railroads located at its manufacturing plants. In its plants in which it engaged in the manufacture of iron and steel, its operations might be likened, the Board said, "to the heart of a self-contained, highly integrated body," drawing in the raw material from Michigan, Minnesota, West Virginia, and Pennsylvania in part through arteries and by means controlled by it, transforming the materials and then pumping them out to all parts of the nation through a vast mechanism which it had elaborated.

In the view of the four dissenting Justices, McReynolds, Van Devanter, Sutherland and Butler, these facts did not serve as an adequate basis upon which to support the constitutional validity of the NLRA. They denied that regulation could be sustained on the theory, urged by the Government, that it affected activity which was part of a stream of commerce. They maintained that two distinct movements were involved in the case at issue. The first, they said, brings in raw materials and there ends. "Then follows manufacture, a separate and local activity." Upon completion, the second distinct movement begins. The SCHECHTER case, they stated, condemned assertion of federal power in respect to commodities which had come to rest after interstate transportation. The CARTER case condemned assertion of federal power in respect to commodities whose interstate transportation had not yet begun.

The contention that the Act validly regulated interstate commerce because in the absence of rights of self-organization and collective bargaining strikes would be engendered which would reduce the volume of goods moving in interstate commerce met the rejoinder that "A more remote and indirect interference with interstate commerce or a more definite invasion of the powers reserved to the states is difficult, if not impossible, to imagine." Manufacturing, they insisted, was not "commerce" and relied upon principles "established" in the SCHECHTER and CARTER cases to the effect that the power of Congress under the commerce clause did not extend to relations between employers and their employees engaged in manufacture.

In differing with the conclusion reached by his dissenting colleagues, it was not necessary, said the Chief Justice, to determine whether the regulatory power could be sustained on the theory that such regulation, as applied to the corporation in this instance, occurred in the "stream" or "flow" of commerce, of which the manufacturing plants in question were a focal point at which industrial strife would cripple the entire movement. "Burdens and obstructions," he stated, "may be due to injurious action springing from other sources."

On what theory, then, might the regulation be upheld? Here he returned to a principle which he had first enunciated in the SHREVEPORT case.

Although activities may be intrastate in character when separately considered, if they have such a close and substantial relation to interstate commerce that their control is essential or appropriate to protect that commerce from burdens and obstructions, Congress cannot be denied the power to exercise that control.

Support for the general proposition that "intrastate activities, by reason of close and intimate relation to interstate commerce, may fall within federal control," he found, not only in the SHREVEPORT and a related case, but also in the application of the federal anti-trust act to combinations of employers in productive industry.

It is thus apparent that the fact that the employees here concerned were engaged in production is not determinative. The question remains as to the effect upon interstate commerce of the labor practice involved. In the SCHECHTER case, *supra*, we found that the effect was so remote as to be beyond the federal power.

"Giving full weight," therefore, to the employer's contention with respect to a break in the continuity of the stream of commerce involved in its manufacturing operations, "the fact remains," he said, "that the stoppage of those operations would have a most serious effect upon interstate commerce. In view of [the corporation's] far-flung activities, it is idle to say that the effect would be indirect and remote." The question of direct and indirect effects cannot be dealt with "in an intellectual vacuum." Whatever may be true of a host of local enterprises throughout the country,

it does not follow that other industrial activities do not have such a close and intimate relation to interstate commerce as to make the presence of industrial strife a matter of the most urgent national concern. . . . We have often said that interstate commerce itself is a practical conception. It is equally true that interference with that commerce must be appraised by a judgment that does not ignore actual experience.

The corporation's enterprise, he added, "presents in a most striking way the close and intimate relation which a manufacturing industry may have to interstate commerce."

The attack upon the Act as one-sided was met by the observation that "we have frequently said that the legislative authority, exerted within its proper field, must not embrace all evils within its reach." Congress may proceed by cautious advance, step by step. So also the procedural provisions of the Act were upheld since the Act established standards to which the Board had to conform and elaborated a set of processes barring arbitrary action and compatible with fair practice. The conclusion of the Chief Justice was that the order of the Board was within its competency and the Act was valid as applied.

At the same time and upon the authority of the decision in the

JONES & LAUGHLIN case, Chief Justice Hughes ruled that the National Labor Relations Act and orders made under it by the National Labor Relations Board could be validly applied to a manufacturer of commercial trailers in its relations with its employees at its factory in Michigan, upon a showing that more than 50 per cent in value of the materials used in the plant came from outside of Michigan and more than 80 per cent of its finished products were shipped outside the state.[11] Similarly, the Act was held validly applied to a manufacturer of garments in its relations with its employees at its factory in Virginia, it being shown that it imported its cloth from other states and sold almost all of the finished garments in other states.[12]

A widespread contention was that the Chief Justice had shifted his position in the JONES & LAUGHLIN case from that taken by him in the SCHECHTER and CARTER cases. Thus, in a typical comment it was said that "Mr. Roosevelt's hypothetical forgotten man, confronted with JONES & LAUGHLIN and asked to reconcile it with the previous SCHECHTER and CARTER decisions, would probably quote Mr. Dooley: 'The Supreme Court follows the election returns.' "[13] That assumption, I have attempted elsewhere to show, misconstrues the scope of the Chief Justice's opinions in the two earlier cases.

The argument that the control of the labor-management relation in the poultry business in the SCHECHTER case and the mining industry in the CARTER case was no more local or "indirect" in its effect upon interstate commerce than the control of that relation in the steel or trailer or clothing industries in the NATIONAL LABOR RELATIONS BOARD cases is, for purposes of judging the consistency of the Chief Justice, beside the point. To have sustained the NIRA and the Bituminous Coal Act, *as these statutes were framed*, in the view of the Chief Justice, was to have sustained the regulation by Congress, under the interstate commerce power, of *all* industry in virtually all phases of its activity without regard to the effect of such activity upon interstate commerce. Such breadth of power, said the Chief Justice, had not been delegated to the federal government. In short, what the Chief Justice insisted upon was that the exercise of power by Congress be appropriately connected with a regulation of interstate commerce if the legislation were to be sustained. The distinction he drew between "direct" and "indirect" effects was, upon analysis, no more than an affirmation of this principle, if lacking in felicity of phrasing. So conceived, the JONES & LAUGHLIN statements that "direct" or "indirect" effects must not be weighed in "an intellectual vacuum" but must have regard for interstate commerce as a "practical conception" that does not ignore "actual experience" and matters of "degree" represent a more realistic approach to a determination of whether the subject is within the regulatory power but not a departure from principle.

After all, even in the absence of the qualifying expressions applied to "direct" and "indirect" in the JONES & LAUGHLIN case, the Chief Justice had shown little disposition to treat the distinction as supplying a mechanical formula. This was reflected in his reasoning in the MINNESOTA RATE CASES, decided in 1913, his dictum in the APPALACHIAN COAL case, decided in 1933, both earlier discussed, and above all, by his SHREVEPORT decision of 1914, upon the reasoning of which the Chief Justice laid principal stress in the JONES & LAUGHLIN decision. In SHREVEPORT, it may be recalled, he affirmed the right of the federal government under its interstate commerce power to control *purely intrastate* railroad rates when because of their close and substantial relation to interstate commerce their control was essential or appropriate to protect interstate commerce from obstructions.

In the light of these decisions of the Chief Justice and the consistent breadth given by him to the power of Congress under the interstate commerce clause, provided Congress itself sought to establish a real and substantial connection between the regulation and such commerce, and my analyses of the SCHECHTER and CARTER cases, it is, I believe, fair to suggest that the decision of the Chief Justice in the JONES & LAUGHLIN case followed logically in the path of his earlier interstate commerce decisions.

It must not be assumed from what has been said with respect to the essential consistency of the Chief Justice, however, that the JONES & LAUGHLIN case disturbed no doctrines of the Court. One such doctrine which had retained considerable vitality despite some glancing blows was the doctrine of "dual federalism." It was based upon the notion that notwithstanding the supremacy of federal action within the sphere of its delegated power, the reservation to the states or to the people of power not delegated to the federal government acted in some general way as a check upon the delegated powers. This was suggested in the case of *Hammer* v. *Dagenhart* when the Court, in invalidating an Act of Congress barring certain products of child labor from the channels of interstate commerce, said, "The grant of authority over a purely federal matter was not intended to destroy the local power always existing and carefully reserved to the States in the Tenth Amendment to the Constitution." It was reiterated in *United States* v. *Butler* when it was stated that "wholly apart" from whether the attempted exercise of power by Congress fell within the scope of a delegated power, it was prohibited by "the reserved rights of the States." And in the CARTER case, in the prevailing opinion of Justice Sutherland, the Court affirmed that no matter how greatly interstate commerce was affected by the evils which come from the struggles between employers and employees over working conditions, "the conclusive answer is that the evils are local evils over which the federal government has no legislative control. The relation of employer and employee is a local relation." The view that the reserved power of the states or that production and the labor relation being local by *their very nature* limited the sphere of delegated federal power was certainly rendered untenable by the decision of the Chief Justice in the JONES & LAUGHLIN case that, given the fact of close and substantial relationship between local activity and interstate commerce, Congress might control such activity. In so far as the doctrine of "dual federalism" had retained its efficacy with the Court, the result of the JONES & LAUGHLIN decision was "to throw down the barriers of dual federalism which had heretofore excluded Congress from the regulation of productive industry." [14]

It was not until *United States* v. *Darby*, however, in the decision of which the Chief Justice acquiesced, that the concept of "dual federalism" as an independently operative limitation on delegated federal power was specifically repudiated. Justice Stone then stated for the entire Court,

The [Tenth] Amendment states but a truism that all is retained which has not been surrendered. There is nothing in the history of its adoption to suggest that it was more than declaratory of the relationship between the national and state governments as it had been established by the Constitution before the Amendment.

About a year after JONES & LAUGHLIN the Chief Justice had occasion to restate his views regarding the constitutional sweep of the National Labor Relations Act. In *Santa Cruz Fruit Packing Company* v. *National Labor Relations Board*,[15] decided in March, 1938, he upheld the applicability of this Act to a company engaged at its plant in Oakland, California, in canning, packing and shipping fruits and vegetables, which at its peak season employed from 1,200 to 1,500 persons, and shipped about 37 per cent of its total "pack" into interstate and foreign commerce.

He rejected the contention that the manufacturing and processing in which the company was engaged constituted local activities beyond the reach of the interstate commerce power. Defining the meaning of the JONES & LAUGHLIN decision, he said, "The close and intimate effect which brings the subject within the reach of federal power may be due to activities in relation to productive industry, although that industry when separately viewed is local."

As for the distinction made between "direct" and "indirect" effects, the terminology, he said, was not crucial. The criterion was necessarily one of degree. "In maintaining the balance of the constitutional grants and limitations, it is inevitable that we should define their applications in the gradual process of inclusion and exclusion." [16]

Just how markedly the logical implications of JONES & LAUGHLIN might be extended was made clear in *Consolidated Edison* v. *National Labor Relations Board*.[17] Consolidated Edison, which produced and sold its electricity solely within the state and was under the "plenary control" of state regulatory agencies, denied the power of the federal government to regulate its relations with its employees under the interstate commerce power and specifically under the National Labor Relations Act.

The decisive factor in encompassing the utility within the Act, said Chief Justice Hughes, was the "effect upon interstate and foreign commerce of an interruption through industrial strife of the service" of the company. In determining the constitutional bounds of the interstate commerce power, he continued, "it is the effect upon interstate or foreign commerce, not the source of the injury, which is the criterion." While the activities of the utility were conducted wholly within the state, it was a matter of federal concern, he ruled, that interruption would immediately and vitally affect interstate railroads, telegraph, telephone, radio, navigation and other facilities. "Congress was entitled to provide reasonable preventive measures and that was the object of the National Labor Relations Act." [18]

The differentiation of the National Labor Relations Act from the statutes in the ADAIR and COPPAGE cases upon which the Chief Justice had relied in attempting to distinguish them proved immaterial when in *Phelps Dodge Corp.* v. *National Labor Relations Board* [19] Mr. Justice Frankfurter, for a majority of the Court, held that the Act not only validly denied to the employer freedom to discriminate against union members in discharging but also forbade similar discrimination in hiring, and added, "The course of decisions in this Court since *Adair* v. *United States*, 208 U.S. 161, and *Coppage* v. *Kansas*, 236 U.S. 1, have completely sapped those cases of their authority."

Chief Justice Hughes did not join in the prevailing opinion but concurred in a separate opinion of Justice Stone who agreed with the determination of the *constitutional* question but dissented on collateral issues relating to the intention of Congress in regard to certain other provisions of the Act. Perhaps out of deference to the Chief Justice, nothing was said in the separate opinion of Justice Stone with respect to the continuing authority of the ADAIR and COPPAGE cases, if any. The logic of events drove the Court to a specific repudiation of the doctrine of these cases but this was accomplished without the explicit consent of the Chief Justice although two of his decisions, *Texas & N.O. R.R.* v. *Ry. Clerks*, and *Labor Board* v. *Jones & Laughlin*, were heavily relied upon to achieve the result.

The JONES & LAUGHLIN case, and those that followed directly from it, viewed in historic perspective, were of tremendous importance. They repudiated the doctrine of dual federalism as a limitation upon federal delegated power. They placed the regulation of the relationships between labor and capital clearly within the province of governmental power, national and state, and thereby struck another blow at the *laissez-faire* conception of liberty under due process which for so long had held dominance in the Court. And fundamental was the growing recognition that with the rise of large-scale industry "while production and commerce are distinguishable for some purposes, they are not distinguishable when it comes to regulating them; that, in short, the issue is between *national* regulation and *no* regulation—not between national and state regulation." [20]

TAXING POWER

Only six weeks after the LABOR BOARD cases, the Supreme Court in two decisions upheld the social security legislation of Congress. In *Stewart Machine Co.* v. *Davis* [21] the unemployment excise tax upon employers, and the grants to the states enacting satisfactory unemployment compensation laws, were upheld as constitutional by a vote of five to four when Chief Justice Hughes and Mr. Justice Roberts joined with the liberals. Justice Cardozo, in speaking for the majority, cast aside the limitation upon the taxing power, deriving from the nature of the federal system, which had been invoked in part to upset the Agricultural Adjustment Act, and said that "the subject matter of taxation open to the power of Congress is as comprehensive as that open to the power of the states." And the credit to the states feature of the law was held not an attempt to coerce the states but rather in the nature of legitimate inducements to federal-state cooperation to serve a national need and purpose.

In the other case, *Helvering* v. *Davis*,[22] only two Justices dissented from the position of Justice Cardozo sustaining the old age tax and benefit provisions of the social security legislation. The old age tax was deemed a valid exercise of taxing power and the benefits provided were supported by the flat assertion that "Congress may spend money in aid of the general welfare." The theory of dual federalism as a principle of limitation on federal power was again repudiated.

BANKRUPTCY POWER

In invalidating the Municipal Bankruptcy Act of 1934 as in excess of federal power and as in derogation of sovereign state authority over its fiscal affairs, the Court had taken the occasion to say that "neither consent nor submission by the states can enlarge the powers of Congress; none can exist except those which are granted." [23] Chief Justice Hughes had been with the minority of four in this case, decided in 1936, but only two years later was able to speak for a majority of six in *United States* v. *Bekins* [24] when a substantially similar amended Bankruptcy Act, with greater verbal deference to the factor of state consent, was upheld as constitutional. This was accomplished with the now not too surprising concurrence of Mr. Justice Roberts.

Giving emphasis to a fact that was not considered material by the majority in the earlier case, Chief Justice Hughes pointed out that "the statute is carefully drawn so as not to impinge upon the sovereignty of the State. The State retains control of its fiscal affairs." With this ineffectual attempt at reconciliation, the Chief Justice proceeded to predicate his decision upon a recognition of practical realities. He pointed to the economic disaster which had made it impossible for these local agencies to meet their obligations. He alluded to the drying up of tax sources and to the lack of legal power of states limited by the contract clause, and concluded,

The bankruptcy power is competent to give relief to debtors in such a plight and, if there is any obstacle to its exercise in the case of the districts organized under state law it lies in the right of the State to oppose federal interference. The State moves in to remove that obstacle. The State acts in aid, and not in derogation, of its sovereign powers.

THE POWER TO SUE

The fear that the narrow and tenuous basis of the decision of the Court in the ASHWANDER case [25] would engender a spate of lawsuits was not long in being vindicated. Nineteen electric power companies brought action challenging the validity of the Tennessee Valley Authority Act of May 18, 1933, which authorized the development by a series of dams on the Tennessee River and its tributaries of a system of navigation and flood control, and the sale of the power created by the dams. The right of the Tennessee Valley Authority to construct the dams affecting the 650-mile length of the river and to generate excess current and sell it to municipalities, rural cooperatives and industrial consumers was subjected to fundamental challenge.

In *Tennessee Electric Power Co.* v. *Tennessee Valley Authority*,[26] in an opinion by Mr. Justice Roberts in which the Chief Justice, *inter alia*, joined, the Court ruled that the validity of a statutory grant of power could not be challenged *merely* because its exercise results in harmful competition with private utilities whose franchises were held not to grant exclusive rights. Accordingly, the Court was unwilling to consider the constitutionality of the Act in question.

The only intimation in the opinion of the Court that a basis for suit *might* be found lay in its reference to the finding of the District Court that the Authority had not indulged in coercion, duress, fraud, or misrepresentation in procuring contracts, had not acted with malicious or malevolent motive and had not conspired with municipalities or other purchasers of power. The inference, perhaps warranted, is that if such conduct were present, suit would lie.[27]

THE INTERSTATE COMMERCE POWER

The plenary conception of the interstate commerce power of Congress reaffirmed in the LABOR ACT cases served as the basis for sustaining a series of far-reaching regulations in the public interest of many aspects of the economy.

After a bitter contest in its halls, Congress had enacted the Public Utility Act of 1935. At issue in *Electric Bond & Share Co.* v. *Securities and Exchange Commission* [28] were the registration provisions of the Act which at this stage alone were being enforced. These required holding companies to register with the Securities and Exchange Commission and to file registration statements giving information with respect to their organization, financial structure, nature of their business and other details and prohibited the use of the mails and the instrumentalities of interstate commerce to companies failing to do so.

Chief Justice Hughes ruled for a majority of the Court that the constitutionality of the registration provisions might be separately considered since the declaration of separability in the legislation reversed the presumption of inseparability and they were not so interwoven with the "control" provisions as to present any practical difficulty in separation and independent enforcement.

With respect to constitutionality, the Chief Justice said,

We have no reason to doubt that from these defendants, with their highly important relation to interstate commerce and the national economy, Congress was entitled to demand the fullest information as to organization, financial structure and all the activities which could have any bearing upon the exercise of congressional authority.

And, he added, "in the imposition of penalties for the violation of its rules, Congress has a wide discretion." [29]

Consistent with the principle that industrial production having a close and intimate relation to the flow of interstate commerce may be made the subject of federal regulatory power was the decision of the Court in *Currin* v. *Wallace* [30] that such power may be used to establish and enforce standards of tobacco at markets where tobacco, bought and sold at auction, moved in interstate and foreign commerce. Disposing of the argument emphasized in the CARTER case that the standards were being enforced before the movement in commerce had actually begun, Chief Justice Hughes said, "Where goods are purchased in one State for transportation to another the commerce includes the purchase quite as much as it does the transportation." [31]

That same year, in *Mulford* v. *Smith*,[32] the Court upheld the validity of the new Agricultural Adjustment Act against the claim of several tobacco growers, who objected to the quotas set for them, that the law regulated production, control over which was vested in the states. Mr. Justice Roberts, who had written the majority decision in the BUTLER case, in this case, with the acquiescence of six members of the Court, including the Chief Justice, sustained the new law on the theory that it did not control production but imposed market regulations at the "throat" of interstate commerce. To the argument that the real purpose of Congress was to control production, he answered that "the motive of Congress in asserting the power to regulate commerce is irrelevant to the validity of the legislation." He did not even consider it necessary to mention the BUTLER case. Yet it was presumably the "real" intention of Congress that led Mr. Justice Roberts in the BUTLER case to hold that the admittedly delegated power to tax was not being used to tax at all.

Another earlier ruling of the Court was virtually repudiated that same year when Justice Stone spoke for the entire Court in upholding an order of the Interstate Commerce Commission which prescribed as a condition for its approval of a railroad lease that certain employees receive partial compensation for the loss which they would suffer as a result of discharge or transfer.[33] Such a provision Justice Stone found to be validly related to the maintenance of an adequate and efficient transportation system and said that there was increasing recognition that "just and reasonable treatment of railroad employees is not only an essential aid to the maintenance of a service uninterrupted by labor disputes, but that it promotes efficiency, which suffers through loss of morale when the demands of justice are ignored." This reasoning was in marked contrast with that which had prevailed in *Railroad Retirement Board* v. *Alton R.R.* and vindicated the position that the Chief Justice had then taken in sharp dissent.

The following year, in *Sunshine Anthracite Coal Co.* v. *Adkins*,[34] a radically altered Court, in an opinion of Mr. Justice Douglas, which met with the concurrence of the entire Court except Justice McReynolds, sustained the constitutionality of the Bituminous Coal Act of 1937 which replaced that invalidated in the CARTER case. This time, however, while the price-fixing provisions were substantially similar to those in the CARTER case, the labor provisions were omitted. Regulation of the industry in the light of its "strategic character" and "the chaotic conditions" which have prevailed in it was upheld as an appropriate exercise of the commerce power of Congress and the penalty tax provisions were deemed a legitimate aid to enforcement. Repudiating the notion that the nature of our federal system might require that a vital industry remain unregulated, Mr. Justice Douglas said that while there were limits that did not mean "that there is a no man's land between state and federal domains."

The Delegation of Legislative Power

That the "reconstructed" Court would not insist with full rigor upon the doctrine laid down in the CARTER case, that the legislative authority could not vest power in individuals to make policy binding other individuals who did not agree, was made apparent in 1939 when in *Currin* v. *Wallace* the Court, in addition to sustaining the regulatory features of the law, also upheld the delegation of authority to two-thirds of the growers affected, voting in a prescribed referendum, to designate markets at which no tobacco could be offered for sale except in compliance with certain standards. "This is not a case," wrote the Chief Justice, "where a group of producers may make the law and force it upon a minority." This did not, he said, involve Congressional abdication, for here "it is Congress that exercises its legislative authority in making the regulation and in prescribing the conditions of its application. The required favorable vote upon the referendum is one of these conditions."

An impressive illustration of the fact that the necessity for large delegations of legislative power to government agencies, only generally circumscribed, had come to be accepted by the Court as an inevitable concomitant of modern government, was its unanimous decision in 1941 in *Opp Cotton Mills, Inc.* v. *Administrator of the Wage & Hour Division.*[35] That case sustained the validity of the Fair Labor Standards Act of 1938 against the claim, *inter alia*, that it involved an unlawful delegation of legislative power to the Administrator since the standards prescribed for the fixing of minimum wages between 30 and 40 cents per hour were too vague and indefinite to admit of any judicial determination as to whether they were within the standards prescribed. The standards laid down by Congress required a determination that classification would not give a competitive advantage to any group in the particular industry, would not substantially curtail employment, and "among other relevant factors" had to take into consideration competitive conditions as affected by transportation and other stated factors. With keen appreciation for practical realities, Justice Stone said,

In an increasingly complex society Congress obviously could not perform its functions if it were obliged to find all the facts subsidiary to the basic conclusions which support the defined legislative policy in fixing, for example, a tariff rate, a railroad rate or the rate of wages to be applied in particular industries by a minimum wage law. The Constitution, viewed as a continuously operative charter of government, is not to be interpreted as demanding the impossible or the impracticable. The essentials of the legislative function are the determination of the legislative policy and its formulation as a rule of conduct. Those essentials are preserved when Congress specifies the basic conclusions of fact upon ascertainment of which, from relevant data by a designated administrative agency, it ordains that its statutory command is to be effective. The present statute satisfies those requirements.

It must be recognized that, despite the vague contours of some of the standards set in the Act, they had greater precision than the standards established in the National Industrial Recovery Act. Nevertheless, it is reasonable to suppose that if the Fair Labor Standards Act had come before the Court in 1935 instead of 1941 it would have been invalidated as involving an illegal delegation of legislative power. Again men and circumstances, and not the Constitution, dictated the decision. The Constitution, whatever its language and the precedents of the Court, whatever their weight, are "not to be interpreted as demanding the impossible or the impracticable."

SUMMARY STATEMENT

From March, 1937, until the close of the 1940 term in June, 1941, when the Chief Justice retired, not a single Act of Congress was invalidated by the Supreme Court although there came before it in the period a whole series of Congressional measures many of which not only involved great extensions of control over the economy but also the exercise of power whose constitutionality had earlier been rejected by the Court. This is an amazing fact when compared to the record of the Court between January 7, 1935, and May 25, 1936, in which period twelve Congressional laws were wholly or partially invalidated.[36] This "great retreat" has been taken by many to constitute, for all practical purposes, an end to judicial intervention in national economic legislation and to betoken the "long-range decline in the importance of the Supreme Court in the American constitutional system." [37]

That judgment may prove to be correct, but it must not be overlooked that the constitutional "revolution" effected after 1937 has largely been the product of emergency conditions, the threat to the Court and the reconstruction of its personnel by President Franklin D. Roosevelt during twelve years in office. The Court has in the past shown striking ambivalence, and the demise of its doctrines and of its power have often been prematurely predicted. So long as the Court retains the power, there can be no assurance that with other men and under other circumstances, it may not again be broadly used to prevent the will of the nation from being translated into valid law.

VI. Charles Evans Hughes and Judicial Review

CHAPTER 21

AN EVALUATION

On June 2, 1941, Chief Justice Hughes, then seventy-nine years of age, wrote President Roosevelt that "considerations of health and age make it necessary that I should be relieved of the duties which I have been discharging with increasing difficulty." For this reason, said the Chief Justice, he availed himself of the opportunity of retiring effective "on and after July first, 1941."

Addressing Mr. Hughes as "My dear Mr. Chief Justice," and signing himself "Sincerely and affectionately yours," the President replied the same day:

I am deeply distressed by your letter of June second. . . . This comes to me, as I know it will to the whole nation, as a great shock for all of us had counted on your continuing your splendid service for many years to come. My every inclination is to beg you to remain; but my deep concern for your health and strength must be paramount.

Whether the President's warmth was wholly genuine is, of course, uncertain. But, it must be realized that the Court reorganization battle was now long since past and that not only had the composition of the Court been radically altered but the Chief Justice had joined in voting to sustain much of the New Deal legislation.

Thus ended a period of more than eleven years of service by Charles Evans Hughes as Chief Justice of the United States. Conservative and liberal journals alike praised the character and record of the retiring Chief Justice although the latter did so in more restrained and qualified fashion than upon his resignation from the Court in 1916.

The New York *Times,* associating his name with that of the greatest of our Chief Justices, said that "to the best loved of them all history will add the name of the forthright, able man who now lays aside his duties after a long life whose best years were spent in public service." [1]

The New York *Herald Tribune,* asserting that he had brought "distinction" to every position he had held, harked back to the Senate fight over his confirmation, and asserted that his record had proved the assumption that his ideas were "solidified and unprogressive" to be "ridiculous." It was a "higher tribute" to him that he had baffled "every attempt at political classification," and remained the "judge *par excellence* with no tag line to his integrity." "Incidentally," added the *Herald Tribune,* "the court itself owes in large part to his skillful resistance its escape from the 'packing' which would have destroyed it." [2]

The *Nation,* which had opposed Hughes' confirmation in 1930, commented that "though he did not fully grasp the needs of a changing time," he "amply refuted our fear that he would bring to the office the outlook of the typical corporation lawyer." While it criticized Hughes for failing consistently to apply to the New Deal program the emergency test, it added that

the Chief Justice earned esteem by realizing that it was not sufficient merely to block the court plan. The principal reforms of the New Deal were approved before vacancies permitted the President to name a majority. . . . Hughes had the acumen to recognize the inevitable, and that is the larger part of statesmanship.

It praised his record in civil liberties and minority rights cases, and, with regard to his entire public record, stated that "the balance sheet of his accomplishments, struck at the close of an extraordinarily long and variegated career, does him honor." [3]

The *New Republic* thought that Chief Justice Hughes would probably be remembered as a "great judicial statesman." And this characterization it connected with his "dramatic shift" during the fight over the court bill, when "he may well have been concerned about the prestige of the Court and its influence on the life of the nation as well as about the political stability of the nation itself." [4]

On August 27, 1948, at the age of eighty-six Mr. Charles Evans

Hughes died in a cottage on Cape Cod where he had gone to recuperate from an illness. Despite the fact that he had lived in Washington for more than seven years in complete retirement from public life, the news of his death received front-page attention throughout the nation and evoked widespread eulogies of his character and record of public service. President Truman, in an official proclamation, commented that the "nation has lost one of its most pre-eminent elder sages," and said that "humanitarian understanding, exalted vision, and inspired judgment characterized the long career of Charles Evans Hughes." Chief Justice Vinson called him "one of our greatest jurists, statesmen and Americans." Secretary of State Marshall thought he "represented the ideal in judicial integrity," and former President Hoover, who had appointed Mr. Hughes Chief Justice, alluding to his "magnificent mind," "elevated character" and record of public service, said, "If there were a few hundred men of his stature scattered throughout the world, civilization would have nothing to fear." [5]

THE RECORD OF CHIEF JUSTICE CHARLES EVANS HUGHES

It is a simple truism that our institutions, whether well or ill-adapted to their purposes, are subjected to little, if any, critical analyses or attack in periods of relative prosperity and stability. The great significance of the decade of the 1930's, during which Mr. Hughes presided over the deliberations of the Supreme Court, is that it put to the severest test, in the crucible of a devastating economic crisis, the capacity of men and the value of institutions. In a very real sense, it posed the question of the survival-value of democracy itself. "One may search in vain," wrote Harlan F. Stone, Mr. Hughes' successor as Chief Justice, "for a period in the history of the Supreme Court in which the burden resting on the Chief Justice has been so heavy or when his task has been more beset with difficulties." [6] It is precisely for this reason that this period offers, in a unique sense, an appropriate occasion for an appraisal of the leadership of Mr. Hughes as Chief Justice of our highest Court, and for a reevaluation of the institution of judicial review. How did the Chief Justice, personally, and the Court, generally, measure up to that test?

Pointing out that the historic shift in emphasis in constitutional interpretation in this period engendered differences of opinion which were strongly held and stoutly maintained, Chief Justice Stone concluded, "That despite all this the Chief Justice can now lay down his labors amid universal expressions of regret and of personal regard is a high tribute to the dignity, fidelity and skill with which he has conducted his great office." [7]

It may justly, I believe, be regarded as a tribute to the leadership of the Chief Justice that he never permitted the sometimes bitter differences within the Court to disrupt it. He sought, virtually above all else, to maintain the dignity and prestige of the Court and this he thought in no small measure depended upon the stability of its decisions. This attitude was reflected not only in formal expression of his views but in the great lengths to which he sometimes went, while often supporting departures, in attempting to find distinctions to avoid overruling precedent. But he refused to carry this process to the point of stubbornness characteristic of the conservatives, who were apparently determined to stand by the foundation even if the edifice were to fall. When the pressure for innovation became great, and the risks to the nation and to the Court itself apparent, reluctantly at first, but increasingly he went along with change. Having sedulously sought to protect the precedents of the Court, sometimes at the risk of offending logic, he witnessed and often participated in the shattering of one precedent after another. He stood thus as a kind of heroic and, in a sense, tragic figure, torn between the old and the new, seeking at first to stem the tide but then relentlessly caught up and moving with it.

There is no better illustration of the skill with which he resolved the dilemma involved in safeguarding the old, that is, the prestige and prerogatives of the Court, while accepting the new, that is, that amplitude of federal power necessary to cope with the problems of our day, than in the ambivalent role he played in the defeat of the President's Court reorganization plan. There can be little doubt that his letter to Senator Wheeler indicating the inadequacies of the arguments originally advanced by the President in support of the plan was a significant and timely factor in its defeat. On the other hand, with the four conservatives usually opposed to extensions of governmental power, national and state, the support of the Chief Justice, while the Court fight was raging, and the influence he exerted in winning Mr. Justice Roberts' support of the constitutionality of the New Deal measures proved decisive in sustaining such legislation.

Apart from the role he played in the critical period when the Court was under direct attack, and in the exercise of a balance of power position, the prestige he commanded as Chief Justice, and the privilege he assumed of writing many of the most important decisions and dissents in a period of reexamination of many of the foundation principles of constitutional law, made him easily the most important member of the Court during the period of his service. It may, in fact, be confidently asserted that no other Justice, excepting John Marshall, played as vital a part and one so fraught with historic consequences in our constitutional history as did Chief Justice Hughes.

Many of the doctrines of which he was the leading proponent or to which he lent effective support are of first importance and may exert long-range influence. Those which related to his period of service as an Associate Justice have been summarized earlier. It remains to summarize briefly some of his significant contributions as Chief Justice.

In relation to due process affecting procedure, Chief Justice Hughes, in the interests of justice, and without regard to historic modes of procedure, refused to uphold convictions for crime resting upon confessions extorted by force or knowingly perjured testimony. In this area, to be sure, the distinction he fostered between so-called "jurisdictional" or "constitutional" and other facts did not stand the test of time but his insistence upon "judicializing" administrative procedure by assurance of a "fair" and "full" hearing, when important interests were affected, is likely to constitute one of the most important bases of continuing judicial supervision of federal economic legislation.[8]

In regard to substantive due process, he imposed the first significant check on the theretofore unrestricted martial law powers of governors but aided in the broad expansion generally of the police powers of states to legislate in the public interest free from policy-making intervention by the Court, except in the field of taxation when he thought the action of the state created dangers of multiple burdens.[9] Similarly, the contract clause limitation and contract rights were reconciled with and to a considerable degree subordinated to the power of the state to legislate reasonably in the interests of the people. In addition, he lent effective assistance to the limitation and reduction of intergovernmental tax immunity, and upheld a plenary interpretation of the interstate commerce power provided Congress itself sought to establish a rational connection between its regulation and such commerce.

Most noteworthy, perhaps, were his decisions affecting civil liberties and the rights of minorities. Here he led in the progressive incorporation of the basic civil liberties into the protection of due process under the Fourteenth Amendment and gave these liberties broad scope and meaning. He denounced the doctrine of guilt by association, sought to reconcile the demands of conscience and authority and affirmed that the safety of the Republic lay in responsiveness to the people and in their opportunity for the airing of grievances. To that much discriminated against and suffering segment of our population, the Negro, he sought generally to assure fair criminal procedures, the right to vote and equality of access to facilities of the state.

THE NATURE OF THE JUDICIAL PROCESS

In the course of his decisions the Chief Justice repeatedly differentiated between "justice and reasonableness," which he regarded as pertinent considerations for the Court, and wisdom, policy or social advantage, which he deemed questions addressed solely to the legislative discretion. This distinction he affirmed in his formal work on the Supreme Court when he wrote that it was an "established principle" that "the Supreme Court does not undertake to review questions of legislative policy. . . . For the purposes of the courts, the legislature within its sphere is deemed to possess all available knowledge and to be the treasure house of wisdom." [10] This view has found very considerable verbal approval in the Court.[11]

Whatever may be said of the disposition of the recent Court to accord considerable discretion to the legislative judgment, the history of judicial review, in cases of large economic or social significance, and certainly the record of the Hughes Court, establish that this distinction, if real in theory, was little honored in practice. The incorporation of substantive content into the due process clause, and the varying meanings imported into procedural and substantive due process, the gyrations of the Court on the scope of Congressional power to regulate interstate and intrastate commerce and to delegate its authority, the drastic change in the limitation imposed upon the states by the contract clause, the inconsistencies with respect to the reach of federal bankruptcy power, the complete emasculation of the privileges and immunities clause, and the vicissitudes of intergovernmental tax immunity, to cite some instances, show that considerations of policy, wisdom and social advantage, consciously or unconsciously, avowed or inarticulate, are inherent in the process of judicial review.

Much more realistic, in the light of this history, is the statement of Mr. Justice Frankfurter that the "words of the Constitution" on which the solution of constitutional problems are based "are so unrestricted by their intrinsic meaning or by their history or by tradition or by prior decisions that they leave the individual justice free, if indeed they do not compel him, to gather meaning not from reading the Constitution but from reading life." "The words he must construe," Judge Learned Hand tells us, "are empty vessels into which he can pour nearly anything he will." [12] And Justice Holmes, with penetrating insight, has written:

The very considerations which judges most rarely mention, and always with an apology, are the secret root from which the law draws all the juices of life. I mean, of course, considerations of what is expedient for the community concerned. Every important principle which is developed by litigation is in fact and at bottom the result of more or less definitely understood views of public policy; most generally, to be sure, under our practice and traditions, the unconscious result of instinctive preferences and inarticulate convictions, but none the less traceable to views of public policy in the last analysis.[13]

In face of the difficulty of differentiating between justice and wisdom the attempt is sometimes made to base a distinction upon the spirit with which judges approach their task. Thus Justice Cardozo has said that the standard of the judge must be "an objective one," and that "the thing that counts is not what I believe to be right. It is what I may reasonably believe that some other man of normal intellect and conscience might reasonably look upon as right." [14] Similarly, Mr. Hughes has written that the "conscientious judge" does his work in "an objective spirit" which will lead him to sustain the validity of legislation which, as a legislator, he might condemn.[15]

Concede that such a spirit has sometimes led Justices, such as Holmes, Brandeis and Cardozo, to sustain legislation the wisdom of which they doubted; the fact remains that in practice only a minority gave evidence of such a spirit. In the early Hughes Court the chief defenders of the "objective" approach were the chief dissenters.

The fact is, too, that it is an almost impossible standard to uphold. It is not surprising that "men holding strong convictions as to the unwisdom of legislation may easily pass to the position that it is wholly unreasonable." [16] How else account, in the light of the professed acceptance of the principle of restraint by every member of the "reconstructed" Court, for the charge that so many were reading their own views of ethics and wisdom into decisions? To cite a few instances: In one case Justices Black and Murphy said of a Frankfurter opinion, "for judges to rest their interpretation of statutes on nothing but their own conceptions of 'morals' and 'ethics' is, to say the least, dangerous business." [17] Mr. Justice Frankfurter countered, in another, that the majority was assuming "however unwittingly, a legislative responsibility that does not belong to it," and warned that "it can never be emphasized too much that one's own opinion about the wisdom or evil of a law should be excluded altogether when one is doing one's duty on the bench." [18] The majority opinion, charged Mr. Justice Jackson, in a third case, "rationalizes . . . an order to show that it conforms to the Constitution, or rather rationalizes the Constitution to show that the Constitution sanctions such an order," [19] and, in another, claimed that the minority were willing to enforce the Constitution "only if the outcome pleases." [20] So, too, Justice Rutledge said with reference to a decision of the Court delivered by Mr. Justice Reed with the concurrence, *inter alia*, of President Truman's appointees, Chief Justice Vinson and Mr. Justice Burton:

I doubt that upon any matter of construction the Court has heretofore so far presumed to override the plainly and incontrovertibly stated judgment of all participants in the legislative process with its own tortuously fashioned view. This is not construction under the doctrine of strict necessity. It is invasion of the legislative process by emasculation of the statute.[21]

And, more recently, Mr. Justice Douglas broke with his liberal colleagues, Justices Black, Murphy and Rutledge, to charge that they, as well as Justices Reed and Frankfurter, were not acting "unwittingly" in encouraging "the virulent growth of monopoly." "The Court," he added, "approves what the Anti-Trust Laws were designed to prevent. It helps remake America in the image of the cartels." [22]

In general, the whole practice of the "New Deal" majority in overruling long established precedents brought the caustic lament from Mr. Justice Roberts that "this tendency indicates an intolerance for what those who have composed this court in the past have conscientiously and deliberately concluded, and involves an assumption that knowledge and wisdom reside in us which was denied to our predecessors." [23] It is singularly interesting to find a similar complaint from Mr. Justice Frankfurter with respect to the change wrought by "Fair Deal" appointments to the Court. Commenting upon a decision written by Mr. Justice Minton with the concurrence of Chief Justice Vinson and Justices Reed, Burton and Clark, he said,

We are asked to overrule decisions based on a long course of prior unanimous decisions, drawn from history and legislative experience. . . . These are not outmoded decisions eroded by time. . . . Especially ought the Court not to reenforce the instabilities of our day by giving fair ground for the belief that Law is the expression of chance—for instance, of unexpected changes in the Court's composition and the contingencies in the choice of successors.[24]

It is a little late to argue that "courts are the mere instruments of the law, and can will nothing." The fact is that the Court, in the guise of constitutional interpretation, necessarily and inevitably, in considerable degree, exercises the function of a "super-legislature," limited though it be to the negation of laws. Or, perhaps more accurately, it may be said to sit as a continuous constitutional convention, since its construction of the Constitution, except when it changes its mind, cannot be overruled except by constitutional amendment.

But a recognition of the true nature of the judicial process in constitutional cases does not dispose of the case for judicial review. How valid is this case when judged in historic context and particularly in the context of the philosophy and decisions of Chief Justice Hughes and the Court over which he presided? [25]

THE CASE FOR JUDICIAL REVIEW OVER ACTS OF CONGRESS

Judicial review, in a fundamental sense, rests upon the sometimes avowed and sometimes tacit assumption of the superiority of our economic, political and social system which it is maintained is better protected and preserved because of this power of the Court. In a more immediate sense, it finds support in the arguments that judicial review gives assurance of a more just and reasonable balance between public and private interests in the enactment and administration of our laws, tends to maintain stability in our institutions, safeguards the federal system and protects civil liberties and our democracy against the force of temporary majorities.

Justice and Reasonableness. The progressive tendency of the Court in recent years, particularly in the contest between public and private interest, has been to make justice and reasonableness the cardinal tests of constitutionality. Due process which has been the primary basis upon which constitutional challenge has been made to legislation, has, in general, whether affecting the nation or the state, and whether in relation to procedure or substance, been tested by justice and reasonableness. So also in regard to the conflict of federal and state power, the decisions are often comprehensible only in terms of the conceptions of the Justices in relation to the demands of justice and reason. Conceding that "the Courts . . . are free in marking the limits of the individual's immunities to shape their judgments in accordance with reason and justice," and asserting that the value of judicial review could not be measured by the occasions of its exercise, Justice Cardozo stated,

By conscious or subconscious influence, the presence of this restraining power, aloof in the background, but none the less always in reserve, tends to stabilize and rationalize the legislative judgment, to infuse it with the glow of principle, to hold the standard aloft and visible for those who must run the race and keep the faith.[26]

That judicial review, because of the very nature of the position and practice of the Justices, brings greater assurance of justice and reasonableness is a view to which Mr. Hughes gave repeated affirmation. In most lucid form he set it forth in his work on the Supreme Court when he wrote:

In our system, the individual finds security in his rights because he is entitled to the protection of tribunals that represent the capacity of the community for impartial judgment as free as possible from the passion of the moment and the demands of interest or prejudice. The ends of social justice are achieved through a process by which every step is examined in the light of the principles which are our inheritance as a free people. The spirit of the work of the Supreme Court permeates every legislative assembly and every important discussion of reforms by legislative action. We largely subject our political thinking to the conception of law, not as an arbitrary edict of power, but as governed by the fundamental conceptions of justice. . . . The Supreme Court is the embodiment of this conception of our law, the exemplar of its application, and the assurance that in the complexities of an extraordinarily expanded life, we have not forgotten the ancient faith by which we have pledged ourselves to render to each one his due,—a faith which alone makes it possible to look to the coming years with confidence as well as hope.[27]

Implicit in these statements of eminent Justices is the assumption that there are fixed or inherited principles of justice and reasonableness, apart from the people's conception of them, which may serve as guides to the Court in setting aside legislation commanding the support of the people. But what are justice and reasonableness? Certainly there are no eternal verities to which reference may be made. Men, it must be recognized, have defended a great variety of divergent ideas in their name. To Plato these dictated a kind of authoritarian state in which each person was limited to that task he could best perform. Aristotle justified slavery in these terms. Hobbes used these concepts to defend absolutism and Locke to defend both the rights of revolution and of private property. To Marx they had no validity apart from our capitalist ideology. To the Pope they forbid socialism. As applied to concrete controversies before the Supreme Court "the principles which are our inheritance as a free people" have been invoked on both sides to support or to defeat social legislation and have seldom furnished any accepted guide to decisions. The Supreme Court, it has been observed, has repeatedly altered its view of the dictates of justice and reason. "Justice," wrote a legal scholar, "is a symbol for the recognition that law is not given but is constantly being made." [28] The assumption, therefore, that these concepts have meaning apart from the people's view of them which may be applied to the solution of important economic and social conflicts by the Court, must be rejected for these are not fixed but changing concepts depending upon the mores of the people. And, it may be asked, in translating mores into the law of any democratic land what better, if imperfect, assurance of justice and reason is possible than that the law reflects the will of the majority? To paraphrase Holmes, the tests of justice and reason, like the test of truth, are references to either a present or an imagined future majority in favor of our view.[29]

Apart from the difficulty of attaching meaning to justice and reasonableness other than the people's conception of them, the argument that Justices "as free as possible from the passions of the moment and the demands of interest and prejudice" and from "the deflections of worldly ambition" are likely to act with greater regard to these ends than the people's representatives meets objection on the score of theory and practice. Who today would seek to breathe substance into the electoral college plan for selecting a President, or restore the indirect election of Senators, or provide a life term for the President or for Senators, although many similar arguments were advanced for each of these practices or proposals? The fact is that no technique of government has ever been devised which will place in the hands of a minority, acting through Courts or other instrumentalities, the power to strike down unjust or unreasonable legislation which will not enable it to defeat just and reasonable legislation it happens to dislike.

The essential weakness of the argument, it must be recognized, is that it posits a specious analogy between the role of a court in regard to purely private litigation and the contests between public and private interests. In the first, courts generally have maintained an Olympian impartiality. It would be difficult to argue, however, that freedom from the immediacy of legislative struggles or popular pressures, in circumstances involving large economic, social or political issues, has brought greater assurance of "justice and reasonableness" than subordination to those processes. "Especially is this the case since, as has been often recognized, of all the branches of government the courts have the least opportunity to be fully advised of all the implications of the cases before them. They are compelled to rely almost entirely upon briefs submitted by lawyers and a few hours of argument.

But, specifically, the record of the Supreme Court in constitutional cases furnishes little support for asserting that the Justices have usually demonstrated a more highly developed sense of justice and reasonableness than the Congress. It is part of that record, supported, I believe, by this study, that for the Court justice and reasonableness were frequently identified with a special regard for property and privilege. If that identification was in accord with the demands of justice and reason, it is a conclusion with which majorities then and now, including many later Justices of the Court, found reason to quarrel.

Nor is that identification difficult to understand. Our Justices are not, like Plato's guardians, schooled in abstract truth, justice and goodness. Judges, we were told in 1933 by a legal philosopher,

are selected from those who are regarded as having been successful at the bar, and this generally means having served the interests of the large property owners. This experience at least serves to make our courts more sensitive to the claims of property owners than to those of workers in shops and factories.[30]

While in recent years there has been less direct connection between success at the bar and appointment to the bench, the fact remains that Justices are drawn only from the legal profession and that the social status, philosophy, interest, and training of the legal profession generally tend toward conservatism. The duty of the Court, therefore, "to enforce explicit constitutional provisions even in opposition to the majority is easily rationalized into enforcing its own views of good policy." [31] And, viewed historically, that writer, now himself a member of the high Court, as late as 1941, concluded that

The alternation of our national moods are such that a cycle of liberal government seldom exceeds eight years, and by living through them the Court could go on without decisive liberal infusions. So well has this strategy worked that never in its entire history can the Supreme Court be said to have for a single hour been representative of anything except the relatively conservative forces of its day.[32]

Of course, it cannot be denied that while the nature of the judicial function makes it easier for the Court to ignore the people's view of justice and wisdom in preference for its own, the President and Congress may also do so. There is this important difference, however. Within relatively little time a President and Congress that have flouted the will of the people can be replaced. Relief from the decisions of the Supreme Court, however, under ordinary circumstances, can be obtained only by heavenly intervention, or, what may prove even more protracted, through amendment to the Constitution.

Stability. It is argued that judicial review brings greater assurance of stability and thereby safeguards our institutions and our democracy. Stability in an age when democracies in many parts of the world have been overturned must be measured as of great value. So far as this argument relates to the protection of civil liberties it is the subject of separate analysis. So far as it relates to economic innovations, several observations appear to be pertinent. I believe, first, that the generalization rests upon questionable assumptions, and second, that to the extent that judicial review has meant stability it has often been a greater source of danger to than safeguard of our institutions and our democracy.

A questionable assumption upon which the argument rests is that it is probable that legislatures will act too quickly rather than too slowly. Anyone familiar with the tortuous process that a piece of social legislation must undergo, subject to the many checks of our system, including generally those of the radio and press, largely controlled by conservative interests, the committee system, two legislative chambers, and executive veto, may doubt that the problem is one of too much speed, at least for those who have urgent wants as against those who seek to preserve the status quo.[33] Another questionable assumption is that legislative innovations necessarily disturb stability. This takes insufficient account of the fact that the stability enjoined by the Court, in the sense of barring innovations, may disturb the more basic stability achieved in the political and economic arena among contending social forces. With its invalidation in 1857 of the Missouri Compromise Act of 1820, the Supreme Court disturbed the delicate balance that Congress had worked out and, in the view of many, thereby contributed to the

solution of the slave problem by force of arms. And with the invalidation by the Court of some of the vital New Deal measures,
and but for one vote in regard to others, we were well on the way
to stabilizing depression and unemployment. Few would question
today that some of these decisions were a greater source of danger
to our democracy than the legislative innovations. For, it must be
recognized that the success of a democratic system depends in considerable degree upon the responsiveness of government to discontent and demands for change before these assume revolutionary
form and avail themselves of non-democratic means.

Guardian of the Federal System.   One of the strongest virtues of
judicial review is said to lie in its preservation of the essential duality
of our constitutional system. Mr. Hughes, as has been shown, repeatedly paid tribute to this role of the Court.[34] Typical was his
insistence in his volume on the Court, in defending judicial review
over Acts of Congress, that "the dual system of government implies
the maintenance of the constitutional restrictions of the powers of
Congress as well as those of the States." He found support for this
conclusion in the argument that

the expansion of the country has vastly increased the volume of legislative measures and there is severe pressure toward an *undue* [my italics]
centralization. In Congress, theories of State autonomy may easily yield
to the demands of interests seeking Federal support. Many of our citizens
in their zeal for particular measures have little regard for any of the
limitations of Federal authority. We have entered upon an era of regulation with a great variety of legislative proposals, constantly multiplying
governmental contacts with the activities of industry and trade. These
proposals raise more frequently than in the past questions of National,
as opposed to State, power. If our dual system with its recognition of
local authority in local concerns is worth maintaining, judicial review is
likely to be of increasing value.[35]

The argument of Mr. Hughes, in relation to curbing national
power as a means of safeguarding our federal system, whether considered in constitutional or extra-legal terms, contains certain weak-
nesses. It must be recognized, for instance, that the power of the
Court to prevent an "undue" centralization necessarily carries with it
the power to prevent a "due" centralization. Thus the Court in a
critical period in the nation's history, in a manner which the Court

itself subsequently criticized, breathed substantive content into the Tenth Amendment as a means of frustrating social legislation passed under the *duly* delegated powers of Congress.

If, on the other hand, reference is made to the struggle among vital economic and local interests which lies back of the controversies over the federal system, although masked in constitutional formulae, it may be doubted whether Congress containing representatives elected under a decentralized party system from states jealous of their local authority will agree to, or in any event persist in, any greater centralization than is likely to be long past "due." A disadvantage of judicial review in fact is that it has acted, and may act again, to prevent that degree of centralization of power in the federal government which is essential to cope with the power of integrated capital. In his final statement as chairman of the Temporary National Economic Committee, Senator O'Mahoney said, "Local business, little business, private enterprise, and local government, even the government of the States themselves, are in truth and in fact submerged by modern business organizations." [36] And Professor Laski has added that "for forty-eight separate units to seek to compete with the integrated power of giant capitalism is to invite defeat." [37]

Whatever may be said of their legality in strict constitutional terms, and whatever disagreement may exist as to their desirability in economic terms, it is incomprehensible that the enforceability of great economic measures, enacted in the face of the impotency of the states and designed to regulate and succor industry, like the NIRA, or restore agricultural prosperity, like the AAA, or aid labor, like the NLRA (or curb labor like the Taft-Hartley law), or develop great resources, like the TVA, or control the monetary system, should be again permitted to depend upon the consent of nine judges basing their decisions upon their conceptions of constitutional mandates principally devised in 1787 and shortly thereafter. And, it must be recognized, in this connection, that while there is little disposition on the part of the present, largely New Deal–Fair Deal Court, to deny full amplitude to federal power, the attitude of a Court appointed by new and different administrations and facing new problems of crisis or change remains an incalculable factor.

Guardian of Civil Liberty. The most persuasive argument for judicial review is that it tends to preserve our civil liberties, and thus our democracy, against the power and force of transient majorities represented by Congress and the President.[38] In specific defense of judicial review over acts of the national government, Mr. Hughes wrote that "the bill of rights in the Federal Constitution, sustained by the judicial power, must still be regarded as of importance to the liberty of the citizen." [39]

In this postwar period with feeling against unpopular minorities running high, it must be admitted that this argument has considerable appeal. The virtues of judicial review in this area, as elsewhere, must be weighed, however, in the light of its disadvantages.

The argument, it seems to me, reveals an implicit distrust of the capacity of the people to govern themselves, attaches too little importance to the educational and political value of having civil liberties issues fought out in the mind and in the political arena, lays too much stress upon the value of legal safeguards and ignores the dangers to democracy and civil liberty involved in the process of judicial review.

The basic premise of this argument is undemocratic because it assumes the necessity of looking to the judiciary to preserve our civil liberties, implying that the majority is not to be trusted, despite occasional abuses, to protect and defend its democratic way of life. If that is true we might well despair of democracy altogether, for if the people lack the restraint necessary in this most vital respect what reason is there to assume it will be revealed in other, less crucial, respects?

There is danger, too, that in focusing attention on questions of constitutionality, the struggle will be removed from the conscience of men into the courts. Much legislation that may be constitutional may be undemocratic in spirit. There is undeniable value in a democracy in the political experience and education that are derived by the people in the process of correcting their own errors.[40] Even more important is the fact that unless the struggle is won in the political arena it cannot be won at all. If the majority has lost its belief in democratic values, the Supreme Court, if not carried along with the tide of popular opinion, will prove a slim reed upon which to rest. For if experience teaches anything it teaches that real security for democracy lies not in judicial safeguards but in the determination of a people to preserve it. That is why democracy is as secure in Britain without judicial review as in the United States; and elaborate constitutional safeguards cannot secure democracy for some South American countries.

The fact is, too, that whatever the record of the Court in regard to state legislation, it has shown little capacity to safeguard civil liberties against federal attack. Thus the Court, in its entire history, has not invalidated a single important federal act alleged to invade civil liberties and has invalidated several designed to protect such liberties. This, no doubt, is in part explained by the relatively few cases to come before the Court challenging the validity of federal anti-civil-liberties legislation and, in part, by the fact that the Court enjoys greater freedom of statutory construction in cases involving federal legislation enabling it to give an interpretation that does not offend civil liberties.[41] It remains true, however, as one scholar concludes, that "the history of judicial review does not furnish the evidence to indicate that the Supreme Court will, in periods of intense feeling or of hysteria, afford a sanctuary to those whose views run counter to the popular will." [42] The Court has a rare opportunity to belie this generalization in the case, shortly to receive its consideration, involving eleven Communist party leaders who were convicted in 1949 under a provision of law which makes it a crime merely to *organize* a group that *teaches* or *advocates* overthrow of the Government by force or violence. No attempt was made by the Government at the trial to establish that, in the conditions of 1948, when indictment was obtained, a clear and present danger of consummation of this design actually existed. It will be seen whether the Court will adhere to the principle and spirit of its decisions in the DE JONGE, *Herndon* v. *Lowry* and *Thomas* v. *Collins* cases, previously discussed, or find rationalizations to sustain the convictions.

Finally, even conceding that judicial review retains some potential value as a bulwark to civil liberties under federal attack, this must be weighed against the danger to democracy which derives from the practice of judicial review in non-civil-liberties cases.[43] Since democracy basically depends upon popular support, the danger is that the repeated frustration of the will of the people, dictated, as so often has been the case, by conscious or unconscious interest or bias only remotely related to any questions of constitutionality, may in periods of crisis demanding far-reaching change, invite solutions of our problems through the arbitrament of force and revolution. It is no answer to point out that this has not happened. That we have escaped these dangers in the past under less compelling conditions gives no assurance for the future. "The vice of judicial supremacy as exerted for 90 years in the field of policy," wrote Robert Jackson, "has been its progressive closing of the avenues to peaceful and democratic conciliation of our social and economic conflicts." [44] In a world that offers alternatives, in the long run the survival of democracy will depend upon the loyalty and support it can command from the people, and this may in no small measure, in turn, depend upon the degree of responsiveness of government to *their* conceptions of justice and reasonableness.

The Case for Judicial Review over Acts of the States

Many of the arguments urged against judicial review of national legislation are obviously equally applicable to review of state legislation. It is, for example, true that a Court empowered to invalidate "unjust" or "unreasonable" legislation may with equal facility strike down "just" and "reasonable" legislation. But there are some essential differences, and the risks to the general welfare involved in denying judicial review over the acts of states (as distinguished from Acts of Congress), seem to me greater than those involved in conceding it.

The reasons that support this view are first, assuming the end of judicial review of Congressional legislation, undesirable decisions affecting states, if serious and widespread in effect, could probably be corrected by Congressional action. Second, greater confidence in the rule of the representatives of a national majority in the general interest is warranted than is true in the case of representatives of a local majority. The President and Congress function under the spotlight of continuous and intense publicity which gives some assurance that they may be trusted in the long run to respond to the people's wishes. Much of the activity of state legislatures is masked in obscurity and confusion. Furthermore, under any conceivable set of circumstances, for the foreseeable future, minority views will receive substantial representation in Congress. Many of our states, on the other hand, are blanketed by the rule of a single party. It is true, too, that Presidents and national parties, in the interests of success at the polls, if for no other reasons, are likely to show more sedulous regard for the rights of minorities than is likely to be true of most governors and local parties. Experience shows that no national party based on intolerance and race prejudice can hope to survive. That is why the remark of one of Blaine's supporters that the Democratic party was the party of "Rum, Romanism and Rebellion" proved so costly to Blaine. It is to the national forum rather than to the local forum that the Negro must, for the most part, look for consideration of his elementary interests.

A distinction suggested by Marshall seems to me also pertinent. All the people are represented in Congress and in the election of a President, and if Congress and the President abuse their power the entire nation, or a substantial part of it, is likely to be affected. The whole faith in democracy rests upon the assumption that normal political processes can be relied upon to correct that abuse. If the state abuses its power, on the other hand, it may, as in the McCul-loch case, benefit the state at the expense of the nation and normal political processes cannot be as fully relied upon to correct that abuse. To free the states from federal control would, for example, enable them to impede national commerce, in the local interest. It was in this connection that Justice Holmes wrote that "one in my place sees how often a local policy prevails with those who are not trained to national views and how often action is taken that embodies what the Commerce Clause was meant to end." [45]

Finally, it is part of the record, supported by this study, that while the Court has, on the occasions when the nation and Congress have been swept by hysteria and bias adverse to minorities, shown little capacity for resistance, it has, for understandable reasons, more often resisted the hysteria and bias which have dominated local majorities and legislatures. On any showing, some of the most valuable and effective work of the Court has been in striking down local legislation attacking the civil liberties of minorities or discriminating against them.

"I do not think the United States would come to an end if we lost our power to declare an Act of Congress void," wrote Justice Holmes.[46] I would go further and maintain that, on balance, the record of the Court, and particularly its record in the early period during which Mr. Hughes served as Chief Justice of the United States, supports the proposition that the democratic progress of the United States has been and may again, in crisis, be impeded unless the Court is deprived of this power. I do, however, unreservedly agree with the position of Justice Holmes that the nation would be imperilled if the Court were denied the power to invalidate the laws of the several states.[47]

NOTES

1. "LEARNING, WISDOM AND CHARACTER"

1. *Osborn* v. *Bank of the United States*, 9 Wheaton 738, 866. Contrast this with the statement of Mr. (now Associate Justice) Frankfurter that "Marshall had, as it were, the duty of creation to a degree greater than falls to the lot of even most great judges." Felix Frankfurter, *The Commerce Clause* (Chapel Hill: University of North Carolina Press, 1937), p. 12.

2. Benjamin N. Cardozo, *The Nature of the Judicial Process* (New Haven: Yale University Press, 1921), p. 88.

3. Oliver Wendell Holmes, "The Path of Law," *Harvard Law Review*, X (March, 1897), 467.

4. The account of the career of Charles Evans Hughes in this chapter, except when otherwise indicated by specific reference, is based upon the following biographical sources which are in general agreement upon the essential facts: William L. Ransom, *Charles E. Hughes* (New York: E. P. Dutton & Company, 1916); Kenneth Bernard Umbreit, *Our Eleven Chief Justices* (New York: Harper & Brothers, 1938), pp. 451–500; Charles Evans Hughes, *Addresses of Charles Evans Hughes, 1906–1916, with an Introduction by Jacob Gould Schurman* (New York: G. P. Putnam's Sons, rev. ed., 1916), pp. xliii–lxiii; *Current Biography, 1941* (New York: The H. W. Wilson Company), pp. 417–420; Drew Pearson and Robert S. Allen, *The Nine Old Men* (New York: Doubleday, Doran & Company, 1936), pp. 74–97; Henry F. Pringle, "Profile of Chief Justice Hughes," The *New Yorker*, June 29, July 6, and July 13, 1935; Silas Hardy Strawn, "Chief Justice Hughes," New York *Herald Tribune*, February 23, 1930; New York *Herald Tribune*, June 3, 1941; United States *Congressional Directory*, May, 1941.

5. An excellent summary account appears in Mark Sullivan, *Our Times* (New York: Charles Scribner's Sons, 1930), III, 49–66.

6. Gustavus Myers, in his highly critical *History of the Supreme Court of the United States* (Chicago: Charles H. Kerr & Company, 1925), pp. 739–766, denies that concentration of control was affected. On the contrary, he maintains that the Morgan, Harriman and Ryan interests strengthened their domination in the insurance field.

7. See Theodore Roosevelt and Henry Cabot Lodge, *Selections from the Correspondence of Theodore Roosevelt and Henry Cabot Lodge* (New York: Charles Scribner's Sons, 1925), II, 248.

8. *Ibid.*, p. 239. Quoted with permission of the publisher.

9. Hughes, *Addresses*, pp. 55–64.

10. *Ibid.*, pp. 65–69.

11. *Ibid.*, p. 68.

12. Charles Evans Hughes, *Conditions of Progress in Democratic Government* (New Haven: Yale University Press, 1910), pp. 33–34.

13. *Ibid.*, p. 46.

14. *Ibid.*, p. 44.

15. *Ibid.*, p. 13.

16. Charles Evans Hughes, *Public Papers of Charles E. Hughes, Governor, 1907* (Albany: J. B. Lyon Company, 1908), p. 90.

17. Hughes, *Public Papers, 1908*, p. 94.

18. Hughes, *Addresses*, p. 247.

19. Hughes, *Conditions*, p. 24.

20. Hughes, *Addresses*, pp. 96–97.

21. *Ibid.*, pp. 97–98. Some months earlier he had expressed similar views. *Ibid.*, p. 233.

22. Hughes, *Public Papers, 1910*, pp. 71–76.

23. Hughes, *Addresses*, pp. 95–96.

24. *Ibid.*, pp. 120–121. See also p. 98.

25. *Ibid.*, pp. 179–192.

26. *Ibid.*, p. 307.

27. *Ibid.*, pp. 307–308.

28. *World*, April 26, 1910.

29. *Ibid.*

30. Roosevelt and Lodge, *Selections*, II, 377–378.

31. *Ibid.*, p. 380. Quoted with permission of the publisher, Charles Scribner's Sons.

32. New York *Times*, April 26, 1910.

33. New York *Daily Tribune*, April 26, 1910.

34. *World*, April 26, 1910.

35. *Wall Street Journal*, April 29, 1910.

36. New York *American*, April 26, 1910.

37. *World*, April 26, 1910.

38. *Ibid.*

39. *Nation*, May 12, 1910, p. 471.

40. *Ibid.*, October 13, 1910, p. 331.

2. THE RECONCILIATION OF LIBERTY AND AUTHORITY

1. Woodrow Wilson, *Congressional Government* (Boston: Houghton Mifflin Co., 1925), p. 4.

2. *Marbury* v. *Madison*, 1 Cranch 137 (1803), was the root decision. Whether it was intended by the Framers that the Court exercise this power, particularly with respect to acts of Congress, has been a matter of historic dispute.

3. The vacancy filled by Mr. Hughes' appointment was that of Justice David J. Brewer, who had died on March 28, 1910. After Mr. Hughes' nomination but before he took his seat, Chief Justice Melville W. Fuller died. On December 12, 1910, President Taft nominated Associate Justice Edward D. White to succeed Mr. Fuller as Chief Justice, Willis Van Devanter to succeed Mr. White as an Associate Justice, and Joseph R. Lamar to succeed Mr. William H. Moody who had retired on November 20, 1910. The Court was considerably reconstituted as a result and early in 1911 consisted of Edward Douglass White of Louisiana as Chief Justice and of the following Associate Justices: John Marshall Harlan of Kentucky, Joseph McKenna of California, Oliver Wendell Holmes of Massachusetts, William R. Day of Ohio, Horace Harmon Lurton of Tennessee, Charles Evans Hughes of New York, Willis Van Devanter of Wyoming, and Joseph Rucker Lamar of Georgia.

On October 14, 1911, Justice Harlan died. He was succeeded by Mr. Mahlon Pitney of New Jersey, who took his seat as an Associate Justice on March 18, 1912. On July 12, 1914, Justice Lurton died and was succeeded by Attorney-General James Clark McReynolds of Tennessee, who took his oath of office on September 5, 1914 by appointment of President Woodrow Wilson. Justice Lamar died on January 2, 1916. On January 28 President Wilson nominated Louis Dembitz Brandeis of Massachusetts to fill the vacancy. After a bitter fight, Mr. Brandeis' nomination was confirmed by the Senate on June 1, and he took his seat as an Associate Justice on June 5, 1916, a few days before Mr. Hughes' resignation of June 10 to accept the nomination of the Republican party as its candidate for the presidency of the United States.

4. For a complete table, see Ransom, *Charles E. Hughes*, pp. 282 ff.

5. *Ibid.*, p. 13.

6. 219 U.S. 219 (1911).

7. See "Labor Contract Laws and the Thirteenth Amendment," *Harvard Law Review*, XXIV (March, 1911), 392.

8. "Criminal Enforcement of Contracts for Labor as Involuntary Servitude," *Columbia Law Review*, XI (April, 1911), 364.

9. "Labor Contract Laws and the Thirteenth Amendment," p. 392.

10. For an exposition of the importance attached to contract obligations by Justice Holmes, see particularly his opinion in *Pennsylvania Coal Co.* v. *Mahon*, 260 U.S. 393 (1922). See also his opinion in *Wright* v. *Central of Georgia R.R.* discussed in chapter 4.

3. DUE PROCESS, EQUAL PROTECTION AND THE POLICE POWER

1. See chapter 11.
2. 219 U.S. 549 (1911).
3. See chapter 21.
4. 226 U.S. 192 (1912).
5. 231 U.S. 320 (1913).
6. 238 U.S. 446 (1915).
7. 208 U.S. 161 (1908).
8. 236 U.S. 1.
9. See chapter 20. It is noteworthy that he sought to distinguish the ADAIR and COPPAGE decisions.
10. Charles Evans Hughes, *The Supreme Court of the United States* (New York: Columbia University Press, 1936), p. 53.
11. 169 U.S. 366.
12. 198 U.S. 45 (1905).
13. 208 U.S. 412 (1908).
14. 236 U.S. 373 (1915).
15. *United States* v. *Darby*, 312 U.S. 100.
16. *Steward Machine Co.* v. *Davis*, 301 U.S. 548 (1937).
17. 226 U.S. 184 (1912).
18. This question receives fuller attention in chapter 13.
19. 235 U.S. 151 (1914).
20. A minority of the Court, Chief Justice White and Justices Holmes, Lamar and McReynolds, simply concurred in the result.
21. 239 U.S. 33 (1915).
22. Justice McReynolds dissented on the technical ground that the suit was against the state and thus barred by the Eleventh Amendment.
23. Justice Hughes in *Miller* v. *Wilson*, 236 U.S. 373 (1915).
24. *Quaker City Cab Co.* v. *Pennsylvania*, 277 U.S. 389 (1928), in dissenting.
25. Recognition of these facts, while disposing of some of the pre-

tensions of the Justices, does not necessarily dispose of the arguments in defense of judicial review. Those arguments are considered in the concluding chapter of this book.

4. PUBLIC CONTRACTS, THE CONTRACT CLAUSE AND THE POLICE POWER

1. Benjamin Fletcher Wright, Jr., *The Contract Clause of the Constitution* (Cambridge: Harvard University Press, 1938), p. xiii.

2. The history of the development of the limitations of the contract clause upon the impairment of private contracts is separately traced in connection with Mr. Hughes' services as Chief Justice.

3. Wright, *The Contract Clause of the Constitution*, p. 16.

4. 6 Cranch 87 (1810).

5. The decision only partly rested upon the contract clause. It was suggested that the state was also restrained by "the nature of society and of government" and perhaps by the *ex post facto* and bill of attainder provisions of the Constitution.

6. Wright, *The Contract Clause of the Constitution*, p. 35.

7. 7 Cranch 164 (1812).

8. Wright, *The Contract Clause of the Constitution*, p. 179.

9. 4 Wheat. 518 (1819).

10. "In the Dartmouth College case," comments Benjamin F. Wright, "it was difficult indeed to see in a charter, granted by the crown, a contract, much less one of the sort which could possibly have been in the minds of the Framers." *The Contract Clause of the Constitution*, p. 43.

11. 11 Pet. 420 (1837).

12. The adverse effect of any other decision upon the development of the nation is too obvious to require comment.

13. 227 U.S. 544 (1913).

14. 235 U.S. 179 (1914).

15. 233 U.S. 195 (1914).

16. 230 U.S. 58 (1913).

17. 230 U.S. 537 (1913).

18. 231 U.S. 298 (1913).

19. 236 U.S. 687 (1915).

20. 236 U.S. 674 (1915).

21. Justice Lamar took no part in the consideration or decision of the case and Justice McReynolds dissented without opinion.

22. "Upon no other matter did Justice Hughes find himself so often or so sharply at variance with the prevailing judgment of his gifted

colleagues as concerning the assertions of the perpetual character of granted franchises and denials of the reserved power of the public to repeal, modify or revoke such grants." Ransom, *Charles E. Hughes*, p. 168.

5. THE CONTROL OF COMMERCE: NATIONAL AND STATE POWER

1. Article 1, Section 8.
2. 9 Wheat. 1.
3. Charles Warren, *The Supreme Court in United States History* (Boston: Little, Brown & Company, 1937), II, 735.
4. 221 U.S. 612 (1911).
5. Discussed in the last pages of this chapter.
6. 223 U.S. 1 (1912).
7. 224 U.S. 603 (1912).
8. 239 U.S. 510 (1916).
9. 221 U.S. 488 (1911).
10. 12 Wheat. 419 (1827).
11. 12 How. 299.
12. 135 U.S. 100.
13. 232 U.S. 14 (1914).
14. 234 U.S. 333 (1914).
15. 234 U.S. 317 (1914).
16. 236 U.S. 151 (1915).
17. Ransom, *Charles E. Hughes*, p. 15.
18. 230 U.S. 352 (1913).
19. Further analysis of this distinction appears at a later point.
20. See, however, Justice Hughes' decisions in the PORT RICHMOND and WILMINGTON TRANSPORTATION cases previously discussed.
21. I. L. Sharfman, *The Interstate Commerce Commission* (New York: Commonwealth Fund, 1931–1937), II, 227.
22. John Bauer, "The Minnesota Rate Cases," *Political Science Quarterly*, XXIX (March, 1914), 79.
23. Hannis Taylor, "The Minnesota Rate Cases," *Harvard Law Review*, XXVII (Nov., 1913), 25–26.
24. 234 U.S. 342 (1914).
25. Justices Lurton and Pitney dissented without opinion.
26. The basis upon which Justice Hughes rested this part of his decision had been suggested by counsel in the MINNESOTA RATE CASES but was then ignored. See 230 U.S. 352, at pages 361–362.

27. Sharfman, *The Interstate Commerce Commission*, II, 238.

28. George G. Reynolds, *The Distribution of Power to Regulate Interstate Carriers between the Nation and the States* (New York: Columbia University Press, 1928), p. 211.

29. Frankfurter, *The Commerce Clause*, p. 34.

30. Hughes, *Addresses*, pp. 338, 340.

31. 301 U.S. 1 (1937).

32. Hughes, *Addresses*, p. 343.

33. Edward S. Corwin, *The Twilight of the Supreme Court* (New Haven: Yale University Press, 1934), p. 50.

34. Frankfurter, *The Commerce Clause*, pp. 21–22.

6. A SUMMARY EVALUATION

1. Arthur M. Allen, "The Opinions of Mr. Justice Hughes," *Columbia Law Review*, XVI (Nov., 1916), 566.

2. Hughes, *Addresses*, p. 351.

3. In *Frank* v. *Mangum*, 237 U.S. 309 (1915), Justice Hughes alone had joined with Holmes in dissenting from the decision of the Court which attached considerable weight, amounting almost to finality, to the determination of the highest state court on the issue of whether the trial of an individual convicted of a crime against state law had been fair and in accord with due process under circumstances suggesting that the trial may have been conducted under the domination of a hostile mob.

4. Hughes, *Addresses*, p. 341.

5. *Ibid.*, p. 340.

6. *Ibid.*, p. 352.

7. *Ibid.*, p. 351.

8. *Ibid.*, p. 342.

9. See chapter 21.

10. While the criteria on the basis of which the judgment was arrived at are not supplied, it is at least suggestive to note that Pearson and Allen, who are sparing in their praise of Mr. Hughes, assert that "in the six years that he served on the Court, he voted with the liberal wing 51 times, with the conservatives only 10 times, as against a record for Justice Holmes of 37 votes on the liberal side and 32 on the conservative." Pearson and Allen, *The Nine Old Men*, p. 80. See also New York *Herald Tribune*, June 3, 1941.

11. "McReynolds, Roberts and Hughes," *New Republic* (July 1, 1936), p. 233.

12. *Nation* (June 14, 1941), p. 685.

7. PRIVATE CITIZEN AND PUBLIC SERVANT

1. Sullivan, *Our Times*, III, 68.

2. New York *Times*, June 19, 1912. In 1915, he again refused to be considered. See *Congressional Record*, LXXII (1930), 3560.

3. John D. Hicks, *The American Nation* (Boston: Houghton Mifflin, 1946), p. 488.

4. New York *Evening World*, June 13, 1916.

5. New York *Times*, June 11, 1916.

6. *New Republic* (June 17, 1916), p. 158.

7. *Nation* (June 15, 1916), p. 632.

8. Hughes, *Addresses*, pp. 8–46.

9. New York *Times*, September 6, 1917.

10. The right of Congress to raise an army by conscription was upheld by the Supreme Court in the SELECTIVE DRAFT LAW CASES, 245 U.S. 366 (1918).

11. The whole episode is fully discussed in Zechariah Chafee, Jr., *Free Speech in the United States* (Cambridge: Harvard University Press, 1941), pp. 269–282.

12. Quoted in *ibid.*, pp. 273–274.

13. Quoted in *ibid.*, p. 165.

14. Quoted in *ibid.*, p. 162.

15. Thomas A. Bailey, *A Diplomatic History of the American People* (New York: F. S. Crofts, 1947), pp. 681–682.

16. Samuel Flagg Bemis, *A Diplomatic History of the United States* (New York: Henry Holt, 1942), p. 656.

17. Bailey, *A Diplomatic History of the American People*, p. 682.

18. Quoted in *ibid.*, p. 682.

19. Nelson P. Mead, *The Development of the United States since 1865* (New York: Harcourt, Brace, 1935), p. 571.

20. Bemis, *A Diplomatic History of the United States*, p. 501.

21. Mead, *The Development of the United States since 1865*, pp. 475–476.

22. Pearson and Allen, *The Nine Old Men*, p. 84.

23. Frederick L. Schuman, *Soviet Politics* (New York: Alfred A. Knopf, 1946), pp. 190, 227–228.

24. Bailey, *A Diplomatic History of the American People*, pp. 689–699.

25. Thomas A. Bailey, *A Diplomatic History of the American People* (New York: Appleton-Century-Crofts, Inc., 1950), p. 699. Quoted with permission of the publisher.

26. Pearson and Allen, *The Nine Old Men*, p. 83.

27. New York *Times*, October 16, 1924.

28. In 1927 Mr. Hughes delivered a series of lectures on the Supreme Court to which repeated reference will be made in connection with his service as Chief Justice.

29. *Congressional Directory*, May, 1941.

8. A HISTORIC DEBATE

1. *Congressional Record*, LXXII (1930), 3372.

2. *Ibid.*, pp. 3372–3373.

3. *Ibid.*, pp. 3448–3451.

4. Earlier Senator Borah had stated, "if the Shreveport case is followed to its logical conclusion, all State regulation, all State control of utilities has passed out of existence." *Ibid.*, p. 3450.

5. *Ibid.*, pp. 3451–3452.

6. *Ibid.*, p. 3452.

7. *Ibid.*

8. *Ibid.*, pp. 3452–3453.

9. *Ibid.*, pp. 3499–3503.

10. *Ibid.*, p. 3503.

11. *Ibid.*, pp. 3508–3514.

12. *Ibid.*, pp. 3516–3517.

13. *Ibid.*, pp. 3517–3519.

14. *Ibid.*, pp. 3553–3560.

15. *Ibid.*, pp. 3560–3561.

16. *Ibid.*, pp. 3561–3564.

17. *Ibid.*, pp. 3564–3581.

18. *Ibid.*, pp. 3581–3583.

19. *Ibid.*, p. 3588.

20. *Ibid.*, pp. 3588–3589.

21. *Ibid.*, pp. 3589–3590.

22. *Ibid.*, pp. 3590–3591.

23. New York *Herald Tribune*, February 14, 1930.

24. New York *Times*, February 15, 1930.

25. *Wall Street Journal*, February 14, 1930.

26. *Nation* (February 12, 1930), p. 165.

27. *New Republic* (February 26, 1930), p. 31.

28. Cortez A. M. Ewing, *The Judges of the Supreme Court, 1788–1937* (Minneapolis: The University of Minnesota Press, 1938), pp. 37–38.

9. THE SETTING

1. Alfred H. Kelly and Winfred A. Harbison, *The American Constitution: Its Origins and Development* (New York: W. W. Norton & Company, 1948), p. 681.

2. Carl Brent Swisher, *American Constitutional Development* (Boston: Houghton Mifflin Company, 1943), p. 592.

3. Subsequent changes in the Court were: Justice Willis Van Devanter retired June 2, 1937, and was succeeded by Mr. Hugo L. Black on October 4, 1937; Justice Sutherland retired on January 18, 1938, and was replaced by Mr. Stanley Reed on January 31, 1938; Justice Cardozo died on July 9, 1938, and Mr. Felix Frankfurter took his seat on January 30, 1939; Justice Brandeis retired on February 13, 1939, to be succeeded by Mr. William O. Douglas on April 17, 1939; Justice Butler died on November 16, 1939, to be replaced by Mr. Frank Murphy on February 5, 1940; Justice McReynolds retired on February 1, 1940, and Chief Justice Hughes announced his retirement on June 2, 1941 effective July 1, 1941.

4. Merle Fainsod and Lincoln Gordon, *Government and the American Economy* (New York: W. W. Norton & Company, 1941), p. 13. The figures are derived from the T.N.E.C. *Hearings*, Part 1 (1939). The quote is with the permission of the publisher.

5. For an analysis of the prerogatives of the Chief Justice, see Hughes, *Supreme Court*, pp. 56–65.

6. *Ibid.*, p. 59.

7. A complete table of the opinions of Chief Justice Hughes is to be found in the Appendix to F. D. G. Ribble, "The Constitutional Doctrines of Chief Justice Hughes," *Columbia Law Review*, XLI (Nov., 1941), 1210–1215.

8. "With the exception of John Marshall, no man has, within the space of a few years, written opinions in cases of such far reaching import, as did Chief Justice Hughes." *Ibid.*, p. 1192.

10. PROCEDURAL DUE PROCESS AND GOVERNMENTAL POWER

1. For an earlier discussion of this topic, see chapter 3.

2. See *Hurtado* v. *California*, 110 U.S. 516 (1884), which held that the due process clause does not impose on states the requirement of grand jury indictment since such procedure was specifically imposed upon

the federal government under another clause of the Fifth Amendment. See also *Twining* v. *New Jersey*, 211 U.S. 78 (1908).

3. A particularly lucid explanation of the rationale involved appears in a decision by Justice Cardozo which came in 1937, *Palko* v. *Connecticut*, 302 U.S. 319.

4. 287 U.S. 45 (1932).

5. 294 U.S. 103 (1935).

6. 297 U.S. 278 (1936).

7. Charles Evans Hughes, *The Pathway of Peace* (New York: Harper & Bros., 1925), p. 208.

8. New York *Times*, February 13, 1931.

9. 285 U.S. 22 (1932).

10. In support of this proposition he cited a number of cases including utility cases involving a claim of confiscation and the determination in deportation cases of whether the person is a citizen or an alien.

11. The decision of the Chief Justice that trial *de novo* before a Court was required in regard to "fundamental and jurisdictional" facts was apparently rested on Article 3 of the Constitution and not upon due process. Since Article 3 is not applicable to the states, it may, perhaps, be concluded that, so far as "fundamental and jurisdictional" facts are concerned, the states were left free to attach finality to the determinations of administrative agencies, if supported by evidence, without violating the requirements of due process.

12. See James M. Landis, *The Administrative Process* (New Haven: Yale University Press, 1938), p. 133.

13. Professor Carl Brent Swisher has commented that "the decision was a long step backward in the movement to lighten the burden of the courts and relieve them of tasks they were not equipped to perform." *American Constitutional Development* (Boston: Houghton Mifflin Company, 1943), pp. 921–922.

14. 288 U.S. 162 (1932).

15. See also *South Chicago Coal Dock Co.* v. *Bassett*, 309 U.S. 251 (1940), *Shields* v. *Utah Idaho Central R.R.*, 305 U.S. 177 (1938), *L'Hote* v. *Crowell*, 286 U.S. 528 (1932), *Del Vecchio* v. *Bowers*, 296 U.S. 280 (1935), *Parker* v. *Motor Boat Sales Co.*, 314 U.S. 244 (1941), *Cardillo* v. *Liberty Mutual Insurance Co.*, 330 U.S. 469 (1947).

16. 298 U.S. 1 (1936).

17. Robert H. Jackson, *The Struggle for Judicial Supremacy* (New York: A. A. Knopf, 1941), p. 152. See also Landis, *The Administrative Process*, pp. 136–140.

18. 253 U.S. 287.

19. 298 U.S. 38 (1936).

20. Apparently no request was made by the company for an opportunity to present additional evidence before the District Court in this case. Had such a request been made, the issue would then have been raised whether due process not only requires an independent judicial judgment upon the facts on the record before the administrative agency but, if requested, upon an independent record in a *de novo* hearing. So far as this case was concerned that remained an open question.

21. Mr. Justice Roberts concurred only in the result without opinion.

22. 310 U.S. 573 (1940).

23. 298 U.S. 468 (1936).

24. That might have raised a question simply of whether such delegation was authorized by the statute.

25. *Morgan* v. *United States*, 304 U.S. 1 (1938).

26. Mr. Justice Black alone dissented but without opinion. Justices Reed and Cardozo took no part in the case.

27. National Farm and Home Hour, April 28, 1938.

28. New York *Times*, May 8, 1938.

29. *Ibid.*, May 13, 1938.

30. *Morgan* v. *United States*, 304 U.S. 23 (1938).

31. *United States* v. *Morgan*, 307 U.S. 183, 191 (1939). Justices Butler, McReynolds and Roberts dissented.

32. *United States* v. *Morgan*, 313 U.S. 409 (1941).

11. DUE PROCESS AFFECTING ECONOMIC INTERESTS

1. Edward S. Corwin, "The Doctrine of Due Process of Law Before the Civil War," *Harvard Law Review*, XXIV (Mar., 1911), 460.

2. "The Role of the Supreme Court in a Democratic Nation," Edmund Janes James Lecture at the University of Illinois, March 9, 1938. Reprinted in Hillman M. Bishop and Samuel Hendel, *Basic Issues of American Democracy* (New York: Appleton-Century-Crofts, Inc., 1948), p. 174.

3. Hughes, *Supreme Court*, pp. 187–188. Quoted with permission of the publisher, Columbia University Press.

4. *Whitney* v. *Cailfornia*, 274 U.S. 357, 373 (1927).

5. Edward S. Corwin, *Constitutional Revolution, Ltd.* (Claremont, Cal.: Claremont Colleges, 1941), p. 26.

6. Corwin, *The Twilight of the Supreme Court*, p. 56.

7. John Marshall in *Fletcher* v. *Peck*, 6 Cranch 87 (1810). See Corwin,

The Twilight of the Supreme Court, pp. 56–65 and note 7, pp. 197–198.

8. *Ibid.*, pp. 65–68.

9. SLAUGHTER-HOUSE CASES, 16 Wall. 36 (1873). See also Edward S. Corwin, "The Supreme Court and the Fourteenth Amendment," *Michigan Law Review*, VII (June, 1909), 672.

10. *Munn* v. *Illinois*, 94 U.S. 113 (1876), and *Davidson* v. *New Orleans*, 96 U.S. 97, 104 (1877).

11. 287 U.S. 378 (1932).

12. Charles Fairman, "Martial Rule, in the Light of Sterling v. Constantin," *Cornell Law Quarterly*, XIX (Dec., 1933), 29–30.

13. 212 U.S. 78 (1909).

14. Fairman, "Martial Rule in the Light of Sterling v. Constantin," p. 30.

15. 94 U.S. 113.

16. *Munn* v. *Illinois, Budd* v. *New York*, 143 U.S. 517 (1892), *Brass* v. *Stoeser*, 153 U.S. 391 (1894), *German Alliance Insurance Co.* v. *Kansas*, 233 U.S. 389 (1914).

17. *Wolff Packing Co.* v. *Court of Industrial Relations*, 262 U.S. 522, 535.

18. *Tyson* v. *Banton*, 273 U.S. 418.

19. *Ribnik* v. *McBride*, 277 U.S. 350.

20. *Williams* v. *Standard Oil Co.*, 278 U.S. 235.

21. *O'Gorman & Young* v. *Hartford Fire Ins. Co.*, 282 U.S. 251 (1931). The four "conservatives" dissented.

22. 285 U.S. 262 (1932).

23. The majority was composed, in addition, of Justices Van Devanter, McReynolds, Butler and Roberts.

24. 291 U.S. 502 (1934).

25. 290 U.S. 398 (1934).

26. See chapter 14.

27. Jackson, *The Struggle for Judicial Supremacy*, pp. 84–85.

28. 298 U.S. 587 (1936).

29. 243 U.S. 629 (1917).

30. 261 U.S. 525 (1923). Justice Brandeis again disqualified himself, this time because his daughter was a member of the minimum wage commission.

31. Morris R. Cohen, *Law and the Social Order* (New York: Harcourt, Brace & Co., 1933), p. 150.

32. Thomas Reed Powell, "The Judiciality of Minimum-Wage Legislation," *Harvard Law Review*, XXXVII (March, 1924), 549.

33. *Ibid.*, p. 548.

34. *Murphy* v. *Sardell*, 269 U.S. 530, and *Donham* v. *West-Nelson Mfg. Co.*, 273 U.S. 657.

35. Justices Brandeis, Stone and Cardozo joined in this dissent.

36. Justices Brandeis and Cardozo joined in this dissent.

37. *Morehead* v. *People, ex rel. Tipaldo*, 299 U.S. 619 (1936).

38. *Erie R.R.* v. *Tompkins*, 304 U.S. 64 (1938).

39. 300 U.S. 379 (1937).

40. *United States* v. *Butler*, 297 U.S. 1, 62 (1936). It is ironical that this statement occurred in the very decision in which Justice Stone maintained, in dissent, that Justice Roberts' opinion involved "a tortured construction of the Constitution" and that its suppositions were "addressed to the mind accustomed to believe that it is the business of courts to sit in judgment on the wisdom of legislative action." At p. 87.

41. This opinion had the concurrence of Justices Van Devanter, McReynolds and Butler.

42. Benjamin F. Wright, *The Growth of American Constitutional Law* (Boston: Houghton Mifflin Company, 1942), p. 221.

43. *United States* v. *Darby*, 312 U.S. 100.

44. *Lochner* v. *New York*, 195 U. S. 45, 75.

45. *Baldwin* v. *Missouri*, 281 U.S. 586, 595. "In short," says Edward S. Corwin, "the 'due process' clause came to arm the Court with a supervisory power over governmental function virtually without statable limits—to render it, in the words of Justice Brandeis, a 'super-legislature.' " *Constitutional Revolution, Ltd.*, p. 30.

12. INTELLECTUAL LIBERTY UNDER THE CONSTITUTION

1. For classic formulations of the values of freedom, see John Stuart Mill, *On Liberty* (New York: Henry Holt and Co., 1898), and Justice Holmes, dissenting opinion, in *Abrams* v. *United States*, 250 U.S. 616, 624 (1919).

2. Hughes, *The Supreme Court*, pp. 162–163.

3. Chafee, *Free Speech in the United States*, pp. 5–6.

4. *Barron* v. *Baltimore*, 7 Peters 243.

5. Horace E. Flack, *The Adoption of the Fourteenth Amendment* (Baltimore: The Johns Hopkins Press, 1908), pp. 55–97.

6. 16 Wall. 36 (1873).

7. 268 U.S. 652 (1925).

8. *Frohwerk* v. *United States*, 249 U.S. 204 (1919), and *Schenck* v. *United States*, 249 U.S. 47 (1919).

9. Chafee, *Free Speech in the United States*, pp. 15, 16.

10. 283 U.S. 359 (1931).

11. Only two Justices dissented. Justice McReynolds dissented on the technical ground that decision had not been requested upon any question arising out of the charge and it was sufficient therefore if conviction could be sustained under any one of the clauses, "some of which were certainly good." Justice Butler dissented on the further ground that in his view the record affirmatively showed that the defendant was not convicted for violation of the first clause.

12. And as Prof. Chafee points out, and the Chief Justice might well have noted in the case at issue, "The indefiniteness of the broad words 'symbol of opposition to organized government' is shown by the fact that they were applied . . . to the flag of Soviet Russia, one of the most rigidly organized governments on earth." *Free Speech in the United States*, p. 365.

13. This was the position he had taken in condemning the ouster of the Socialist members of the New York State Assembly.

14. 283 U.S. 605 (1931).

15. Justices Van Devanter, McReynolds, Butler and Roberts concurred.

16. 279 U.S. 644 (1929). In that case, an uncompromising pacifist with no sense of nationalism "and only a cosmic sense of belonging to the human family" who testified that she would not take up arms in defense of this country and expressed a willingness to be treated as a conscientious objector was denied citizenship. That case had been decided by a vote of six to three. Changes in the Court encouraged the belief that the MACINTOSH case would bring a different result. Justices Holmes and Brandeis, who had dissented in the former case, were still on the bench and the hope was that the two new appointees, Chief Justice Hughes and Mr. Justice Roberts, would join with them. Only one member of the Schwimmer majority—possibly Justice Stone—would then have to be won over. The Chief Justice did support the Macintosh application and Justice Stone was brought over but Mr. Justice Roberts joined in the old majority position.

17. He was joined in this dissent by Justices Holmes, Brandeis and Stone.

18. This result was accomplished in *Girouard* v. *United States*, 328 U.S. 61 (1946), when the Court reversed the SCHWIMMER and MACINTOSH decisions and upheld the right to citizenship of a Seventh Day Adventist who although expressing an unwillingness to bear arms because of religious scruples was willing to perform non-combatant services in war.

19. 283 U.S. 697 (1931). Justices Holmes, Brandeis, Stone and Roberts concurred in the opinion of the Chief Justice. Justice Butler wrote a dissenting opinion with the concurrence of Justices Van Devanter, McReynolds and Sutherland.

20. See *Cornell Law Quarterly*, XVII (Dec., 1931), 130.

21. Chafee, *Free Speech in the United States*, p. 381.

22. New York *Herald Tribune*, June 3, 1931. In *Grosjean* v. *American Press Co.*, 297 U.S. 233 (1936), a unanimous Court, in an opinion by Justice Sutherland, upset as an unconstitutional denial of freedom of the press, contrary to due process, a Louisiana statute imposing a license tax of two per cent on the gross receipts of all publishers of any publication having a circulation of more than 20,000 copies per week which sold advertising.

23. 299 U.S. 353.

24. Justice Stone took no part in this case.

25. 116 U.S. 252

26. See *California Law Review*, XXV (May, 1937), 496.

27. Arguing that the decision had a "very limited application," one writer says, "Contributing nothing to the definition of the word 'peaceable,' it merely says that a peaceable assembly may not be prohibited merely because its sponsors are criminal. Nor is the dictum helpful in determining the extent of 'liberty' protected by the due process clause." *University of Chicago Law Review*, IV (April, 1937), 489.

28. 301 U.S. 242 (1937).

29. The Chief Justice and Justices Brandeis, Stone, and Cardozo concurred in this opinion. Justices Van Devanter, McReynolds, Sutherland and Butler dissented. This was the last time the four conservatives stood together in a civil liberties case. A few months thereafter Justice Van Devanter retired and was succeeded by Mr. Justice Black.

30. Shortly after Chief Justice Hughes retired from the bench the Court specifically reinvoked the "clear and present danger" doctrine as the test of constitutionality in all cases involving freedom of speech, press, assembly and religion. It is clearly formulated in *Thomas* v. *Collins*, 323 U.S. 516 (1944).

31. 303 U.S. 444 (1938).

32. The entire Court, except for Justice Cardozo who took no part in the consideration or decision of the case, concurred in the opinion.

33. Chafee, *Free Speech in the United States*, pp. 401, 405.

34. 310 U.S. 296 (1940).

35. *Minersville School District* v. *Gobitis*, 310 U.S. 586 (1940). After

the Chief Justice retired, the Court reversed itself. *West Virginia State Board of Education* v. *Barnette,* 319 U.S. 624 (1943).

36. 312 U.S. 569 (1941).

37. 301 U.S. 468 (1937).

38. Justices Butler, Van Devanter, McReynolds and Sutherland dissented.

39. 303 U.S. 323 (1938).

40. 303 U.S. 552 (1938).

41. Justices Butler and McReynolds alone dissented.

42. 307 U.S. 496 (1939).

43. Justices McReynolds and Butler dissented. Justices Frankfurter and Douglas took no part in the case.

44. 310 U.S. 88 (1940).

45. 310 U.S. 106 (1940).

46. Justice McReynolds alone dissented.

47. 312 U.S. 287 (1941).

48. Justices Black, Douglas and Reed dissented.

49. 312 U.S. 321 (1941).

50. See Samuel J. Konefsky, *Chief Justice Stone and the Supreme Court* (New York: The Macmillan Co., 1945), pp. 193–196, 230–234, and Robert E. Cushman, "Ten Years of the Supreme Court: 1937–1947: Civil Liberties," *American Political Science Review,* XLII (Feb., 1948), 43.

51. Joseph Percival Pollard, "An Unexpected Champion," *North American Review,* CCXXXVII (April, 1934), 357.

52. Robert Jackson, "The Judicial Career of Chief Justice Hughes," *American Bar Association Journal,* XXVII (July, 1941), 409.

53. *Nation* (June 14, 1941), p. 685.

13. EQUALITY BEFORE THE LAW AND THE POLICE POWER

1. *Powell* v. *Alabama.*

2. 294 U.S. 587 (1935).

3. Justice McReynolds took no part in the consideration and decision of this case.

4. 294 U.S. 600 (1935).

5. In fact in the NORRIS case this issue was based upon the evidence submitted in the PATTERSON case.

6. Justice McReynolds did not participate in this case.

7. 238 U.S. 347.

8. 307 U.S. 268 (1939).

9. 286 U.S. 73 (1932).

10. Justices McReynolds, Van Devanter, Sutherland and Butler dissented.

11. *Grovey* v. *Townsend*, 295 U.S. 45 (1935).

12. 313 U.S. 299.

13. Thereafter, in *Smith* v. *Allwright*, 321 U.S. 649 (1944), the barring of Negroes from participating in primaries was specifically outlawed. Chief Justice Hughes was no longer a member of the Court.

14. 109 U.S. 3.

15. 163 U.S. 537.

16. 305 U.S. 337.

17. Justice Butler concurred in his views.

18. 313 U.S. 80 (1941).

19. 235 U.S. 151 (1914). See chapter 3 of this book.

20. The President's Committee on Civil Rights, *To Secure These Rights* (Washington: United States Government Printing Office, 1947), pp. 81–82.

21. *Henderson* v. *United States*, 339 U.S. 816.

22. *McLaurin* v. *Oklahoma State Regents*, 339 U.S. 637.

23. *Sweatt* v. *Painter*, 339 U.S. 629.

24. New York *Herald Tribune*, April 4, 1950.

14. PRIVATE CONTRACTS, THE CONTRACT CLAUSE AND THE POLICE POWER

1. 290 U.S. 398.

2. "This case has probably been the subject of more written comment than any other contract case except the Dartmouth College case." Wright, *The Contract Clause of the Constitution*, footnote, p. 109.

3. For an earlier discussion in this book on the historic development of the contract clause limitation upon public contracts, see chapter 4.

4. Wright, *The Contract Clause of the Constitution*, p. 8.

5. *Ibid.*, p. 9.

6. Allan Nevins, *The American States during and after the Revolution, 1775–1789* (New York: The Macmillan Co., 1924), pp. 386, 389, 390, 405, 457, 525, 526, 537, 538, 571; Wright, *The Contract Clause of the Constitution*, pp. 4, 13; and A. H. Feller, "Moratory Legislation: a Comparative Study," *Harvard Law Review*, XLVI (May, 1933), 1061.

7. United States *Code* (Vol. XLIV, Part I, of the Statutes at Large), 1851.

8. Article 1, Section 10. Wright, *The Contract Clause of the Constitution*, p. 5.

9. "There can be no doubt of the accuracy of the classic theory that the insertion of the obligations of contract clause was a victory of the creditor class over their debtors," wrote Feller, "Moratory Legislation: a Comparative Study," p. 1067.

10. The *Federalist*, No. XLIV, p. 279.

11. *Ibid.*, No. VII, p. 38.

12. Wright, *The Contract Clause of the Constitution*, p. 101.

13. 1 How. 311.

14. Justice McLean dissented. He said in part, "Every contract is entered into with a supposed knowledge by the parties, that the law-making power may modify the remedy. And this it may do, at its discretion, so far as it acts only on the remedy." The argument that a state might in this view repeal all remedy he met by the observation that a state might as easily fail to appoint judges and officers essential to the administration of justice.

15. 2 How. 608 (1844).

16. There was no dissent. Justice Catron, however, concurred in a separate opinion. The principle of the BRONSON case was again reaffirmed by the Taney Court in 1845, *Lessee of Gantly* v. *Ewing*, 3 How. 707, and, in 1861, *Howard* v. *Bugbee*, 24 How. 461.

17. See Wright, *The Contract Clause of the Constitution*, p. 70. That despite the adverse effect of the decisions of the Marshall and Taney Courts upon debtors, these decisions "did fit in with the prevailing economic and political thought of the years of democratic development" is made evident by the widespread adoption, in their midst, of contract clauses in state constitutions. *Ibid.*, pp. 60–61, 87.

18. See *Gunn* v. *Barry*, 15 Wall. 610, decided in 1872, *Edwards* v. *Kearzey*, 96 U.S. 595, decided in 1877, *Barnitz* v. *Beverly*, 163 U.S. 118, decided in 1896, *Bradley* v. *Lightcap*, 195 U.S. 1, decided in 1904, *Bank of Minden* v. *Clement*, 256 U.S. 126, decided in 1921.

19. *Block* v. *Hirsh*, 256 U.S. 135 (1921), *Marcus Brown Holding Co.* v. *Feldman*, 256 U.S. 170 (1921), *Edgar A. Levy Leasing Co.* v. *Siegel*, 258 U.S. 242 (1922).

20. T.N.E.C. *Hearings*, Part 1 (1939), p. 194.

21. The contrast with the decline of production and prices for industrial products is revealing. See G. C. Means, *Industrial Prices and Their Relative Inflexibility* (1935), Senate Doc. 13, 74th Cong., 1st Sess. (1935).

22. William L. Prosser, "The Minnesota Mortgage Moratorium," *Southern California Law Review*, VII (May, 1934), 353–355.

23. Professor Corwin, pointing out that the Chief Justice, after declaring that emergency does not enlarge power, went on to hold that Minnesota had the power to enact the statute precisely because of the emergency, adds: "Surely our judges ought to relinquish the idea that the judicial robe invests them with Humpty-Dumpty's facile prerogative over words." Edward S. Corwin, "Moratorium Over Minnesota," *University of Pennsylvania Law Review*, LXXXII (Feb., 1934), 315.

24. Justice Sutherland's italics. "There is no reason to doubt," writes Mr. Prosser, "that this provision was inserted in the Constitution for the purpose of preventing precisely the type of legislation which was contemplated in Minnesota in 1933." "The Minnesota Mortgage Moratorium," p. 357.

25. The statute was passed on April 18, 1933. As applied to the present case, it extended the period of redemption absolutely from May 2 to May 18, 1933.

26. Benjamin F. Wright has commented that "it seems quite clear that the historical argument of the minority is not and cannot fully be answered, save by reference to principles not discussed in the BRONSON case and those following it." *The Contract Clause of the Constitution*, p. 111.

27. *Chastleton Corp.* v. *Sinclair*, 264 U.S. 543, 547–548.

28. "The contract clause, which has now been reduced to mean little more than due process, presents no substantial obstacle to the power of the state to make reasonable provision for the general welfare." *Columbia Law Review*, XXXIV (June, 1934), 1134.

29. *Harvard Law Review*, XLVII (Feb., 1934), 668.

30. Corwin, "Moratorium over Minnesota," p. 315.

31. *New Republic* (January 24, 1934), p. 307. See also *Columbia Law Review*, XXXIV (Feb., 1934), 1134, and Wright, *The Contract Clause of the Constitution*, p. 111.

32. 292 U.S. 426 (1934).

33. 295 U.S. 56.

34. 300 U.S. 124 (1937).

35. 306 U.S. 539 (1939).

36. See *Louisville Joint Stock Land Bank* v. *Radford*, 295 U.S. 555 (1935).

15. THE FEDERAL SYSTEM: TAX IMMUNITY OF GOVERNMENTAL INSTRUMENTALITIES

1. 4 Wheat. 316 (1819).

2. 11 Wall. 113.

3. Concurring opinion in *Graves* v. *New York ex rel. O'Keefe*, 306 U.S. 466, 491 (1939).

4. *Ibid.*, p. 489.

5. Dissenting opinion in *Panhandle Oil Co.* v. *Mississippi*, 277 U.S. 218, 223 (1928).

6. *Metcalf and Eddy* v. *Mitchell*, 269 U.S. 524 (1926). See, in connection with Stone's contribution to the revision of this doctrine the discussion by Konefsky, *Chief Justice Stone and the Supreme Court*, pp. 10–47.

7. 281 U.S. 313 (1930).

8. 282 U.S. 216 (1931).

9. 286 U.S. 132 (1932).

10. 288 U.S. 325 (1933).

11. *Helvering* v. *Mountain Producers Corp.*, 303 U.S. 376 (1938).

12. *Gillespie* v. *Oklahoma*, 257 U.S. 501 (1922) and *Burnet* v. *Coronada Oil & Gas Co.*, 285 U.S. 393 (1932). Justices Butler and McReynolds, dissenting, did not believe that "the urgency of governmental demand for money" justified overturning precedents nor "so sweeping a change of construction of the Constitution."

13. 302 U.S. 134 (1937).

14. 277 U.S. 218 (1928).

15. Justices McReynolds, Sutherland and Butler joined in this dissent.

16. 293 U.S. 214 (1934).

17. 299 U.S. 401 (1937).

18. 300 U.S. 352 (1937).

19. Justices Stone and Cardozo concurred in the result on technical grounds without expressing an opinion "as to the need for revision of the doctrine of implied immunities declared in earlier decisions." Justices Roberts and Brandeis dissented for the reason that salaries received "by those rendering to a municipality services of the same kind as are rendered to private employers" should not be exempt from federal taxation.

20. 304 U.S. 405 (1938).

21. Mr. Justice Black concurred in a separate opinion but finding it difficult to reconcile the result with the principle announced in *Collector* v. *Day* and later decisions applying that principle urged repudiation especially in the light of the grant of power to Congress, under the Sixteenth Amendment, to levy a tax on incomes "from whatever source derived."

Justice Butler dissented with the concurrence of Justice McReynolds urging that "the salaries paid by the Port Authority to its officers and employees are not distinguishable from salaries paid by States to their officers and employees." In the light of a century of precedents, he said, these salaries should be held exempt from federal taxation.

22. 306 U.S. 466 (1939).

23. *Metcalf and Eddy* v. *Mitchell.*

24. At pp. 491–492.

16. SOME IMPORTANT FEDERAL LEGISLATION

1. 295 U.S. 555 (1935).

2. Wright, *The Contract Clause of the Constitution*, p. 116.

3. Franklin D. Roosevelt, *The Public Papers and Addresses of Franklin D. Roosevelt* (New York: Random House, 1938), IV, 10.

4. 297 U.S. 1 (1936).

5. See Jackson, *The Struggle for Judicial Supremacy*, pp. 166–169.

6. 298 U.S. 513.

7. The author is principally indebted for the factual background to Jackson, *The Struggle for Judicial Supremacy*, pp. 96–100.

8. Franklin D. Roosevelt, "The Fight Goes On," *Collier's* (Sept. 13, 1941), p. 46.

9. 294 U.S. 240.

10. 294 U.S. 317.

11. 294 U.S. 330.

12. Eight Justices of the Court agreed in this conclusion.

13. See Alfred H. Kelly & Winfred A. Harbison, *The American Constitution: Its Origins and Development* (New York: W. W. Norton & Company, 1948), p. 732.

14. 297 U.S. 288 (1936).

15. Jackson, *The Struggle for Judicial Supremacy*, p. 144.

16. Justice McReynolds concurred in the view that a justiciable issue was presented by the plaintiffs and that position thus commanded the support of a narrow majority of the Court.

17. In effect, by calling for a more extended inquiry, Justice McReynolds consented, at least, to the limited inquiry.

18. Justices Brandeis, Stone, Roberts and Cardozo indicated their agreement with the conclusion reached by the Chief Justice on the constitutional question.

19. Jackson, *The Struggle for Judicial Supremacy*, p. 146.

17. THE DELEGATION OF LEGISLATIVE POWER

1. Aristotle, *Politics* (London: George Bell & Sons, 1898), pp. 155–156.

2. John Locke, *Of Civil Government* (New York: E. P. Dutton & Co., Inc., 1924), pp. 189, 190–191. Locke believed, however, that in emergencies, the executive might be justified in the public interest in acting according to discretion "without the prescription of law and sometimes against it." At p. 199.

3. Baron de Montesquieu, *The Spirit of Laws* (New York: The Colonial Press, 1900), I, 151–152.

4. The separation of powers doctrine received its most rigid interpretation in the writings of Blackstone, J. L. DeLolme and David Hume and was adopted in the first Massachusetts Constitution of 1780 in completely unqualified form in the very language of John Adams.

5. *The Writings of Thomas Jefferson* (Washington: The Thomas Jefferson Memorial Association, 1903), II, 163.

6. The limitation is not made applicable by the federal Constitution to the states. Accordingly, subject to the provisions of their own constitutions, and in extreme cases, to due process, states are free to unite governmental powers as they desire.

7. *The Federalist*, No. XLVII (New York: G. P. Putnam's Sons, 1888), pp. 301–302.

8. *The Federalist*, No. LI, pp. 322–327.

9. J. Allen Smith, *Spirit of American Government* (New York: The Macmillan Company, 1907), p. 129.

10. Herman Finer, *The Theory and Practice of Modern Government* (New York: Dial Press, Inc., 1934), pp. 84–85.

11. Landis, *The Administrative Process*, p. 1.

12. "Separation of Powers," *Encyclopedia of Social Science*, XIII, 664.

13. O. Douglas Weeks, "Legislative Power versus Delegated Legislative Power," *Georgetown Law Journal*, XXV (Jan., 1937), 314.

14. Landis, *The Administrative Process*, p. 2.

15. 287 U.S. 12.

16. 293 U.S. 389 (1935).

17. That the ground upon which the decision was based, the non-delegability of legislative power, came as surprise to the Administration is evidenced by the fact that the Government's brief of 227 pages plus 200 pages of appendix devoted only thirteen pages to that question. Jackson, *The Struggle for Judicial Supremacy*, p. 92.

18. 295 U.S. 495 (1935).

19. The declarations of Title 1 are described in the PANAMA REFINING Co. case.

20. Justice Stone joined in this opinion.

21. The interstate commerce phase of the case is discussed in the next chapter.

22. 298 U.S. 238 (1936).

23. The other grounds are dealt with in the next chapter.

24. E. E. Schattschneider, *Politics, Pressures and the Tariff* (New York: Prentice-Hall, Inc., 1935), p. 9.

25. J. D. McGowen, "An Economic Interpretation of the Doctrine of Delegation of Governmental Powers," *Tulane Law Review*, XII (Feb., 1938), 179.

26. 306 U.S. 1 (1939).

27. Quoted by Walter Gellhorn, *Administrative Law* (Chicago: The Foundation Press, Inc., 1st ed., 1940), p. 278.

28. *Old Dearborn Distributing Co.* v. *Seagram-Distillers Corp.*, 299 U.S. 183 (1936).

18. THE CONTROL OF COMMERCE

1. An earlier discussion of the development of this power appears in chapter 5.

2. 281 U.S. 548 (1930).

3. These cases were discussed in chapter 3.

4. 289 U.S. 266.

5. 295 U.S. 330 (1935).

6. *Second Employers Liability Cases*, 233 U.S. 1, 47 (1912).

7. The other two cases were *Adair* v. *United States*, 208 U.S. 161 (1908) and *Employers' Liability Cases*, 207 U.S. 463 (1908).

8. Thomas Reed Powell, "Commerce, Pensions and Codes," *Harvard Law Review*, XLIX (November, 1935), 12.

9. See chapter 17.

10. For a statement of these policies, see the Panama Refining Co. case discussed in Chapter 17.

11. Edward S. Corwin, "The Schechter Case—Landmark or What?" *New York University Law Quarterly Review*, XIII (January, 1936), 151, 155.

12. Thomas R. Powell, "Commerce, Pensions and Codes," II, *Harvard Law Review*, XLIX (November, 1935), 215.

13. *DiSanto* v. *Pennsylvania*, 273 U.S. 34, 44 (1927). Thomas R. Powell voiced similar criticism of the use of the terms "direct" and "indirect" in commerce cases. He wrote, "One objection to them is that they speak with the tongue of physics rather than with the tongue of economics. They point to a process more mechanical than any that can

give wise results in the world of human affairs. They tend to make the judicial enterprise look easier and simpler than it really is. The poles they point to are not so fixed that from them we may locate the equator. Some distinction may be fundamental, but no particular phrasing can demand acceptance as exclusive legal tender." "Commerce, Pensions, and Codes," p. 208.

14. Edward S. Corwin, *The Commerce Power versus States Rights* (Princeton: Princeton University Press, 1936), p. 205.

15. Thomas R. Powell, in a well-reasoned statement, maintains that Hughes' argument amounts to this, that "if Congress could regulate the costs of the Schechters it could regulate the costs of any and all enterprise and that such a wide power would mean a centralized system not provided for by the Constitution. So it seems that the Chief Justice is saying that Congress may not regulate all the processes of production and distribution that enter into cost, and that he is saying no more." "Commerce, Pensions, and Codes," p. 224.

16. *Ibid.*, p. 225.

17. Justice Stone joined in this opinion.

18. 301 U.S. 1, 40–41 (1937).

19. Jackson, *The Struggle for Judicial Supremacy*, pp. 154–155. An excellent factual summary of the background of the legislation is found in pp. 153–158.

20. *Appalachian Coals, Inc.* v. *United States*, 288 U.S. 344, 372.

21. This phase of the decision has been discussed in chapter 17.

22. In a separate opinion joined in by Justices Brandeis and Stone, Justice Cardozo agreed with the Chief Justice that the price-fixing provisions were valid and separable from the labor provisions. He maintained, however, that the suits were premature in so far as they sought a judicial declaration on the regulations with respect to labor. It will be time enough, he reasoned, to consider them "when there is a threat or even the possibility of imminent enforcement." Since a decree was sought to restrain the enforcement of the statute in "all or any" of its provisions, if some parts are valid and separable, he said, the injunction could not issue.

19. THE COURT UNDER ATTACK

1. The Beards wrote that "the Court had never succeeded in paralyzing a statute of major interest to any great political party without encountering a powerful recoil." Charles A. Beard and Mary R. Beard, *America in Midpassage* (New York: The Macmillan Co., 1939), p. 348.

2. Roosevelt, "The Fight Goes On," *Collier's* (Sept. 20, 1941), p. 17.

3. *Ibid.* (Sept. 13, 1941), p. 48.

4. Most of these decisions have been discussed elsewhere in this volume and will therefore be alluded to only briefly at this point.

5. *Panama Refining Co.* v. *Ryan.*

6. *Norman* v. *Baltimore & Ohio R.R.*

7. *Perry* v. *United States.*

8. *Railroad Retirement Board* v. *Alton R.R.*

9. *Louisville Joint Stock Bank* v. *Radford.*

10. *Humphrey's Executor* v. *United States,* 295 U.S. 602 (1935).

11. 272 U.S. 52 (1926).

12. *Schechter Poultry Corp.* v. *United States.*

13. *United States* v. *Butler,* 297 U.S. 1.

14. *Ashwander* v. *Tennessee Valley Authority.*

15. *Jones* v. *Securities and Exchange Commission.*

16. Roosevelt, *The Public Papers and Addresses of Franklin D. Roosevelt,* IV, 11.

17. *Carter* v. *Carter Coal Co.*

18. *Morehead* v. *New York ex rel. Tipaldo.*

19. The only important decision the president neglected to include among the cases he cited was *Ashton* v. *Cameron County District,* in which Justice McReynolds spoke for a majority of five members in invalidating the Municipal Bankruptcy Act of 1934.

20. In the public gold clause case he sustained the Administration on technical rather than substantive grounds.

21. The whole story of the formulation and struggle for the adoption of the reorganization plan is told in racy, largely undocumented but substantially accurate fashion by Joseph Alsop and Turner Catledge, *The 168 Days* (New York: Doubleday, Doran & Co., Inc., 1938).

22. Roosevelt, "The Fight Goes On," *Collier's* (Sept. 20, 1941), p. 16.

23. Robert E. Sherwood, *Roosevelt and Hopkins* (New York: Harper & Bros., 1948), p. 89.

24. Many who favored reorganization of the Supreme Court deplored the deviousness involved. Senator Norris, for example, who supported the plan made no secret of his dislike of its indirection. And Justice Brandeis was alienated by a charge which seemed to base the President's case on the inefficiency and infirmity of the Court rather than its judicial record. Jackson, *The Struggle for Judicial Supremacy,* pp. 189–190. Franklin D. Roosevelt later said, "I made one major mistake when I first presented the plan. I did not place enough emphasis upon the real mischief—the kind of decisions which, as a studied and continued policy,

had been coming down from the Supreme Court. I soon corrected that mistake—in the speeches which I later made about the plan." Roosevelt, "The Fight Goes On," *Collier's* (Sept. 20, 1941), p. 37.

25. The division in the nation and the course of developments are ably and fairly presented in Charles A. and Mary R. Beard, *America in Midpassage*, pp. 348–362.

26. New York *Times*, March 23, 1937.

27. In 1927 Mr. Hughes in one of his lectures on the Supreme Court had said, "Everyone who has worked in a group knows the necessity of limiting size to obtain efficiency. And this is peculiarly true of a judicial body. It is too much to say that the Supreme Court could not do its work if two more members were added, but I think that the consensus of competent opinion is that it is now large enough." Hughes, *The Supreme Court*, p. 238.

28. The *New Republic* editorially commented that the Chief Justice had invoked "the taboo of constitutionality on such a procedure without any case before him, at the request of an opponent of the administration, to be used as an argument in a political controversy." "The Chief Justice's Letter" (April 7, 1937), p. 254.

29. *West Coast Hotel Co.* v. *Parrish.*

30. *Virginia Railway Co.* v. *System Federation No. 40*, 300 U.S. 515 (1937).

31. *Wright* v. *Vinton Branch of the Mountain Trust Bank of Roanoke*, 300 U.S. 440 (1937).

32. *National Labor Relations Board* v. *Jones and Laughlin Steel Corp.*, 301 U.S. 1 (1937).

33. *National Labor Relations Board* v. *Fruehauf Trailer Co.*, 301 U.S. 49 (1937).

34. *National Labor Relations Board* v. *Freedman–Harry Marks Clothing Co.*, 301 U.S. 58 (1937). These cases are discussed in the next chapter.

35. *Steward Machine Co.* v. *Davis*, 301 U.S. 548 (1937) and *Helvering* v. *Davis*, 301 U.S. 619 (1937).

36. *Carmichael* v. *Southern Coal and Coke Co.*, 301 U.S. 495 (1937). The Chief Justice voted for constitutionality in each of the above cases.

37. In the opinion of Franklin D. Roosevelt, "It would be a little naive to refuse to recognize some connection between these decisions and the Supreme Court fight." Roosevelt, "The Fight Goes On," *Collier's* (Sept. 20, 1941), p. 38.

38. Jackson, *The Struggle for Judicial Supremacy*, pp. 192–193.

39. Adverse report of the Committee on the Judiciary on a Bill to

Reorganize the Judicial Branch of the Government, Senate Report No. 711, 75th Cong., 1st sess.

40. Jackson, *The Struggle for Judicial Supremacy*, p. 196.

20. THE END OF AN ERA: REEXAMINATION AND RETREAT

1. See *United States* v. *Curtiss-Wright Export Corp.*, 299 U.S. 304 (1936).

2. 299 U.S. 334 (1937).

3. 247 U.S. 251 (1918).

4. "The opinion," writes Dean Ribble, "is thus a logical antecedent of the decision sustaining the Fair Labor Standards Act, *United States* v. *Darby*, 312 U.S. 100 (1941), and is inconsistent with *Hammer* v. *Dagenhart* notwithstanding the Chief Justice's careful and typical effort to distinguish that case." F. D. G. Ribble, "The Constitutional Doctrines of Chief Justice Hughes," *Columbia Law Review*, XLI (Nov., 1941), 1202.

5. 312 U.S. 100.

6. See chapter 18.

7. 301 U.S. 1.

8. The four conservatives dissented.

9. The ADAIR and COPPAGE cases are discussed in chapter 3.

10. One distinction, it might be argued, was that in the earlier cases criminal penalties were fixed by the statutes while in the JONES & LAUGHLIN case punishment followed from a violation of the court order. But such a distinction was not suggested by the Court and has never been considered fundamental. *California Law Review*, XXV (May, 1937), 605. In any event, whatever tenuous basis existed for any distinction was specifically repudiated in *Phelps Dodge Corp.* v. *National Labor Relations Board*, 313 U.S. 177 (1941).

11. *National Labor Relations Board* v. *Fruehauf*, 301 U.S. 49 (1937).

12. *National Labor Relations Board* v. *Freedman–Harry Marks Clothing Company, Inc.*, 301 U.S. 58 (1937).

13. *Cornell Law Quarterly*, XXII (June, 1937), 569. See also the explanation for the alleged shift suggested by Professor Wright that "Chief Justice Hughes was evidently more concerned with the pending threat to the Court's independence than he was with the dissenters' lament for the end of state rights." *The Growth of American Constitutional Law*, p. 205.

14. Edward S. Corwin, *Court over Constitution* (Princeton: Princeton University Press, 1938), p. 124.

15. 303 U.S. 453.

16. In dissent, Justice Butler with the concurrence of Justice Mc-Reynolds argued that both the JONES & LAUGHLIN and this decision were in clear conflict with the CARTER case, and added, "At least until this Court definitely overrules that decision, it should be followed."

17. 305 U.S. 197 (1938).

18. Justices McReynolds and Butler dissented on the ground that the decision was inconsistent with the limits set on the interstate commerce power in the SCHECHTER and CARTER cases.

19. 313 U.S. 177 (1941).

20. Corwin, *The Commerce Power versus States Rights,* pp. 193-194.

21. 301 U.S. 548 (1937).

22. 301 U.S. 619 (1937).

23. *Ashton* v. *Cameron County District.*

24. 304 U.S. 27 (1938).

25. See chapter 16.

26. 306 U.S. 118 (1939).

27. Justice McReynolds joined in a strong dissent by Justice Butler. As Robert Jackson put it the "utilities had then lost their last stand. The practical upshot of the case was that the private utility interests sold many existing facilities and retired from Tennessee Valley territory." *The Struggle for Judicial Supremacy,* p. 260.

28. 303 U.S. 419 (1938).

29. Justice McReynolds dissented without opinion. After Chief Justice Hughes retired from the bench, the Court upheld several substantive provisions of the Act, including the so-called death sentence. See *North American Co.* v. *Securities & Exchange Commission,* 327 U.S. 686 (1946), and *American Power and Light Co.* v. *Securities & Exchange Commission,* 329 U.S. 90 (1946).

30. 306 U.S. 1 (1939).

31. Justices McReynolds and Butler dissented without opinion.

32. 307 U.S. 38 (1939).

33. *United States* v. *Lowden,* 308 U.S. 225 (1939).

34. 310 U.S. 381 (1940).

35. 312 U.S. 126.

36. Wright, *The Growth of American Constitutional Law,* pp. 207, 180.

37. Kelly and Harbison, *The American Constitution,* p. 789.

21. AN EVALUATION

1. New York *Times,* June 4, 1941.
2. New York *Herald Tribune,* June 4, 1941.

3. *Nation* (June 14, 1941), p. 685.

4. *New Republic* (June 9, 1941), p. 776.

5. New York *Times*, August 29, 1948.

6. Harlan F. Stone, "The Chief Justice," *American Bar Association Journal*, XXVII (July, 1941), 407.

7. *Ibid.*

8. "Procedural due process is not gone. Its importance may even be on the increase, particularly in the field where the courts are reviewing the actions of administrative officers and commissions." Wright, *The Growth of American Constitutional Law*, p. 240.

9. See, in the latter connection, his decision in *Beidler* v. *South Carolina*, 282 U.S. 1 (1930), and his dissenting opinions in *Graves* v. *Elliott*, 307 U.S. 383 (1939) and *McGoldrick* v. *Berwind-White Coal Mining Co.*, 309 U.S. 33 (1940). Commenting upon the record of Chief Justice Hughes on the occasion of his retirement, then Attorney General Robert Jackson said, "Apart from the field of taxation . . . the Chief Justice has gone very far in sustaining state regulatory statutes." "The Judicial Career of Chief Justice Hughes," *American Bar Association Journal*, XXVII (July, 1941), 410.

10. Hughes, *Supreme Court*, p. 37. It is interesting that the principal illustrations he cited in support of this distinction were the decisions of the Court invalidating the anti-child-labor laws passed by Congress under its interstate commerce and taxing powers. These laws, he said, had been struck down because of lack of power rather than disapproval of policy. *Ibid.*, pp. 38–39. Yet, oddly enough, this was accomplished when a distinction was created which the Court itself subsequently characterized as "novel when made and unsupported by any provision of the Constitution." *United States* v. *Darby*, 312 U.S. 100 (1941).

11. See, for example, Justice Stone, in *United States* v. *Butler*, 297 U.S. 1, 67 (1936).

12. Felix Frankfurter, "The Supreme Court," Parliamentary Affairs, III (Winter, 1949), 68, 69.

13. Oliver Wendell Holmes, Jr., *The Common Law* (Boston: Little, Brown and Company, 1938), pp. 35–36. Later he wrote: "I think that the judges have failed adequately to recognize their duty of weighing considerations of social advantage. The duty is *inevitable*, and the result of the often proclaimed judicial aversion to deal with such considerations is simply to leave the very ground and foundation of judgments inarticulate and often unconscious." "The Path of Law," *Harvard Law Review*, X (Mar., 1897), 467.

14. Cardozo, *The Nature of the Judicial Process*, p. 89.

15. Hughes, *Supreme Court*, p. 38.

16. *Ibid.*

17. *Mercoid Corp.* v. *Mid-Continent Inv. Co.*, 320 U.S. 661 (1944).

18. *West Virginia Board of Education* v. *Barnette*, 319 U.S. 624 (1943).

19. *Korematsu* v. *United States*, 323 U.S. 214 (1944).

20. *Magnolia Petroleum Co.* v. *Hunt*, 320 U.S. 430 (1943).

21. *United States* v. *Congress of Industrial Organizations*, 335 U.S. 106 (1948).

22. *Standard Oil Co.* v. *United States*, 337 U.S. 293 (1949).

23. *Smith* v. *Allwright*, 321 U.S. 649 (1944).

24. *United States* v. *Rabinowitz*, 339 U.S. 56 (1950).

25. The case for judicial review over state legislation rests in part upon a different foundation than that in regard to acts of Congress and will be dealt with separately.

26. Cardozo, *The Nature of the Judicial Process*, pp. 88, 92–93.

27. Hughes, *Supreme Court*, pp. 241–242. Quoted with permission of the publisher, Columbia University Press. "Our system," wrote Mr. Justice Frankfurter, "is built on the faith that men set apart for this special function, freed from the deflections of worldly ambition, will be able to take a view of longer range than the period of responsibility entrusted to Congress and Legislatures." *West Virginia Board of Education* v. *Barnette*, 319 U.S. 624, 665 (1943).

28. Edwin N. Garlan, *Legal Realism and Justice* (New York: Columbia University Press, 1941), p. 126.

29. If, on the other hand, it is suggested that these concepts mean no more than what "some other man of normal intellect and conscience might reasonably look upon as right," in the phrase of Justice Cardozo, then the Court should have had little occasion to exercise its power to invalidate legislation unless we assume that legislators frequently demonstrate a lack of normal intellect and conscience.

30. Cohen, *Law and the Social Order*, p. 149. As early as 1875 before the philosophy of *laissez-faire* had thoroughly impregnated the Court, Justice Miller found it necessary to say: "It is vain to contend with judges who have been at the bar the advocates for forty years of railroad companies, and all the forms of associated capital, when they are called upon to decide cases where such interests are in contest. All their training, all their feelings are from the start in favor of those who need no such influence." Charles Fairman, *Mr. Justice Miller and the Supreme Court* (Cambridge: Harvard University Press, 1939), p. 374.

31. Jackson, *The Struggle for Judicial Supremacy*, pp. 313, 315.

32. *Ibid.*, p. 187. The exceptions, which came about as a result of the election of Franklin D. Roosevelt to four terms as president and thereafter of Harry Truman, would appear to be the "New Deal" and possibly "Fair Deal" Courts.

33. For an excellent discussion along these lines, see Henry Steele Commager, *Majority Rule and Minority Rights* (New York: Oxford University Press, 1943).

34. Attack upon the duality of our system may come from two sources, the national government and the states. Only judicial review as a defense against national attack upon our federal system is dealt with at this point.

35. Hughes, *Supreme Court*, pp. 95–96. Quoted with permission of the publisher, Columbia University Press.

36. Joseph C. O'Mahoney, "The Preservation of Economic Freedom," 77th Cong., 1st Sess., Document No. 39.

37. Harold J. Laski, "The Obsolescence of Federalism," *New Republic* (May 3, 1939), pp. 367–369.

38. Again discussion of this argument is limited to its applicability to actions of the federal government.

39. Hughes, *The Supreme Court*, p. 96.

40. For an excellent presentation of these essential views, see Frankfurter, J., dissenting, in *West Virginia State Board of Education* v. *Barnette*, 319 U.S. 624 (1943).

41. See for example the decision of the Court in *United States* v. *Congress of Industrial Organizations*, 335 U.S. 106 (1948).

42. Wright, *The Growth of American Constitutional Law*, p. 254. See also Henry W. Edgerton, "The Incidence of Judicial Control over Congress," *Cornell Law Quarterly*, XXII (Apr., 1937), 299.

43. Experience shows that there is no practical way of differentiating the two types of cases so that judicial review may be maintained in "economic" cases and denied in the other. Commager, *Majority Rule and Minority Rights*, pp. 68–70.

44. Jackson, *The Struggle for Judicial Supremacy*, p. 321. In this connection it must be realized that mass unemployment was dissolved only by war and its aftermath and there is every indication that some of the fundamental problems of our economy remain unsolved.

45. Oliver Wendell Holmes, *Collected Legal Papers* (New York: Harcourt, Brace & Co., 1921), p. 296.

46. *Ibid.*, pp. 295–296.

47. *Ibid.*, p. 296.

TABLE OF CASES

Adair v. United States, 27, 29, 228, 260, 268, 320

Adams Express Co. v. New York, 52-53

Adkins v. Children's Hospital, 126, 127, 128, 129, 130, 252

American Federation of Labor v. Swing, 157

American Power and Light Co. v. Securities & Exchange Commission, 325

Appalachian Coals, Inc. v. United States, 265, 321

Ashton v. Cameron County District, 200, 322, 325

Ashwander v. Tennessee Valley Authority, 205-210, 270, 322

Bailey v. Alabama, 18-22

Baltimore & Ohio R.R. v. Interstate Commerce Commission, 48-49

Bank of Minden v. Clement, 315

Barnitz v. Beverly, 315

Barron v. Baltimore, 310

Beidler v. South Carolina, 326

Blaisdell case, see Home Building & Loan Association v. Blaisdell

Block v. Hirsh, 315

Bradley v. Lightcap, 315

Brass v. Stoeser, 309

Bronson v. Kinzie, 170, 171, 176, 181, 315, 316

Brown v. Maryland, 52

Brown v. Mississippi, 97

Brush v. Commissioner, 192, 194

Budd v. New York, 309

Burnet v. Coronada Oil & Gas Co., 317

Cantwell v. Connecticut, 154

Cardillo v. Liberty Mutual Insurance Co., 307

Carlson v. California, 156

Carmichael v. Southern Coal and Coke Co., 323

Carter v. Carter Coal Co., 223, 225, 241-244, 252, 257, 262, 264, 265, 266, 272, 273, 322, 325

Charles River Bridge v. Warren Bridge, 37-38

Chastleton Corp. v. Sinclair, 316

Chicago, B.&Q.R.R. v. McGuire, 24-25

City of Sault Ste. Marie v. International Transit Co., 53

Civil Rights Cases, 162

Collector v. Day, 186, 193, 194

Consolidated Edison v. National Labor Relations Board, 267-268

Cooley v. Board of Wardens, 52

Coppage v. Kansas, 27-29, 228, 260, 268

Cox v. New Hampshire, 155

Crowell v. Benson, 99-103, 104, 106

Currin v. Wallace, 225, 272, 273-274

Dartmouth College v. Woodward, 37

Davidson v. New Orleans, 309

De Jonge v. Oregon, 150-151

Del Vecchio v. Bowers, 307

DiSanto v. Pennsylvania, 320

Donham v. West-Nelson Mfg. Co., 310

Edgar A. Levy Leasing Co. v. Siegel, 315

Edwards v. Kearzey, 171

Electric Bond & Share Co. v. Securities & Exchange Commission, 271-272

Employers' Liability Cases, 320

Erie R.R. v. Tompkins, 310

Federal Radio Commission v. Nelson Bros., 228-229

Fletcher v. Peck, 37, 308

Fox Film Corp. v. Doyal, 189

Frank v. Mangum, 97, 303

Frohwerk v. United States, 310

German Alliance Insurance Co. v. Kansas, 309

Gibbons v. Ogden, 46-47, 51-52, 53, 227

Gillespie v. Oklahoma, 317

Girouard v. United States, 311

Gitlow v. New York, 138, 139

Grand Trunk Western R.R. v. South Bend, 38-39, 40

Graves v. Elliott, 326

Graves v. New York ex rel. O'Keefe, 195, 317

Grosjean v. American Press Co., 312

Grovey v. Townsend, 314

Guinn v. United States, 161

Gunn v. Barry, 315

Hague v. Committee for Industrial Organization, 156

Hammer v. Dagenhart, 256-257, 258, 266, 324

Helvering v. Davis, 323

Helvering v. Gerhardt, 192, 195

Helvering v. Mountain Producers Corp., 317

Helvering v. Powers, 191

Henderson v. United States, 314

Herndon v. Lowry, 152-153

Holden v. Hardy, 29

Home Building & Loan Association v. Blaisdell, 125, 168, 171-181, 182, 183, 184, 198, 235

Honeyman v. Jacobs, 184

Houston, E. and W. Texas R.R. v. United States, *see Shreveport Case*

Howard v. Bugbee, 315

Humphrey's Executor v. United States, 322

Hurtado v. California, 306-307

Indian Territory Illuminating Oil Co. v. Board of Equalization, 189

James v. Dravo Contracting Co., 189-190

Jones v. Securities & Exchange Commission, 103-104, 322

Jones & Laughlin case, *see* National Labor Relations Board v. Jones & Laughlin Steel Corp.

Kentucky Whip & Collar Co. v. Illinois Central R.R., 255-257

Korematsu v. United States, 327

Lane v. Wilson, 161

Lauf v. Shinner & Co., 156

Leisy v. Hardin, 52

Lessee of Gantly v. Ewing, 315

L'Hote v. Crowell, 307

Lochner v. New York, 29-30

Louisville & Nashville R.R. v. Garrett, 42

Louisville Joint Stock Land Bank v. Radford, 198, 258, 316, 322

Lovell v. Griffin, 153-154

McCabe v. Atchison, T.&S.F.R.R., 33, 165

McCracken v. Hayward, 171

McCulloch v. Maryland, 185, 193, 194, 295

McGoldrick v. Berwind-White Coal Mining Co., 326

McLaurin v. Oklahoma State Regents, 314

Magnolia Petroleum Co. v. Hunt, 327

Marbury v. Madison, 299

Marcus Brown Holding Co. v. Feldman, 315

Mercoid Corp. v. Mid-Continent Inv. Co., 327

Metcalf and Eddy v. Mitchell, 190, 317, 318

Milk Wagon Drivers Union v. Meadowmoor Dairies, Inc., 157

Miller v. Wilson, 30

Minersville School District v. Gobitis, 312

Minnesota Rate Cases (Simpson v. Shepard), 55, 58, 59, 60, 61-62, 265, 302; *see also State Rate Cases*

Missouri ex rel. Gaines v. Canada, 163-164, 165

Missouri ex rel. Missouri Insurance Co. v. Gehner, 187

Mitchell v. United States, 164-165, 166

Mooney v. Holohan, 96

Morehead v. People ex rel. Tipaldo, 125, 126-130, 131, 132, 133, 322

Morgan v. United States, first of four companion cases, 109-111; *see also* United States v. Morgan

Morgan v. United States, second of four companion cases, 111-113; *see also* United States v. Morgan

Moyer v. Peabody, 121

Mulford v. Smith, 272

Muller v. Oregon, 30

Munn v. Illinois, 122, 309

Murphy v. Sardell, 310

Myers v. United States, 247

National Labor Relations Board v. Freedman-Harry Marks Clothing Co., 323, 324

National Labor Relations Board v. Fruehauf Trailer Co., 323, 324

National Labor Relations Board v. Jones & Laughlin Steel Corp., 62, 240, 258-266, 267, 268, 323, 324, 325

National Life Insurance Co. v. United States, 187

Near v. Minnesota, 144-150

Nebbia v. New York, 124, 129, 182

New Jersey v. Wilson, 37

New Negro Alliance v. Sanitary Grocery Co., 156

New State Ice Co. v. Liebmann, 123-124, 125

New York Central Securities Corp. v. United States, 214

New York Electric Line Co. v. Empire City Subway System, 39-40

New York ex rel. Rogers v. Graves, 191, 194

Nixon v. Condon, 162

Norman v. Baltimore & Ohio R.R., 201-202, 322

Norris v. Alabama, 160, 161

North American Co. v. Securities & Exchange Commission, 325

Nortz v. United States, 202

O'Gorman & Young v. Hartford Fire Ins. Co., 309

Ohio Valley Water Co. v. Ben Avon Borough, 104, 107

Old Dearborn Distributing Co. v. Seagram-Distillers Corp., 320

Opp Cotton Mills, Inc. v. Administrator of the Wage & Hour Division, 274

Osborn v. Bank of the United States, 297

Owensboro v. Cumberland Telephone and Telegraph Co., 40

Palko v. Connecticut, 307

Panama Refining Co. v. Ryan, 214-219, 220, 222, 224, 319, 320, 322

Panhandle Oil Co. v. Mississippi, 190, 317

Parker v. Motor Boat Sales Co., 307

Patterson v. Alabama, 160-161

Pennsylvania Coal Co. v. Mahon, 300

Perry v. United States, 202-204, 322

Phelps Dodge Corp. v. National Labor Relations Board, 268, 324

Phil., Balt., & Wash. R.R. v. Schubert, 49-50

Plessy v. Ferguson, 162-163, 167

Port Richmond Ferry v. Hudson County, 53-54, 55, 57

Powell v. Alabama, 96, 313

Presser v. Illinois, 151

Price v. Illinois, 26-27

Purity Extract & Tonic Co. v. Lynch, 26, 29

Quaker City Cab Co. v. Pennsylvania, 300

Radford case, see Louisville Joint Stock Land Bank v. Radford

Railroad Commission v. Rowan & Nichols Oil Co., 108

Railroad Retirement Board v. Alton Railroad Co., 229-233, 273, 322

Ribnik v. McBride, 309

Richmond Mortgage and Loan Corp. v. Wachovia Bank and Trust Co., 183-184

Russell v. Sebastian, 40

St. Joseph Stock Yards Co. v. United States, 105-107, 158

Santa Cruz Fruit Packing Company v. National Labor Relations Board, 267

Schechter Poultry Corp. v. United States, 219-223, 224, 233-240, 252, 262, 263, 264, 265, 322, 325

Schenck v. United States, 139

Second Employers' Liability Cases, 49, 320

Selective Draft Law Cases, 304

Senn v. Tile Layers Protective Union, 156

Seven Cases v. United States, 50-51

Shields v. Utah Idaho Central R.R., 307

Shreveport Case (Houston, E. and W. Texas R.R. v. United States) 59-63, 81, 86-87, 262, 263, 265, 305; see also State Rate Cases

Simpson v. Shepard, see Minnesota Rate Cases

Slaughter-House Cases, 138, 309

Smith v. Allwright, 314, 327

South Chicago Coal Dock Co. v. Bassett, 307

Southern Pacific Co. v. Campbell, 41-42

Standard Oil Co. v. United States, 327

State Rate Cases, 49, 55, 61-62; see also Minnesota Rate Cases, Shreveport Case

Sterling v. Constantin, 118-122

Stettler v. O'Hara, 125-126

Steward Machine Co. v. Davis, 269, 300, 323

Stromberg v. California, 139-140

Sturges & Burn Manufacturing Co. v. Beauchamp, 26, 29

Sunshine Anthracite Coal Co. v. Adkins, 273

Sweatt v. Painter, 314

Tennessee Electric Power Co. v. Tennessee Valley Authority, 270-271
Texas & New Orleans R.R. v. Brotherhood of Railway & Steamship Clerks, 227-228, 268
Thomas v. Collins, 311
Thornhill v. Alabama, 156
Toyota v. Hawaii, 32
Truax v. Raich, 33-34
Twining v. New Jersey, 307
Tyson v. Banton, 309

United States v. Bekins, 270
United States v. Butler, 199, 266, 272, 310, 322, 326
United States v. Classic, 162
United States v. Congress of Industrial Organizations, 327, 328
United States v. Curtiss-Wright Export Corp., 324
United States v. Darby, 257-258, 266, 300, 310, 324, 326
United States v. Johnson, 50-51
United States v. Lowden, 325
United States v. Macintosh, 141-144, 311
United States v. Morgan, third of four companion cases, 111-113; see also Morgan v. United States

United States v. Morgan, last of four companion cases, 114-115; see also Morgan v. United States
United States v. Rabinowitz, 327
United States v. Schwimmer, 142, 143, 311

Virginia Railway Co. v. System Federation No. 40, 323
Voehl v. Indemnity Insurance Co., 103

W. B. Worthen Co. v. Kavanaugh, 183
W. B. Worthen Co. v. Thomas, 182
West Coast Hotel Co. v. Parrish, 130-134, 323
West Virginia State Board of Education v. Barnette, 313, 326, 327, 328
Whitney v. California, 308
Willcuts v. Bunn, 188
Williams v. Standard Oil Co., 309
Wilmington Transportation Co. v. California R.R. Commission, 54, 55
Wolff Packing Co. v. Court of Industrial Relations, 309
Wright v. Central of Georgia R.R., 43-45, 300
Wright v. Louisville & Nashville R.R., 43
Wright v. Vinton Branch, 323

INDEX

Adams, John, 319
"Affected with a public interest," 72, 122-125
Agricultural Adjustment Act, 199, 247, 269
Allen, Arthur M., quoted on Justice Hughes' record, 64
Alsop, Joseph, and Turner Catledge, 250, 322
Aristotle, 211, 286
Authority, reconciliation with liberty, 16-18, 137

Bailey, Thomas A., quoted on achievements of Washington Disarmament Conference, 76
Baldwin, Henry, 171
Bankruptcy, power of national government over, 197-198, 199-200, 269-270
Bates, Ernest Sutherland, 67
Bauer, John, 58
Beard, Charles A., 92; and Mary R. Beard, 321, 323
Bituminous Coal Conservation Acts, 223, 240, 241, 248, 264, 273
Black, Hugo L., 156, 283, 284, 306, 317
Blackstone, 319
Blaine, John J., 84-85
Borah, William E., 15, 80-81, 305
Brandeis, Louis B., 34, 91, 101-102, 106, 107, 117, 123, 124, 125-126, 198, 206, 249, 250, 251, 317, 322
Bryan, William Jennings, 14-15
Burton, Harold H., 283, 284
Butler, Pierce, 92, 127-128, 147-148, 161, 187, 194, 249, 250, 306, 311, 317, 325

Cardozo, Benjamin N., 90, 91, 92, 104, 107, 162, 183, 200, 204, 217-219, 222, 224, 240, 249, 269, 282, 285, 306, 317, 321, 327
Cases, see separate TABLE OF CASES
Chafee, Zechariah, Jr., 149-150; quoted on decisions of Court before 1917, 139; calls Lovell v. Griffin a "turning-point in the law," 154; on Stromberg v. California, 311
Civil liberty, see Liberty, civil

Clark, Tom C., 284
Cohen, Morris Raphael, 126; quoted on selection of judges, 288
Commager, Henry Steele, 328
Commerce, control of, see Interstate commerce clause, Intrastate commerce
Contract clause, private contracts, 168-184; Home Building and Loan Ass'n v. Blaisdell, 171-181; public contracts, 36-45
Coolidge, Calvin, 91-92
Copeland, Royal S., 81-82
Corcoran, Thomas J., 249
Corwin, Edward S., 63, 117, 181, 239, 310, 316; quoted on effect of JONES & LAUGHLIN on "dual federalism," 266; quoted on distinction between production and commerce, 268-269
Cummings, Homer S., 249
Cushman, Robert E., 116

Daugherty, Harry M., 81, 85
Day, William R., 28, 40-41
Delegation of legislative power, 224-226; genesis of doctrine, 211-214; cases under, 214-223, 273-275
DeLolme, J. L., 319
Denby, Edwin, 85
Depression, facts and problems posed, 92-93, 171-172, 197, 199, 200-201, 211, 215, 240-241
Dill, Clarence C., 82-83, 85
"Direct" and "indirect" effects doctrines, 54, 57, 188-189, 236-238, 242, 261, 263, 264-265, 267, 320-321
Douglas, William O., 273, 284, 306
Dual federalism, 8-10, 51, 62-63, 65, 236-237, 242, 257, 265-266, 268, 269, 273, 290-291
Due process of law, substantive, 23-31, 35, 116-136, 259, 260; procedural, 95-115, 159-160, 280, 303; see also Hughes, Liberty, civil

Emergency, governmental power in time of, 173-174, 180-181, 234-236, 316
Emergency Banking Act of 1933, 200

"Equal but separate" doctrine, 33, 162-167
Equal Protection of the laws, 31-35, 159, 160, 161-167

Fair Labor Standards Act, 274, 275, 324
Fairman, Charles, 121; quoted on martial law decision, 122
Fall, Albert B., 85, 89
Federal system, see Dual federalism, Governmental instrumentalities, Hughes
Feller, A. H., 315
Finer, Herman, 213
Frankfurter, Felix, 61, 63, 108, 114-115, 154, 157, 186, 195, 268, 282, 283, 284, 297, 306, 327, 328
Frazier-Lemke Act, 198, 247, 252, 258
Friedrich, Carl J., 213-214
Fuller, Melville W., 13

Garlan, Edwin N., quoted on justice as a symbol, 286-287
Gillette, Guy M., 82
Glass, Carter, 81
Glenn, Otis F., 83-84
Gold clause cases, 200-204
Governmental instrumentalities, tax immunity, 185-196

Hamilton, Alexander, 169
Hand, Learned, 282
Harding, Warren G., 74, 75, 92
Harlan, John Marshall, 13
Holmes, Oliver Wendell, 2, 20-22, 28, 43-44, 45, 90, 91, 133, 135-136, 138, 186, 282, 295, 296, 300, 303, 326
Hoover, Herbert, 90, 92, 93, 278
Hopkins, Harry, 249
Hughes, Charles Evans, to 1910: early years, 2-3; lawyer, 3; counsel to Stevens Committee, 3-4; counsel to Armstrong Committee, 4; suggested for mayoralty, 4; candidate for governor, 4-5; his philosophy of government, 5-13; on selection of competent officials, 5; on administrative discretion, 6; on "just" balance of freedom and control, 6-8; on federal system, 8-10; on income tax amendment, 9; on judicial review of administrative action, 10-11; on role of Supreme Court generally, 10-12; nominated as Associate Justice, 12-13; reception of nomination of, 13-15; sources relating to career of, 297

—— Justice, 1910–1916: assumes seat, 18; on "peonage" legislation, 18-22; on social legislation under due process, 24-31; concurs in dissent in *Coppage* v. *Kansas*, 28-29; on equal protection of the laws, 32-34, 35; on "equal but separate" doctrine, 32-33; on contract clause and public contracts, 38-45; on national power under interstate commerce clause, 48-51; on state power over interstate commerce, 53-54; on state and national power over intrastate commerce, 55-63; in MINNESOTA RATE CASES, 56-58; in SHREVEPORT CASE, 59-61; New York State Bar Ass'n address, 62, 64, 65; evaluation of record of, 64-67; on judicial review, 64-65; on federal system, 65; record as "liberal," 67; source reference to table of opinions of, 299; concurs in dissent in *Frank* v. *Mangum*, 303
—— Private Citizen and Public Servant, 1916–1930: on stability of judicial decisions, 29; nominated for presidency, 68-69; candidacy, 69-71; returns to law practice, 71; on constitutionality of conscription, 71-72; on expulsion of Socialist assemblymen, 72-74; on abuse of war powers, 74; named Secretary of State, 74; on League of Nations and World Court, 74-75; relations with South America, 75; on Soviet Russia, 75; at Washington Disarmament Conference, 75-76; estimate of record of as Secretary of State, 76; opposes enabling Congress to reenact invalidated law, 76-77; resigns as Secretary of State, 77; "leader" of American bar, 77; nominated as Chief Justice of the United States, 78; debate over nomination, 78-90; Westminster Hall address on dangers of uncontrolled administrative authority, 98; on meaning of due process, 116-117; on judicial review, 137, 281, 282-283, 286, 290, 292; on federal system, 290; lectures on Supreme Court, 305; on size of Supreme Court, 323; on child labor cases, 326
—— Chief Justice, 1930–1941: 155, 156, 161-162, 199, 269, 270, 306; assumes seat, 91; setting, 91-94; presides over divided court, 91-92, 93; opportunity for leadership, 93-94; number of opinions of, 94; on procedural due process, 96-

115; on due process in administrative proceedings, 97-115; Federal Bar Ass'n address, 98, 102; American Law Institute address, 113; on due process affecting economic interests, 116, 118-136; on martial law, 118-122; balance of power position of, 124, 249, 253; on minimum wages for women, 128-129, 130-133; on symbolic expression, 139-141; on conscientious objectors, 142-144; on freedom of the press, 144-147; on Communist activities, 150-152; on freedom of religion, 153-154, 155; civil liberties contribution of evaluated, 157-158; in Scottsboro cases, 160-161; on equality for Negroes, 163-165; on "equal but separate" doctrine, 163-164; in BLAISDELL case, 171-181; in other private contract cases, 182-184; in tax immunity cases, 186-194; in municipal bankruptcy cases, 200, 269; in gold clause cases, 201-204; in T.V.A. case, 205-210; on delegation of legislative power, 214-217, 219-222, 223, 274; on national power under interstate commerce clause, 227-229, 230-232, 234-240, 241, 242-244, 256-258, 259-269, 271-272, 273; decisions of his Court attacked by President, 246-248; his position in such cases, 248, 249; could retire, 250; position on Court reorganization plan, 250-252; on federal "police power," 256-258; letter of resignation, 276; evaluation of his record, 276-281; dies, 277-278; quoted on "men holding strong convictions," 283; source reference to table of opinions of, 306
Hume, David, 319

Interstate commerce clause, genesis of doctrine, 46-47; national power under, 48-51, 227-245, 255-269, 271-273; state power under, 51-54
Intrastate commerce, state and national power over, 55-63

Jackson, Robert H., 104, 113, 125, 158, 206, 209, 240-241, 253, 283, 294, 325, 326; quoted on rationalization of duty of court, and on effect of alternation of national moods, 288
Jefferson, Thomas, 212
Johnson, Hiram, 71
Judicial review in cases of constitution-

ality, nature and significance of, 1-2, 16-17, 30-31, 34-35, 45, 63, 96, 102-103, 107, 115, 126, 131, 135-136, 149, 157, 181, 182, 195-196, 204-205, 210, 275, 281-295; Hughes on, 10-12, 64-65, 66-67, 281, 282-283, 286, 290, 292; intention of Framers, 299

Kelly, Alfred H., and Winfred A. Harbison, quoted on decline in importance of Supreme Court, 275

LaFollette, Robert M., 85-86
Lamar, Joseph R., 39
Landis, James M., 213
Laski, Harold J., 291
Liberty, reconciliation with authority, 16-18, 137; civil, 137-158, 291-294; see also Hughes
Locke, John, 117, 211, 319
Lodge, Henry Cabot, 13
Long, Huey, 121
Lurton, Horace H., 40

McGowen, J. D., 224-225
McKellar, Kenneth D., 87-88
McLean, John, 315
McReynolds, James C., 92, 161, 163-164, 194, 200, 204, 207, 208, 209, 249, 250, 261-262, 306, 311, 317, 318, 325
Madison, James, 169, 212
Marshall, George C., 278
Marshall, John, 2, 37, 46-47, 48, 51-52, 94, 185-186, 280, 295, 297
Martial law, 118-122
Miller, Samuel Freeman, 327
Minimum wages, for women, 125-134; for men and women, 135
Minton, Sherman, 284
Montesquieu, 211-212
Municipal Bankruptcy Act, 199, 269
Murphy, Frank, 283, 284, 306
Myers, Gustavus, History of the Supreme Court, 85, 297

Nation, 15, 67, 69, 88-89, 277; quoted on Hughes' civil liberties and minorities record, 158
National Industrial Recovery Act, 214-215, 233-234, 247, 264, 275
National Labor Relations Act, 247, 252, 258, 267, 268
Newberry, Truman H. (NEWBERRY case), 80, 83

New Republic, 69, 89, 277, 323
New York *American*, 14
New York *Daily Tribune*, 14
New York *Evening World*, 69
New York *Herald Tribune*, 88, 150, 277
New York *Times*, 14, 69, 88, 277
Norris, George W., 78-79, 86, 322
Nye, James W., 85

O'Mahoney, Joseph C., 291

Packers and Stockyards Act of 1921, 109
Parker, John J., 90
Pearson, Drew, and Robert S. Allen, 75,
  303; quoted on Hughes as Secretary
  of State, 76
Pitney, Mahlon, 27-28, 39
Pollard, Joseph Percival, 158
Powell, Thomas Reed, 126, 232, 235-236,
  239, 320-321
Precedents, Hughes' reluctance to over-
  rule, 29, 130, 144, 151, 179, 187, 189,
  194, 228, 256-257, 260, 270, 279
President's Committee on Civil Rights,
  166
Prosser, William L., 316
Public Utility Holding Company Act,
  247

Railroad Retirement Act of 1934, 229,
  247
Ransdell, Joseph E., 86-87
Ransom, William, 55, 301-302; quoted
  on Hughes' record, 18
Reed, Stanley, 156, 249, 283, 284, 306
Reynolds, George G., quoted on "im-
  plications" of SHREVEPORT decision, 61
Ribble, F. D. G., 324; on importance of
  Hughes' opinions, 306
Roberts, Owen J., 90, 91, 92, 108, 124-
  125, 131-132, 152-153, 154, 156, 157,
  162, 183-184, 229-230, 249, 252, 253,
  269, 270-271, 272, 279, 284, 310, 317
Robinson, Joseph, 253
Roosevelt, Franklin D., 90, 93, 131, 201,
  233; attacks decisions of Supreme
  Court, 246-248; proposes to reorganize
  Court, 249-250; contest over his proposal, 250-254; letter to Hughes on
  resignation, 276; on mistake made in
  Court reorganization contest, 322-323;
  on connection between Court fight
  and its decisions, 323

Roosevelt, Theodore, 4, 13-14
Rutledge, Wiley B., 283, 284

Schattschneider, E. E., 224
Scottsboro cases, 159-161
Sharfman, I. L., 61; calls MINNESOTA
  RATE CASES an "important step,"
  58
Shortridge, Samuel M., 81, 83
Smith, J. Allen, 213
Social Security Act, 247, 252
Stanchfield, John V., 11
Stone, Harlan F., 91-92, 107, 114, 129-130,
  133, 154, 156, 158, 186, 187, 192, 193-
  194, 195, 237, 249, 258, 266, 272-273,
  274, 278, 279, 310, 317
Sullivan, Mark, 297
Supreme Court, 90; composition of
  during Hughes' service as Chief Justice, 91, 92, 306; change in attitude toward social legislation, 134-135; attack
  by Franklin D. Roosevelt on decisions
  of, 246-248; contest over proposal to
  reorganize, 249-254, 279-280; reexamination and retreat, nature and scope,
  255-275; composition of during
  Hughes' service as Associate Justice,
  299; *see also* Judicial review
Sutherland, George, 92, 96, 103-104, 123-
  124, 133-134, 141-142, 173-181, 182-183,
  191, 192, 223, 225, 241-242, 249, 250,
  257, 312
Swisher, Carl Brent, calls *Crowell* v.
  Benson a "long step backward," 307

Taft, William Howard, 13, 78, 92, 122-
  123
Taney, Roger B., 37-38, 78, 170
Taxing power, national, 269
Teapot Dome investigation, 81, 91
Tennessee Valley Authority, cases af-
  fecting, 205-210, 270-271
T. R. B. (*New Republic*), 181-182
Truman, Harry S., 278

Van Devanter, Willis, 49, 92, 249, 250,
  251, 253, 306
Vinson, Fred M., 278, 283, 284

Wagner, Robert F., 81
Waite, Morrison R., on businesses "af-
  fected with a public interest," 122
Wallace, Henry A., 112-113, 114-115

Wall Street Journal, 14, 88
Walsh, Thomas J., 87
Washington Disarmament Conference, 88
Wheeler, Burton K., 84, 250, 251
Wilson, Woodrow, 16, 68, 91, 92

World, 14
Wright, Benjamin Fletcher, Jr., 199, 301, 314, 315, 316, 324, 326; quoted on intention of Framers, 36-37, 170; quoted on Supreme Court in periods of "intense feeling," 293